Governing California in the Twenty-First Century

SEVENTH EDITION

THE POLITICAL DYNAMICS OF THE GOLDEN STATE

J. Theodore Anagnoson
California State University, Los Angeles

Gerald Bonetto
Vice President, Government Affairs, Printing Industries of California

J. Vincent Buck
California State University, Fullerton

Jolly Emrey
University of Wisconsin–Whitewater

James J. Kelleher
College of the Canyons

Nadine Koch
California State University, Los Angeles

Melissa Michelson
Menlo College

W. W. NORTON & COMPANY
INDEPENDENT PUBLISHERS SINCE 1923

W. W. Norton & Company has been independent since its founding in 1923, when William Warder Norton and Mary D. Herter Norton first published lectures delivered at the People's Institute, the adult education division of New York City's Cooper Union. The firm soon expanded its program beyond the Institute, publishing books by celebrated academics from America and abroad. By midcentury, the two major pillars of Norton's publishing program—trade books and college texts—were firmly established. In the 1950s, the Norton family transferred control of the company to its employees, and today—with a staff of four hundred and a comparable number of trade, college, and professional titles published each year—W. W. Norton & Company stands as the largest publishing house owned wholly by its employees.

Copyright © 2019, 2017, 2015, 2013, 2011, 2009, 2008 by W. W. Norton & Company, Inc.

All rights reserved.

Printed in Canada.

The text of this book is composed in Berlin with the display set in Interstate.

Book design: Lissi Sigillo

Composition: Achorn International

Manufacturing: Transcontinental

Editor: Laura Wilk

Editorial Assistant: Chris Howard-Woods

Project Editor: Laura Dragonette

Managing Editor, College: Marian Johnson

Managing Editor, College Digital Media: Kim Yi

Production Manager, College: Ashley Horna

Media Editor: Spencer Richardson-Jones

Associate Media Editor: Michael Jaoui

Media Project Editor: Marcus Van Harpen

Media Editorial Assistant: Tricia Vuong

Design Director: Jillian Burr

Marketing Manager, Political Science: Erin Brown

Director of College Permissions: Megan Schindel

Permissions Specialist: Bethany Salminen

Photo Editor: Ted Szczepanski

Library of Congress Cataloging-in-Publication Data

Names: Anagnoson, J. Theodore, editor.

Title: Governing California in the twenty-first century : the political dynamics of the Golden
    State / J. Theodore Anagnoson, California State University, Los Angeles, Gerald Bonetto,
    Vice President, Government Affairs, Printing Industries of California, J. Vincent Buck,
    California State University, Fullerton, Jolly Emrey, University of Wisconsin-Whitewater,
    James J. Kelleher, California State University, Dominguez Hills, Nadine Koch, California
    State University, Los Angeles, Melissa Michelson, Menlo College.

Description: Seventh Edition. | New York : W.W. Norton & Company, [2019] |
    Previous edition: 2017. | Includes bibliographical references and index.

Identifiers: LCCN 2018053633 | ISBN 9780393664881 (paperback)

Subjects: LCSH: California—Politics and government—21st century—Textbooks.

Classification: LCC JK8716 .G67 2019 | DDC 320.4794—dc23 LC record available at
    https://lccn.loc.gov/2018053633

W. W. Norton & Company, Inc., 500 Fifth Avenue, New York, N.Y. 10110

www.wwnorton.com

W. W. Norton & Company Ltd., Castle House, 75/76 Wells Street, London W1T 3QT

1 2 3 4 5 6 7 8 9 0

Contents

Preface

In 2017 and 2018, California assumed a new role: the epicenter of resistance to the Trump administration. Ever since Trump became president, California has been at odds with his administration over many of its policy directives, including immigration, the environment, trade, and numerous social issues, among others. While these conflicts demonstrate federalism in action, and underscore what makes California politics unique, the state is far from homogenous. The same issues that challenged the country heading into the 2018 midterm elections divided the state along demographic, geographic, and economic lines. In this new edition, we explore California's new role as well as the political history that brought us to this point.

The Seventh Edition features updated scholarship throughout the book, building on the foundation that has made *Governing California* a success. We began this project over a decade ago with a working title asking whether California's political system and its politics were simply "broken." That is, politicians were caught within a system that was so contradictory in its rules, norms, and mores that budgets couldn't be passed on time or balanced, programs and departments couldn't be managed under the existing set of rules, and citizen expectations were so out of line with the ability of the political system to satisfy them that the level of negativism and cynicism was as bad as could be found anywhere in the nation.

We think after a decade of false and halting starts that the picture needs some modification. California has begun to repair its infrastructure. The state has new incentives for politicians to be less ideologically extreme on the right or the left, in particular the "top two" primary system and the commission that is now drawing new districts for the Assembly, the state Senate, and congressional districts every 10 years after the census. Decision rules in Sacramento still leave much to be desired, but at least a budget can be passed with majority rule instead of a two-thirds vote, a rule that necessitated some votes from the minority party and, unfortunately, some pork projects or other incentives to gain those votes. And the nation's strictest term-limit rules have been modified to allow members of the Assembly or state Senate to serve 12 years in a single house before being "termed out" and forced to seek another office outside the state legislature. Hopefully, this will increase the level of expertise available among legislators.

The Seventh Edition of *Governing California* offers a ray of hope but also the reality of a long distance to go. We hope you enjoy our analysis of California's politics as not quite "broken" but as not yet "fixed" either.

Highlights of this revision include the following:

- NEW co-author Melissa Michelson (Menlo College) brings fresh scholarship to Chapters 2, 6, and 9. In Chapter 2, a new discussion of California's complicated legacy of discrimination provides deeper insight into the evolution of the state constitution. Additionally, Chapter 6 provides an overview of the new governor and administration, while Chapter 9 provides new data on the housing crisis.

- NEW coverage of the 2018 midterm elections (Chapter 4) explores the issues that were at stake and the propositions that were on the ballots, and provides a thorough analysis of the election results and what they say about where California is heading as the country looks toward the next presidential election in 2020.

- NEW "Who Are Californians?" features by contributing author R. Allen Bolar (Bakersfield College), explore diversity in the legislature (Chapter 5) and the growing population of uninsured in the state (Chapter 10). In addition, all of the other features have been thoroughly updated to help students understand the data behind big questions about state government.

- NEW information on California's political landscape provides points of comparison and contrast on divisive issues across the country, including the WeSaidEnough movement (Chapter 4) in the state capitol, which echoed the sentiments of the national #MeToo movement against sexual harassment.

- A thoroughly revised InQuizitive course helps reinforce the key topics and concepts in each chapter by quizzing students on what they still need to learn, not on what they've already mastered. InQuizitive is customizable to align the chapters and sections that you assign to your students. In addition, a test bank is available for all your assessment needs.

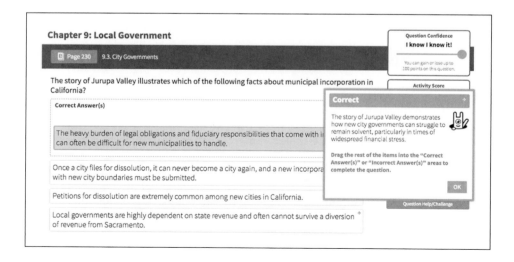

In order to provide the most knowledgeable analysis of the diverse topics in the table of contents, we divided the writing of this book as follows:

1. California Government: Promise and Practice—Anagnoson (tanagno@calstatela.edu)
2. The Constitution and the Progressive Legacy—Michelson (melissa.michelson@menlo.edu)
3. Interest Groups and the Media in California—Bonetto (gbonetto@roadrunner.com)
4. Parties and Elections in California—Koch (nkoch@calstatela.edu)
5. The California Legislature—Buck (vbuck@fullerton.edu)
6. The Governor and the Executive Branch—Michelson
7. The California Judiciary—Emrey (emreyj@uww.edu)
8. The State Budget and Budgetary Limitations—Anagnoson (tanagno@calstatela.edu)
9. Local Government—Michelson
10. Public Policy in California—Emrey

We would like to acknowledge the helpful recommendations from professors who have reviewed the book. Their comments have assisted us in updating events and materials. For the Seventh Edition, we thank the following reviewers:

John Vento, Antelope Valley College
Betty Chan, American River College, Sierra College
James E. Starkey, College of the Canyons
Anthony O'Regan, Los Angeles Valley College
Cameron Billeci, California State University, Sacramento
Janice Shiu, California State University, Sacramento
Allen K. Settle, California Polytechnic State University
Christopher Arns, California State University, Sacramento

We also thank the several students who have communicated their comments.

We would be glad to hear from you about the book. Please use the email addresses above to communicate with us.

J. Theodore Anagnoson
Professor of Political Science
California State University, Los Angeles

1

California Government: Promise and Practice

WHAT CALIFORNIA GOVERNMENT DOES AND WHY IT MATTERS

In the morning you drive to work on the freeway, stopping first at the gas station on the corner to fill up, then at the corner grocery store to buy an apple for a midday snack. Next you drive across a bridge to get to the university where you are currently taking general education courses. You are already considering what will follow after graduation. Perhaps you'll work for the California Highway Patrol (CHP), a private security guard service, or for a technology company. In the evening you are ready to relax after a full day of school, so you go out to a restaurant.

How is the government of California relevant to your day? Let's start at the beginning. Your car is built to conform to government safety standards. The freeways are built by the state government, with a mixture of federal and state money, to conform to federal and state standards. Traffic is monitored by the CHP. The gas station has to meet local safety regulations—it uses gasoline that conforms to federal standards for automobiles. Additionally, you paid a gas tax of 41.7 cents per gallon, which was increased by 12 cents on November 1, 2017 (to pay for increased construction and maintenance on the state's roads), and was the subject of a referendum on the November 2018 ballot to repeal the 12 cent increase. The grocery store relies on scales that are certified by county government; both imported and domestic fruit must meet U.S. and state Department of Agriculture standards. The bridge was built by government and is maintained by government (although a large proportion of the bridges nationally and in California are behind on their scheduled maintenance). If you attend a K-12 school, the school must comply with state standards for curriculum at each grade level and administer tests to determine whether it is meeting those standards. If you are in higher education, the public university you attend must have a general education program that conforms to state regulations. If you are enrolled in a community college, California State University, or the University of California, the cost of your education is partially subsidized by state funds. If you attend a private college, you might be receiving federal student aid. If you eventually go to work for the CHP, you will work under state laws and regulations. The private security service is regulated by the state as well, and the tech industry must conform to state and federal privacy regulations. The restaurant in which you enjoy your evening meal is inspected periodically by the local government health department, and in some locations the department will post the summary score (A, B, or C).

The California Dream?

For almost 200 years the **California dream** has attracted residents from other parts of the United States as well as immigrants from abroad. Former governor Arnold Schwarzenegger, in his 2004 State of the State address, said that California represents "an empire of hope and aspiration," a place where "Californians do great things." To some, the California dream is sun and surf; to others, the warm winter season and a house on the coast amid redwoods and acres of untrammeled wilderness, and to still others, the luxury of three or four cars per family.

The core of the dream is the ability to live a middle-class lifestyle in the most congenial climate in the nation, but that lifestyle is becoming increasingly difficult to attain in California. A 2018 analysis of the California dream posted on CalMatters.org shows that by 2014, median California families made only 8 percent more than they did in 1980. The median U.S. family made 22 percent more.[1] The modern conception of the California dream seems to have become finding a way to stick it out here. "California is a struggle, so we dream of the good struggle, of finding our footing, of figuring out some way to beat the statistics and buy a house and educate our kids."[2]

No matter what the conception, some of the dream is attainable for many—California's winter weather is the envy of most of the nation—but much of it is not. One of the themes of this book is the conflict between dreams and reality, between the ideals that we set for ourselves and the reality of our everyday lives. Particularly vivid for politicians is the conflict between our expectations of them and the constraints we place upon them.

Why Study California Politics?

The obvious answer is that you have to: your California history course meets some requirement for graduation or your major, since the state of California decided that every college student should know something about the California Constitution and California government and politics. But more important—why *care* about California politics?

- You are **the residents and voters of the present and future**. The policies and political trends occurring today will impact your lives, affecting everything from university tuition fees to the strength of the job market.

- California politics is plagued by **low levels of participation and turnout**, so much so that the electorate is older, more conservative, wealthier, more educated, and less ethnically diverse than would be the case if every eligible adult voted. So your vote and participation really can make a difference.

- California politics also suffers from **too much interest-group participation and not enough citizen participation**. The general interests of large groups of citizens need to be represented at the table.

That's the narrow answer. The broad answer is that California's government and politics are distinctive and worthy of study. How is California different from other states?

- We have much more **cultural diversity** than other states, including a much higher proportion of Latino and Asian residents. By some measures, we are the country's multicultural trendsetter. Our diversity affects our politics, and our solutions to multicultural issues have become an example for other states.

- We are **one of the five largest economies in the world**. The California economy in 2017, according to the federal Bureau of Economic Analysis, is the fifth largest in the world, surpassing Russia, Italy, Brazil, the United Kingdom, and India. Only the United States without California, and China, Japan, and Germany have larger economies. California's large and diverse economy means that we are able, in theory, to weather economic downturns more easily than other states. The fact that budget crises continue to plague California indicates that our taxing and spending system has fundamental problems (see below and Chapter 8).

- We are **the most populous state, with about 39.5 million people, and we have grown more quickly than other states**. In 1960, New York had 41 members in the U.S. House of Representatives; California had 38. The 2010 census gave California 53 seats, followed by Texas with 36 and Florida and New York with 27 each. In the past, California was forced to develop creative solutions to the problems engendered by high growth—problems such as uneven population distribution among various regions of the state and the need for housing and schools. However, California is currently losing more people to other states than it is gaining, and in recent years the exodus has grown as a result of high housing costs, taxes, and other costs of living. (The most popular destination for those leaving is Texas.) California's population is still slowly increasing on account of our having more births than deaths in recent years, but internally the population changes mean that the average age is growing and that the state has more senior citizens than it has had in the past. In the near future, we could even see California's population decline slightly each year. Current projections show the number of congressional seats staying at 53 after the 2020 Census, or even declining by a seat if the undercount is significant.

- We are **more majoritarian than other states**, meaning that we rely more on the measures for direct democracy—the initiative, the referendum, and

The initiative was added to the California Constitution by the Progressive movement in 1911 as a way to promote the involvement of the people in public policy and affairs. In November 2018 there were 11 propositions on the ballot, including Proposition 6, on which Californians had to decide whether or not to repeal a gas tax enacted in 2017. This proposition ultimately failed.

the recall—that were added to the state constitution by the Progressive movement in 1911. Every state uses majority rule for most decisions, but in a majoritarian state the public is more likely than elected representatives to make important policy decisions.

Consider the following continuum:

majoritarian   republican

A **majoritarian** government is one that is highly influenced by the public at large, through public-opinion polls and measures such as the initiative, the referendum, and the recall that enable voters to decide government policies directly.

A **republican** government is one in which we elect representatives to make our decisions for us, based on the Madisonian model for the federal government.

California government has moved much more toward the majoritarian model than other states. Initiatives to amend the constitution are routine, and interest groups often collect signatures for an initiative in order to pressure the legislature into voting in their favor. By voting directly on public policies and constitutional amendments that are placed on the ballot, California voters can influence policy in their state more than voters can in other states.

And Californians like being majoritarian. Surveys show that most don't want to restrict use of the initiative in spite of its extensive use and manipulation by interest groups as well as other problems. Ballotpedia lists 364 initiatives from 1912 through 2016, and we had another eleven in November 2018, for a total of 373.[3] California's number of initiatives historically is second only to Oregon's. Twenty-seven states do not have the initiative at all, and the top five states account for more than half of all initiatives considered from 1904 to 2012.[4] In other words, interest in and use of the initiative is highly concentrated in just a few states, one of which is ours.

What Determines the Content and Character of California's Politics?

Three factors shape the content and character of California's politics:

- the underlying demographic and sociopolitical trends that affect California and the other states;
- the rules of the game, as set out in the federal and state constitutions and in state laws;
- and the decisions of voters and politicians.

In Chapters 1 and 2 we will discuss the underlying demographic and sociopolitical trends and the rules of the game. The decisions of voters and politicians, and the way they shape California politics, will be discussed later in the text.

Who Are Californians?

The preamble to the California State Constitution begins, "We, the People of the State of California, . . ." This is fitting for a democratic form of government, which seeks to give voice to the people in the governing of their community affairs. So, who are Californians? Do the demographic characteristics of California differ from those of the United States as a whole? And how have changing demographic and socioeconomic trends contributed to the political challenges that face California voters and politicians? (See the "Who Are Californians?" feature.)

RACE AND ETHNICITY In many respects, California's population has a notable degree of **racial and ethnic diversity** compared with the U.S. population. **Latino or Hispanic** is not a racial category in the official census, but a separate census question asks about Hispanic or Latino origin. Answers to this question reveal that about 17 percent of the United States is Latino but that Latinos make up about 39 percent of California's population.[5] Almost 60 percent of that population is of Mexican heritage.

AGE California's population is relatively young, mostly because of immigration. Immigrants tend to be younger and have larger families than those who have been residents for longer periods. However, in recent decades the proportion of senior citizens has been increasing, from 10.6 percent in 2000 to 11.4 percent in 2010 and to an estimated 13.6 percent in 2017. California is therefore still a relatively young state. Nevertheless, because of the increase in the number and proportion of senior citizens, there has been an increased need for caregivers. Issues regarding the quality of care in nursing homes in the state have persisted for many years.

EDUCATION Californians are relatively well educated, with a greater proportion having gone to college or completed a bachelor's degree or higher than in the

How Is the California Population Changing?

California's demographics are changing rapidly. The state used to be predominately comprised of non-Latino whites (Anglos), but since 2000 the state has had a majority minority population. Latinos and Asians in particular are fast-growing populations, while whites and blacks are an increasingly small proportion. If these trends continue, by 2060, less than 31 percent of Californians will be white, while close to half (45 percent) will be Latino.

At the same time, the total size of the state's population is expected to continue to grow rapidly, from 40 million people in 2019 to 51 million in 2060. Population density will increase in the state's urban areas as well as inland areas, particularly in the Central Valley and Inland Empire, where housing is substantially less expensive.

Projected population growth by demographic group

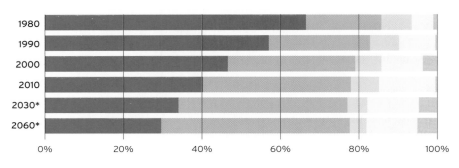

Legend:
- White / Anglo
- Latino
- Black / African American
- Asian
- Other

* Data for 2030 and 2060 are estimates.

Projected population growth between 2019 and 2060 by county

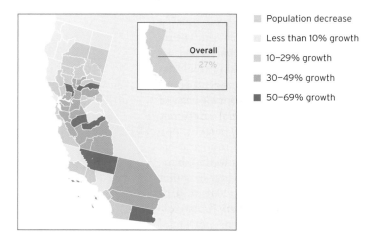

Legend:
- Population decrease
- Less than 10% growth
- 10–29% growth
- 30–49% growth
- 50–69% growth

Overall 27%

SOURCE: Frank Hobbs and Nicole Stoops, "Demographic Trends in the 20th Century," U.S. Census Bureau, www.census.gov/prod/2002pubs/censr-4.pdf (accessed 7/26/18); Jonathan Vespa, David M. Armstrong, and Lauren Medina, "Demographic Turning Points for the United States: Population Projections for 2020 to 2060," U.S. Census Bureau, https://www.census.gov/content/dam/Census/library/publications/2018/demo/P25_1144.pdf (accessed 7/26/18); and "Projections," State of California Department of Finance, www.dof.ca.gov/Forecasting/Demographics/projections/ (accessed 7/26/18).

forcriticalanalysis

1. What impact are these shifting demographics likely to have on politics? Will they change the issues that the state government focuses on? Will they change the issues that are the subject of citizen-driven initiatives?

2. California's coastal regions have traditionally been more densely populated, but rapid population growth and rising housing costs are increasingly driving populations to settle further inland. How will this change California politics in the inland counties, particularly in areas traditionally dedicated to agriculture?

United States as a whole. Fewer, however, have graduated from high school in recent years (83 percent from 2015 to 2016 versus 84 percent for the United States as a whole from 2015 to 2016). About three-quarters of California's two million college students attend a UC, CSU, or community college campus, with 44 percent of the total attending community colleges. Even with those numbers, analysts anticipate the state in 2030 will face a long-term shortage of college-educated workers, with about 33 percent of the state's workers having a college education in 2030 but with over 38 percent of all jobs requiring a college education.[6]

MOBILITY AND FOREIGN-BORN RESIDENTS About 60 percent of all Americans live in the state in which they were born, but only 50 percent of all Californians were born in California. In fact, 27.0 percent are **foreign-born**, more than twice the percentage of foreign-born residents in the United States as a whole (13.2 percent). "About half (49%) of California's immigrants are naturalized US citizens, and another 26% have . . . legal status."[7] As one might expect with such a large foreign-born population, only 61 percent of those over age five speak English at home in California, as opposed to 82 percent nationwide. That is a substantial difference by the standards of social science. Many political issues have arisen from this, ranging from debates over whether local store signs should be written in foreign languages to the "English as the official state language" movement.

INCOME The U.S. Census Bureau has estimated California's median household income at $63,783 for 2012–16, $8,461 higher than the national figure of $55,322. The state poverty rate is almost the same as the national figure: 14.3 percent (California) compared to 12.7 percent (United States). The official poverty line does not account for California's costs, particularly housing costs. A California-based poverty line calculated by the respected Public Policy Institute of California (PPIC) and the Stanford Center on Poverty and Inequality puts the 2016 poverty line at 19.4 percent, about 7.4 million people. Another 19 percent of Californians live within 1.5 times of the poverty line, which means that 38.2 percent of state residents were poor or near-poor.[8]

Income inequality in California has increased in the last 35 years. A study by the PPIC found that pretax cash incomes of top earners in California are 40 percent higher than they were in 1980, but middle incomes are only 5 percent higher and low incomes 19 percent lower. Bay Area incomes are twice those in the Central Valley, on average. The report did find that California's safety net, including tax credits as well as nutrition, cash, and housing assistance, had played a significant role in lessening inequality in the state. When local, state, and federal safety net programs are included, the amount of inequality shrinks by about 40 percent.[9]

GEOGRAPHY AND POLITICS Over the last 40 years, the population of California has shifted so that the coastal regions have become significantly more liberal and aligned with the Democratic Party than have the inland regions, which in turn have become more conservative and aligned with the Republican Party. These liberal coastal regions include every county on the coast from Del Norte County near Oregon to Los Angeles County. The Central Valley and Inland Empire (Riverside and San Bernardino counties) are disproportionately Republican. Orange and San Diego counties have been very Republican in the past but less so in recent elections. Local politics, on the other hand, are quite different even among Democratic- or

Republican-leaning cities (for example, San Francisco's local politics are very liberal compared with Los Angeles's more moderate politics).

POPULATION GROWTH Except for the four years from 1993 to 1996, California's population has grown by about 450,000 people per year for more than two decades until the early 2000s. The 2010 census listed California's population as 37,691,912; at the end of 2015 the state Department of Finance estimated the population at 39.5 million. California's current rate of growth has slowed: the rate for the 10 years preceding 2016 was 310,000 per year. Regardless of this slowdown, which includes outmigration, many of the problems that have plagued the state in the past will continue to raise issues in the future. The following are some of these issues:

- **Housing and Transportation** Even with the decline brought on by the recession of 2008–09, housing prices and rents in many areas have skyrocketed in recent years. Many lower- and middle-class people who work in San Francisco's Bay Area must live in the Central Valley, while many of those who work in the Los Angeles area must live in Riverside and San Bernardino counties. Commutes of one to two hours each way are common for residents of these areas. Housing costs in 2018 have risen so much that many younger families are leaving the state for other states. And our transportation systems, built for a much smaller population, have not kept pace with this growth.

- **Schools** Population growth means more schoolchildren and thus a higher demand for teachers across the state. In recent years, California has lacked enough fully qualified or credentialed teachers to meet this demand, particularly in many urban areas. Projections of the educational requirements of the future job market indicate that approximately 38 percent of jobs will require a college degree in 2030. The University of California, California State University, and community college systems do not produce sufficient numbers of graduates to meet this goal, which means that well-educated workers from other states will move in to fill these positions. The proportion of students who receive a college degree should be rising to meet future job requirements; instead, it is falling. More evidence on the inadequacy of California's degree production comes from data on high school graduates and where they go to college. The numbers who go out of state are up markedly from just a decade ago, with data from the U.S. Department of Education showing that about 40,000 high school graduates left the state for college in 2016, compared with the 22,000 who did so in 2006.[10]

- **Immigration** California has experienced high levels of immigration since the 1950s—so high in some areas that candidates for Mexico's presidency have campaigned here. Between 1970 and 2016 the number of immigrants in California's population increased from 1.8 million to about 10.2 million; 27 percent of the state's population in 2016 was foreign-born, a much higher proportion than the 13 percent nationwide. Most of California's immigrants were born in either Latin America (51 percent) or Asia (39 percent); 4.3 million come from Mexico alone, composing some 43 percent of the total immigrant population in California. Immigrants live in all parts of the state,

TABLE 1.1 ● Leading Countries of Origin of Immigrants in California, 2016

Country	Number of Immigrants in California
Mexico	4,200,000
China (including Taiwan)	936,000
Philippines	813,000
Vietnam	534,000
India	482,000

SOURCE: Public Policy Institute of California, "Just the Facts: Immigrants in California." ppic.org/publication /immigrants-in-California/ (accessed 10/23/18).

with those from Latin America more likely to live in Southern California and those from Asia more likely to live in Northern California. Immigrants are younger than nonimmigrant Californians and are more likely to be poor, and although some have relatively high levels of education, most are less educated than the native population.[11] Table 1.1 shows the five largest countries of origin for immigrants in California in 2016.

As of 2014 there were approximately 2.35 million **undocumented immigrants** in California, according to the Urban Institute and the Public Policy Institute of California, which used the census figures on the foreign-born population and subtracted the numbers of people who are naturalized or here on legal visas and work permits.[12] Undocumented immigrants are a continuing political issue, with politicians arguing over the public services to which they should have access: Should they be treated in hospital emergency rooms? Should they be allowed to buy insurance on the state exchange under the federal Affordable Care Act? As of January 1, 2015, one issue was decided: California residents who cannot establish legal presence in the United States can apply for a California driver's license if they can establish proof of identification and state residency. As of March 31, 2018, 1,001,000 such licenses had been issued. Table 1.2 lists the number of undocumented immigrants by state, along with the share they compose of that state's total population. California and Texas have the highest numbers of undocumented immigrants, at 2.3 and 1.6 million respectively.

Reflecting the controversies over both documented and undocumented immigration in recent years, a number of demonstrations have taken place in California on the immigration issue. These demonstrations have represented different views: against more immigration, in favor of closing the borders, in favor of a "path to citizenship," both for and against the Arizona immigration law of 2010, against housing undocumented children who have been taken into custody before their court hearings, and so forth. At least one of the demonstrations involved more than 1 million people, the largest ever seen in Southern California to date. But aside from the 2013 law that allowed undocumented immigrants to obtain driver's permits starting in 2015 (see above), little policy action has taken place at the state level.

TABLE 1.2 ● Undocumented Immigrants by State, 2014

State	Number of Undocumented Immigrants	Share of State's Total Population (%)
California	2,350,000	6.0%
Texas	1,650,000	6.1
Florida	850,000	4.2
New York	775,000	3.9
New Jersey	500,000	5.4
Illinois	450,000	3.5
Georgia	375,000	3.6
North Carolina	350,000	3.4
Arizona	325,000	4.9
Virginia	300,000	3.5
Other States	3,175,000	2.0
All states	11,100,000	3.5

SOURCE: Pew Research Center, Hispanic Trends, "U.S. Unauthorized Immigration Population Estimates." www.pew hispanic.org/interactives/unauthorized-immigrants/ (accessed 10/23/18).

The Crisis of California Politics

Is California government capable of making the decisions needed for the state to thrive and preserve its standard of living through the twenty-first century? The general sentiment among informed observers is that California is hamstrung by voter-approved rules and regulations, some of which are admirable on an individual level but make for a collective nightmare. However, some progress toward effective decision making began during the 2003–11 Schwarzenegger administration and continued under Governor Jerry Brown, who left office in 2019:

- Proposition 11, approved in November 2008, took the power to apportion the districts of the Assembly and state Senate (**redistricting**) away from those bodies and gave it to a citizens' commission. Later, the voters added apportioning congressional districts to the duties of the new citizens' commission. In the first years the new districts have been used, they seem to be fair (that is, not gerrymandered). Future years will establish whether unbiased districts will produce more moderate legislators who are willing to compromise for the good of the state as a whole, which was the goal of changing the reapportionment method. So far, elections have been more competitive.

- In 2010 the voters opted to change the state's party primary elections to a new **top-two primary** system, used for the first time in June 2012. Under the new system, there is no party primary. Instead, the election system is like a swim meet or a track meet, in which there are preliminary heats and finals. Following the preliminary election, the top two candidates advance to the finals in November, even if they are from the same party or are not in a major party. Third parties such as the Green Party are strongly opposed to the new system, since they rarely finish in the top two candidates in the primary election and thus have no access to the general election ballot during the two months when voter attention is highest. Two problems have arisen recently with the new system. First, if a party wishes to replace its candidate on the ballot, there are no provisions for that action or even for a candidate to withdraw—once on the ballot, the candidate is on for good. And second, no write-ins are allowed on the November ballot, so the two candidates approved in the June primary are the ones the voters are stuck with in November, no matter what.

- In 2010 the voters also approved of a change in the legislative process for approving the state budget. The previous requirement was a **two-thirds vote** of the total number of legislators in each chamber (the Assembly and the state Senate). It is now a simple majority (50 percent plus one). The budget approved in June 2011 was the first to use the new system. In order to raise or lower taxes, however, the state constitution still requires a two-thirds majority of both houses of the state legislature, plus the governor's signature.

After the election of Governor Jerry Brown in November 2010, California's frustrating budget stalemate initially continued in spite of the new majority rule, largely because the taxation system had not changed. In June 2012 the budget gap was $16 billion—more than the total revenues received for the general fund in 40 of the 50 states. By mid-2014, however, the budget had a surplus almost as large as the deficit from two years before, and this surplus has lasted into the 2018–19 budget year. The California taxation system is highly dependent on its **capital gains tax**—income taxes paid on capital gains (funds received from selling stock). It produced a huge surplus in 2013 and 2014 when the stock market rose, inducing many investors to sell shares. The governor and legislature agreed to use the surplus to build up a "rainy day" fund and to pay off many old bonds issued when the budget was in deficit.

In contrast to the decade beginning in 2010, the first decade of the 2000s was one long downward trend, the result of difficult and tough decisions. The budgets of all three segments of public higher education deteriorated substantially in the face of ever rising numbers of entering students. Other budget reductions included rates and services of Medi-Cal (California's medical program for the poor), many cost-containment measures in state programs for the developmentally disabled, and the elimination of local government redevelopment agencies and their state funding (see Chapter 9). Prisoners were sent from the state prisons to local jails, and many state responsibilities were passed to the local level of government. The fiscal years around 2014 show that California can have budget-surplus years as well as deficits, but no one should think that a permanent era of plenty has arrived. California's budget is unduly responsive to the economy and especially to capital gains. When the next recession arrives, and it *will* arrive, revenues will dive again. As Governor Jerry Brown said after delivering his 2018 budget (a budget with a strong surplus) message: "What's out there is darkness, uncertainty, decline and recession," meaning that the problem is that no one knows when the next recession will begin or how severe it will be.

California state government thus faces a series of paradoxes. On the one hand, we see progress in cutting the deficit and in making the hard decisions necessary to weather the national economic storm. On the other hand, the difficulty of those decisions and the fact that taxes can be raised only by a two-thirds majority has meant that a budget crisis occurred every year from 2000 to 2012 and to a lesser extent through 2016. Every decision in the state government became—and still is—a budget decision, a decision made solely, or almost solely, on the basis of whether there is enough money and a budget source for the considered activity.

Let us take a closer look at some reasons for the recurring crises despite the promise of California state government.

The Ease of Passing Initiatives

One factor in these recurring crises is certainly the ease with which **special interests** collect signatures to propose, campaign for, and sometimes pass initiatives to help their own causes. The initiative was added to the California Constitution by the Progressive movement in 1911 as a way to promote the involvement of the people in public policy and affairs. One recent example of a special interest using the initiative for its own gain was Proposition 15 on the June 2010 ballot, which ostensibly allowed taxpayers to have more control over their government but was in fact designed to keep local public utilities from competing against Pacific Gas and Electric (PG&E). Similarly, Proposition 33 on the November 2012 ballot ostensibly allowed insurance companies to give longevity discounts to drivers who had continuous insurance coverage from another insurance company; in fact, this initiative was designed to give one insurance company the ability to raise rates on drivers who had lapses in insurance coverage. Another example was the November 2016 referendum on the law banning single-use plastic bags statewide. The sponsors of the referendum, opposed to the law, made—you guessed it—plastic bags. In general, the initiative has ceased to promote direct democracy for at least the last two decades. Instead, it has mostly become just another method by which special interests convince voters who are paying little attention to government and politics to enact rules, laws, and constitutional amendments that benefit a particular interest at the expense of the public as a whole. While there are exceptions, far too many initiatives fall into this category.

To place an initiative on the ballot requires 5 percent of the votes at the last gubernatorial election for an initiative statute and 8 percent for initiative constitutional amendments. With the number of votes cast for governor in 2014 at 7,317,581 (only 42.2 percent of registered voters and 29.9 percent of voter-eligible adults), the number of signatures was lowered to 365,880 for an initiative statute and 585,407 for an initiative constitutional amendment, the lowest number since the 1975–78 period. It is thus easier to place an initiative on the ballot today than it has been in some time.

Term Limits

The **term limit** movement found fertile ground in California in the 1980s and 1990s. Proposition 140 in 1990 imposed what were then the severest term limits in the nation on the legislature and the elected officials of the executive branch. The voters in many California cities instituted term limits on their local leaders as well. Part of the statewide anger and consequent push for term limit legislation was directed against Willie Brown, then speaker of the California Assembly, whose flamboyant lifestyle and prolific fund-raising provoked the ire of voters.

The term limits movement's theory is that term limits will encourage members of the Assembly and state Senate to pay more attention to their jobs and spend less time raising money for future campaigns, and that the limits will make the legislative bodies more welcoming to minority and female candidates. Since term limits have been imposed, the proportion of Latino legislators has indeed risen; however, members now have much less expertise on the matters they vote on, and by the time they acquire this expertise they are term-limited out. Additionally, many—perhaps most—members of the legislature spend a good deal of their time in office worrying about their next job and raising funds for future campaigns. Most observers believe that term limits have worsened the legislature, not bettered it, and increased the power of lobbyists and interest groups as inexperienced legislators rely on them for expertise.

While voters strongly support term limits, they recently took a step to address some of the institutional problems that have resulted from them. In June 2012 the voters approved Proposition 28, which allows legislators to serve as many as 12 years in the legislature, as long as those 12 years are served in one house. (The previous total service time was actually higher—14 years—but was capped at 6 years in the Assembly and 8 in the Senate.) Currently, the term limits are 12 years (six terms) for the Assembly, 12 years (three terms) for the state Senate, and 8 years (two terms) for all statewide officials (governor, lieutenant governor, attorney general, controller, secretary of state, treasurer, superintendent of public instruction, insurance commissioner, and the four elected members of the Board of Equalization).

The Two-Thirds Requirement for Raising Taxes

As noted earlier, until the voters passed Proposition 25 in November 2010, California's constitution required a two-thirds vote of the total membership—not just those present and voting—in each house of the legislature to pass the budget. Only three states, Arkansas, California, and Rhode Island, required such a strong **supermajority** to pass the budget. Proposition 25 lowered the required vote to 50 percent plus one. So far, all the budgets passed under the new rules, which financially penalize legislators if the budget is not passed on time, have been passed around June 15, the constitutional deadline.

However, a two-thirds vote of the absolute number of legislators in both houses of the state legislature is still necessary to raise or lower any tax level. With a Republican Party that refuses to countenance tax increases of any kind (plus the taxpayer groups that promise to sue the instant any tax increase is passed), the burden of balancing the state budget has fallen on low- and moderate-income state residents, who benefit disproportionately from the state programs that have been cut. For higher-income state residents, state services are at least partially irrelevant—their major "service" is a low tax rate, as well as exemptions and deductions that enable some of their income to be taxed at a lower rate.

The Democratic Party has had a two-thirds majority in the legislature three times during the last several years. The 2012 elections saw the Democrats win a short-lived supermajority of seats in the legislature, which meant they had enough votes to raise taxes without any Republican support (see Chapter 5). Raising taxes, however, requires the approval of the governor, and former governor Jerry Brown had consistently wanted a balanced budget without additional tax increases beyond those instituted by Proposition 30, approved by voters in November 2012. This proposition enacted a four-year increase in the state sales tax and seven-year increases in the tax rates for citizens making over $250,000 in income (see Chapter 8). The supermajority lasted a little over a year, until early 2014 when three Democrats in the state Senate were suspended over corruption allegations. In 2017 the Democrats again had a two-thirds supermajority, and they did indeed raise a tax: the gas tax, in order to fund highway development and repair, long considered to be sorely needed. Repealing the gas tax increase was a referendum item on the November 2018 ballot, which did not pass. The basic structure of California's tax system, however, has been frozen since the 1960s.

Lack of Consensus on Fundamental Questions

Another reason for California's perpetual state of crisis is the inability of legislators to unify on matters of policy and principle. In order to be effective, a political system must overcome the inertia generated by narrow interests to make decisions that benefit the broader public interest. This is a persistent issue in a large, complex state such as California, but in the past, California politicians have been able to overcome the lack of **consensus** to make progress on significant questions. Has California changed? Why do interest groups cause impasse in the 2000s, when their influence was relatively minimal back in the 1970s and 1980s? After all, we have always had interest groups, and we had the two-thirds decision rule for adopting the budget or raising taxes in the legislature from 1935 until 2010.

Journalist Dan Walters suggests that the blame heaped on the legislature is inappropriate:

> In fact, California's governance maladies stem from the complex, often contradictory nature of the state itself. With its immense geographic, economic, and cultural diversity, California has myriad policy issues, but those same factors also have become an impediment to governance. The state lost its vital consensus on public policy issues, and without that civic compass, its politicians tend to ignore major

Passing a balanced state budget is a perennially contentious issue in California. However, the budget surplus in early 2014 allowed Governor Jerry Brown—shown here breaking down certain state expenditures—to propose budgets for 2014-17 that increased state funding for education and paid off some of the debt that the state had accrued over previous years.

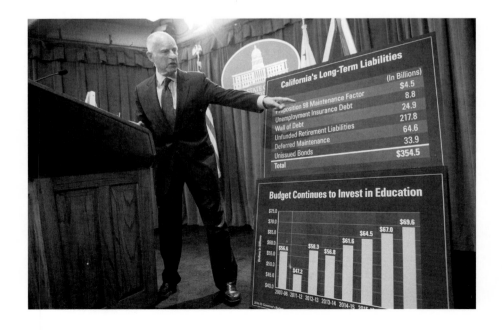

issues and pursue trivial ones. . . . The real issue is whether the public's anger at Gray Davis will morph into a new sense of civic purpose or whether California is destined to be . . . ungovernable.[13]

If you combine the lack of consensus with the swift-moving news cycle typified by Twitter and other social media, you can get a sense of the problem. So far, the events following the recall of Governor Gray Davis in 2003 have indicated very slow progress, with no "new sense of civic purpose." The same old problems seem to vex California's political class over and over.

A recent example concerns the legislature declaring California to be a **sanctuary state**, meaning that the state limits its cooperation with the federal government in accelerating deportations for violations of the immigration laws. SB (Senate Bill) 54 limits state and local law enforcement in helping the federal government enforce the immigration laws, unless the individual concerned has been convicted of one of several hundred serious or violent crimes (in the latter situation, state and local officials cooperate with the federal government in deporting the person concerned). For incarcerated inmates, the state fully cooperates with the federal government. AB (Assembly Bill) 450 generally prohibits both public and private employers from giving federal immigration workers access to the nonpublic areas of a business or government agency unless the federal workers have a warrant. AB 103, the third bill in this area, prevents local governments from contracting with the federal Immigration and Customs Enforcement agency to house immigrant detainees in local jails.

Within a few months, at least six counties and 13 California cities passed resolutions voicing their opposition to the laws or have joined the U.S. Department of Justice lawsuit filed against California. One question is the extent to which a state can refuse to cooperate with the federal government. Another is the extent to which state law can compel local cities and counties to comply. The traditional rule has been "Dillon's Rule" (see Chapter 9), under which subgovernmental units within states lack the rights of a federal state and can be governed as a state wishes, subject to the state's own constitution and laws. Whether that will apply in this case we shall have to see.

Reform Ideas

In addition to the steps already taken (as discussed earlier), numerous reforms have been suggested over the years to address the institutional hindrances to effective California governance. Some of the standard ones are listed below. See how many you agree with as you begin reading this book. You might check this section at the end of your course to see if you still have the same opinion. You might not!

On the liberal side:

- **Instituting public financing of election campaigns. Public financing** would reduce the impact of money on Assembly, state Senate, and congressional campaigns because all or most campaign funding would come from the state, not from interests who want something in return for these donations. It would also lessen the impact of fund-raising on members of the legislature, some of whom spend up to half their time in Sacramento raising money. However, it would be difficult to devise a system that would not unduly benefit incumbents, who are typically better known than their challengers.

- **Lowering the required supermajority to raise taxes** from two-thirds to some lower, more achievable, percentage, such as 55 or 60 percent. This proposal would require an amendment to the state constitution, probably impossible on a tax issue such as this unless it is proposed as part of a broad package of tax relief and reform.

- **Restricting the initiative process** to allow more citizen participation and lessen the need to hire professional firms to collect signatures and run initiative campaigns. This would require lengthening the time allowed to collect signatures even more than the recent change from 150 days to 180. Changing an initiative process that California's citizens hold in high regard would be a tough sell, and the industry that sponsors initiatives and makes money from them might well oppose it, making the campaign expensive.

- **Realigning the tax structure** to match the state's shift from a manufacturing economy to a service-based one (see Chapter 8). The most powerful method for doing this would be to change the sales tax to make it apply to services such as medical care and automobile repair. In order to pass, this would have to be sold as decreasing the sales-tax rate. Several recent commissions have indicated interest, but few politicians want to be associated with the cause.

On the conservative side:

- **Changing the legislature from full time to part time.** This idea is popular in Tea Party circles, reflecting their nostalgia for an earlier era and their desire for a less expensive government, not to mention the typical Californian's distrust of the legislature. However, it would weaken the legislature's level of expertise on the programs it is expected to enact and oversee. Term limits, another measure taken to limit the legislature, have clearly weakened the average legislator's knowledge of the subject areas the legislature oversees.

- **Lowering California's tax rates**, making the system less progressive in the process. This is popular among conservatives but is a tough sell for liberals and Democrats.

- **Improving California's business climate** with lower taxes and fewer regulations. Almost everyone agrees that this goal is laudable, but there is little agreement on what taxes to lower (or how to make up the difference financially) and what regulations to simplify or abolish.

Most of these ideas involve so much controversy that they have little chance of being enacted, at least in the short run. Enacting major reforms such as those just listed is much easier through the ballot box (that is, via an initiative) than it is through the legislature, where constitutional changes require a two-thirds vote of the Assembly and the Senate before being placed on the ballot for ratification.

Conclusion

In this book we are going to consider the real world of California politics and the possibilities, both fascinating and frustrating, of the present, as well as changes that might make the future more positive for both politicians and the public. We will investigate what makes California different from other states and examine its unique political problems, which include the following:

- the inability to balance the budget year after year (the most recent years under Governor Jerry Brown are an exception)
- the malapportioned districts for the California legislature that, in combination with the primary system, produce legislators who are more liberal than the public on the Democratic side and more conservative than the public on the Republican side (we shall see whether the new top-two primary system and the non-gerrymandered legislative districts make any difference in this area)
- the public's attachment to the strict term limits
- the public's attachment to extreme majoritarianism, which produces the longest ballots in the nation as well as low turnout rates

Our coverage includes subjects that newspapers and bloggers discuss in great detail, as well as some subjects, such as the California tax system and the impact of Proposition 13, that receive little coverage in the media. Welcome to the journey.

A Guide to This Book

Chapter 2, "The Constitution and the Progressive Legacy," deals with California's state constitution and the Progressives, the two crucial factors that define the shape and direction of today's California government.

Chapters 3 and 4 consider the bodies outside government that influence what government can accomplish. Chapter 3, "Interest Groups and the Media in California," takes a look at the groups that are as prevalent and influential in California as they are in our nation's capital. Chapter 4, "Parties and Elections in California," examines how both parties and voters influence government through elections and campaigns.

Chapters 5, 6, and 7 cover the institutions of government. Chapter 5, "The California Legislature," discusses the legislature, the body we love to hate. We try in this book to understand the legislature and why it functions as it does rather than simply to condemn it. Chapter 6, "The Governor and the Executive Branch," asks whether California has become ungovernable. Chapter 7, "The California Judiciary," deals with judges and the criminal justice system.

Chapters 8, 9, and 10 provide an in-depth guide to policy problems and governmental structures that are particularly relevant today. Chapter 8, "The State Budget and Budgetary Limitations," addresses taxes, spending, and the California budget, asking whether the budget can be controlled in today's political and policy environment with the tools we have available to us. Chapter 9, "Local Government," considers local government and its dependency on the state, a dependency that localities are taking action to eliminate in part through the initiative process. Chapter 10, "Public Policy in California," delves into several contemporary public policy problems, illustrating how the institutions and voters have acted in these areas.

Study Guide

FOR FURTHER READING

Bonn, Sarah, and Caroline Danielson. *Income Inequality and the Safety Net in California*. Public Policy Institute of California, May 2016. http://ppic.org/main/publication.asp?i=1190. Accessed 7/1/18.

Davis, Mike. *City of Quartz: Excavating the Future in Los Angeles*. New York: Vintage, 1990.

Hill, Laura, and Joseph Hayes. "Just the Facts: Undocumented Immigrants." Public Policy Institute of California, March 2017. http://www.ppic.org/publication/undocumented-immigrants-in-california/. Accessed 7/1/18.

Horwitz, Sasha. *Termed Out: Reforming California's Term Limits*. Center for Governmental Studies, October 2007. www.policyarchive.org/handle/10207/2047. Accessed 7/1/18.

Lewis, Michael. "California and Bust." *Vanity Fair*, November 2011.

Mathews, Joe, and Mark Paul. *California Crackup: How Reform Broke the Golden State and How We Can Fix It*. Berkeley: University of California Press, 2010.

McGhee, Eric, and Daniel Krimm. *California's Political Geography*. Public Policy Institute of California, February 2012. www.ppic.org/main/publication_quick.asp?i=1007. Accessed 7/1/18.

Mejia, Marisol Cuellar, and Hans Johnson. "Just the Facts: Immigrants in California." Public Policy Institute of California, May 2018. http://www.ppic.org/publication/immigrants-in-california/. Accessed 7/1/18.

Olin, Spencer C. *California's Prodigal Sons: Hiram Johnson and the Progressives, 1911–1917*. Berkeley: University of California Press, 1968.

Skelton, George. "California's Capitol—The Long View. A Columnist Looks Back on 50 Years Covering the Ups and Downs of Sacramento." *Los Angeles Times*, December 1, 2011.

ON THE WEB

California Choices. www.californiachoices.org. Accessed 7/1/18.

California Forward. "How to Fix CA's Government." www.cafwd-action.org/pages/how-to-fix-CA-government. Accessed 7/1/18.

Los Angeles Times. www.latimes.com. Accessed 7/1/18.

Public Policy Institute of California. www.ppic.org. Accessed 7/1/18. A think tank devoted to nonpartisan research on how to improve California policy.

Sacramento Bee. www.sacbee.com. Accessed 7/1/18.

San Francisco Chronicle. www.sfgate.com. Accessed 7/1/18.

SUMMARY

I. California politics are important for several reasons.
   A. California is the most populous state, has the fifth largest economy in the world, and has a population more multicultural and diverse than the rest of the nation.
   B. California is strongly majoritarian, and its citizens like it that way.
   C. California is younger than many states, has a greater percentage of college-educated citizens, and is richer than most states.
   D. California has experienced some of the strongest population growth of any state, resulting in a number of political conflicts over the years. The high price of housing, in particular, has been difficult to solve.
   E. California has more immigrants, and more undocumented immigrants, than any other state, although Texas has almost the same proportion of undocumented immigrants.

II. Progress in dealing with California's problems has occurred in the last decade, in spite of the fact that the state is generally considered to be hamstrung by voter-approved rules and regulations.
   A. Redistricting, once the province of the legislature, is now done by a citizens' commission. The new districts (used from 2012 forward) seem to have considerably less gerrymandering than the old.
   B. The party primary election system has been changed to the new "top-two" system, in which the two top vote-getters from the primary election, regardless of party, move to the general election for a runoff.
      1. The new system is more like a swim meet or track meet, with a preliminary heat and final, than a party primary.
   C. In 2010 the voters approved a change to the state constitution so that the legislature could approve the state budget by a majority vote, instead of the prior rule of two-thirds of the total membership of each house of the legislature.
      1. The state constitution still requires any tax increase to be approved by a two-thirds vote of

each house of the legislature, plus the governor's signature.

D. These changes have not resolved the underlying problems with the state's taxation system, which result in soaring surpluses when the stock market is high and the opposite during recessions.

III. Some reasons for the continual crisis in California state government include the following:

A. The ease of passing initiatives. Special interests find that the state has a congenial atmosphere in which they can spend several million dollars to collect signatures and fund a campaign to pass a law or change the state constitution in order to benefit the initiative's proposer.

B. Term limits, in spite of the 2012 change that lengthened the maximum time to 12 years in either the Assembly or the state Senate, still hamper the legislature. By the time legislators learn their jobs, they are often looking for new ones.

C. The two-thirds vote requirement in the Assembly and state Senate to raise taxes has meant that the only realistic way to balance declining budgets has been to cut services disproportionately used by the lower-middle class and the poor.

D. The lack of consensus on fundamental questions among both politicians and citizens has made it difficult to build the broad consensus that major change requires.

IV. Reform ideas are abundant but few have the political support necessary for enactment in the short run. Several ideas from both sides of the political spectrum are listed in the text.

PRACTICE QUIZ

1. The budget must be passed by a majority of those present and voting in both chambers of the legislature.
   a) true
   b) false

2. Most states require a two-thirds majority to pass their budgets each year.
   a) true
   b) false

3. According to the text, California's total population, its foreign-born population, and the approximate number of undocumented immigrants living in the state are
   a) 50 million, 5 million, and 2 million.
   b) 34 million, 8.8 million, and 2.4 million.
   c) 25 million, 20 million, and 18 million.
   d) 39.5 million, 10.2 million, and 2.35 million.

4. "Latino" or "Hispanic" is one of the racial categories in the U.S. Census, which is taken every 10 years.
   a) true
   b) false

5. Compared to the proportion of immigrants who speak English at home in the U.S. population, the proportion of immigrants in California who speak English at home is
   a) greater.
   b) lesser.
   c) the same.

6. According to this book, the inability of the California legislature to make decisions that benefit the state as a whole is due to
   a) the influence of interest groups.
   b) the two-thirds requirement to raise taxes.
   c) California's size and diversity.
   d) all of the above

7. California's current term limits are
   a) 8 years for the governor, 4 years for the Assembly, and 6 years for the state Senate.
   b) 6 years for the governor, 6 years for the Assembly, and 8 years for the state Senate.
   c) 8 years for the governor, 12 years for the Assembly, and 12 years for the state Senate.
   d) 8 years for the governor, 8 years for the Assembly, and 12 years for the state Senate.

8. Undocumented immigrants were able to obtain a driver's permit in California as of 2015.
   a) true
   b) false

9. "Majoritarian" as applied to California government means that
   a) the state requires majority rule in all major decisions.
   b) the state does not have a "republican" form of government; it has a "majoritarian" form.
   c) the state makes many important decisions through direct democracy and the initiative process.
   d) the California legislature uses majority rule for all decisions.

10. California's institutions of higher education produce sufficient numbers of graduates to meet the the state's workforce needs in the foreseeable future.
    a) true
    b) false

11. California's "top-two" primary is more like an athletic event with preliminary heats and finals than it is a political party primary.
    a) true
    b) false

CRITICAL-THINKING QUESTIONS

1. How distinctive is California compared with other states? Are we really that different from citizens in the rest of the country?
2. California's population differs from that of other states on several levels. What are the two or three that are most significant, and why are they significant?
3. What are the advantages and disadvantages of the "majoritarian" form of government? Of the "republican" form of government?
4. Consider the disparity between the number of college-educated workers required for the California economy in the future compared with the number that the state will be producing. What happens to a state when it doesn't produce enough college-educated workers for its needs? When it doesn't have housing that workers can afford?

KEY TERMS

California dream (p. 2)
capital gains tax (p. 11)
consensus (p. 14)
cultural diversity (p. 3)
foreign-born (p. 7)
Latino or Hispanic (p. 5)

majoritarian (p. 4)
public financing (p. 15)
racial and ethnic diversity (p. 5)
redistricting (p. 10)
republican (p. 4)
sanctuary state (p. 15)

special interests (p. 12)
supermajority (p. 13)
term limit (p. 12)
top-two primary (p. 10)
two-thirds vote (p. 11)
undocumented immigrants (p. 9)

2 The Constitution and the Progressive Legacy

WHAT CALIFORNIA GOVERNMENT DOES AND WHY IT MATTERS

The purpose of a constitution is to define the rules under which political actors and citizens interact with each other to fulfill their goals as individuals, as members of a group, and as a population as a whole. The California Constitution is long and very detailed, with numerous amendments added over the years that deal with both the fundamental principles and power of government as well as commonplace issues such as the right to fish on government property, English as the state's official language, and grants for stem cell research. Today, California has the second highest number of constitutional amendments (over 500 by some counts), behind Alabama, and the second longest state constitution, behind Louisiana.

One distinctive feature of the California Constitution is that it allows the people to enact both constitutional amendments and legislation through a majority vote without going through the legislature. The process through which citizens make legislation at the ballot box is called the initiative. The initiative developed out of a political movement called Progressivism, which opposed the influence of moneyed special interests in politics and called for political power to be returned to the people. Any individual or group can propose a statute or an amendment to the California Constitution. In 2018 there were five statewide propositions on the June primary ballot and eleven statewide propositions on the November ballot.[1]

However, the initiative process has not always lived up to its progressive ideals. Today, wealthy individuals and special interest groups spend hundreds of millions of dollars on campaigns for and against initiatives. In the November 2016 general election, more than $485 million was spent by both sides on 17 propositions; in 2018, initiative spending topped $379 million. Although the initiative does put legislative power in the hands of the general public, it does not eliminate the influence of money in politics, and—ironically—it bypasses the more careful debate and compromise that might take place in the legislature.

The most expensive ballot proposition battle in 2016 was over Proposition 61, a high-profile initiative to limit state spending on prescription drugs. Supporters of the measure, led by the Los Angeles–based AIDS Healthcare Foundation, spent over $19 million, while pharmaceutical industry opponents, led by Merck, Pfizer, and Johnson & Johnson, spent $109 million. Just two years later, spending on Proposition 8 broke a new record with spending of over $131 million. Proposition 8 would have added new regulations for outpatient kidney dialysis clinics, requiring those clinics to limit the amounts they could charge (and thus to limit their profits). Supporters, led by local unions including the Service Employees International Union-United Healthcare Workers West, spent over $20 million; opponents, led by health care companies specializing in dialysis care clinics, DaVita and Fresenius, spent more than $111 million.

The impetus behind Proposition 8 was a failed effort by the unions to pressure those two companies, who control 70 percent of the dialysis clinics in the state, to allow workers at those clinics to unionize. In short, a labor dispute led to the most expensive ballot initiative battle in California history, and asked regular voters to make a decision that, if the campaign commercials on both sides were to be believed, would endanger the lives of dialysis patients. Many voters were left confused by the competing claims, emphasizing a major weakness of the modern use of the initiative process: it often asks voters to make decisions about issues on which they lack reliable information and expertise.

In the end, Proposition 8 was defeated, losing by a vote of 38.9 percent to 61.1 percent. Overall spending on Proposition 8 was not a record—that distinction falls to the $156 million spent in 2006's battle over Proposition 87, which proposed to reduce petroleum consumption. In that instance, supporters contributed $69.9 million, and opponents contributed $94.4 million. Yet, while spending on Proposition 8 was lower overall, it marks a record spent in opposition to a state ballot proposition. These are just a few examples of an overall pattern: initiative battles in California often are waged with television commercial battles funded by multimillion-dollar donations, a far cry from the return of power to the people that the Progressives intended.

In Chapter 1 we discussed some of the demographic differences between California and other states. We also mentioned that the institutional design of California's government prevents it from solving critical state issues. Here are some of the unique features of the state's political process:

- The **sheer size of the state** increases the cost of political campaigns and media outreach programs.

- The **competing networks of interest groups** cause groups to jockey for position and influence.

- The **increasing use of the initiative** significantly affects state and local governance and policy.

- The **divided executive branch**, composed of nine separately elected officials, each with their own area of authority and responsibility, leads to overlapping responsibilities and fragmentation in the execution of state policy.

- The **widespread, almost universal use of nonpartisan elections at the local level of government** eliminates a valuable clue that helps voters identify the policy positions of the candidates on the ballot.

Aside from the size of the state and its interest-group network, the other characteristics listed above are a result of the **Progressive movement**, which flourished in California from 1900 to 1917. The leaders of this movement focused on one goal: making government more responsive to the political, social, and economic concerns of the people. Their reforms continue to shape California's government and politics in ways that sharply differentiate it from other states. To some, these features hamper the political process and should be changed. To others, they form part of the essence of California. Were they to be changed, that essence would be destroyed.

California's political history is also heavily influenced by the extreme diversity that resulted from the Gold Rush, which took place before the Civil War, from 1848 to 1855. Forty-niners, as the miners were called, came from around the world to make their fortunes—by wagon train across the county or by ship from the west, either sailing around Cape Horn or crossing by canoe and donkey train through the jungles of Panama (the Panama Canal did not exist until half a century later). Canadian merchant William Perkins described the mining town of Sonora in 1849: "Here were to be seen people of every nation in all varieties of costume, and speaking 50 different languages, and yet all mixing together amicably and socially."[2]

At the same time, this diversity, combined with competition over mining claims and other resources, also led to significant racism and discrimination. The vigilante justice of the Gold Rush included violence against Mexicans, South Americans, Chinese, and other foreigners, as well as against the few free Blacks in the area, whom white miners did not believe were entitled to "their" gold. Cycles of violence against Native Americans reduced the state's native population from 150,000 in 1848 to just 30,000 by 1870. As we will see, this racism was often institutionalized in early California's laws and constitutions.

The Rules of the Game: California's Constitution

The California Constitution has a long and storied history that can be divided into four stages:

- **The 1849 Constitution**   Written by residents of the territory in anticipation of statehood, this constitution contains many of the basic ideas underlying California's government today.

- **The 1879 Constitution**   Written by a constitutional convention in 1878, this is the basic governing document, with amendments, that is in force today.

- **From 1900 to 1917**   During this period, the Progressives amended the constitution and passed laws to temper the power of special interests and make government responsive to the people's desires and needs. The most prominent reforms of this period are the initiative, referendum, and recall.

- **From 1918 to the present**   Amendment after amendment lengthened the state's constitution, resulting in a document that at one point was almost 100,000 words long. Several commissions proposed substantive changes, but only two commissions, one in the 1960s and the other in the 1990s, saw their proposals realized: the constitution's language was shortened and clarified, but no substantial changes were made to its provisions.

The 1849 Constitution

Gold was discovered in California in January 1848; news spread slowly until President James Polk mentioned it in his State of the Union message to Congress on December 5, 1848. In 1849, 80,000 fortune seekers from around the world moved to California, tripling the area's non-native population past the minimum needed to apply for statehood and also increasing the need for a formal government to impose order.[3] Yet, since the start of the Mexican-American War, Americans had been bitterly divided over whether to allow slavery in any new acquired territories. During congressional debate on a bill sought by President Polk to fund treaty negotiations, Pennsylvania congressman David Wilmot proposed the Wilmot Proviso, an amendment to eliminate slavery within any land acquired as a result of the Mexican-American War. Although the amendment was killed in the Senate, it enflamed the growing controversy over slavery, as the South understood that slavery was now seriously under attack. In 1849 newly elected president Zachary Taylor proposed that California and New Mexico be admitted as free states (states, unlike formal territories, had the power to decide for themselves whether to allow slavery). As Congress debated over what to do with the newly acquired lands, including border disputes between Texas and New Mexico, California citizens elected delegates to a constitutional convention. These included famous pre-1846 settlers such as John Sutter, as well as eight *Californios*, among them General Mariano Guadalupe Vallejo.

Meeting in Monterey, the 48 elected delegates met for 37 days between September 1 and October 13, 1849. They drafted a constitution that relied heavily on the Iowa Constitution and to a lesser degree on the New York Constitution. The

California electorate ratified the constitution in November 1849, and on December 15 California formally petitioned Congress for admission to the Union.

The basic provisions of the 1849 Constitution are still in force:

- The framework of the government rests on a separation of powers—executive, legislative, and judicial—interacting through a system of checks and balances, like the federal government.

- Executive power is divided, with the separate election and jurisdiction of the governor, lieutenant governor, comptroller, treasurer, attorney general, surveyor general, and superintendent of public instruction. This division weakens the governor, who cannot appoint—or remove—senior members of his or her own administration. Moreover, each of these statewide officials is a potential competitor for the governor's office, and each can release statements that contradict what the governor is saying.

- An extensive bill of rights begins the constitution.

- The legislature is elected and consists of two houses, one called the Senate, the other the Assembly.

However, there are notable differences between the 1849 Constitution and the framework that exists today:

- The right to vote at that time was limited to white (including white Mexican) males 21 years of age or older who had lived in California for at least six months. Another provision denied citizenship to African Americans, Chinese Americans, and Native Americans; they were also prohibited from testifying against whites in court. The legislature could, by a two-thirds vote, enfranchise Native Americans "in such special cases as such proportion of the legislative body may deem just and proper."

- The judiciary was elected, as judges are today, but they were organized into four levels—as Mexico's judiciary was at the time.

- All laws and other provisions were to be published in both English and Spanish, since California was a bilingual state.

The nativism and racism in the 1849 Constitution reflected the competitive greed of the Gold Rush. Miners overran Native American territories and organized themselves into gangs to drive natives away. Volunteer infantries attacked and massacred villages. As mining became more difficult and fortunes more elusive, white miners increasingly believed they were entitled to the gold and that people of color were not. They defended this privilege with violence, as well as with laws and constitutional provisions. Mexican Americans, whose claims to citizenship and property ownership had been promised in the Treaty of Guadalupe Hidalgo, were victims of state-sanctioned violence and claim jumping, and lost their land to white settlers.

In July 1850 the sudden death of President Taylor, who wanted to exclude slavery from the Southwest, and the accession of Vice President Millard Fillmore, who was anxious to resolve the border dispute between Texas and New Mexico, paved the way for the federal government to pass a series of five bills that together composed the Compromise of 1850. The package balanced the interests of slave owners and abolitionists, allowing California admission to the Union as a free state on September 9, 1850.

California's 1849 Constitution quickly proved to be problematic. Its framers had neglected to include provisions for the financial stability of the new government; within the first five years, California was in deficit. There were few provisions for taxation but no limits on spending, legislative salaries, or the governor's pardon power.[4] Four times between 1859 and 1873 the legislature called for a new constitutional convention to fix obvious defects; each time, too many voters left their ballots blank to achieve the necessary majority to approve the convention.

Additionally, the provision that California was a free state was not immediately successful. Proslavery lawmakers and judges worked to undermine the constitution and cement the rights of slave owners, culminating in the California Fugitive Slave Law of 1852. Slaves and free Blacks found themselves dragged before state courts and remanded to their self-professed owners, even if they had earned or purchased their emancipation. The law expired in 1855, but proslavery sentiment (and legal victories) continued until 1858, coinciding with the rise of the free soil Republican Party.

The 1879 Constitution

The call for a new constitutional convention finally succeeded in 1877, as California suffered from the worst recession in the brief history of the nation. The Panic of 1873 began in September 1873 with a series of bank failures and the closing of the New York Stock Exchange. As railroads went bankrupt and businesses failed, wages were cut and unemployment spiked, leading to the Great Railroad Strike of 1877. Although the depression technically ended in the spring of 1879, the tension in the labor market persisted. This included increased resentment of Chinese railroad workers, who were often willing to work for much lower wages. For example, in 1870, Union Pacific in Wyoming hired Chinese laborers for $32.50 a month, while whites were asking for $52 a month.

At a July 1877 rally in San Francisco meant to organize support for striking railroad workers in the East, a mob of hundreds broke away from the meeting and charged through the center of the city, sparking a riot that lasted for three nights and spread throughout the city. Rioters attacked Chinese homes and businesses, mostly laundries, and threatened establishments that employed Chinese workers. Several people died over the course of the riots and dozens were injured.

The riots created a movement determined to settle "the Chinese question" and workers' grievances. Called the Workingmen's Party of California, the movement was led by Irish immigrant Denis Kearney. Under Kearney's leadership, the party adopted a platform to break up monopolies, redistribute wealth, and remove Chinese residents from California. His rallying cry was, "The Chinese must go!"[5] The Workingmen became a force in Bay Area politics, winning a seat in the state Senate in early 1878 and electing officials in San Francisco, Oakland, and Alameda. The Kearneyites also won almost all of the San Francisco delegate seats for the 1878 constitutional convention, where they worked to include their anti-Chinese demands in the new constitution.

Article XIX of the 1879 Constitution banned private and public employment of Chinese workers. The laws enacting these provisions were swiftly struck down in federal courts that ruled they violated the Fourteenth Amendment's guarantee of equal protection, infringed on rights due to Chinese immigrants under treaty, and trampled upon corporate rights. However, anti-Chinese sentiment persisted. (The voters of California formally repealed Article XIX in 1952.)

Anti-Chinese sentiment didn't suddenly appear in the 1870s; it had been brewing for decades. In the peak year of gold rush immigration in 1852, 20,000 Chinese immigrants came to San Francisco in search of gold. Mirroring the racist attitudes that stripped Mexicans of their claims, white miners also believed Chinese immigrants were not entitled to "their" gold. Anti-Chinese prejudice led to a ruling that Chinese miners could only work claims that white miners had abandoned as worthless, and white prospectors often attacked Chinese miners. In 1850 the California legislature adopted a Foreign Miners License Law, charging all non-U.S. citizens $20 per month. The exorbitant fee led many Chinese (and others, including thousands of Mexicans) to abandon the mining camps and move to San Francisco, where they created America's first Chinatown, before the law was repealed in 1851. A new foreign miners' tax of $4 per month soon followed, and anti-Chinese feeling persisted in the mining camps.

In the 1840s and 1850s most of the country saw the rise of the American Party (the "Know Nothing" Party), which focused on protecting Americans from the influx of Catholic immigrants. The San Francisco chapter of the Know Nothings, founded in 1854, focused instead on opposing Chinese immigration. The party enjoyed sweeping victories in the state election of 1855, including that of 30-year-old gubernatorial candidate James Neely Johnson (the youngest governor in California history), and large majorities in both houses of the legislature. While the party soon faded, xenophobia and racism persisted.

In 1863 work began on the Central Pacific railroad line, to run from Sacramento to the East, and Chinese workers had the physical courage and intellectual

Decades of xenophobia and racism against Chinese immigrants in California culminated in the largest mass lynching in American history. The lives lost in the Chinese Massacre are memorialized here in this bilingual plaque in Los Angeles.

resourcefulness to lay the track and blast routes through the Sierras. They were also willing to work for lower wages, as noted above. When the railroads were completed in the early 1870s, Chinese workers moved into new jobs, including in agriculture as farm workers. As the economy worsened in the 1870s, white Californians blamed Chinese residents for their economic woes. Newspaper editorials attacked Chinese residents as inferior and immoral. Calls for an end to Chinese immigration grew louder, and incidents of anti-Chinese violence became more frequent. White mobs attacked Chinese communities throughout California in the 1870s. On October 24, 1871, a mob in Los Angeles massacred at least 17 Chinese men and boys in the largest mass lynching in American history, and looted the Chinese section of town.

It was in this context of economic anxiety and hostility toward Chinese immigrants that delegates met to decide how best to reorganize the government of California. The delegates at the 1878–79 constitutional convention adopted a large number of diverse provisions. Among these were the shifting of responsibility for the debts of a corporation to stockholders and various new rules regarding the railroads: the railroads could not give free passes to those holding political office, they could not raise rates on one line to compensate for reductions made to compete on alternative lines, and they would be regulated by a railroad commission.

These provisions added words—almost doubling the constitution's size—and policies that read very much like a series of laws rather than a fundamental framework within which laws could operate. In this way, the California Constitution differs greatly from the federal U.S. Constitution, whose articles and amendments deal strictly with institutional procedures and rules that construct a governmental framework. The Eighteenth Amendment stands as the only experiment in establishing a substantive policy in the U.S. Constitution; it prohibits the manufacture, sale, import, or export of alcohol and was repealed with the Twenty-First Amendment just 14 years later.

At the time, however, the many specific, substantive policies in the drafted California Constitution were viewed as beneficial, and it was approved by a vote of 54 to 46 percent in May 1879, with 90 percent of those eligible to vote participating. Most of the reform measures were not put into practice right away, as corporate and railroad power continued to dominate the state and sued to block their implementation. These setbacks were temporary, however. In a matter of three decades the broad reforms of the Progressive movement gained passage, weakening the grip of these special interests in the legislature and reshaping the landscape of California politics.

One notable feature of the 1879 Constitution is the procedures it established for amendment. The federal Constitution and every state constitution in the United States include procedures for their own amendment, but these procedures vary considerably. The U.S. Constitution is one of the most difficult to amend in the world, requiring a two-thirds majority vote in the House and Senate followed by ratification by three-fourths of the states.[6] This very high hurdle explains in part why the U.S. Constitution has only been amended 27 times since 1789. In contrast, the California Constitution is much easier to amend. (See Figure 2.1 for an overview of the different paths through which the constitution can be amended.) Convening a constitutional convention is a more dramatic method of reform and has rarely been used. It is not particularly difficult, however, to get 8 percent of voters in the most recent gubernatorial election to sign a petition adding an amendment to the next ballot; the amendment then needs a simple majority vote to

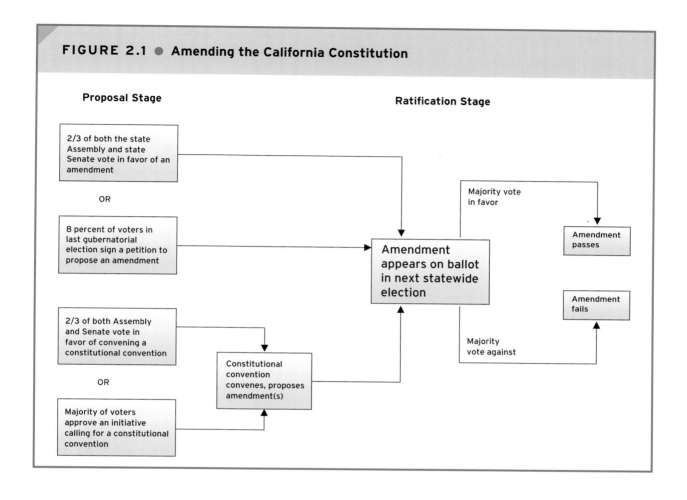

FIGURE 2.1 ● Amending the California Constitution

Proposal Stage

Ratification Stage

2/3 of both the state Assembly and state Senate vote in favor of an amendment

OR

8 percent of voters in last gubernatorial election sign a petition to propose an amendment

2/3 of both Assembly and Senate vote in favor of convening a constitutional convention

OR

Majority of voters approve an initiative calling for a constitutional convention

Constitutional convention convenes, proposes amendment(s)

Amendment appears on ballot in next statewide election

Majority vote in favor

Majority vote against

Amendment passes

Amendment fails

pass. This method has been used more than any other to amend the California Constitution.

You can get a sense of the California Constitution and how different it is from the U.S. Constitution by examining California's bill of rights, called the "Declaration of Rights." The federal Bill of Rights consists of the first 10 amendments to the U.S. Constitution, and while other amendments may be passed, the first 10 will remain the Bill of Rights as they were written. California's bill of rights, meanwhile, can be expanded or rewritten as times change, and it therefore reflects the political changes and conflicts that have occurred over time, with some of the rights described in much greater specificity than the corresponding federal rights. You can see an example of this specificity in the provisions for freedom of speech as they apply to a newspaper. The federal Constitution has the familiar First Amendment:

> Congress shall make no law respecting an establishment of religion, or prohibiting the free exercise thereof; or abridging the freedom of speech, or of the press; or the right of the people peaceably to assemble, and to petition the Government for a redress of grievances.

California's corresponding section has both more detail and more specificity, since it has been amended over time.

> SEC. 2. (a) Every person may freely speak, write and publish his or her sentiments on all subjects, being responsible for the abuse of this right. A law may not restrain or abridge liberty of speech or press.
>
> (b) A publisher, editor, reporter, or other person connected with or employed upon a newspaper, magazine, or other periodical publication, or by a press association or wire service, or any person who has been so connected or employed, shall not be adjudged in contempt by a judicial, legislative, or administrative body, or any other body having the power to issue subpoenas, for refusing to disclose the source of any information procured while so connected or employed for publication in a newspaper, magazine, or other periodical publication, or for refusing to disclose any unpublished information obtained or prepared in gathering, receiving, or processing of information for communication to the public. Nor shall a radio or television news reporter or other person connected with or employed by a radio or television station, or any person who has been so connected or employed, be so adjudged in contempt for refusing to disclose the source of any information procured while so connected or employed for news or news commentary purposes on radio or television, or for refusing to disclose any unpublished information obtained or prepared in gathering, receiving, or processing of information for communication to the public.

Note the use of modern language, such as *wire service* and *television*.

From 1900 to 1917: The Progressive Movement

Pressure for political reform did not end with the 1879 Constitution. Beginning at the turn of the twentieth century, the Progressives pursued three goals: reduce corporate political influence, eliminate the political corruption that accompanied such influence, and democratize the political process.[7]

The Progressives understood that these goals had to be accomplished before they could address equally pressing but more mundane concerns of the time. They accomplished all of their goals—and much more. Beginning with the 1911 legislative session, these reformers passed dozens of constitutional amendments and statutes that changed the face of California government and politics.[8] The most prominent of the political reforms were the following:

- **Nonpartisanship**   This is the norm in local elections and means that no party label is affixed to the candidates' names on the ballot. Of the more than 19,000 elected public officials in California, fewer than 300 are elected in partisan races.

- **Primary elections**   Before the institution of primary elections, political parties chose their candidates in party conventions (the stereotypical smoky back room) or caucuses—meetings of party members at the local level. In a primary election, each prospective party nominee has to obtain more votes than any other prospective nominee in order to run as the party's candidate in the November general election. (This system was changed again in 2010; see next section.)

- **The office block ballot**   This is the ballot that we vote on today, with a "block" for each office and the candidates listed for that office. Before this reform, in some elections, voters cast ballots for their preferred party, not for individual candidates.

- **Direct democracy**   These grassroots processes—the initiative, referendum, and recall—give citizens the ability to exert some control over both the legislative and executive branches. In this way, citizens can rein in the abuse of power by elected officials or reignite officials who have become paralyzed by inaction and partisan bickering. These processes will be examined in detail later in the chapter.

- **The civil service**   An essential element of the Progressive reform movement was the implementation of a civil service in which government employees are selected on the basis of merit, replacing the spoils system in which employees are selected based on their personal connections to the party in power. In California, the 1913 Civil Service Act created a Civil Service Commission to eliminate politics and the spoils system among the state's public employees.

During this period, the California Constitution grew substantially as the legislature enacted dozens of constitutional amendments and statutes. In the first three months of 1911 alone, the legislature passed more than 800 statutes and 23 constitutional amendments.

From 1960 to the Present: Late Revisions

In 1963 the legislature created a constitution revision commission as a result of a 1962 initiative. The commission, composed of 50 citizens, 3 state senators, and 3 Assembly members, submitted two major reports containing recommended revisions to the state constitution. The legislature incorporated these into 14 constitutional amendments and submitted them to the voters for approval between 1966 and 1976; the voters approved 10. These amendments simplified, shortened, and reorganized the constitution but made few substantive changes to it.

In 1993 the legislature again established a constitution revision commission, which proposed a number of substantial changes, some of which reformers had discussed for generations. For a variety of reasons, including the difficulty of achieving the two-thirds vote in the Assembly and Senate required to place the proposed changes on the ballot, they were never submitted to the voters.

In 2010 the voters implemented a change to the primary election system that echoed the effort of many Progressive Era reforms to further democratize the political process. This change replaced the party primaries with a "top-two" primary election, in which the top two candidates from a list of all candidates, regardless of party, proceed to the November runoff. The new system is no longer a party primary; instead it is like a swim meet or track meet, with preliminary and final races.

Despite its numerous amendments, the California Constitution is not well suited to a state that is 25 times larger than it was in 1900. The legislature is the same size, with 40 state senators and 80 Assembly members, but each state Senate district has grown from just over 60,000 persons to almost 1 million; legislators are able to offer far less individualized attention to their constituents than they could in an earlier era (see the "Who Are Californians?" feature on the facing page). In the early twentieth century, small amateur groups could utilize the initiative, but well-funded interest groups are now uniquely able to take advantage of it. Unfortunately, serious efforts to modernize state government have been few and far between, and when they have occurred, as with the constitutional revision commission of the 1990s, the results have been subject to partisan voting and have not achieved the majorities necessary to send them to the people for a final decision.

The Progressive Movement and Its Impact on California Politics

The development of California's distinctive constitution has been influenced by many different groups over the course of the state's history. One group whose influence is still deeply felt in California politics is the Progressives. The Progressive movement had roots in the economic and political changes that swept the United States after the Civil War. It was foreshadowed by the Populist movement, which dominated American politics from 1870 to 1896.

Some of the political concerns and much of the moral indignation expressed by the Populists about the changes taking place in the United States were subsequently reflected in the Progressive movement. From the Civil War on, the country rapidly industrialized, and wealth became concentrated in the hands of a new breed of corporate entrepreneurs. *Monopoly* was the word of the day. These corporate giants dictated economic policy, with significant social and political consequences. One huge corporation, the Southern Pacific Railroad, held a monopoly on shipping in California and could charge producers and retailers exorbitant prices. Its vast wealth and power gave it undue influence not only economically but also politically; along with a web of associated interests, it ruled the state to a degree previously unparalleled in the nation. Bribing public officials was not unusual, nor was handpicking candidates for the two major political parties.[9]

The Progressives countered the powerful corporations, specifically the Southern Pacific Railroad, by prosecuting the corrupt politicians who served them. Eventually, this tactic led to a series of regulatory reforms that loosened the choke hold of the railroad, corrupt politicians, and interest groups on state and local politics.

Local Politics

Progressive reforms began at the local level. The battle against the Southern Pacific Railroad and corporate influence in general started in San Francisco in 1906, with the reform movement fighting to rid city government of graft and bribery. President Theodore Roosevelt stepped in to help. Working hand in hand with James D. Phelan, the former mayor of San Francisco, Roosevelt sent in federal agents led by William J. Burns to investigate bribery and corruption charges.[10] Public officials were put on trial for bribery, bringing to the public's attention the extent of graft and political corruption in municipal government, and 17 supervisors and a number of corporate leaders were indicted.[11] The mayor was forced to resign, and his henchman, Abraham Reuf, who implicated officials of the Southern Pacific Railroad and several utility companies, was convicted and sentenced to 14 years in jail. Although the graft trials largely failed to convict those indicted (Reuf was an

Who Draws the Lines in California?

The Constitution of 1879 provided for 80 Assembly and 40 Senate districts based on population, and after each U.S. Census the lines were supposed to be redrawn by the state legislature (to account for births, deaths, and people moving). This procedure was followed until 1910, when conflict between urban and rural areas led to the Reapportionment Act of 1911, which shortchanged the growing urban areas of Los Angeles and San Francisco. In 1926, a constitutional amendment made representation in the California Senate even more unequal. In 1964, this unequal representation was declared unconstitutional by the U.S. Supreme Court (in Reynolds v. Sims), leading to new districts of roughly equivalent populations.

In 2008, California voters approved a constitutional amendment that placed redistricting in the hands of the new Citizens Redistricting Commission. The new districts took effect for the June 5, 2012 primary. The commission drew new districts that followed a set of nonpartisan rules, such as creating geographically compact districts that kept existing cities and communities intact, and they are not allowed to take into consideration where incumbents live or the partisan tilt of district voters. How do the most recent changes compare to the districts in 1961 and 2001, before the amendment that assigned restricting to the Citizens Redistricting Commission?

Population per district

■ 50,000 or less ■ 50,001 – 99,999 ■ 100,000 – 199,999 ■ 200,000 – 499,999 ■ 500,000 – 999,999 ■ 1,000,000 or more

State Senate Districts, 1961

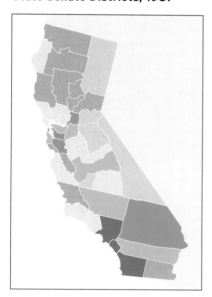

State Senate Districts, 2001

State Senate Districts, 2016

SOURCES: Join California, "Election History for the State of California" www.joincalifornia.com/; Don A. Allen Sr., Legislative Sourcebook (1965); California Citizens Redistricting Commission, www.wedrawthelines.ca.gov (accessed 12/07/18).

forcriticalanalysis

1. Does the large population size of current Assembly and State Senate districts make it difficult for Californians to truly be represented in the legislature?

2. If the plan adopted by California in 1926 is unconstitutional because representation is unequal, why is it that the representation in the U.S. Senate is not invalid?

This cartoon from 1882 depicts the Southern Pacific Railroad as a destructive octopus with farmers, miners, lumber dealers, and other victims of the company's monopoly on shipping entangled in its tentacles. The faces of Mark Hopkins and Leland Stanford, two of the railroad's founders, form the creature's eyes.

THE CURSE OF CALIFORNIA.

exception), they were nonetheless an important step in breaking the power of the Southern Pacific Railroad and its political allies.

In 1906 the Southern Pacific Railroad also dominated local politics in Los Angeles.[12] During this time, a group dedicated to good government, the Non-Partisan Committee of One Hundred, was formed. They selected a reform candidate for mayor who was opposed by the two major parties, labor groups, and the *Los Angeles Times*. While the reform candidate lost his bid for the mayoralty, 17 of 23 reform candidates for other city positions were elected.[13] The nonpartisan reformers were on their way to ridding the city of the Southern Pacific machine.

State Politics

The 1907 legislative session was one of the most corrupt on record, heavily controlled by the political operatives of the Southern Pacific Railroad. At the end of the session, the editor of the *Fresno Republican*, Chester Rowell, wrote, "If we are fit to govern ourselves, this is the last time we will submit to be governed by the hired bosses of the Southern Pacific Railroad Company."[14]

At the same time, Rowell and Edward Dickson of the *Los Angeles Express* began to organize a statewide movement to attack Southern Pacific's power. At Dickson's invitation, a group of lawyers, newspaper publishers, and other political reformers met in Los Angeles. They founded the Lincoln Republicans, later to become the League of Lincoln-Roosevelt Republican Clubs (also known as the Lincoln-Roosevelt League), dedicated to ending the control of California politics by the Southern Pacific Railroad and linking themselves to the national Progressive movement.

The Lincoln-Roosevelt League participated in the statewide legislative elections of 1908 and managed to elect a small group of reformers to the legislature. Two years later it fielded a full-party slate, from governor down to local candidates.

STATEHOUSE VICTORY In 1910, Hiram Johnson became the Lincoln-Roosevelt League candidate for governor. He campaigned up and down the state, focusing on one issue: the Southern Pacific Railroad. He claimed that the company, acting in concert with criminal elements, had corrupted the political process in California. He defined the battle as one between decent, law-abiding citizens and a few corrupt, powerful individuals who were determined to run the state in their own best interests.

Johnson won the election and met with leading national Progressives—Theodore Roosevelt, Robert La Follette, and Lincoln Steffens—to discuss a reform program for California. The new administration in Sacramento set out to eliminate every special interest from the government and to make government solely responsive to the people and Johnson. Through a series of legislative acts and constitutional amendments, they made significant progress in that direction. In 1911 the voters passed the initiative, the referendum, and the recall. These three reforms, widely known as **direct democracy**, placed enormous power and control over government in the hands of the voters. Now citizens could write their laws or amend the constitution through the initiative, approve or reject constitutional amendments through the referendum, and remove corrupt politicians from office through the recall.

In addition to these reforms, a new law set up a railroad commission that had power to fix rates beginning in 1911. Other reforms included the direct primary, which gave ordinary citizens the power to select the candidates of the political parties for national and state offices. Women obtained the right to vote in California in 1911. Legislation was also enacted that limited women to an eight-hour workday, set up a workmen's compensation system, put into practice a weekly pay law, and required employers to inform strikebreakers that they were being hired to replace employees on strike (and therefore might face verbal abuse and physical violence). These reforms were in part a reaction to what were viewed as harsh employment practices by Southern Pacific Railroad.

The Progressives in California made significant headway in limiting the influence of corporations and political parties in politics. In its first two years in office, the Johnson administration succeeded in breaking the power of the Southern Pacific Railroad.[15]

LAST HURRAH The national Progressive Party lost its bid to capture the White House in 1912 with Theodore Roosevelt on the ticket for president and Hiram Johnson for vice president. The failure to win an important national office weakened the party by lessening the enthusiasm of its supporters. It also meant that the party had no patronage with which to reward its followers between elections. Electoral failure was just one of several major problems that plagued the Progressives. Several other factors also contributed to the decline of the party: the public grew tired of reform; there was a major falling out among the leadership in California; the Progressives generally opposed World War I, which was supported by the overwhelming majority of the American public once the country got into the war; and the party failed to support reforms that labor badly wanted.

When the Progressives learned that the Republican Party would not nominate Roosevelt in 1916, they offered him the nomination. Roosevelt declined. At a dinner in San Francisco in July 1916, the California Progressive Party disbanded and Hiram Johnson urged his followers to join either the Republican or the Democratic Party. Later that year Johnson, now a Republican, was elected to the U.S. Senate, where he served for 28 years.

Despite the success of the Progressive reforms mentioned above, one major flaw in Progressive thinking was the belief in an active, informed citizenry willing to participate in politics. Progressives believed that, given the opportunity, citizens would be happy to support the democratic process and spend whatever time and effort was needed to participate in politics. Since the late 1940s, however, a host of studies have shown that many people neither vote nor pay attention to politics. Nevertheless, the Progressives left behind the significant legacy of having gained tremendous political power for the people of California, if and when they choose to use it. As noted later in this chapter, however, many of these powers are most often used by moneyed interests rather than by members of the general public.

Another flaw was that although Progressives wanted to increase political participation, that support applied only to white citizens. Many Progressives were racists, believing Blacks and immigrants from Eastern and Southern Europe to be genetically inferior to immigrants from Western Europe. Federal immigration policies of the era, including the Immigration Act of 1917 and the National Quota Law of 1921, were designed to increase immigration from Western and Northern Europe, to decrease immigration from Southern and Eastern Europe, and to exclude immigration from Asia.

Progressives particularly discriminated against Japanese Americans. In 1913 state legislators passed the California Alien Land Law of 1913, prohibiting "aliens ineligible from citizenship" from owning land or possessing long-term leases. The law applied to all Asian immigrants but was mainly aimed at Japanese farmers, with the further aim of reducing Japanese immigration. Japanese immigration had surged beginning in 1900, with many Japanese immigrants settling in rural areas of southern California to work in agriculture and fishing. Anti-Japanese sentiment soon followed; the California legislature in January 1901 urged Congress to protect American labor by restricting Japanese immigration; a second resolution was approved in March 1905. In 1920 voters approved by a 75–25 percent margin a ballot proposition to close loopholes in the 1913 measure, stoked by fears that Japanese people could not assimilate and that their birth rate was so high that they would eventually replace white people. While the two laws failed to have much effect, and were eventually struck down as unconstitutional, their passage reflects the era's hostility.

The Progressives' strategies to gain power for the people were appropriate for 1910, when California had a population of 2.4 million. Since then, however, California has grown so much and so quickly that its constitution has been unable to catch up. In a state of 39.5 million people, reforms that allowed "the people" to propose initiatives and recall public officials cannot now be exercised on a statewide[16] level without a great deal of money, organization, and professional help. The last initiative that did *not* use paid, professional signature gatherers was introduced in 1990, and it relied on a paid campaign coordinator. An initiative organized completely by volunteers has not been successful since 1984.

Direct Democracy

The Progressives established civil service reforms, nonpartisan commissions to control key state regulatory functions, nonpartisan elections to cripple local machines, office block voting, and primary elections. Even if these innovations have failed to check the power of special interests, they have given voters the power of direct action through the initiative, referendum, and recall. Citizens can activate these three mechanisms by circulating petitions to gather a required number of signatures and bring the measure to statewide vote. The number of signatures, as we shall see, varies depending on the mechanism.

Initiative

THE PROCESS Of the three direct voices in government, the **initiative** is the most well known and most frequently used. The process, also known as direct legislation, requires the proponent to obtain a title (for example, "Farm Animals Confinement Standards") and summary of the proposed initiative from the state attorney general. Upon obtaining the title and summary, the proponents have 150 days to circulate a petition to gather the required number of signatures to qualify for the ballot—5 percent of voters in the last gubernatorial election for statutes, and 8 percent for constitutional amendments. The secretary of state submits the measure at the next general election held at least 131 days after it qualifies or at any special election held before the next general election. The governor may call a special election for the measure.

Before 1960 initiatives appeared only on the general election ballot, thus limiting their use to the two-year election cycle. From 1960 to 2012 they appeared on the primary, general, and special election ballots. In 2012 a new law, propelled by the Democratic majority in the legislature, again required that ballot propositions appear only on the general election ballot in November, motivated by the general consensus that the smaller and more conservative primary electorates disadvantage more liberal initiatives.

FREQUENCY OF USE Initiatives have become indispensable to California's political fabric. From 1912 to 2018 over 2,000 initiatives were titled and summarized for circulation. Of this number, 397 qualified for the ballot, 4 were removed by court order, and 142 were approved by the voters—for an overall passage rate of 36 percent. Of the 142 initiatives approved, 42 were constitutional amendments and 13 were constitutional/stationary changes.[17]

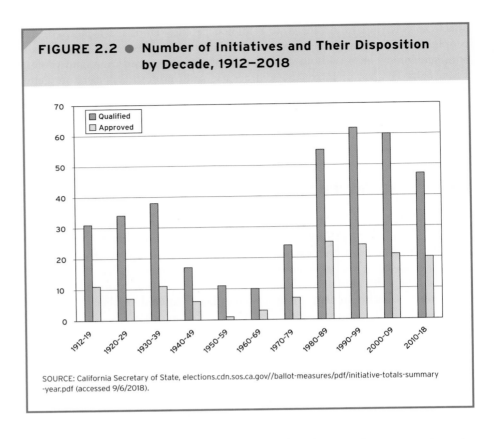

FIGURE 2.2 ● Number of Initiatives and Their Disposition by Decade, 1912–2018

SOURCE: California Secretary of State, elections.cdn.sos.ca.gov//ballot-measures/pdf/initiative-totals-summary-year.pdf (accessed 9/6/2018).

Figure 2.2 presents the use of initiative by decade. Note these two points: the increasing frequency of initiatives since 1970, and the varying, but generally low level of success for the measures that made it to the ballot.

For discussion purposes, we can compress the 100-year history of initiatives into four time periods: 1912–39, 1940–69, 1970–99, and 2000–18.

1912–39 From the beginning, various individuals and special interests understood that the initiative could be used to forward their special causes. Social and cultural issues, such as outlawing professional fighting, prostitution, gambling on horse races, and land ownership by Asian Americans, drew the highest voter turnout during this period. Labor issues (closed versus open shops) and tax propositions were also volatile issues.

No single issue, however, dominated the initiative process during this period more than the so-called "liquor question."[18] These initiatives were among the most controversial, and they drew high voter turnouts. Twelve measures related to liquor control appeared on the ballot between 1914 and 1936: measures for and against full prohibition, anti-saloon measures, and measures related to state regulation versus local control. Voting was consistent throughout this period, with the anti-Prohibition forces generally prevailing on every measure. The issue, however, wouldn't go away—until 1948 when, after many failures to qualify an initiative, the anti-liquor forces qualified another local option measure, which was rejected by 70 percent of the voters. After this vote, the issue lost its appeal, never to appear on the ballot again.

1940–69 In this time period use of the initiative declined markedly. Compared to the previous 27 years, a higher percentage of proposed measures failed to gather enough signatures to qualify for the ballot. The subject matter of the initiatives also varied from those of 1912–39. Newer issues came to the forefront: race and civil rights, property taxes, and labor and welfare.

Proposition 14 (1964) was the most prominent of a number of initiatives that dealt with fair housing. The initiative was drafted to nullify the Rumford Fair Housing Act, which prohibited discrimination in the rental, lease, or purchase of housing on the basis of race and national origin. The Rumford Act, supporters of Proposition 14 claimed, interfered with their private property rights. Real estate and homeowners' associations led the efforts in support of the proposition; a coalition of Democratic Party leadership, organized labor, churches, and a variety of other groups led the forces against it. The broader issue of race, specifically regarding treatment of and biases toward African Americans, lingered in the background of the campaign; by all accounts, race was the deciding factor in how people voted. Proposition 14 passed by a 2-to-1 margin in November 1964. Its victory was a major impetus for the Watts riots during the summer of 1965, which lasted six days, resulted in 34 deaths, and damaged almost 1,000 buildings.[19] Over the next two years, Proposition 14 was overturned, first by the California Supreme Court and then by the U.S. Supreme Court, for violating the Fourteenth Amendment.

1970–99 In this period initiatives abounded, with over 1,000 initiatives receiving titles, 141 qualifying for ballot, and 56 approved by the voters. The subjects involved social, cultural, and economic issues, including the death penalty, gun control, busing, the property tax, nuclear power, water resources, air quality, coastal preservation, English as the official language, affirmative action, undocumented immigrants, and gay marriage.

The most controversial initiative of this period was Proposition 13, titled the "People's Initiative to Limit Property Taxation" (1978). Sponsored by longtime antitax activists Howard Jarvis and Paul Gann, Proposition 13 was a reaction to the spiraling appreciation of property throughout the 1970s. In just one year, some properties were reassessed at a value 50 to 100 percent higher, and their owners' tax bills jumped accordingly. Proposition 13 included several provisions, one of which dramatically reduced residential property taxes and another that required a two-thirds supermajority in both houses of the legislature to approve tax increases.

Proposition 13 was a grassroots effort, opposed by nearly every state employee and labor union and most Democratic leaders. The pro side raised $2.2 million, and the con side raised $2 million. On June 6, 1978, nearly two-thirds of California's voters passed the proposition, reducing property tax rates by about 57 percent.

Now, almost 40 years later, Proposition 13 is still hotly debated. Critics argue that it creates tax inequities by treating residential and commercial property as equivalent and by assessing similar properties in different ways based solely on when a homeowner bought a house. Supporters argue that pegging property taxes to the value of the property, assessed yearly, exposes homeowners to accelerated yearly property taxes, which leaves them vulnerable to losing their homes. In 2020, California voters will decide whether to revise Proposition 13 to split the rolls.

2000–18 During this period, California voters decided on 105 initiatives in 19 separate elections, 3 of which were special elections, including the special election to recall Governor Gray Davis. Initiatives that passed included measures on farm animal confinement practices, redistricting the state legislative boundaries, victims' rights, and parole procedures. (See Table 2.1 for a list of the top contributors for this period.)

The most controversial and long-lasting ballot issue deals with same-sex marriage, an issue that has been publicly debated for some 35 years. In 1977 the state legislature passed a law stating that marriage was a "personal relation arising out of a civil contract between a man and a woman." This was reaffirmed in 2000 when the voters passed Proposition 22, a statutory—not constitutional—amendment that revised the California Family Code to define marriage as between a man and a woman. However, in May 2008, the California Supreme Court ruled Proposition 22 invalid. At about the same time, fearing such a decision, proponents of Proposition 8 ("Eliminates Right of Same-Sex Couples to Marry") had already begun to qualify the initiative for the ballot, relying on a **constitutional amendment**, not a **statute**, to end debate on the issue.

The campaign over Proposition 8 was fiercely contested. In the end, the initiative passed by a margin of 52.3 to 47.7 percent. Both sides raised significant amounts of money: those supporting Proposition 8 contributed $39 million, while those opposing contributed $44 million, making it one of the most expensive initiative campaigns in state history and the highest expenditure on a same-sex marriage initiative campaign in the nation. After the election, six lawsuits were filed with the California Supreme Court by same-sex couples and government bodies challenging the constitutionality of Proposition 8. The court consented to hear three of the six jointly, but it denied the request to stay the enforcement of

---

TABLE 2.1 ● Top Contributors to Initiative Ballot Committees, 2000–18

Contributor	Amount ($)
California Teachers Association	$159,281,213
Philip Morris	107,037,384
Pharmaceutical Research & Manufacturers of America	71,159,206
DaVita Inc	66,974,313
California State Council of Service Employees	65,023,920
RJ Reynolds Tobacco Company	64,475,932
Pacific Gas & Electric Company	62,718,850
California Association of Hospital and Health Systems	61,195,522
Charles Munger, Jr.	59,123,466
Stephen L. Bing	51,066,372
Thomas Steyer	49,434,000
Pechanga Band of Luiseno Mission Indians	48,931,480
Morongo Casino Resort Spa	46,660,977
AIDS Healthcare Foundation	46,397,012
Chevron Corporation	44,777,500

SOURCE: National Institute on Money in State Politics, www.followthemoney.org/show-me?s=CA&y=2018,2017,2016, 2015,2014,2013,2012,2011,2010,2009,2008,2007,2006,2005,2004,2003,2002,2001,2000&m-exi=1#[{3|(1|gro=d -eid,d-ad-st,d-ins (accessed 11/12/18).

Two same-sex couples–Paul Katami and Jeffrey Zarrillo, and Kristin Perry and Sandra Stier–pictured here outside the U.S. Supreme Court, were the plaintiffs in *Hollingsworth v. Perry*. The Court held that the sponsors of Proposition 8 "lacked standing" to appeal the federal court ruling that upheld same-sex marriage under the Equal Protection Clause of the federal Constitution and thus paved the way for same-sex marriage in California.

Proposition 8. On May 26, 2009, the court ruled that Proposition 8 was valid but allowed existing same-sex marriages to stand (in *Strauss v. Horton*).

Opponents of Proposition 8 then took their fight to federal court, which, on August 4, 2010, declared the ban unconstitutional in *Perry v. Schwarzenegger* (renamed *Perry v. Brown* to reflect the changing governorship). This decision was upheld by the Ninth Circuit in February 2012. The supporters of Proposition 8 (but not the state government) then appealed to the U.S. Supreme Court. The Court ruled in *Hollingsworth v. Perry* in June 2013 that the proposition's supporters could not appeal the case; only the state government could defend a proposition approved by the voters, and the state had declined to do so. As a result of this decision, same-sex marriage became legal in California. Two years later, same-sex marriage became legal throughout the United States as a result of the U.S. Supreme Court decision in *Obergefell v. Hodges*.

How can we account for the increase in initiatives over the past four decades? The simplest explanation is that it is a consequence of several factors, including the complexity of modern society and the increased willingness of the government to regulate decisions previously left to citizens. Additionally, the legislature went from part to full time in 1968, which had a number of significant effects on California politics: more politicians made a career in the field, more legislation was passed, the budget grew, and decision making and power shifted to Sacramento.

These shifts, coupled with the other Progressive reforms designed to rid the capital of political corruption and an unresponsive legislature—direct primaries, term limits, regulation of campaign contributions, and various tactics to weaken political parties—undermined voters' influence on elected officials. Frustrated by the action or inaction of the legislature, voters have turned to the initiative to get what they want.

In addition to voters, special interests frequently turned to initiatives during this period to promote policies they could not get through the legislature. Money has increasingly become the only requirement for a successful initiative campaign. As a result, an industry of professional campaign managers and signature gatherers is flourishing. These so-called policy managers identify hot issues and then search for clients who will pay for the privilege of sponsoring the initiative.

Referendum

THE PROCESS The referendum allows voters to approve or reject constitutional amendments or statutes proposed or passed by the state legislature. There are two types of referendum: the legislative referendum and the popular referendum.[20]

The **legislative referendum** exists when the legislature proposes a constitutional amendment or revision, or the issuing of the majority of bonds (long-term borrowing to finance capital projects such as construction of buildings and infrastructure). This type of referendum must be approved by a two-thirds vote of both houses of the legislature before it appears on the ballot. In contrast to other direct democracy measures, legislative referenda are brought before the voters automatically, without the need for qualifying petitions.

The **popular referendum** is employed when voters are displeased with a law that was passed by the legislature. The requirements are the same as those for the initiative, and the two are sometimes confused. The process is as follows: the measure may be proposed by presenting to the secretary of state a petition with signatures equal to 5 percent of the voters in the last gubernatorial election. The filing of the signatures must take place within a 90-day period after the enactment of the statute. If the measure qualifies to be on the ballot, the law in question may not take effect until the electorate decides whether it should become a law.

FREQUENCY OF USE The referendum is used infrequently. In fact, it has almost faded from use. Between 1912 and 2016, 50 referenda have appeared on the ballot. Voters rejected 29 laws and approved 21. Of the seven approved since 1982, five dealt with Indian gaming. Proposition 29 (2000) rejected repeal of the Pala Indian tribe compact that authorized the operation of "video lottery terminals" if operated as lotteries, not slot machines. Propositions 94, 95, 96, and 97 (2008) allowed four individual tribes to operate additional slot machines and revised the environmental impact procedures. In 2012 voters rejected a veto referendum funded by Charles Munger, Jr., keeping intact the state Senate districts drawn by the Citizens Redistricting Commission.[21] In the 2016 general election, voters upheld a law passed by the state legislature that prohibited grocery and other retail stores from providing single-use plastic or paper carryout bags at point of sale and placed a 10-cent charge on reusable paper bags. The referendum to repeal the plastic bag fee, Proposition 65, was mostly funded by the plastics industry; environmental groups and grocers supported the fee.

Recall

THE PROCESS The **recall** allows voters to determine whether to eject an elected official from office before his or her term expires. Proponents first submit a petition alleging the reason for recall. They then have 150 days to present to the secretary of state a petition with the required number of signatures to qualify for the ballot. If the sitting official is recalled, a successor is elected. Most recalls are of school board or city council members at the local level.

For statewide offices, the number of signatures must be equal to 12 percent of the last vote for the office, with signatures from at least five counties equal to 1 percent of the last vote for the office in the county. For the Senate, Assembly, members of the Board of Equalization, and judges, the number of signatures must be equal to 20 percent of the last vote for the office. Upon receiving the petitions, an election must be held between 60 and 80 days from the date of certification of sufficient signatures.

FREQUENCY OF USE Recall of statewide offices or the state legislature are rare. There have been eight recall elections out of 118 filings against state officeholders. Seven of the eight were state legislators; Governor Gray Davis in 2003 was the other. Four of the state legislators were expelled from office. The recall was put into use against three state legislators almost immediately after its passage—twice in 1913, against Senator Marshall Black for involvement in a banking scandal, which succeeded, and against Senator James Owen for corruption, which failed. The next year, Senator Edwin Grant, who represented the red-light district in San Francisco, was successfully recalled for opposing prostitution.

Four other state legislators faced a recall vote in 1994 and 1995. The National Rifle Association failed in its attempt to recall Senator David Roberti for his position on gun control legislation. Two Republican members of the Assembly, Doris Allen and Paul Horcher, were voted out of office for supporting Democrat Willie Brown for speaker in a battle between the parties for control of the Assembly. Similarly, an attempt to recall Democratic Assemblyman Mike Machado for backing Republicans failed.[22]

The most notorious recall was that of Governor Davis. He is the only California governor to have been recalled, although there have been over two dozen previous attempts, including three against Ronald Reagan in the 1960s and one against Pete Wilson in the 1990s. During the 2002 campaign for governor, Davis, the incumbent governor, had claimed that the budget deficit was $18 billion, but a week after his election he revealed it was actually $35 billion. Proponents of the recall immediately accused Davis of misleading voters about the severity of the state's budget crisis during his reelection campaign. Other actions prompting the recall included the governor's efforts to prevent the anti-immigrant Proposition 187 from being appealed to the U.S. Supreme Court and his approval of two gun control measures. The public also held Governor Davis partially responsible for the electricity crisis, during which some people's electricity bills doubled and even tripled. Supporters of the recall also blamed Davis for California's generally weak economy. After Representative Darrell Issa, who hoped to run for governor, funded the signature collection effort with a contribution of $2 million, the recall took off on its own momentum. Because the filing requirements to run as Davis's successor were relatively low, 135 candidates filed to replace him. Arnold Schwarzenegger's candidacy quickly gained the most attention, and he easily won the two-part election, in which voters were asked to decide whether Davis should be recalled and to choose his successor. Only 4 of the 135 candidates received more than 1 percent of the vote.

Debating the Merit of Direct Democracy

The debate about the merits of direct democracy has been ongoing since its adoption in the early twentieth century. As we have seen, the initiative has been employed more than the referendum or recall and is generally the focus of the debate on the value of direct democracy.

Many scholars believe that the initiative blurs the complexity of many issues and reduces them to clichés or sound bites for the voter. Large donors with deep pockets dominate the initiative process, undermining the efficacy of representative government with its built-in system of checks and balances. Only millionaires and billionaires, not average citizens, can afford to qualify their ideas for the ballot; once qualified, no contribution limits apply. Single elections often feature competing ballot measures, such as the contest between competing income tax measures Proposition 30 and 38 on the November 2012 ballot. If both had been approved, the one with the most votes would have prevailed (but only Proposition 30 was approved by voters). Similarly, in November 2016 voters were asked to either repeal the death penalty (Proposition 62) or speed up executions (Proposition 66). If both had been approved, only the one receiving more votes would have taken effect, but voters only approved Proposition 66.

Most who have studied the initiative believe it to be a flawed method of forming public policy. Many initiatives are poorly drafted and are difficult to understand even for judges and legislators. The process is complex, proponents cannot correct errors once circulation of petitions has begun, and many are later declared unconstitutional. The legislature is discouraged from participating in the process at all. Reflecting the strong historic bias of its citizens against the legislature, California is the only state that prohibits the legislature from amending initiatives unless permission is written into the initiative itself. Even then, it usually requires a supermajority of two-thirds of the legislature to approve changes, a level of support difficult if not impossible to obtain on significant amendments. Qualifying initiatives by signature is too easy for a signature-gathering firm and too difficult in the five months allowed for those without one, meaning that a large amount of money is necessary in order to qualify an initiative.

Supporters of the initiative, on the other hand, claim that it is a more effective means of serving the majority in California than the legislative process. Therein lies the catch-22 that largely defines California politics: the legislature is supposedly hamstrung by the zealous use of direct democracy, while direct democracy is supposedly necessary to overcome an unproductive legislature.

A 2013 Public Policy Institute of California (PPIC) poll (see Figure 2.3) showed continued strong support for the initiative process, with 72 percent of likely voters viewing as positive the initiative's power to change public policy, and only 40 percent agreeing that major reforms are needed to the initiative process. At the same time, 60 percent said that public policies made through the initiative are superior to those made by the governor and legislature. Likely voters supported several reforms of the initiative process: more public disclosure of funding sources on initiatives; giving the legislature and the initiative's sponsors more time to seek a compromise before the initiative goes on the ballot; and increased public engagement, such as a citizens' commission to hold hearings on initiatives and make ballot recommendations. Oregon established such a program in 2011.

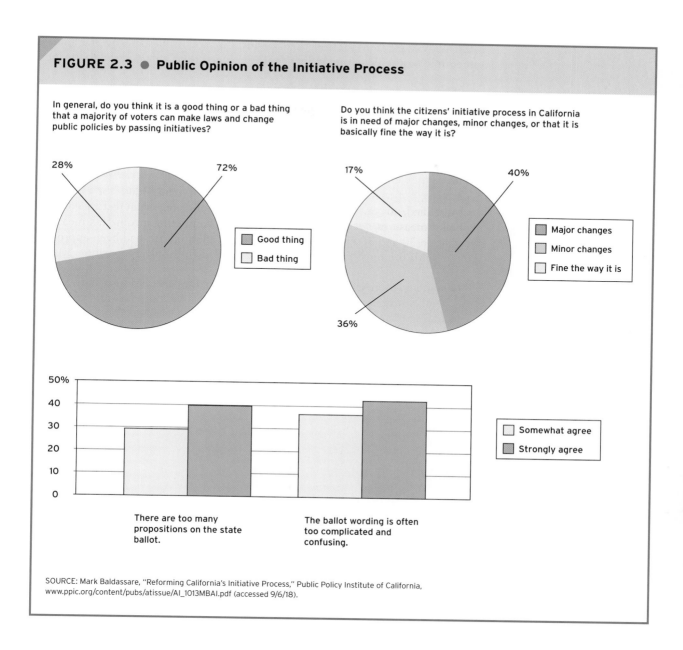

FIGURE 2.3 ● Public Opinion of the Initiative Process

In general, do you think it is a good thing or a bad thing that a majority of voters can make laws and change public policies by passing initiatives?

28% 72%

- Good thing
- Bad thing

Do you think the citizens' initiative process in California is in need of major changes, minor changes, or that it is basically fine the way it is?

17% 40% 36%

- Major changes
- Minor changes
- Fine the way it is

50%
40
30
20
10
0

There are too many propositions on the state ballot.

The ballot wording is often too complicated and confusing.

- Somewhat agree
- Strongly agree

SOURCE: Mark Baldassare, "Reforming California's Initiative Process," Public Policy Institute of California, www.ppic.org/content/pubs/atissue/AI_1013MBAI.pdf (accessed 9/6/18).

California's Constitution: Where Are We Now?

California's constitution has been through three stages—establishment in the mid-1800s, rewriting in 1879, and extensive amendment during the Progressive Era. Since then, a fourth, ongoing stage has been defined by political scientists and others, in which numerous suggestions have been made to update the constitutional framework. Most notably, the 1996 California Constitutional Revision Commission made many suggestions to strengthen the governor and make state government less susceptible to interest-group influence. These suggestions included the following:

- Having the governor and lieutenant governor run as a team. Because the governor and lieutenant governor currently are elected separately, their political agendas may diverge.

- Having the other elected members of the executive branch appointed by the governor. The governor currently has no supervisory responsibility over the lieutenant governor, the secretary of state, the treasurer, the controller, the attorney general, the insurance commissioner, and the state superintendent of public instruction. The lack of supervisory authority significantly weakens the governor as a leader (see Chapter 6).

- Merging the several tax administration agencies. The state currently has three tax administration agencies; merging them would save money (see Chapter 6).

- Lengthening term limits for legislators. In 2012 the term limit for state Assembly members was lengthened from 6 years to 12 and for state senators from 8 years to 12, provided the total time in both chambers is limited to 12 years. This is an improvement over the stricter limits enacted in 1990, but the term limits still increase the likelihood that major, complex state legislation will be enacted by inexperienced legislators (see Chapter 5).

Most of these proposals have never come before the voters.

Study Guide

FOR FURTHER READING

Broder, David. *Democracy Derailed: Initiative Campaigns and the Power of Money*. New York: Harcourt, 2000.

California Secretary of State. "History of California Initiatives." www.sos.ca.gov/elections/ballot-measures/resources-and -historical-information/history-california-initiatives/. Accessed 6/19/18.

Donovan, Todd, S. Bowler, D. McCuan, and K. Fernandez. "Contending Players and Strategies: Opposition Advantages in Initiative Elections." In *Citizens as Legislators: Direct Democracy in the United States*, edited by S. Bowler, T. Donovan, and C. Tolbert, 133–52. Columbus: Ohio State University Press, 1998.

Gerber, Elisabeth. *The Populist Paradox: Interest Group Influence on the Promise of Direct Legislation*. Princeton, NJ: Princeton University Press, 1999.

Hofstadter, Richard. *The Age of Reform*. New York: Washington Square Press, 1988.

HoSang, Daniel Martinez. *Racial Propositions: Ballot Initiatives and the Making of Postwar California*. Berkeley: University of California Press, 2010.

Hui, Iris and David O. Sears. "Reexamining the Effect of Racial Propositions on Latinos' Partisanship in California." *Political Behavior* 40, 1 (March 2018): 149–174.

Johnson, Hiram. "First Inaugural Address." January 3, 1913. http://governors.library.ca.gov/addresses/23-hjohnson01 .html. Accessed 6/20/16.

Levy, JoAnn. *They Saw the Elephant: Women in the California Gold Rush*. Norman: University of Oklahoma Press, 2014.

Lustig, R. Jeffrey, ed. *Remaking California: Reclaiming the Public Good*. Berkeley: Heyday, 2010.

Madley, Benjamin. *An American Genocide: The United States and the California Indian Catastrophe, 1846–1873*. New Haven: Yale University Press, 2017.

Matthews, Joe, and Mark Paul. *California Crackup, How Reforms Broke the Golden State and How We Can Fix It*. Berkeley: University of California Press, 2010.

Romero, Mindy, and Greg Keidan. 2018. "California's 2014 Ballot Initiative Transparency Act (BITA) and Its Impact on Public Involvement in the Ballot Initiative Process." *California Journal of Politics and Policy* 9, 2. DOI: 10.5070/P2CJPP9234891

Starr, Kevin. *Inventing the Dream: California through the Progressive Era*. New York: Oxford University Press, 1985.

———. *California: A History*. New York: The Modern Library, 2005.

Smith, Daniel A. and Caroline J. Tolbert. "The Initiative to Party: Partisanship and Ballot Initiatives in California," *Party Politics* 7, 6 (November 2001): 739–57. DOI: 10.1177/1354068801007006004

———. *Educated by Initiative: The Effects of Direct Democracy on Citizens and Political Organizations in the United States*. Ann Arbor: University of Michigan Press, 2004.

ON THE WEB

Baldassare, Mark. *At Issue, Reforming California's Initiative Process*. Public Policy Institute of California, 2013. www.ppic.org/main/publication.asp?i=1071. Accessed 6/20/16.

Baldassare, Mark, Dean Bonner, Sonja Petek, and Jui Shrestha. *The Initiative Process in California*. Public Policy Institute of California, 2013. www.ppic.org/main/publication_show.asp?i=1072. Accessed 6/20/16.

Bruno, Carson. "Is it time to reconsider California's initiative system?" *Eureka: California's Policy, Economics, and Politics*. The Hoover Institution, Aug. 30, 2016, https://www.hoover.org/research/it-time-reconsider-californias-initiative-system. Accessed 6/19/18.

California Secretary of State. *Ballot Measures*. www.sos.ca.gov/elections. Accessed 6/20/16.

California State Constitution. www.leginfo.ca.gov/const.html. Accessed 6/20/16. This site makes the California State Constitution searchable by keyword.

Center for Governmental Studies. *Democracy by Initiative*. May 2008. www.policyarchive.org/collections/cgs/index?section=5&id=5800. Accessed 6/20/16. Search for "Democracy by Initiative."

Initiative & Referendum Institute. www.iandrinstitute.org. Accessed 7/20/16.

Southern Pacific Historical & Technical Society. www.sphts.org. Accessed 6/20/16.

KQED. "Boomtown, 1870s: Decade of Bonanza, Bust and Unbridled Racism." *KQED News*. https://www.kqed.org/news/10413670/draft-boomtown-history-2a. Accessed 6/19/18.

KQED. "The California Gold Rush." *The American Experience*. https://www.pbs.org/wgbh/americanexperience/features/goldrush-california/. Accessed 6/19/18.

SUMMARY

I. The history of the California Constitution comprises four stages.
   A. 1849: basic structure of government established. Includes separation of powers, bicameralism, federalism, and popular election of most state offices.
   B. 1879: a constitutional convention adds nine new articles and 8,000 words to respond to the reform needs of the time.
   C. 1910–17: the Progressive Era adds the initiative, referendum, and recall, as well as hundreds of reform laws.
   D. 1960–present: California voters have authorized a few significant reforms.

II. Proposing an amendment to the California Constitution is easy.
   A. Amendments can be proposed in three ways:
      1. Through a constitutional convention. The legislature can convene the convention by a two-thirds vote, or it can be convened by a majority vote of the electorate from an initiative. A Bay Area business group tried to collect sufficient signatures for a new constitutional convention in 2009–10 but gave up because professional signature-gathering firms refused to work with the group, feeling that the effort would imperil their future existence.
      2. Amendments may be proposed by collecting signatures through the initiative process.
         a) Signatures totaling 8 percent of the vote in the last gubernatorial election are required, collected over a five-month period.
         b) Most amendments are proposed this way. The cost is approximately $1 million to $2 million, mostly for signature gathering.
      3. The legislature may propose an amendment by a two-thirds vote.
   B. Amendments must go through a ratification stage. Regardless of the way in which an amendment is proposed, the electorate must then ratify the amendment before it goes into the constitution. A majority vote is required.

III. The Progressive reformers had several key goals.
   A. Ending the dominance of big business, especially the Southern Pacific Railroad, over the state.

B. Reforming the corrupt political process.

C. Removing from office corrupt political officials at the state and local levels of government.

D. Returning political power to the people.

IV. Progressive laws and constitutional amendments wrought many significant changes.

  A. Enacted protections for working people

  B. Established nonpartisan elections

  C. Instituted primary elections

  D. Created office block voting

  E. Set in motion the process of direct democracy—the initiative, referendum, and recall

  F. Resulted in the great number of Progressive reforms that are still in operation today

V. Direct democracy is a vital aspect of California politics.

  A. The initiative is the most popular of the three direct democracy mechanisms.

    1. Proponents need to gather signatures equal to 5 percent of voters in the last gubernatorial election for statutes and 8 percent of the voters for constitutional amendments.

    2. Since 1912 roughly 36 percent of initiatives that have been voted on have passed.

    3. The initiative has increasingly become a mechanism by which special interests or wealthy individuals can pass legislation by circumventing the legislature.

B. The referendum refers legislation to the voters for a direct decision. There are two types of referendum: legislative and popular.

  1. Legislative referendum allows voters to decide on statutes or constitutional amendments as well as most bond measures proposed by the legislature; it takes a two-thirds vote of the legislature to place a referendum on the ballot.

  2. Popular referendum allows voters to approve or repeal an act of the legislature. If the legislature passes a law that voters do not approve of, they may gather signatures to demand a popular vote on the law. Proponents need to gather signatures equal to 5 percent of voters in the last gubernatorial election.

  3. The referendum is infrequently used and has appeared on the ballot 50 times since 1912.

C. The recall allows voters to remove a public official from elected office before his or her term is up.

  1. The number of signatures that needs to be gathered depends on the office: 12 percent of the last vote for statewide office from at least five counties equal to 1 percent of the last vote in the county; 20 percent of the last vote for office for Senate, Assembly, and Board of Equalization.

  2. Since 1912 there have been only eight recalls of statewide officials and legislative members.

  3. Governor Gray Davis is the only statewide official to have been recalled.

PRACTICE QUIZ

1. The popular direct-democracy process by which citizens can place a constitutional amendment or statute on the ballot is called a(n)
   a) referendum.
   b) initiative.
   c) recall.
   d) nonpartisan election.

2. The individual who served as governor during much of the Progressive Era was
   a) Chester Rowell.
   b) Edward Dickson.
   c) Hiram Johnson.
   d) Samuel P. Huntington.

3. The process by which a petition signed by a specific percentage of those who cast votes in the last gubernatorial election enables voters to approve or reject a law enacted by the legislature is a(n)

   a) popular referendum.
   b) initiative.
   c) recall.
   d) nonpartisan election.

4. The process by which an elected official is removed from office before his or her term expires is called a(n)
   a) referendum.
   b) initiative.
   c) recall.
   d) nonpartisan election.

5. Progressive reformers pointed to this company whenever they spoke about machine politics and corporate privilege in Sacramento.
   a) Standard Oil Company
   b) Bank of America
   c) Southern Pacific Railroad
   d) Northern Securities Company

6. The only sitting California governor to be recalled from office was
   a) Ronald Reagan.
   b) Jerry Brown.
   c) Gray Davis.
   d) Pete Wilson.

7. Which of the following direct-democracy devices allows voters to approve or reject constitutional amendments or statutes and the majority of bond measures put on the ballot by the legislature?
   a) initiative
   b) direct primary
   c) legislative referendum
   d) recall

8. In which historical block was the greatest number of initiatives titled?
   a) 1912–39
   b) 1940–69

   c) 1970–99
   d) 2000–16

9. Which of the following is not a Progressive Era reform?
   a) nonpartisan elections
   b) primary elections
   c) the office block vote
   d) party caucuses

10. Which of the following is *not* a legal way to amend the California Constitution?
   a) The legislature can convene a constitutional convention by a two-thirds vote.
   b) The governor can sign into law a proposed amendment passed by the legislature.
   c) The legislature may propose a constitutional amendment by a two-thirds vote.
   d) The electorate can propose a constitutional amendment through the initiative process.

CRITICAL-THINKING QUESTIONS

1. The California Constitution has gone through a series of revisions. Identify the periods of those revisions and discuss the contributions that each made to the state's political structure.
2. How did the extreme diversity of the state, which began with the Gold Rush, shape the California Constitution?
3. Suppose you worked for a coalition of interest groups supporting legislation to increase the state sales tax to fund a state-run health care system. The coalition is frustrated by the lack of action in the legislature. They come to you for advice about the initiative process and the possibility of success. What would you tell them, based on what you've learned in this chapter?
4. Some people argue that direct democracy provides citizens with another way to correct the behavior and decision

making of public officials. Others argue that it is merely the instrument of those special interest groups that have enough money to manipulate the political process. Present an argument for each position. Where do you stand in this debate?
5. California is the model Progressive state. The key components of the Progressive agenda, however, greatly weakened the role of political parties in the state. Identify and discuss how some of these Progressive reforms have weakened the state's party system. Is this a good or a bad thing? Do you think there are any correlations between weak parties and the increasing use of the initiative process?

KEY TERMS

constitutional amendment (p. 40)
direct democracy (p. 35)
initiative (p. 37)

Progressive movement (p. 23)
recall (p. 42)
legislative referendum (p. 42)

popular referendum (p. 42)
statute (p. 40)

3 Interest Groups and the Media in California

WHAT INTEREST GROUPS DO AND WHY THEY MATTER IN CALIFORNIA POLITICS

Consider the diversity of organizations that try to influence governmental policy or legislation:

- A **student organization** opposes legislation to raise tuition at state universities.
- A **business trade association** supports legislation that would reform the state's workers' compensation insurance system.
- A **beverage company** opposes legislation to tax sugar-sweetened soft drinks and label them with warnings of health hazards.
- A **citizens' group** supports legislation that would impose stricter penalties on people convicted of drunk driving.
- An **association of county governments** opposes legislation that prohibits the placing of certain juvenile offenders into group homes that are located in residential neighborhoods.
- A **public employees' union** supports legislation that prohibits state agencies from contracting with businesses unless the businesses pay their employees the equivalent of a living wage.

Each of these organizations is an interest group. Interest groups have always been part of California's (and the United States') political landscape. They are a product of freedom of association, a First Amendment right under our democratic system of government.

Interest groups are associations of individuals who seek to influence policy decisions in the legislature, the executive branch, and administrative agencies, as well as through direct legislation (the initiative). They are one method, as is voting, for individuals to voice their opinions on issues that concern them.

Interest groups are also called pressure groups, political advocacy groups, special interest groups, and lobbying groups. Because they focus primarily on influencing policy decisions in the legislature, interest groups are often referred to as the **third house**, a term that describes their standing and influence in the legislative process.[1]

In California, interest groups are especially influential because of the state's unique political landscape. As we shall see, open primaries, top-two primary elections, term limits, and nonpartisan elections at the local level have freed candidates from party dependence and pushed them toward interest groups for financial backing and help with mobilizing voters. At the same time, interest groups have realized that they can successfully use the initiative process to achieve political goals and have spared no expense in launching propositions, even when they are in conflict with broad-based citizen interests.

Character of Interest Groups

All Californians are represented, whether wittingly or not, by interest groups such as county and city governments, trade associations, labor unions, professional and religious organizations, educational institutions, and environmental groups. When a government recognizes the right of association, citizens will exercise that right, and groups of all types will form. There is much debate about the influence of interest groups in the political arena, especially about whether the theories of **pluralism** or **elitism** best explain their status and power in the political process.

Pluralist theory considers the political system as a marketplace in which a multitude of interests compete, where no single interest or combination of interests is powerful enough to dominate and government sits outside as an umpire or a referee. Pluralist theory argues that power is dispersed. To achieve success, interests often have to join together to bargain and negotiate with opposition interests, producing, by the end of the process, policy decisions. Pluralist theory acknowledges that some groups are stronger and more successful than others; however, it also contends that these groups do not necessarily succeed all or even a majority of the time—weaker but well-organized groups do sometimes succeed in achieving their goals or checking stronger groups.

Elitist theory acknowledges that there are many interest groups active in the political process but argues that most of them have minimal power. Power rests in the hands of a few groups, such as large national and multinational corporations, universities, foundations, and public policy institutes, where leaders (elites) set the agenda and determine the policy outcomes of government. Accordingly, when it comes to important policy matters, such as the economy and noteworthy social issues, elites representing a narrow range of groups determine the basic direction of public policy. Still, elite theory recognizes that less powerful groups, most commonly in coalition with other less powerful groups, are occasionally able to check the proposals of the elites. This is especially true when elites can't agree among themselves on policy choices.

But neither of these theories perfectly describes interest groups in California; in practice, California politics is a blend of pluralism and elitism. In each legislative session, there is widespread interest group activity, with literally thousands of interests competing for influence on more than 2,000 bills. Most of these groups, from child care facilities and auto repair shops to environmental organizations, trade unions, and businesses, focus on measures that directly affect their interests. Often these issues are of limited concern to the public at large. In these circumstances, the groups involved in the issue, whether supporting or opposed to it, work to create policy through competition and compromise. Here the pluralism theory fits well. Yet on some broad-based issues, a small number of (elite) groups, such as public employee unions and multinational corporations, influence decision making to favor their own special interests. They are able to exert power on the legislature, the public, and other interest groups because of their economic clout and ability to contribute great sums of money to candidates, independent committees, ballot initiatives, and public relations campaigns. In the end, California politics is a mixture of pluralism and elitism, depending on the issue in question and the stakes presented.

Diversity of Interest Groups

The term *interest group* is all inclusive, covering a wide range of businesses and organizations. The California secretary of state classifies interest groups into 19 categories and indicates the amount spent by each category for lobbying during a two-year legislative session. Table 3.1 lists the figures for the 2015–16 session.

Many organizations openly state under the About tab on their websites that **lobbying** or advocacy is a major part of their activity; this is a principal reason why many individuals and businesses join a group. For example, the California Applicants' Attorneys Association claims to be "the most powerful and most knowledgeable legal voice for the injured workers of California"; the California Labor Federation, AFL-CIO, professes to promote "the interests of working people and their families for the betterment of California communities"; and the California Alliance of Child and Family Services claims it is "the champion and leading voice for organizations that advocate for children and families, and for advancing policies and services on their behalves."

Table 3.2 lists the top employers of lobbyists. This list has remained relatively stable over the past several years, with three or four groups moving in and out of the ranks from one year to the next, depending on their agenda in the legislative session. By most standards, the lobbyists for these groups are some of the most successful in Sacramento. Note how the top employers of lobbyists match up with the categories in Table 3.1. The health sector, for instance, is third in total contributions, and the California Hospital Association and Kaiser Foundation Health Plan both make the list.

Individual businesses and educational institutions, however, rarely identify lobbying as one of their activities. This is understandable and perfectly legitimate: lobbying is not a primary reason for the existence of these organizations. They participate in politics to protect their chief interests: profits and education. But they are careful not to call attention to their involvement in politics out of fear that they may alienate customers or tarnish their image. Accordingly, information about their lobbying activity must be obtained from newspaper accounts and public disclosure documents.

Many businesses do join professional or **trade associations** to give them a voice on issues that affect their industry. "We're the champion of California businesses, large and small," the California Chamber of Commerce proudly asserts on its website. "For more than 125 years, CalChamber has worked to make California a better place to live, work, and do business by giving private-sector employers a voice in state politics." Its more than 13,000 member businesses give the chamber tremendous clout and stature. In turn, individual members enjoy several advantages—sharing of cost, strength in numbers, and, perhaps most important, anonymity.

Government also lobbies government. Taxpayer protection groups have come to call these interests—education, health, special districts, local government, state agencies—"the spending lobby" because they are motivated by the desire to maintain or increase their revenue. In Table 3.1, for instance, government was the second highest spender, after the catchall miscellaneous category, among the 19 categories of lobbyist employers who themselves determine the category in which they wish to be listed.

According to governmental lobbyists, the passage in 1978 of Proposition 13, which limited property tax revenues to local government, is responsible for spurring the growth in governmental lobbying and the competition for funds. John P. Quimby, Sr., a former assemblyman who lobbies for San Bernardino County, told the

TABLE 3.1 ● Lobbying Categories and Spending, 2015–16

Category	Amount (in Millions)
1. Miscellaneous**	$120.1
2. Government	97.0
3. Health	80.7
4. Manufacturing, industrial	44.6
5. Oil and gas	38.5
6. Finance, insurance	37.3
7. Labor unions	32.2
8. Education	32.1
9. Utilities	31.4
10. Professional, trade	30.8
11. Entertainment, recreation	15.5
12. Transportation	12.9
13. Real estate	12.0
14. Agriculture	9.7
15. Legal	9.3
16. Merchandise, retail	9.1
17. Public employees	8.2
18. Lodging, restaurants	3.9
19. Political organizations	.5

**Includes hundreds of interest groups, such as professional and trade associations, environmental organizations, and religious groups.

SOURCE: Data from California Secretary of State, by Employer Category, 2015-16, http://cal-access.sos.ca.gov/Lobbying /Employers/list.aspx?view=category&session=2015 (accessed 6/1/18)

TABLE 3.2 ● Top Lobbyist Employers, 2015–16

Organization	Cumulative Expenditures ($)
Western States Petroleum Association	$18,718,663
California Hospital Association	11,980,669
California State Council of Service Employees	11,799,828
Nextgen Climate Action	9,385,933
Chevron Corporation and subsidiaries	7,179,341
California Chamber of Commerce	7,033,032
Kaiser Foundation Health Plan Inc.	4,525,576
California Teachers Association	4,449,370
AT&T	4,307,774
California School Board Association	3,981,703
California School Employees Association	3,456,039
California Manufacturing & Technology Association	3,430,589

SOURCE: Data from California Secretary of State, http://cal-access.sos.ca.gov/Lobbying/Employers/list.aspx?view=category&session=2015 (accessed 6/1/18). (Compare amounts in each "Employer Category, 2015-16.")

Riverside Press Enterprise in 1997: "I wish government wasn't for sale like this, but the fact is you have to hustle to get your share. Local governments without lobbyists see the ones with representation doing better so they say, 'We need to get our butts on board and get one [lobbyist] or they're going to steal everything from us.'"[2] Or, to put it another way, government agencies spend taxpayers' money to lobby government for more money to spend on taxpayers.

Proliferation of Interest Groups

In California over the last two and a half decades, the number of interest groups and lobbying expenditures has grown steadily. In 1990 lobbyists represented approximately 1,300 interest groups; in 2000 the number nearly doubled to 2,552; in 2012 it increased to 3,468; and in 2016 it swelled to 3,663.[3] During the same period, lobbying expenditures also grew substantially with just a slight dip in 2009–10, as seen in Table 3.3.

Several factors have encouraged the proliferation of interest groups:

WEAK POLITICAL PARTIES California has weak parties for a variety of reasons, but the main one is the Progressive reforms of the 1910s. These reforms were directed at the spoils system in government, the control of the political parties over which candidates would represent the party in general elections, and the influence of interest groups in the legislature. To balance these influences, the Progressive reforms granted voters the direct-democracy practices of initiative, referendum, and recall. These measures and subsequent reforms—many of which were considered citizen initiatives, such as the direct primary, term limits, redistricting by an independent commission, and top-two open primaries—greatly free officials from party structure and discipline. But politicians still need money, resources, and support to win reelection, and so they

TABLE 3.3 ● Growth in Lobbying Expenditures

Legislative	Lobbying ($)	Percent Increase (%)
1993–94	$233,872,097	0%
1995–96	250,119,667	6.9
1997–98	292,615,513	17.0
1999–2000	344,318,650	17.7
2001–02	386,829,719	12.4
2003–04	413,376,146	6.9
2005–06	500,326,710	21.0
2007–08	558,419,109	11.6
2009–10	538,638,251	−3.5
2011–12	563,003,065	4.5
2013–14	579,995,079	3.0
2015–16	623,783,807	7.5

SOURCE: Data from California Secretary of State, Employer Category 2015-16, http://cal-access.sos.ca.gov/Lobbying/Employers/list.aspx?view=category&session=2015 (accessed 6/1/18).

have looked to interest groups in lieu of parties for help. In this way, Progressive attempts to curb interest-group influence have instead strengthened it.

GROWTH OF GOVERNMENT California government has grown substantially over the past half century. Californians, like other Americans, initially were suspicious of government, perceiving it as a force whose powers had to be kept in check to protect individual rights. As time passed, however, citizens began to perceive government as a tool that could be used to solve myriad social and economic problems. The legislature has eagerly taken up the challenge. A by-product of government expansion has been that local levels of government have increased their lobbying efforts in the state legislature. For example, in 2015–16, counties, cities, special districts, school districts, and public employee unions spent over $97 million on lobbying legislation that would affect their interests. (See Table 3.1.)

TERM LIMITS In 1990, California voters approved term limits for all state and legislative offices. Term limits, it was argued, would break the cozy relationship between elected officials and lobbyists. Yet this has not been the case. As legislators with years of institutional memory left office, the legislature became more chaotic and less efficient. This opened the door for the "third house" of special interests to gain influence, as lobbyists had the institutional memory that new legislators lacked. Legislators now often rely on lobbyists to write intricate legislation and council them on the flood of complex issues that come across their desk.[4]

PUBLIC INTEREST GROUPS The growth of **public interest groups**, what some call the New Politics movement, began in the 1970s and continues through today. Examples of such groups are AARP, Sierra Club, and the Foundation for Taxpayers and Consumer Rights. The public interest lobby sought to distinguish itself from other groups—business groups, in particular—by "purporting to represent the general good rather than its own economic interests."[5] Although these so-called public interest groups claim to represent *only* the public interest, they should be judged critically; they are sometimes facades behind which narrow private interests hide.

Interest-Group Strategies

Basically, in California, politics *is* interest groups. Not all interest groups, however, are equal. Some have considerably more clout than others. The success of an interest group depends on several factors: a clear message, group cohesiveness, the alignment of the group's interests with those of other groups and elected officials, an understanding of the political process, technical expertise, and money. As we shall see, money is especially important.

Lobbyists

The people who do the work for interest groups are called lobbyists, and the work they do is called lobbying. Lobbyists are at the forefront of interest-group activity. They coordinate the efforts to secure passage, amendment, or defeat of bills in the legislature and the approval or veto of bills by the governor. Having a good lobbyist is paramount to the success of any group.

There are citizen lobbyists and professional lobbyists. A **citizen lobbyist** is not paid to advocate for a particular issue or set of issues. Citizen lobbyists interact with their representatives to express their personal views on an issue and to attempt to influence legislation on that issue. Professional lobbyists are paid for their services

Lobbyists and special interests are often seen as the driving force behind politics in California, as illustrated by this cartoon from the *Los Angeles Daily News*.

and must register with the secretary of state. They also must submit quarterly disclosure reports detailing for whom they are working, the amount of money earned, and payment such as gifts and honoraria made to public officials they lobby.

There are two types of professional lobbyists: contract and in-house. **Contract lobbyists** make up 50 percent of all lobbyists in Sacramento; **in-house lobbyists** account for the other half.[6] Contract lobbyists offer their services to the general public; they are advocates for hire and often represent multiple clients on a variety of issues at the same time. In-house lobbyists are employees of a trade, professional, or labor association and represent that group's interest only. Many of these interest groups also use contract lobbyists because the group is involved in too many issues for its in-house staff to handle, or it may want to use a lobbyist who specializes in a specific subject area such as health insurance. A group may also want to use a lobbyist who has a close relationship with a particular legislator or members of a specific committee whose support is vital for the group's success.

LOBBYING THE LEGISLATURE Few issues are just lobbied—that is, discussed with legislators or their staff during the legislative process. Most issues are managed using a combination of techniques: public relations (marketing), grassroots mobilization, and coalition building.

The first job of the lobbyist is to know the group's objective. Is the goal new legislation? Is it to amend existing law? Or is it to stop another business or interest group from passing new legislation or amending an existing law that may affect the group's interest? The goal may not even be legislation. The group may want to amend current regulatory policy or shape the content of new regulations that will affect its members.

The lobbyist must also identify other groups that may have an interest in the issue and assess whether these groups, as well as legislators, the executive branch, regulators, or the general public, will support or oppose the group's activity. Moreover, lobbyists who can rely on the group's members, especially if they reside in the legislator's district, can more easily influence policy making. The most successful efforts are built around networks of activists who have made it a point to know their elected officials. These relationships can be built in many ways: working on election campaigns, commending them in writing for actions they have taken, contributing to political campaigns, and connecting in other ways so as to have a positive relationship with these officials.

With this preparation in hand, the lobbyist has a greater chance of success. Of course, several other factors are also important: knowledge of the legislation process, strong communication skills, established relationships, credibility, adaptability to change, and the ability to negotiate.

LOBBYING THE EXECUTIVE BRANCH The techniques used to lobby the executive branch are similar to those used in lobbying the state legislature. There are, however, two main differences between these two branches that make lobbying the executive more challenging. First, unlike most other states, California has a number (seven) of statewide elected administration offices composing the plural executive. This makes it more difficult to coordinate lobbying, especially when the elected officials of those offices are from different political parties. Second, the executive branch includes more than 85 agencies, 325 state commissions and boards, and 30 educational institutions (see Chapter 6). The agencies write and oversee the implementation of thousands of regulations that have a powerful impact on different sectors of society at different times. The regulations they write and implement are generally subject-specific and often very technical. This forces a lobbyist to develop expertise—and relationships—with a number of different agencies.

Campaign Contributions to Candidates

Many interest groups also make campaign contributions, which enable them to become familiar with and gain access to legislators. They do so through **political action committees (PACs)**. There are, however, interest groups that don't make campaign contributions, and for a variety of reasons: they don't have the means and resources to do so, or the group opposes making campaign contributions out of principle (for example, the belief that PACs weaken the democratic process by making it more expensive to run for office or that PACs reduce competition because of their overwhelming support of incumbents).

There is a connection between lobbying success and campaign contributions. Those who invest heavily in lobbying generally invest heavily in PAC contributions, and vice versa.[7] Table 3.4 lists the top 11 contributors for the 2015–16 legislative session. The table shows only the amount directly contributed to candidates for the state legislature—the total of which from all contributors was $166,822,059.[8] This figure does not include what these organizations may have spent on independent expenditures for candidates for the state legislature or ballot initiatives, ($83,604,001),[9] the Democratic or Republican Party committees ($41,266,977),[10] or direct contributions to ballot initiatives committees ($469,851,572),[11] which, when totaled, comes to an additional $594,722,550. Campaign contributions enable a lobbyist to gain access to legislators. The lobbyist can then make his or her argument—at which time he or she can provide the legislator with important, often technical information. To put these numbers in perspective, consider that the average cost of a winning seat in the California Assembly was $1,010,528 and in the California Senate was $1,877,994 for the 2015–16 election cycle.

TABLE 3.4 ● Top Eleven Contributors to Legislative Candidates, 2015–16

Organization	Amount ($)
California State Council of Laborers	$1,188,550
California Association of Realtors	1,092,500
California State Council of Service Employees	1,066,100
State Building & Construction Trades Council	970,400
AT&T	818,689
California Teachers Association	776,200
California Faculty Association	768,225
Pechanga Band of Luiseno Mission Indians	763,930
California Nurses Association	694,400
California State Association of Electrical Workers	682,600
The Doctors Company	628,300

SOURCE: National Institute on Money in State Politics, https://www.followthemoney.org/show-me?s=CA&y=2016&c-exi=1&c-r-ot=S,H#[(1|gro=d-eid (accessed 6/1/18).

Studies show that incumbency (currently holding political office) is a strong factor in being elected to office. Incumbents hold an advantage over their opponents for a number of reasons: high visibility and name recognition; media attention; history of constituency service; experience in managing a successful political campaign; and, most important, strong ties to the fund-raising pipeline.[12]

For example, in the 2016 campaign for state Senate, 20 seats were up for election—11 incumbents and 9 open seats. All 11 incumbents won re-election handily. The winning incumbents raised $14.6 million—an average of $1.3 million per incumbent—compared to their opponents who raised a combined $548,411.

In the 2016 campaign for state Assembly, all 80 seats were up for election. Sixty-two of the candidates were incumbents who raised $63.9 million—an average of $1.0 million per incumbent. Their opponents raised $16.7 million—an average of $208,750 per candidate. Needless to say, the incumbents dominated, as all but five won re-election. Of the five, four were interparty contests. In three of these contests the Democrat challengers defeated the Republican incumbent, who ironically had unseated these same individuals in 2014. A fourth Democrat unseated another Republican incumbent. The fifth was an intraparty contest in which the Democrat challenger defeated the Democrat incumbent, with the challenger winning back the seat he had lost to this same individual in 2014. The winning challengers raised $13.0 million, and the losing incumbents raised $8.5 million, making these five races the most expensive Assembly contests in 2016.

In the Senate, the campaign for the nine open seats (seats not held by an incumbent) showed expenditures of $22.9 million. Overall, the winning candidates raised 31 percent more money than the losing candidates. In competition for the 18 open seats in the Assembly, candidates raised $27.6 million. The competition for monetary support was ongoing and spirited. In the end, the winning candidates outraised their competitors by a margin of 18 percent.

In the Senate and Assembly together, 93 percent of incumbents were re-elected to office, and 79 percent of those running for open seats who raised more money than their opponent won. What is the source of the campaign funds? The majority of contributions (91 percent) came from non-individual sources—that is, primarily from interest groups and to a much lesser extent from the candidate's political party, which also received significant contributions from the same interest groups that contributed to the candidate.[13] (See the "Who Are Californians?" feature for more on top interest-group contributors.)

Incumbency and interest groups (and their campaign contributions) go hand-in-hand, since their interrelationship, as we have seen, plays a crucial role in sitting legislators being re-elected. As Jesse Unruh, former speaker of the Assembly, once said, "Money is the mother's milk of politics."[14] This adage still holds true today. Most interest groups and PACs carefully target their campaign contributions. They support individuals who are in positions of power, such as incumbent state officers, party leaders in the legislature, committee chairs, and rising stars. Contributions have little to do with a legislator's or their party's political ideology. The only question is this: Can this legislator help me achieve my goals?

CALIFORNIA CORRECTIONAL PEACE OFFICERS ASSOCIATION An example of the dynamics of campaign contributions and lobbying can be seen in the California Correctional Peace Officers Association (CCPOA), one of the most powerful interest groups in Sacramento. It has achieved this status through a combination of aggressive lobbying, large campaign contributions, and skillful public relations.

Who Spends Money in California Politics?

Funds Raised for Selected Ballot Measures, 2016

■ Support ■ Oppose ✔ Passed ✖ Rejected

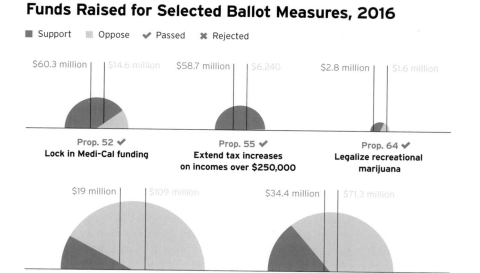

$60.3 million | $14.6 million

Prop. 52 ✔
Lock in Medi-Cal funding

$58.7 million | $6,240

Prop. 55 ✔
**Extend tax increases
on incomes over $250,000**

$2.8 million | $1.6 million

Prop. 64 ✔
**Legalize recreational
marijuana**

$19 million | $109 million

Prop. 61 ✖
Regulate drug prices

$34.4 million | $71.3 million

Prop. 56 ✔
Increase taxes on tobacco

Every election cycle, interest groups and individual donors spend massive amounts of money in California politics. During the 2018 general election, they contributed $379 million in support of or in opposition to ballot propositions In comparison in 2016 the contribution reached a record total of $473 million in support of or in opposition to ballot propositions, while only $99.5 million was raised by candidates running for the state legislature.

SOURCES: California Secretary of State, "Ballot Measure Total Contributions - 2016," www.sos.ca.gov/campaign-lobbying/cal-access-resources/measure-contributions/ (accessed 09/01/2018); National Institute on Money in State Politics, www.followthemoney.org/show-me ?s=-CA&y=2016 (accessed 09/01/2018).

Top Interest Group Contributors, 2016

■ Donations for ballot initiatives ■ Donations to Democrats ■ Donations to Republicans

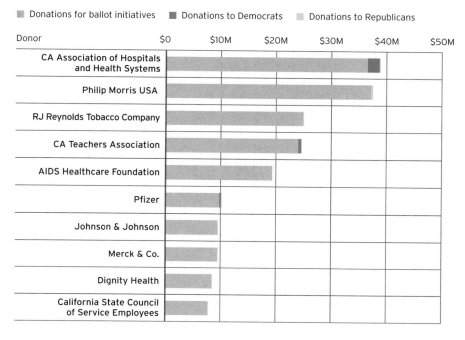

Donor | $0 | $10M | $20M | $30M | $40M | $50M

CA Association of Hospitals and Health Systems
Philip Morris USA
RJ Reynolds Tobacco Company
CA Teachers Association
AIDS Healthcare Foundation
Pfizer
Johnson & Johnson
Merck & Co.
Dignity Health
California State Council of Service Employees

forcriticalanalysis

1. Should more be done to limit the role of wealthy interest groups in California politics, or is this sort of campaign spending an important component of political speech?

2. What do you think contributes to the high cost of candidate and ballot measure campaigns in California?

The CCPOA, a union, is one of the biggest contributors to candidates running for statewide and legislative office. Over the past two decades, the union has spent over $40 million on lobbying,[15] contributing aggressively to the campaigns of its supporters and just as aggressively to defeat those who oppose its agenda. The union is one of the few public employee groups to give generously to both Republicans and Democrats. For example, when Pete Wilson ran for governor in 1990, prison guards gave $1 million to his campaign. Wilson reciprocated with substantial pay increases and stronger sentencing policies. The union made its most significant show of support, however, to Gray Davis. Besides granting him early endorsement in the primary, which guaranteed his selection as the Democratic candidate for governor, it contributed more than $3 million between 1998 and 2002 to his campaign war chest. During the same period, the union gave millions of dollars to members of the legislature, with especially large sums going to the leadership of both parties. Governor Davis responded in kind. Correctional officers' wages were tied to those of highway patrol officers. At that time, highway patrol officers earned only $666 more than correctional officers. Moreover, highway patrol officers' pay, and by implication correctional officers' pay, for each year was brought in line with the pay of police officers in the five largest urban areas.

CCPOA also spent heavily—$1.8 million—in support of Jerry Brown's 2010 gubernatorial victory. In March 2012 the legislature and Governor Brown agreed on a new contract, which the union overwhelmingly approved. The contract increased officers' pension contributions, reduced their yearly pay by requiring one day of unpaid leave each month, and eliminated a state-funded, $42-million-a-year 401(k)-type plan that correctional officers had received in addition to their pensions. These changes sound like losses. However, as the *San Francisco Chronicle* pointed out, the contract eliminated limitations on accrual of vacation time, currently estimated at more than 33 million hours and with costs to the state calculated at $1 billion.[16]

Governor Brown argued that collective bargaining is about "give and take" and claimed that the deal with the correctional officers was comparable to what other public-employee unions received under Governor Schwarzenegger. But some observers allege that the union contract is a bargaining chip to gain union support for the governor's prison reform agenda, which includes closing youth prisons and transferring up to 30,000 low-level offenders from state prisons to local jails. These reforms are intended to save the state millions of dollars. Still, the returns from CCPOA's campaign spending and lobbying suggest that the strategy has paid off handsomely for the union.

In March 2016, Governor Brown announced a new three-year deal with the union that includes an annual across-the-board 3 percent raise for members. As a compromise, union members agreed to pay a small percentage of their salary into a reserve account for retirees' medical benefits. The state will match the employees' contribution. Today, "California's prison guards are the nation's highest paid, a big reason that spending on the state's prison system has rocketed from less than 4.3 percent of the budget in 1986 to more than 11 percent today."[17]

Grassroots Mobilization

Up until now, we have focused on the influence of interest groups on the state legislature and executive branch. Interest groups, however, flex their muscles in other ways in the electoral process: through get-out-the-vote and initiative (direct legislation) campaigns.

GET OUT THE VOTE Many interest groups engage in get-out-the-vote (GOTV) operations among their members to help a candidate (and political party) or an issue win at the ballot box. This is especially true during what are perceived as hotly contested elections. In such instances, GOTV can be the most important activity undertaken because there are many examples of an election being won or lost by a handful of votes.

GOTV operations are often considered "outsider strategies"—that is, they take place outside the traditional arena of interest-group activity (the legislature), and they are supported by groups that feel they have a vital stake in the outcome of the election. Examples of this are Hispanics' interest in 1994 in defeating Proposition 187, which declared undocumented people ineligible for public assistance, and the Protect Marriage Coalition's efforts in 2008 on behalf of Proposition 8, which eliminated same-sex couples' right to marry.

Some interest groups, such as organized labor, religious denominations, and minorities, have a long history of mobilizing their members to vote for or against a candidate or critical issue. Other interest groups, such as the LGBTQ community, environmentalists, and gender-based groups, have more recently begun to participate in GOTV activities. They mobilize their supporters at the grassroots level through a variety of techniques, including direct mail, door-to-door canvassing, telemarketing, poll watching, pickup, phoning, and assistance. Months of work go into planning the campaign. While the goal is simple—delivering members' votes—the outcome is unpredictable until the final tally of ballots.

INITIATIVES Chapter 2 explored the history of the initiative and the impact of some of those that have passed. What was initially considered a tool for citizens to check the actions of elected officials and the influence of interest groups in the legislature is still considered so today. The majority of voters support the use of the initiative because they believe that the public is better suited than elected representatives to decide "important government issues," although many believe that a few narrow economic interests also shape public policy through the initiative process.[18]

Yet, as public policy scholar Elisabeth Gerber shows, this may not be as big of an issue as voters think. Although there are now more initiatives and considerably more money spent on them, groups with different goals use the initiative process differently. On the one hand, narrow (economic) interest groups, whose members join because of their occupation or professional status, rely primarily on the mobilization of money for initiative campaigns. They use these monetary resources and, to a lesser extent, personnel in two ways: "to protect the status quo or to pressure the legislature." When they sponsor initiatives, the measures generally fail. On the other hand, citizen groups, whose members join as free individuals committed to some personal belief or social issue, rely primarily on the mobilization of personnel who "volunteer their personal time and energy . . . to pass new laws by initiative."[19] In the end, the measures that are backed by citizen groups succeed at a higher rate than those that are sponsored by narrow economic interests.

The Legislature, Bribes, and Scandals

Interest-group politics is not new; lobbyists have played a visible and sometimes controversial role in California politics for a long time. The most notorious figure was Arthur Samish, whose influence in the state legislature during the 1930s and 1940s drew national attention. Samish represented the most powerful industries in the state: oil, liquor stores, transportation, breweries, and racing. Samish was not shy about his influence. He once told a grand jury looking into his lobbying activities, "To hell with the governor of California. I'm the governor of the legislature."[20]

Samish's downfall came as a result of two articles in *Collier's* magazine in 1949 about "the man who secretly controls the state."[21] In one of the articles, when asked who had more influence, himself or Samish, Governor Earl Warren responded, "On matters that affect his clients, Artie unquestionably has more power than the governor."[22] Soon after the articles appeared, Governor Warren asked for legislation to regulate lobbyists and require the disclosure of lobbyists' financial activities. The legislature obliged first with the Collier Act and later with the Erwin Act, two of the earliest efforts to regulate lobbying in the state. The legislature also voted to ban Arthur Samish from the capitol building. Somewhat thereafter, Samish was convicted of income tax evasion and sentenced to three years in federal prison, thus ending his career as a Sacramento power broker.

As the preceding incident illustrates, interest-group influence has not remained on the sidelines; quite the opposite, in fact. It is not surprising that with the growth of the "lobbying industrial complex" in California, allegations of influence peddling follow and sometimes turn out to be true. For example, Clay Jackson, one of the most influential lobbyists in Sacramento, was accused in the early 1990s of offering large campaign contributions to Senator Alan Robbins in return for the lawmaker's support on legislation benefiting Jackson's clients. The FBI uncovered Robbins's part in the plan, and he agreed to wear a wire to expose Jackson in exchange for a reduced sentence. In the end, Jackson, Robbins, and former state senator Paul Carpenter (who funneled campaign money through a public relations firm for Robbins's personal use) were convicted of engaging in a money-laundering scheme.

Again, in 2014, the Senate was rocked by the indictment of three members—Rod Wright, Leland Yee, and Ron Calderon. All three were suspended by the Senate but remained on voluntary pay and benefit leave until their cases were ruled upon or their terms expired. This was the first time either the Assembly or Senate suspended members in its 164-year history.

In 2014, Senator Wright was convicted of voter fraud and perjury. He appealed the verdict; however, he lost the appeal. Later that year he was sentenced to 90 days in jail and ordered to complete 1,500 hours of community service. But Wright spent less than one hour in jail. Because of the nonviolent nature of his crime and overcrowding in the jail, he was quietly released. Senator Lee was not so fortunate. In April 2016 he negotiated a plea bargain and avoided a possible 20-year prison sentence. Ultimately he received a five-year prison sentence on the lesser charges of bribes for political favors and coordinating weapons sales to help pay down campaign debts.

In June 2016 former assemblyman Tom Calderon, the brother of Senator Ron Calderon, pleaded guilty to one count of money laundering and implicated his brother in the scheme. His conviction could have carried up to 20 years in prison; however, federal prosecutors recommended a one-year prison sentence. Because of significant health problems, he was ultimately sentenced to six months in prison and six months under house arrest wearing an electronic monitor. Senator Ron Calderon pleaded guilty to mail fraud, acknowledging that he accepted thousands of dollars in bribes from a hospital executive and FBI agents. He was sentenced to three and a half years in federal prison and will be required to do 150 hours of

It is not surprising that with the growth of the "lobbying industrial complex" in California, allegations of influence peddling follow and sometimes turn out to be true. This was the case with Senator Ron Calderon, who in 2016 pled guilty to mail fraud and acknowledged that he had accepted thousands of dollars in bribes from hospital executives.

community service following his release. This brought to a close the FBI's Senate investigation and sting operation.

Because of these scandals, the Senate adopted resolutions to ban members from fund-raising during the last month of the legislative session and the month leading up to a budget vote, when special interests are especially active in trying to influence legislation. The resolutions also required the Senate Rules Committee to appoint an ethics ombudsman to accept allegations of wrongdoing and protect whistle-blowers from retaliation. In 2016, however, the ban on political fund-raising was killed after the Assembly did not adopt a similar rule—perhaps because it didn't suffer similar scandals—so all that is left is the ethics ombudsman position.

In the 2016 primary election, however, voters passed a legislative referendum (Proposition 50) that gave the Senate and Assembly the power to suspend members and prohibit them from receiving pay and benefits during the suspension period. This brought to a close the debate over legislative suspensions and the withholding of pay and benefits of suspended legislators.

These incidents raise questions about the connections among interest groups, money, and power in Sacramento. They reveal how a legal fund-raising system can be used to benefit legislators, especially in an environment in which there is a fine line between campaign contributions and influence over legislators' votes—even when these processes are conducted legally.

Needless to say, the current spotlight on the issue of sexual misconduct, triggered by the Harvey Weinstein revelations and the #MeToo movement, has also negatively impacted the state legislature's interaction among themselves and with lobbyists. In 2018 three Democratic legislators were forced to resign because of sexual misconduct accusations by staffers and a lobbyist. A fourth, a Democratic assemblywoman who was accused of sexual harassment by a staffer and a lobbyist, was exonerated from blame after an independent investigation. In addition, information provided by the *Los Angeles Times* found that, in 2017 alone, 27 sexual harassment allegations were filed against members and staffers of the legislature. The intent of the disclosure is to provide greater transparency in how the legislature deals with such misconduct going forward, and is a warning to legislators and staffers—and lobbyists—that they are no longer immune from scrutiny.

Regulating Campaign Contributions

This dubious history of influence peddling prompted numerous efforts over the years at reform. With the passage of the **California Political Reform Act (PRA)** of 1974, California lobbyists and interest groups are required to report campaign and lobbying expenditures. At the same time, the PRA shifted the filing of lobbying statements from the state legislature to the independent Fair Political Practice Commission.

Since its passage, the PRA has undergone numerous amendments, the most significant being in 2000 with the passage of Proposition 34. The following rules now govern interest groups and lobbyists:

- A lobbyist or lobbying firm cannot present a gift to a state-elected official or legislative official in aggregate of more than $10 a month. Anyone who is not a registered lobbyist can give up to $250 in gifts in any calendar year.

- A lobbyist cannot contribute to state candidates or officeholders if he or she is registered to lobby that candidate or officeholder's agency. However, the various interest groups that employ lobbyists have no such restrictions.

- Interest groups, individuals, and businesses have specific limits on election contributions to candidates or officeholders (see Table 3.5).

A controversial issue involves campaign contributions not directly tied to the candidate or political party. Much of the publicity and discussion of this type of organization, called Super PACs at the national level, centers on presidential, U.S. Senate, and House of Representatives campaigns in which millions of dollars are raised in support of or in opposition to a federal election candidate.

At the state level, these organizations are sometimes referred to as Super PACs but more often as **independent expenditure committees**. Like their federal counterpart, these committees may raise unlimited sums of money from corporations, unions, associations, and individuals and then spend unlimited sums to overtly advocate for or against a political candidate.

Independent expenditure committees have come under scrutiny for a variety of reasons: they infuse large sums of money into a campaign without having to comply with the limits for direct contributions to a candidate; they allow for great sums of money from outside the state to influence the state's politics and elections; and they sometimes make it difficult to identify donors by contributing money to third-party organizations, which then funnel the funds to the independent expenditure committees. Interestingly, for all the focus on it and while not an insignificant amount, independent spending has hovered around 10 percent of total direct contributions to political campaigns. In a recently revised study of independent expenditure committees in California, Linda Casey of the National Institute on Money in State Politics (FollowTheMoney.org) compares the amount of independent expenditure spending to the amount given directly to candidates and ballot measure committees. From

TABLE 3.5 ● California Contribution Limits

	Individuals* ($)	Single Candidates Committees ($)	PACs ($)	Small Contributor Committees** ($)	Political Parties ($)	Super PACs*** ($)
Governor	$29,200	$4,200	$29,200	$29,200	unlimited	$0
Statewide candidate	7,300	4,200	7,300	14,600	unlimited	0
State Senate	4,400	4,200	4,400	8,800	unlimited	0
State Assembly	4,400	4,200	4,400	8,800	unlimited	0
Party committees	36,500	35,000	35,000	35,000	$35,000	0
Ballot measures	unlimited	4,200	unlimited	unlimited	unlimited	0

*Corporate and union contribution limits are the same as individual limits.

**A small contributor committee is one that has been in existence for at least six months, receives contributions from 100 or more persons but no individual contributions of more than $200 in a calendar year, and makes contributions to five or more candidates.

***Super PAC: an independent expenditure organization that can spend unlimited amounts for or against candidates and ballot measures but cannot give directly to candidates, PACs, or committees.

SOURCE: California Fair Political Practices Commission, California State Contribution Limits, http://www.fppc.ca.gov/content/dam/fppc/NS-Documents/TAD/Campaign%20Manuals/Manual_4/Manual_4_Ch_5_State_Contribution_Limits.pdf (accessed 6/1/18).

2008 through 2016, independent expenditure committees spent $333,370,503 on candidates who ran for state offices and ballot measures. As Table 3.6 shows, this number is significantly less than the $2,849,421,255 contributed directly to candidates and ballot measure committees—just 11.7 percent of the total expenditures.

In 2010 the U.S. Supreme Court in *Citizens United v. Federal Elections Commission* held that these independent expenditure committees were legal and could raise unlimited funds. While not directly deliberating on independent expenditure committees in California, *Citizens United* confirmed the practice in California, since California had allowed such open expenditures before the Supreme Court ruling.

In 2015, however, the California Fair Political Practices Commission took action to clarify the meaning of "coordination" between candidates and organizations in order to make sure that independent expenditures were clearly independent of the candidate. It clarified within the definition of "coordination" these activities:

- the group cannot be established or run by former members of the candidate's staff,

- the candidate cannot participate in fund-raising for the outside group,

TABLE 3.6 ● Independent Spending Compared to Direct Campaign Contributions, 2008–16

	Independent State Campaigns and Ballot Measures ($)	Direct Contributions to State Campaigns and Ballot Measures ($)	Independent Spending as Percentage of Direct Campaign Contributions (%)
2008	$35,413,175	$591,753,664	5.98%
2010	84,055,049	640,346,256	13.13
2012	47,638,234	581,215,152	8.20
2014	82,660,044	399,432,572	20.69
2016	83,604,001	636,673,631	13.13
Total	333,370,503	2,849,421,255	11.70

SOURCE: Linda Casey, "Independent Spending in California, 2005-2010," September 20, 2011, revised and updated by Linda Casey, June 1, 2016, National Institute on Money in State Politics, www.followthemoney.org/research /institute-reports/independent-spending-in-california-2005-2010; 2016 update by Gerald Bonetto.

- the group cannot be established or funded by the candidates' family members, and

- political consultants cannot work for both the candidate and the outside group.

While these changes may seem minimal, they are intended, within the scope of law, to help bring transparency to the relationship between candidates and independent expenditure, which topped $90 million in 2014.

In 2017 the legislature took further action on campaign disclosure rules with the passage of AB 249, the **California DISCLOSE Act**. The act requires anonymous PACs or ballot measures and independent spending campaigns to disclose their largest contributions. The act sets disclosure standards for political advertisement in different media: radio, video and television, print and mass mailers, electronic (the internet), and robocalls. The act changes the format of disclosures, of statements required on different media, and of the names of the top two or three contributors to the advertisement. These requirements will bring greater transparency of individuals or groups funding independent spending for candidates and ballot measures.

Some public interest groups, such as Common Cause, Clean Money Campaign, and the League of Women Voters, have called for further restrictions on lobbying expenditures and campaign contributions by both individuals and interest groups. Such measures, they argue, would constrain the power of special interests and allow public-policy decisions to reflect the overall interests of society.

Recommendations to restrict the power of interest groups fall into three categories: clean-money elections, contribution restrictions, and conflict-of-interest laws.

Clean-Money Elections

The first category, clean-money elections, would provide public funding to candidates who demonstrate a base of public support by obtaining a qualifying number of voter signatures and a certain number of small contributions and who agree to forgo any other private donations. Such measures would cover all state legislative and statewide offices and have recently been adopted by Maine and Arizona. In California, it would be difficult to get the political parties and most legislators, who are tied to the current funding system, to support the idea. It would also be difficult to convince the public that they should subsidize campaigns for elective office. Over the years, only 35 to 40 percent of California voters have supported public financing of election campaigns.

Contribution Limits

The second category, contribution limits, has been a focal point of campaign reform for some time. Most of the effort has come from citizen groups disgruntled with the current system. Together they have established stricter reporting requirements, as well as limits on campaign contributions and loans to state candidates and political parties. The changes have been accomplished almost wholly through initiatives sponsored by these groups over the past decade—Propositions 63 and 78 in 1993, Proposition 208 in 1996, and Proposition 34 in 2000. These efforts will continue in the future as various groups attempt to rein in the free flow of money into political campaigns.

Conflict-of-Interest Laws

The last category, conflict-of-interest laws, covers a multitude of situations. These laws are based on the belief that government officials owe their loyalty to the public and that personal gain should not be part of the political process. Conflict-of-interest laws prohibit government officials from participating in decisions in which they have a vested interest, such as a business or real estate investment, or in any variety of situations in which they or their family would stand to gain financially.

There are, however, government-official lobbyist activities that technically fall outside of conflict-of-interest laws but may give the impression of conflict of interest. For example, the California Senate offers lobbyists who contribute to its charity, the California International Relations Foundation, the opportunity to travel with the lawmakers to various foreign countries.[23] Each donor contributes $2,000 to $3,000, which gives the donor a seat on the foundation's board of directors and the invitation to travel with legislators on trade and cultural trips to foreign countries. Since 2004 there have been 18 trips to places such as Tokyo, Jerusalem, and Rio de Janeiro. The foundation operates in the open, and it does not underwrite the expenses of either the traveling legislators or the supporters. Critics, however, contend that it creates a conflict-of-interest situation by providing a unique opportunity for supporters to gain the goodwill of and access to legislators. This is especially convenient when the supporter's interest group has a bill pending in the legislature.

The Media

For most Californians, the **media**—news stories, paid political commercials, public debate, direct mail—are the most influential sources of information on the activity of interest groups, the amount of money spent on lobbying and political campaigns, and the increasing frequency and amount of money spent on initiatives. The media keep citizens actively involved in politics.

The term *media* refers to the dispensers of information, including broadcast media (radio and television), print media (newspapers and magazines), and electronic media (the internet). An individual source is a *medium* (the Latin singular of *media*). Sometimes we speak about mass media but most often the limiting adjective (*mass*) is assumed.

Television

For many years, television has been the medium of choice for obtaining political information for the vast majority of Americans, and Californians are no exception. Although the rise of digital media has challenged television's dominance, TV retains a slight edge.[24] This medium can spread messages quickly, covering a wide variety of topics, including car chases, earthquakes, and the latest political scandal. Television is particularly important for conducting political campaigns in a large state with a diverse population such as California. Yet for all its speed and ability to reach large numbers of viewers, television is a medium that provides little information about government.

Two facts account for this lack of information: (1) California is so big and diverse that it is difficult to cover statewide political and governmental news, and (2) Californians in general are not that interested in state government and policy. These dynamics, along with a fragmented political structure, produce a stark reality—the largest state in the nation, with some of the largest media resources and markets in the nation, provides relatively little political and governmental news, particularly on television news programs.[25] There are few media correspondents in Sacramento. More important, because there is no newspaper distributed statewide, there is no incentive for television networks to cover news on a statewide basis.

The nightly news stations compete with one another for viewers. But the news programs provide little in the way of important political information. The half-hour news format is crammed with commercials, weather reports, entertainment news, sports coverage, and a host of other topics that do little to inform the viewer about the political problems that affect the state and the nation. Those topics that are reported with any depth are calculated to achieve ratings and are structured to last over several newscasts.

Each local station has its own version of some type of "action" news team or consumer protection group bringing audiences the latest artificially hyped crisis. From the nature of the issues covered, it is clear that local television, for the most part, has made a concerted effort to treat political news as a secondary issue. Issues related to political parties, government, or interest groups in California don't have the power to reach and energize large populations on a day-to-day basis.

Local television stations focus our attention on issues such as crime in a way that government representatives cannot. Sensational undercover stories are frequently broadcast, such as the financial deceptions practiced by automobile dealers, the unsanitary conditions in local restaurants, and the health risks of cosmetic surgeries. These exposés help identify dishonest practices in our communities, but they are also examples of how the ability to identify important political issues has passed from the political parties to the media. The media place an issue on the agenda, often based more on its sensational appeal than its practical importance, and the next day government representatives are telling the public what must be done to fix the problem. They are reacting to the media's promotion of the issue.

In California, where voters have the ability to put statutes and constitutional initiatives on the ballot, local television plays a major role in disseminating information to voters about these issues through extensive advertising campaigns. These messages are drafted and paid for by the interest groups that support the initiatives, and the political parties may or may not play a role in the process. The broadcast media have the power to reach a vast audience, something the parties cannot do on their own.

Newspapers

The number of newspapers across the United States has fallen during the last 25 years, and newspaper circulations have steadily declined in every recent year as well. Those who claim to get most of their information about politics from newspapers has rapidly dropped from 87 percent in 2007 to 20 percent in 2016, as consumers rely more on digital outlets for news.[26]

Newspapers, however, still remain active in identifying political corruption, reporting the workings of state and local government, covering political campaigns, and helping to keep the public focused on important political issues. But in the final analysis, newspapers are businesses and must be able to generate revenues and profits. To adequately cover state government, reporters and news staff have to be located in Sacramento. At the same time, on-the-spot coverage of county and local government requires a second set of reporters and news staff. The expense is prohibitive, and, over time, newspaper coverage at the state and local levels has noticeably declined. The public is not as fully informed about the activities of its various levels of government as it needs to be. The *Los Angeles Times* and the *Sacramento Bee* cover developments in Sacramento more extensively than other newspapers, but both have become victim to cost pressures and the need to reduce news reporting staffs.

The drive for profits has reduced the news-reporting capabilities of broadcast and print media, which cover only the big stories at the state government level. Ultimately, this means the public receives little information about the political activities of state and local government. This leads to a public that constantly finds itself surprised by political crises that seem to develop suddenly, such as rising state deficits, electricity shortages, declining state bond ratings, school facilities that are falling apart, and an overwhelmed freeway system. But for all their failings, broadcast and print media still play an important role in the election process and in formulating the political agenda. The media continue to identify the major political issues, report on the political progress of candidates at all levels, question the candidates and officeholders, and edit the replies the public is allowed to hear and read. These powers continue to undermine the role of political parties in California.

With Arnold Schwarzenegger's election as governor in October 2003, the public gained a renewed interest in state politics. People were curious. A few stations that had closed their Sacramento news bureaus announced their reopening. This wasn't surprising: nationally known figures have generally drawn more media attention than regional or local personalities. There was more coverage of governors Edmund G. Brown, Ronald Reagan, and Jerry Brown, each of whom was a presidential contender, than of governors Deukmejian, Wilson, and Davis, who were not.[27]

As time passed, the increase in coverage remained; however, it was no longer due to Schwarzenegger's celebrity but to the state's economic woes: record budget deficits, sinking bond ratings, high unemployment, and staggering foreclosure filings. These concerns persisted under Governor Jerry Brown and will continue under Governor Gavin Newsom. Local government, interest groups (especially public employee unions whose members are affected by the budget deficits), and the general public have turned to Sacramento for solutions. Economic, environmental, and social justice issues are the big concern, not the political personalities to whom have been thrown the responsibility for resolving these problems.

The Internet

Online and digital news are the only forms of news media that have increased in the number of users over the past six years. Americans are turning more frequently to their computers (desktops or laptops) and mobile devices—31 percent of computer owners and 45 percent of mobile device owners use them for news on a daily basis.[28]

Mobile devices offer instant access to political information and the opportunity to quickly communicate one's views to political leaders, news outlets, interest groups, and other individuals through blogs, Twitter, Snapchat, Facebook, other social media channels, and YouTube videos. Twitter and Facebook have become instrumental in organizing campaigns. The "share" function on Facebook and "retweet" feature of Twitter allow like-minded activists to easily share news and information such as fund-raising appeals and get-out-the-vote efforts.

The internet doesn't change politics, but it does make it easier for elected officials to share with the public their opinions unfiltered by traditional media, and for the public to share their unfiltered opinions with public officials.

At the state level, Californians are at the forefront in experimenting with the internet by using crowdsourcing techniques and wiki-style websites to reach into the political arena. While still in its infancy, **crowdsourcing** is proving to be a useful fund-raising tool. In 2012, Steve Hansen was running for the Sacramento City Council. Hansen, a young openly gay Democrat, had very little name recognition or backing from community leaders. But that didn't stop him. "In just one day, Hansen built a website on WordPress, joined MailChimp, and set up an account on Rally. Hansen's campaign raised more than $80,000 from donors who contributed $250 or less."[29] He now sits on the Sacramento City Council.

In the California state legislature, then assemblyman Mike Gatto became the first lawmaker nationally to utilize the internet to encourage citizens to craft legislation. In 2016, for the second session in a row, Gatto encouraged individuals to draft legislation directly by going to "Wikibill," a now inactive website that had an interface similar to Wikipedia's. There, users could propose, draft, or edit a bill, which, after a consensus emerged, Gatto committed to introducing. We have no analytics on the number of respondents, but the outcome appears to be Assembly Bill 83, which requires businesses and corporations to strengthen privacy standards for personal information including Social Security numbers, driver's license numbers, financial information, medical information, and travel information (such as one's Uber trip log). The bill made it through the Assembly (66 yea, 4 nay) but ended up on the inactive file in the Senate.

The most ambitious use of the internet came in 2014, when Tim Draper, a California venture capitalist, initiated a campaign using a web page to gain support for a ballot initiative. The measure was to divide California into six states. The effort failed and didn't make it to the ballot. But this didn't stop Draper. In 2015 he founded a nonprofit organization called Innovate Your State and launched the Fix California Challenge to allow citizens to help draft what would become the first crowdsourced initiative in the nation. The idea was that a 'Venture Governance' approach would "produce fresh, innovative ideas that effectively address the problems that California faces."[30]

The campaign generated over 500 ideas, 1,100 comments, and 8,000 votes. The campaign selected the best idea, submitted by Assemblyman Sam Blakeslee, for a 2016 ballot initiative. The initiative, Proposition 54 (the California Legislature Transparency Act) passed by a margin of 65 to 35 percent. The act implements a number of open government reforms, for instance that a bill must be in print and posted online 72 hours before it may pass out of the legislature, and requires the legislature to make a video recording of every official public legislative meeting available online within 24 hours.[31] Political consultants and elected officials watched this campaign closely, and, even though it was successful, they have yet to consider incorporating some sort of crowdsourcing approach to drafting future legislation and initiatives.

Many experts see the internet as a catalyst for enhancing the democratic process. It offers candidates the opportunity to communicate rapidly with supporters and to recruit campaign workers. During the presidential election season, it has proven to be an excellent tool for raising campaign funds. The internet offers political parties the opportunity to disseminate their issue positions quickly and inexpensively to millions of potential voters. Whether it will restore some of the power that political parties have lost remains to be seen. The internet is open to all users, and in that environment, political parties will still have lots of competition over control of the political agenda.

Even with these innovative uses of the internet, when it comes to social media, politics still lags behind other domains such as advertising and marketing. Most often, political campaigns use the internet to develop websites that outline a candidate's or party's position on important issues in hopes that possible supporters will visit the websites and donate to the campaigns they represent. However, campaigns are beginning to recognize and harness the power of social media networks and digital media to influence the electorate.

The example of Proposition 32, a 2012 initiative, demonstrates how the strategic implementation of new media campaigns can transform voting behavior. Proposition 32 sought to limit the money that unions could spend on lobbying and prohibit them from putting money that had been gained through automatic dues deductions from members' paychecks toward campaign contributions. By the end, the amount spent in the election was great—$75 million against and $60 million for the proposition. Midway through the campaign, however, with support for the "No on Proposition 32" cohort lagging, union leaders concluded that young voters—those under 30 years old—weren't being influenced by union television ads because they weren't watching them. Therefore, the unions switched tactics. Employing sophisticated data-mining techniques and research via Facebook, they identified patterns of behavior among younger voters that gave clues about their political beliefs. In turn, the unions began speaking the language of these voters through their medium of choice, particularly through smartphones and tablets, in an attempt to influence their voting. They sent online messages, ads, and even some direct mail to individuals whom they had targeted through their research. Within a couple of weeks, support for "No on Proposition 32" among young voters

TABLE 3.7 ● Online Sources Covering California Politics
MAJOR NEWSPAPERS *Capitol Weekly* (www.capitolweekly.net) *Los Angeles Times* (www.latimes.com) *Sacramento Bee* (www.sacbee.com) *San Francisco Chronicle* (www.sfgate.com)
ORGANIZATIONS Around the Capitol (www.aroundthecapitol.com) Calitics (www.calitics.com) Calbuzz (www.calbuzz.com) Cal Matters (https://calmatters.org/) California Political Review (www.capoliticalreview.com) Flashreport (www.flashreport.org) Fox & Hounds (www.foxandhoundsdaily.com) Rough & Tumble (www.rtumble.com)
PUBLIC POLICY SITES Public Policy Institute of California (www.ppic.org) California Health Care Foundation (www.chcf.org) California Policy Center (http://californiapolicycenter.org)
UNIVERSITIES University of California at Berkeley, Institute of Governmental Studies   (http://igs.berkeley.edu) The Pat Brown Institute for Public Affairs (https://calstatela.patbrowninstitute.org/)
MAJOR COLUMNISTS Joe Garofoli of the *San Francisco Chronicle* (www.sfgate.com) George Skelton of the *Los Angeles Times* (www.latimes.com) Michael Smolens, *San Diego Union Tribune* (www.sandiegouniontribune.com/)

rose from 40 percent to 60 percent, and the measure was ultimately defeated in the statewide election.[32]

With the growth of social and digital media, access to California's political and news sources has expanded exponentially. Today, major newspapers provide daily emails that focus on their readers' topics of interest, while research organizations, libraries, and blogs provide political information, background, and research. A list of some of the major sources covering California politics is provided in Table 3.7.

Media and Political Campaigns

Running for office is a very expensive endeavor, and it requires highly focused political messages. Because of these requirements, electronic media are the media of choice to reach large numbers of citizens. The media are also very useful in mobilizing supporters on Election Day. Mobilizing a candidate's base of support is essential to winning elections. Without the media, no effective message is conveyed to the electorate, and consequently no money can be raised to fuel the modern type of media campaign that candidates must use to get elected.

In some cases, the media themselves and their coverage can become a central issue in the campaign, with a candidate running against the media and positioning him- or herself outside the political establishment. During the recall election of 2003, the *Los Angeles Times* ran a story just before the election about inappropriate sexual behavior on the part of Schwarzenegger during his acting days. Many citizens reacted by asserting that the newspaper was taking incumbent Governor Gray Davis's side, not that it was uncovering important information that citizens might want to consider in their voting decisions.[33]

Interest-Group Politics in California: Where Are We Now?

Interest groups play an important and often dominant role in California politics. The continued growth in the number of groups and their lobbying expenditures attests to this fact. Moreover, if the past decade is any indication, the number of interest groups doing business in Sacramento will continue to grow, and lobbying expenditures will continue to increase. The size and structural deficit of the state budget, weak political parties, mandated term limits, the increase in public interest groups, and the continued dependence of local governments on Sacramento for financial assistance are all factors that will continue to promote interest-group politics.

Much of the time, these groups are self-regulating, checking one another and forging broad-based coalitions of interests to achieve important policy decisions. Of course, interest groups will always be able to win on narrow issues affecting their members, and the most powerful will generally be the most successful, as long as they can convince a group of legislators to fall in behind them. That's why interest-group disclosure rules, campaign expenditure limits, and other reporting requirements are necessary. They enable us to keep these groups in check. That's the theory, at least.

Today, however, there is a disjunction between theory and practice. Interest groups have undue influence on politics in the state. Without some limit on the amount of money an interest group can spend on lobbying and campaign contributions, the only check on their power may be divided government, whereby one party controls the executive and one controls one or both houses of the legislature, so that no single interest or coalition of interests can ride roughshod over government.

That's the state of affairs in California today. California's politics is not broken, but unless these concerns are addressed, California will continue to hobble along, and interest groups will continue to flourish and prosper at the expense of the general public.

Study Guide

FOR FURTHER READING

Alexander, Robert, *Interest Group Involvement in Ballot Campaigns*. Westport, CT: Praeger Publishers, 2002.

Baldassare, Mark. "Reforming California's Initiative Process." Public Policy Institute of California, October 2013. http://www.ppic.org/content/pubs/atissue/AI_1013MBAI.pdf. Accessed 6/7/18.

Boyarsky, Bill. *Jesse Unruh and the Art of Politics*. Berkeley: University of California Press, 2007.

Gerber, Elisabeth R. *Interest Group Influence in the California Initiative Process*. Public Policy Institute of California, 1998. www.ppic.org/main/publication.asp?i=49. Accessed 6/7/18.

Lajos, Maria, "California Interest Groups Hedge Their Bets, Give Cash to Anyone in Power." KQED News, May 14, 2015.

McWilliams, Carey. *California: The Great Exception*. Berkeley: University of California Press, 1999.

Michael, Jay, Dan Walters, and Dan Weintraub. *The Third House: Lobbyists, Power, and Money in Sacramento*. Berkeley: Berkeley Public Policy Press, 2000.

Miller, Kenneth P., Thad Kousser, and Frederick Douzets. *The New Political Geography of California*. Berkeley: Berkeley Public Policy Press, 2008.

Morain, Dan, "An Out of Control System Creates Instant Campaigns and Candidates." *The Sacramento Bee*, June 4, 2016.

www.sacbee.com/opinion/opn-columns-blogs/dan-morain/article81726957.html. Accessed 6/7/18.

Rasky, Susan F. "Covering California: The Press Wrestles with Diversity, Complexity, and Change." In *Governing California: Politics, Government, and Public Policy in the Golden State*, edited by Gerald C. Lubenow and Bruce E. Cain, 157–88. Berkeley: Institute of Government Studies Press, University of California, 1997.

Samish, Arthur H., and Bob Thomas. *The Secret Boss of California*. New York: Crown Publishers, 1971.

ON THE WEB

Around the Capitol. www.aroundthecapitol.com. Accessed 6/7/18. A portal to California legislative information.

Capitol Alert. www.sacbee.com/news/politics-government/capitol-alert/. Accessed 6/7/18. California and national political news and commentary.

Capitol Weekly. www.capitolweekly.net. Accessed 6/7/18.

Lobbying activity. http://cal-access.ss.ca.gov/lobbying. Accessed 6/7/18. The secretary of state's office reports on lobbying in California politics.

SUMMARY

I. Interest groups are at the center of California's campaign and lobbying activities.
   A. Interest groups are associations of individuals who join together for the purpose of influencing governmental or legislative policy. They can be individual businesses, trade and professional associations, or labor unions.
   B. Some believe that interest groups play a necessary role in our democratic society, advocating a pluralist theory to explain their power.
   C. Others see them as detrimental to our political system, because only a few, elite groups have power.

II. The number of interest groups (and registered lobbyists) has grown substantially in each legislative session since 1990.
   A. In the 2015–16 legislature, interest groups employed over 3,600 lobbyists.
   B. In the same legislature, interest groups spent more than $500 million on lobbying activities.

C. Interest groups have proliferated over the past three decades for four reasons: weak political parties, growth of government, term limits, and a greater number of public interest groups.

III. Lobbyists do the work of interest groups. There are three different categories of lobbyists: citizen lobbyists, contract lobbyists, and in-house lobbyists.
   A. Citizen lobbyists are individuals who have an interest in an issue and want to make their view known to their public official.
   B. Contract lobbyists and in-house lobbyists are professionals who must register with the secretary of state and submit a variety of disclosure statements yearly regarding their activities.

IV. Lobbyists perform a variety of activities to accomplish their goals.
   A. The first job of the lobbyist is to know the interest group's objective.

B. The lobbyist must also identify other organizations that could support or oppose their goals.

C. Lobbyists may work with a grassroots network of activists in a legislator's district to establish a relationship with a legislator.

D. Lobbying the executive branch is more difficult to coordinate because of the large number of regulatory agencies and commissions within the branch.

V. There is a strong correlation between lobbying expenditures and campaign contributions.

A. Interest groups that invest heavily in lobbying also invest heavily in political campaigns. Interest groups contribute to candidates' and officeholders' campaigns to leverage their influence.

B. The California Correctional Peace Officers Association (CCPOA) is a prime example.

VI. Many efforts have been made to regulate the relationship between lobbyists and legislators.

A. The Political Reform Act of 1974 was passed to regulate lobbying practices and requires the disclosure of lobbying financial activity.

B. Proposition 34, the most recent amendment to the act, includes new restrictions:

1. Lobbyists cannot contribute to the campaigns of anyone for whom they are lobbying.

2. Lobbyists are limited in the amount of money they can contribute during any election cycle.

VII. The media are important vehicles for mobilizing and informing voters and candidates' supporters.

A. Television and newspapers have traditionally had the greatest influence on politics.

B. Today the internet and social media, as well as the increased use of smartphones and tablets, are changing the way political messages are conveyed. Given the current growth in usage of these devices, digital media, among specific age groups, has surpassed all other media as the primary source for political news and campaign management.

C. Little of this mobilization, however, comes from news programs, which generally provide scant political information. Television news programs cover scandals and dishonest practices of politicians and focus viewers' attention on the latest special investigation, which indirectly mobilizes citizens.

D. California politicians are at the forefront among those in all states in using social media to raise money for campaigns and in enlisting citizens to help draft legislation and initiatives. This demonstrates how the power to set the political agenda has passed from the political parties to the media.

PRACTICE QUIZ

1. The term *third house* refers to which of the following entities?
   a) judicial branch
   b) executive branch
   c) interest groups
   d) media

2. Over the past two decades, interest-group expenditures in California have
   a) declined.
   b) increased.
   c) remained relatively the same.
   d) fluctuated from year to year.

3. An individual who offers his or her lobbying services to multiple clients at the same time is called a(n)
   a) contract lobbyist.
   b) "hired gun."
   c) citizen lobbyist.
   d) in-house lobbyist.

4. The principal function of an interest group is to
   a) provide its members with educational and social opportunities.
   b) contribute money to candidates for public office who favor its programs.
   c) attain favorable decisions from government on issues that it supports.
   d) seek to inform the public on the role of interest in the economy.

5. Political action committees (PACs)
   a) have declined in popularity in recent years.
   b) must disclose campaign contributions and expenditures in connection with state and local elections.
   c) may make unlimited contributions to political candidates.
   d) provide candidates with public funding for their campaign.

6. According to the text, all of the following factors are involved in the media's decision not to cover more political and governmental news except:
   a) Californians are not that interested in political and governmental news.
   b) The ratings for political and governmental news are lower than other kinds of news, such as the weather, consumer news, and sports coverage.

c) So many news programs cover California political and governmental news that there is little for each station to report.

d) Political and governmental news, except during election campaigns, does not lend itself to sensational coverage.

7. Which former speaker of the California Assembly said "Money is the mother's milk of politics"?
   a) Jesse Unruh
   b) Willie Brown
   c) Antonio Villaraigosa
   d) Fabian Nuñez

8. Over the past two decades, the number of newspapers across the United States has _____, and newspaper circulations have _____ in every recent year as well.
   a) risen, increased
   b) remained the same, increased

c) risen, declined
d) fallen, declined

9. Which of the following describes the process of obtaining ideas, fund-raising contributions, or policy support by enlisting online a large group of people?
   a) direct appeal
   b) crowdsourcing
   c) web-based business pattern
   d) outsourcing

10. Many experts see digital media as a catalyst for _____ the democratic process.
   a) threatening
   b) enhancing
   c) having little effect on
   d) undermining

CRITICAL-THINKING QUESTIONS

1. Over the past several decades, interest groups have grown and expanded their influence over public-policy decisions in the legislature and at administrative agencies. Identify the reasons for this phenomenon.

2. Interest groups use a variety of techniques to accomplish their goal. Suppose you worked for an interest group that opposed stricter requirements for the recycling of plastic bottles. Outline a campaign to achieve your goal. Justify why you would take the action you propose.

3. Some people argue that interest groups provide citizens with another way to become involved in the political process. Others argue that interest groups undermine the political process. Discuss the arguments for both positions. Give your opinion on the controversy.

4. Interest groups play a significant role in the funding of political campaigns. Should more restriction be put on their activity? If you decide that interest groups should be limited or altogether prohibited from contributing to political campaigns, how would this policy affect political campaigns? What would be the outcome of this reform?

5. What are the factors that have led to relatively low levels of media coverage of politics and government in California?

KEY TERMS

California DISCLOSE Act (p. 68)
California Political Reform Act (PRA) (p. 66)
citizen lobbyist (p. 57)
contract lobbyist (p. 58)
crowdsourcing (p. 72)
elitism (p. 52)

independent expenditure committees (p. 66)
in-house lobbyist (p. 58)
interest groups (p. 51)
lobbying (p. 53)
media (p. 69)
pluralism (p. 52)

political action committees (PACs) (p. 59)
public interest groups (p. 56)
third house (p. 52)
trade associations (p. 54)

4 Parties and Elections in California

WHAT CALIFORNIA GOVERNMENT DOES AND WHY IT MATTERS

In 2017 and 2018 California assumed a new role: the epicenter of resistance to the Trump administration. Ever since Donald Trump became president, California has been at odds with his administration over many of its policy directives. Many federal policies either passed by Congress or implemented through Trump's signing of executive orders—which do not require approval from both houses of Congress—are in direct conflict with California laws. California's attorney general, Xavier Becerra, has filed over 30 lawsuits against the Trump administration, claiming that specific federal policies violate California law or the U.S. Constitution. Examples of these lawsuits demonstrate the environmental, immigration, and social policies pitting California against the Trump administration:

- California cities have taken on "sanctuary" status to limit how they will cooperate with federal immigration officials.
- California has sued the Environmental Protection Agency for rolling back the requirement that agricultural companies train California workers about the hazards of pesticides.
- California has backed a Planned Parenthood court motion against the Trump administration's plan to withhold funding for women's reproductive health services to any organization that provides abortions or makes referrals for the procedure.
- Along with more than a dozen other states, California has sued the federal government over the lowering of federal automobile emission standards.

- California has sued the federal government over plans to reintroduce a citizenship question for the 2020 Census, arguing this will discourage undocumented individuals from participating.
- California has sued the federal government for ending the Deferred Action for Childhood Arrivals (DACA) program.

These lawsuits demonstrate what many analysts and political observers believe is only natural—that California has taken on the leading role of the anti-Trump resistance. California is dominated by the Democratic Party, its voters favor progressive candidates and policies, and it has historically been on the cutting edge politically, culturally, economically, and socially. The state has the fifth largest economy in the world, is the most populated and diverse state in the country, and is home to some of the most powerful and influential high-tech industries in the world. Other states watch what California does; we are an influential trendsetter.

Political Parties

A political party is an organization of people with roughly similar political or ideological positions who work to win elections in order to gain greater control of the government and change public policy. Political parties perform many valuable functions in a democratic society. One of their most important roles is to mobilize voters at election time. They are directly involved in political campaigns: providing workers, raising money, and identifying important political issues. In theory, parties help bring about consensus on important political issues and serve as two-way communication channels between government and the people. Consequently, most political scientists consider them vital to the health of a democratic state.

California has a **winner-take-all system** of voting in which the candidate receiving the highest number of votes wins the election. Political scientists have long known that such a system promotes two dominant political parties, and, as expected, the Republicans and the Democrats dominate the political process in California. But as you will discover below, California has what is considered a weak political party system, a consequence of the reforms brought about by the Progressive movement, which took a considerable amount of power away from organized political parties.

The Progressive Impact on Political Parties

The Progressive movement (1890s–1920s) viewed political parties as corrupt organizations operating in concert with big corporations to control and manipulate the political system for their own benefit. Historian Spencer Olin describes the attitude of Progressives toward political parties:

> Accompanying their democratic faith in the wisdom of the individual voter was a distrust of formal party organizations, which were viewed as the media of special-interest power. . . . Furthermore, it was argued by progressives that science and

efficient management would solve the problems of government; parties were irrelevant and unnecessary.[1]

The Progressives attacked the power of the political parties with reforms such as party primaries. **Primary elections** are used to select the party candidate who will run for office against other candidates in the **general election**. Before primaries were established, party leaders typically selected their candidates in proverbial "smoke-filled rooms," outside of public view. Primaries were designed to allow voters, not parties, to select candidates for office. The primary system also opened up the opportunity to run for office to anyone capable of meeting the basic qualifications, which included age and residency requirements. Historically, the party leadership and their corporate allies had selected candidates and subsequently manipulated them while they held office; with the Progressive reforms, the people could participate in a whole new class of elections, forcing candidates to direct their political messages and loyalty to the average voter.

The Progressives also introduced a new type of ballot, the **office block ballot**. This type of ballot made it difficult to vote the straight party ticket, a method popular in many other states where ballots list all the candidates running for each office by party. Political parties preferred this party column ballot because it made it easy for voters to select only candidates from their party. The use of the office block ballot in California discourages such behavior by listing each office separately and has resulted in more split-ticket voting, where people vote for candidates from different parties.

Another Progressive reform was the introduction of nonpartisan elections, which further weakened parties by preventing party designations from appearing on the ballot for most local contests (city councils, board of supervisors, school boards, and judges). Instead, voters were given only the current occupational status of the candidate and thus could no longer use their party loyalties to make voting decisions at the county and city level on Election Day. The Progressives wanted the electorate to research the candidates by reading up on them or attending forums.

Political scientists believe that the weakening of political parties through nonpartisan elections at the county and city levels has an impact on voters. Despite the hopes of the Progressives, most voters do not devote a lot of time to conducting research on each candidate to determine how to cast their vote. County and city races are typically low profile; therefore, forbidding party labels on ballots further diminishes the voters' already limited information. Voters who identify with a political party view the party affiliation of candidates as important and rely on it to make their voting decisions. As political scientists Brian Schaffner, Matthew Streb, and Gerald Wright describe it, "Party identification is a, or even the, central component of voter decision making. As an effective attachment, it motivates individuals to participate as a display of party support."[2] Therefore, nonpartisan elections may have lower turnout rates than partisan ones.

The Democratic and Republican Parties in California

Currently, California is considered a very Democratic state. Democratic candidates running for the presidency are fairly confident they will win the popular vote in California (for example, Hillary Clinton won 62 percent of the vote in 2016), and they visit our state not to sway voters but to hold expensive fund-raisers. Republican candidates don't spend too much time campaigning in California, as they are certain they will lose the popular vote—although, like Democrats, they do visit to collect campaign contributions. For over 20 years, our state has had two Democratic U.S. senators, and for over 20 years the Democratic Party has controlled the state legislature.

But California has not always been in the Democratic camp. From 1952 to 1988, Republican presidential candidates won every presidential vote in California except for one (Democrat Lyndon Johnson defeated Republican Barry Goldwater in 1964). Richard Nixon and Ronald Reagan were both hugely popular in California: Nixon represented California in both the U.S. House and Senate before being elected president, and Reagan served two terms as governor of California before serving in the White House.

What caused the Republican Party to lose support? A couple of reasons may help explain this shift. Some scholars point to a series of anti-immigrant initiatives, beginning with Proposition 187 in 1994, which were embraced by the Republican Party. Proposition 187, a ballot measure that prohibited undocumented individuals from receiving nonemergency medical care, public education, and other services, was strenuously supported by Republican Governor Pete Wilson in his re-election bid. Shortly after the passage of Proposition 187 (which was ultimately invalidated), Propositions 209 and 229 sought to outlaw affirmative action and bilingual education. As Figure 4.1 illustrates, there was a spike in Latinos registering with the Democratic Party and voting for Democratic candidates after these propositions were introduced. And Latinos have apparently not forgotten the anti-immigrant positions of the Republican Party. A 2010 survey found that Latino voters had negative views when asked about former governor Pete Wilson's involvement in the campaign of a Republican gubernatorial candidate—this was nearly 20 years after Proposition 187.[3]

Many experts also believe that demographic changes in the state help explain the ascendancy of the Democratic Party. White and older voters, an important part of the Republican Party coalition, are declining in numbers. As of July 2014, Latinos are the largest ethnic group in California, just edging out the white population. It is projected that by 2060, Latinos will make up 49 percent of the state's population. The Asian population has also increased in California. Overall, the Asian population in the United States has grown 72 percent since 2000 and about one-third of the Asian population resides in California.[4] Young and ethnically diverse voters prefer the Democratic Party. Nonwhites now amount to a majority in the state, and these voters have not supported some of the more conservative and strident anti-immigrant policies touted by Republican candidates. Conservative, right-wing Republicans do not do well in statewide elections; California voters largely prefer centrist leaders who advocate moderate policies. And California appears to be a harbinger of national trends. "Where L.A. goes is where the rest of the state goes and where the rest of the country goes," proclaimed one analyst. "We announce, demographically speaking, the future for the rest of the country."[5]

Third Parties in California

The American political system, which is a federal system, delegates power to three levels of government: national, state, and local. One of the powers that states retain is to determine how political parties may organize and gain access to the ballot. By dominating the legislature in California, Republicans and Democrats have not made it easy for third parties to qualify for the ballot, and consequently the two parties

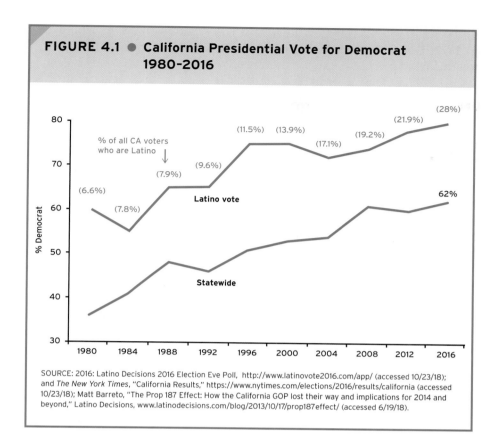

FIGURE 4.1 ● California Presidential Vote for Democrat 1980–2016

% of all CA voters who are Latino ↓

(6.6%)
(7.8%)
(7.9%)
(9.6%)
(11.5%) (13.9%)
(17.1%)
(19.2%)
(21.9%)
(28%)

Latino vote

62%

Statewide

% Democrat

80
70
60
50
40
30

1980 1984 1988 1992 1996 2000 2004 2008 2012 2016

SOURCE: 2016: Latino Decisions 2016 Election Eve Poll, http://www.latinovote2016.com/app/ (accessed 10/23/18); and *The New York Times*, "California Results," https://www.nytimes.com/elections/2016/results/california (accessed 10/23/18); Matt Barreto, "The Prop 187 Effect: How the California GOP lost their way and implications for 2014 and beyond," Latino Decisions, www.latinodecisions.com/blog/2013/10/17/prop187effect/ (accessed 6/19/18).

dominate California politics. Third parties then are defined as any party other than Republican or Democratic.

Traditionally, third-party candidates do not win in a winner-take-all system, a fact that both major parties emphasize to warn voters against throwing their votes away. However, a significant percentage of voters continue to vote for third-party candidates anyway.

There are two ways in which political parties can qualify to get on the ballot in California. The first method is by registration; the second is by petition. To qualify a new party by the registration method, the law requires that one-third of the total number of voters registered on the 154th day before the primary election or the 123rd day before the presidential general election are registered with the new party. The petition method is just as difficult and tedious. New political parties must petition to be included in the upcoming election; the party must collect signatures equal to 10 percent of those who voted in the last gubernatorial election. In 2018 approximately 12 million votes were cast in the governor's race, so the law mandates that over one million signatures must be collected to qualify a new party. Qualifying as a new political party clearly is not an easy task and requires time, personnel, expertise, and resources. In 2018, California had six qualified parties (see Table 4.1): the American Independent

TABLE 4.1 ● Qualified Political Parties in California, 2018

AMERICAN INDEPENDENT PARTY	www.aipca.org
DEMOCRATIC PARTY	www.cadem.org
GREEN PARTY	www.cagreens.org
LIBERTARIAN PARTY	www.ca.lp.org
PEACE AND FREEDOM PARTY	www.peaceandfreedom.org
REPUBLICAN PARTY	www.cagop.org

Party, the Democratic Party, the Green Party, the Libertarian Party, the Peace and Freedom Party, and the Republican Party. So what is the role of third parties in politics, particularly in California? One theory is that third parties act as spoilers, drawing enough votes from one or the other of the two major parties to alter the election outcome. Third parties also help focus public attention on important political issues. Once an issue attracts enough public attention, it will be taken over by one or both of the two major political parties. Sometimes, third parties can motivate people who do not usually vote to turn up at the polls because the third-party candidate better represents their views than do the established Democratic or Republican candidates.

Party Affiliation of California Voters

A plurality of California voters identify with the Democratic Party. As of October 2018 about 44 percent of voters are registered with the Democratic Party compared to 24 percent registered with the Republican Party. A substantial 28 percent of voters have **no party preference**, and 5 percent identify with one of the minor third parties. It should be noted that the name of one of these minor third parties, the American Independent Party, has confused voters who thought they actually were registering as independent voters (no party preference). Because the word *independent* appears in the party's name, tens of thousands of Californians mistakenly registered with this party, a party that was formed in the 1960s by a segregationist and that espouses ultraconservative, antigay, and antiabortion positions. After the *Los Angeles Times*[6] brought to light this confusion on the part of voters, nearly 32,000 voters who had previously registered with the American Independent Party changed their political party registration. The American Independent Party, however, still attracts over half a million voters, the most of any of the minor parties, and because of this the party meets the requirements of California law for ballot access.

Party affiliation is fairly easy to determine because people are asked to declare **political party affiliation** when registering to vote (one of the options, however, is no party preference). As Figure 4.2 illustrates, since 1998 registration in the two major political parties has declined. The percentage of voters registering with the Democratic Party fell by 3 percentage points, while the percentage registering with the Republican Party fell by 12 points. The most dramatic change has been among those who have no political party preference (also referred to as independent voters). This group has more than doubled in size over the past 20 years; more than one in four voters now claim no party preference when they register to vote.

Now let us look at political-party affiliation and some demographic factors. Figure 4.3 presents the results of a California statewide survey conducted in October 2018 that asked respondents about their party affiliation, age, gender, race, educational level, and place of birth. The results suggest that young, middle-aged, and older Californians prefer the Democratic Party over other parties. The survey also found that the Republican Party is becoming the party of senior citizens. Currently, those 55 years of age or older make up the majority of the party, and this number is growing annually as the population ages. Many are questioning what the Republican Party of the future will look like in California with the passing of these older Republicans. Will the party be able to survive this demographic trend? Another important trend is young voters' movement away from organized parties to register instead as independent voters; no party preferences (30 percent) has the second highest affiliation.

We also observe a sizeable gender difference in party affiliation, with many more women affiliating with the Democratic Party (52 percent of women versus 37 percent of men). Also of note is that more men than women are registering as independents. The Democratic Party has more support than the Republican Party regardless of educational level. Race is also a key predictor of party identification, with Latinos preferring the Democratic Party at a much higher rate than do whites (55 percent compared to 40 percent). Similarly, 51 percent of immigrants identify with the Democratic Party compared to 43 percent of those native born. Some of these demographic trends suggest that politics in our state will change in the future. Older white males' proportionate decline in the population will continue to have an impact on the Republican Party as it loses a large segment of its support.

Another important demographic change is the increasing Latino population. Data from the U.S. Census Bureau demonstrate that from 2000 to 2017 the Latino population grew by nearly 30 percent to 15 million, whereas the white population

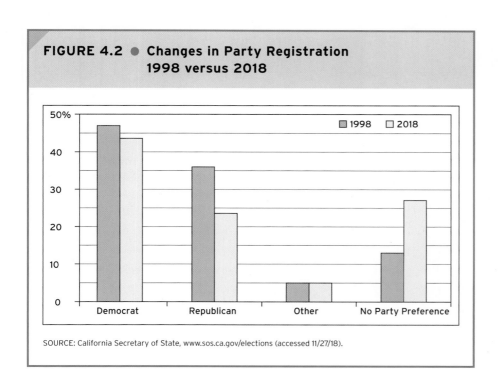

FIGURE 4.2 ● Changes in Party Registration 1998 versus 2018

SOURCE: California Secretary of State, www.sos.ca.gov/elections (accessed 11/27/18).

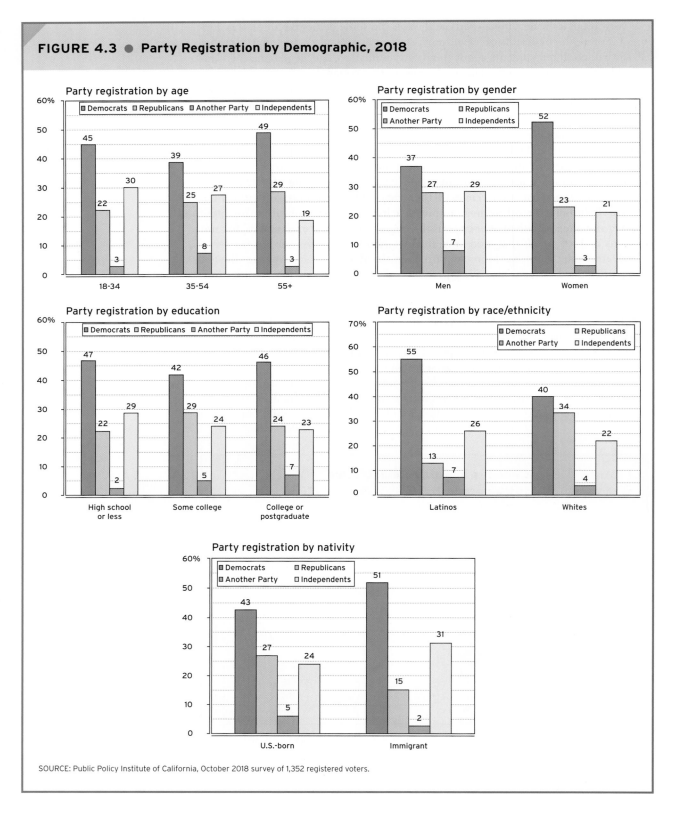

FIGURE 4.3 ● **Party Registration by Demographic, 2018**

Party registration by age

■ Democrats ■ Republicans ■ Another Party □ Independents

18-34: 45, 22, 3, 30
35-54: 39, 25, 8, 27
55+: 49, 29, 3, 19

Party registration by gender

■ Democrats ■ Republicans ■ Another Party □ Independents

Men: 37, 27, 7, 29
Women: 52, 23, 3, 21

Party registration by education

■ Democrats ■ Republicans ■ Another Party □ Independents

High school or less: 47, 22, 2, 29
Some college: 42, 29, 5, 24
College or postgraduate: 46, 24, 7, 23

Party registration by race/ethnicity

■ Democrats ■ Republicans ■ Another Party □ Independents

Latinos: 55, 13, 7, 26
Whites: 40, 34, 4, 22

Party registration by nativity

■ Democrats ■ Republicans ■ Another Party □ Independents

U.S.-born: 43, 27, 5, 24
Immigrant: 51, 15, 2, 31

SOURCE: Public Policy Institute of California, October 2018 survey of 1,352 registered voters.

declined by more than 5 percent to just under 15 million. The California Department of Finance projects that in the next 20 years whites will make up 35 percent of the population and Latinos will make up 43 percent of the population. Currently, Latinos favor the Democratic Party over the Republican Party by a sizable percentage, and there is no reason to expect this to change in the future. Thus, many are predicting an even stronger Democratic Party presence in the state in the future.

THE RED AND THE BLUE IN CALIFORNIA You may recall that most television programs focusing on the 2016 presidential election exhibited a color-coded map of the United States, which represented the states that voted Republican as red and the states that voted Democratic as blue. The map nicely illustrated the national split between urban areas and rural, agricultural, and suburban areas; the West Coast, most of the Northeast, and the major urban areas of the United States were blue; the South, the agricultural regions, and the Great Plains states were red.

As the map in Figure 4.4 illustrates, the same geographic split appears within the state of California, between the coastal counties and the inland counties. Most of the Democratic counties are coastal and encompass major urban areas, whereas most of the Republican counties are inland and rural.

As reported by the *Los Angeles Times*:

> Over the last decade, Republican influence has grown more concentrated in conservative inland California—largely the Central Valley and Inland Empire but also the Antelope Valley, the Sierra and rural north. . . . At the same time Democrats have strengthened their domination of counties along California's coastline, building overwhelming advantages in the San Francisco and Los Angeles areas as Latino voters have expanded the party's base. And from San Diego's beachfront suburbs to the Central Coast, Democrats have eroded Republican support among moderates, especially women.[7]

What does this split mean politically? Overall, the Democratic Party has an electoral advantage in California; nearly 70 percent of the state's population resides in Democratic-leaning coastal regions. Republicans have an uphill battle to win statewide elections and are more likely to succeed if they nominate ideologically moderate candidates who are able to gain the support of Democratic voters. The fact that the urban and coastal population centers are largely Democratic and moderate to liberal, coupled with the tendency of the majority of independent voters to lean toward the Democratic Party, suggests that California will remain a distinctly blue state. However, this ideological split has potentially negative consequences. As described by Mark Baldassare, president of the Public Policy Institute of California, before the 2016 election,

> California seems poised to maintain its blue status this fall (2016). However, the geo-political segregation of the state—with Republican pockets of strength in California's northern, inland, and rural regions—means that federal and state legislators will be elected to represent the views of voters who are worlds apart. Indeed, the political polarization and antipathy of this year's election may result in a California Congressional delegation that will contribute to Washington gridlock and a California Legislature that will struggle to find common ground on solutions to the many challenges facing California's future.[8]

FIGURE 4.4 ● Percent Difference between Democratic and Republican Registration by County, 2018

Del Norte 4%

Siskiyou 8%

Modoc 28%

Humboldt 22%

Trinity <1%

Shasta 23%

Lassen 28%

Tehama 17%

Plumas 13%

Mendocino 27%

Glenn 14%

Butte <1%

Sierra 13%

Colusa 8%

Nevada 2%

Sutter 10%

Yuba 9%

Placer 16%

Lake 12%

Yolo 28%

El Dorado 13%

Alpine 7%

Sonoma 34%

Napa 23%

Sacramento 16%

Amador 16%

Calaveras 14%

Tuolumne 12%

Mono 3%

Solano 25%

Marin 40%

Contra Costa 28%

San Joaquin 12%

Mariposa 16%

San Francisco 50%

Alameda 45%

Stanislaus 2%

Madera 8%

San Mateo 35%

Santa Clara 27%

Merced 15%

Santa Cruz 42%

San Benito 19%

Fresno 3%

Inyo 10%

Tulare 10%

Monterey 28%

Kings 10%

San Luis Obispo 3%

Kern 2%

San Bernardino 8%

Santa Barbara 16%

Los Angeles 33%

Ventura 9%

Orange 4%

Riverside 2%

San Diego 7%

Imperial 30%

Dominant political party affiliation
☐ Democratic advantage
▨ Republican advantage

SOURCE: California Secretary of State, www.sos.ca.gov (accessed 11/26/18).

This is not to imply, however, that all populated coastal regions are the same politically and ideologically. As the next section illustrates, there are some interesting variations.

California's Local Political Cultures from Left to Right

Political culture is difficult to define and to quantify. However, we can offer at least a few statistics to show how three of the state's most populous counties differ in terms of political partisanship, political ideology, political activism, political tolerance, and voting tendencies on important issues. Table 4.2 compares and contrasts the city of San Francisco and counties of Los Angeles and San Diego on these selected indicators of local political culture.

POLITICAL PARTY REGISTRATION As of October 2018, registered Democrats outnumber Republicans in San Francisco by eight to one and by three to one in Los Angeles County. In San Diego County, however, Democrats slightly outnumber Republicans 35 percent to 28 percent.

TABLE 4.2 ● **Regional Political Cultures: Three California Counties Compared from Left to Right**

Indicator	San Francisco (%)	Los Angeles (%)	San Diego (%)
1. Democrats (2018)	57%	50%	35%
2. Republicans (2018)	7	17	28
3. Very liberal (2000)	21	8	6
4. Very conservative (2000)	4	15	14
5. High protest activity (2000)	47	30	30
6. Voter turnout (Nov. 8, 2016)	38	23	33
7. Voter turnout (Nov. 6, 2012)	57	52	56
8. Yes on Proposition 13 (1978)	47	67	60
9. Yes on Proposition 187 (1994)	29	56	68
10. Yes on Proposition 209 (1996)	29	45	63
11. Yes on Proposition 8 (2008)	25	50	54
12. Yes on Proposition 30 (2012)	77	60	46
13. Yes on Proposition 47 (2014)	79	63	55
14. Yes on Proposition 62 (2016)	71	52	44
15. Yes on Proposition 64 (2016)	74	58	56
16. Yes on Proposition 6 (2018)	17	39	51
17. Vote Brown for governor (2014)	88	66	50
18. Vote Obama for president (2012)	83	69	51
19. Vote for Clinton for president (2016)	85	72	56

SOURCE: Indicators 1–2, 6–19: California Secretary of State, various official statements of vote. Indicators 3–5: Analysis of sample survey data obtained from the Social Capital Benchmark Survey 2000.

POLITICAL IDEOLOGY Based on community surveys conducted in late 2000, 21 percent of San Franciscans identify themselves politically as "very liberal" and only 4 percent as "very conservative." In both Los Angeles County and San Diego County, conservatives outnumber liberals by about two to one.[9]

POLITICAL PROTEST AND VOTER TURNOUT Those same surveys show that San Franciscans are much more inclined to engage in political protest than are their counterparts in the southland. Specifically, 47 percent of San Francisco citizens scored "high" on a nationally normed political-protest-activity index, as compared with only 30 percent of citizens in both Los Angeles and San Diego counties. In terms of more conventional forms of political participation, the 2016 presidential election saw San Francisco voters turning out at a slightly higher rate than San Diego voters, with Los Angeles lagging somewhat behind. In November 2018 voter turnout skyrocketed nationally (especially considering this was a non-presidential election year), and a similar turnout pattern held with San Francisco voters leading the way with an historically high turnout rate of 75 percent. San Diego and Los Angeles voters followed with turnout rates slightly higher than the 2016 presidential election.

SUPPORT FOR PROPOSITION 13 Proposition 13, the 1978 initiative that rolled back property tax rates and limited the government's ability to raise local property taxes in the future, is regarded by some observers "as one of the most significant political events in California's history."[10] It won by a landslide vote nearly everywhere in the state, including a 67 percent vote in favor in Los Angeles County and a 60 percent vote in favor in San Diego County. In San Francisco, however, it mustered only a 47 percent vote in favor, not even a majority.

SUPPORT FOR PROGRESSIVE POLICIES AND RACIAL AND CULTURAL DIVERSITY Table 4.2 reports county voting results on different statewide ballot propositions over the period 1994–2018. All results can be viewed as indicators of California voters' political tolerance and level of support for racial and cultural diversity and progressive policies.

- Proposition 187 was a 1994 initiative constitutional amendment that made undocumented immigrants ineligible for various public social services. The state's voters approved it by a wide margin, with 56 percent voting yes in Los Angeles County and 68 percent voting yes in San Diego County. Only 29 percent voted for it in San Francisco. After passage, Proposition 187 was challenged in the courts and was ultimately invalidated.

- Proposition 209 was a 1996 initiative constitutional amendment that prohibited state and local government agencies from giving preferential treatment to any individual or group on the basis of race, sex, color, ethnicity, or national origin. Widely viewed by friends and foes alike as an attack on affirmative action, this measure passed in the statewide vote, with 63 percent support in San Diego County. It received only 45 percent support in Los Angeles County, however, and a mere 29 percent support in San Francisco.

- Proposition 8 was a 2008 initiative constitutional amendment that eliminated the right of same-sex couples to marry. Backers of the proposition placed it on the ballot as a direct challenge to the California Supreme Court's ruling in

May 2008 affirming the constitutionality of same-sex marriage. The measure was approved 52 to 48 percent in the statewide vote. Only 25 percent of San Francisco County's voters voted yes, however, compared with 50 percent in Los Angeles County and 54 percent in San Diego County. In June 2015 the U.S. Supreme Court ruled in favor of same-sex marriage nationwide, declaring Proposition 8 unconstitutional.

- Proposition 30 was a 2012 initiative constitutional amendment that would temporarily raise taxes to fund education. Personal income taxes would increase for those earning over $250,000 for seven years, and the sales tax would increase by 25 cents for four years. This increased state revenue would be used to fund education at the K–12, community college, and university levels, which otherwise faced budget cuts. Teacher unions and Governor Brown campaigned aggressively for the passage of this initiative. Failure of the proposition would result in extensive budget cuts to the already struggling public school and university systems. Proposition 30 was approved statewide by a vote of 54 to 46 percent. Over 75 percent of San Francisco voters approved of the measure, as did 60 percent of Los Angeles County voters. In San Diego County, however, only 46 percent voted yes. Proposition 55 on the November 2016 ballot sought to extend by 12 years the temporary personal income tax increases enacted in 2012. This proposition passed with 62 percent of the statewide vote. San Francisco voters approved it by 72 percent, Los Angeles voters by 67 percent, and San Diego voters by 60 percent.

- Proposition 47 was a 2014 initiative that would reform the state's three strikes law. This law resulted in harsh prison sentences for those convicted of a third felony offense. However, the "third strike" for many was a nonviolent crime. Research has found that the three strikes law has disproportionately affected minority populations; over 45 percent of those serving life sentences under this law are African Americans.[11] Under the law as reformed by the initiative, those convicted of certain drug and property crimes would receive a misdemeanor sentence instead of a felony sentence if they had no prior convictions for serious or violent crimes such as rape, murder, or child molestation. Additionally, this measure would allow offenders currently serving felony sentences for nonviolent crimes to petition to have their felony sentences reduced to misdemeanor sentences. The measure passed with a statewide vote of 59 percent. It passed 79 percent to 21 percent in San Francisco and 63 percent to 37 percent in Los Angeles County. In San Diego County it passed by only 55 percent to 45 percent.

- Proposition 62 was a November 2016 initiative asking voters to approve the repeal of the death penalty and replace it with life imprisonment without the possibility of parole. This measure would apply retroactively to those inmates currently on death row. A very similar measure failed to pass in 2012 with a statewide vote of only 47 percent. November 2016 was no different: 54 percent of voters disapproved of this measure. San Francisco voters were very supportive of repealing the death penalty, with 71 percent voting in favor of the initiative. A slim majority (52 percent) of Los Angeles voters supported repeal. In contrast, only 44 percent of San Diego County voters were in favor of this measure.

- Proposition 64 on the November 2016 ballot legalizes marijuana and hemp under state law. With the support of 56 percent of the voters, this measure passed. Nearly 75 percent of San Francisco voters supported legalization, with

In 2018, Democratic candidate Gavin Newsom (left) and Republican candidate John Cox (right) ran to replace outgoing Governor Jerry Brown.

Los Angeles and San Diego voters supporting passage at 58 and 56 percent respectively.

- Proposition 6 on the November 2018 ballot asked voters to repeal fuel and vehicle tax increases that were enacted in 2017. The law mandated that the funds (about $5 billion per year) be used for road repairs and public transportation. Proposition 6 failed to pass and the fuel and vehicle taxes remain law. Not surprisingly, 83 percent of San Francisco voters were against the repeal of the fuel tax. Sixty percent of Los Angeles voters and only 49 percent of San Diego voters were against the repeal. Again, this exemplifies the progressive character of San Francisco and the comparatively more conservative leanings of San Diego.

THE GUBERNATORIAL ELECTION OF 2018 In the 2018 race for governor, the winner, Democrat Gavin Newsom, easily beat Republican John Cox with 86 percent of the vote in San Francisco and 71 percent in Los Angeles County. In San Diego County, however, support for Newsom stood at only 56 percent.

THE PRESIDENTIAL ELECTION OF 2016 In the November 8, 2016, presidential election, California voters preferred Hillary Clinton over Donald Trump 62 to 33 percent. San Francisco County overwhelmingly voted for Clinton with a resounding 85 percent; voters in Los Angeles County supported her at 72 percent, and San Diego County at 56 percent.

TO SUM UP The statistics in Table 4.2 demonstrate that political life varies dramatically in California from region to region. If you happen to reside in San Francisco, you live in one of the nation's most liberal, tolerant, and activist political cultures.[12] The political environment in San Diego, on the other hand, is more conservative, less tolerant, and more passive. Los Angeles falls somewhere in between. These three regions reflect the range of political cultural differences that exist across the state. You can easily see why local representatives in the state legislature fight so much and so fiercely and why they have such a hard time agreeing on anything.

Elections in California

The Battle over the Primary

The past decade has seen considerable controversy and upheaval and a number of court challenges regarding the type of primary system used in California. In primary elections, voters select their party's nominee for the general election. In the United States, there are three general types of primary-election systems, and states have the authority to determine the system under which they will operate.

- **Closed primary system**   Only voters who declare a party affiliation when they register to vote are permitted to vote in their party's primary election. Each party has its own ballot, listing the names of those who are competing to be the party's candidate in the general election. Voters receive the ballot of the party for which they are registered. Voters who decline to state a party affiliation when they register are not eligible to receive a party ballot; only party members can elect the party's nominees. Approximately 25 states use this system.

- **Open primary system**   Registered voters, regardless of their party affiliation, can vote in the party primary of their choice on primary election day. For example, a registered Democrat can decide if he or she would like to vote in the Republican Party primary and request that ballot. The choice of party ballot on primary election day does not affect the voter's permanent party affiliation. Approximately 20 states operate under this system.

- **Blanket primary system**   One ballot lists all candidates from all of the parties. All registered voters, including those not affiliated with any party, are permitted to vote, and all voters receive the same ballot. For instance, a voter who is not affiliated with a party may vote for a Democrat to run as the nominee for governor and a Republican to run as the nominee for the U.S. Senate. Under this system, voters who are not affiliated with a party help to choose that party's nominees. Alaska, Louisiana, Washington State, and California all use this primary system.

California operated under the closed primary system until the passage of Proposition 198 in 1996. Proposition 198 instituted a blanket primary system in which all voters received a single ballot containing the names of all candidates from all parties. California held two blanket primaries—in June 1998 and March 2000—before the U.S. Supreme Court (in the case of *California Democratic Party v. Jones*) invalidated Proposition 198. The Court ruled that, based on the First Amendment's guarantee of freedom of association, California's political parties have the right to exclude nonparty members from voting in party primaries. In an effort to include the growing number of nonaffiliated voters, California adopted a **modified closed primary system**. Beginning with the March 2002 primary election, political parties still had their own ballots but now had the option of adopting a party rule that would allow unaffiliated voters to vote in their party primary. If an unaffiliated voter was not allowed to request a party's ballot, he or she was given a ballot containing only the names of candidates for nonpartisan races and ballot measures.

Proponents of the blanket primary were not satisfied with the modified closed primary system, arguing that the blanket primary system is more inclusive and would result in more moderate candidates running in primary elections, thus producing more competitive races. The logic is that if independent, ideologically moderate voters participate in the primary election, they will bring a counterbalance to the more extreme and ideological views of traditional primary-party voters, the party loyalists. Primary candidates would, therefore, need to moderate their positions to attract the votes of independent voters. Therefore, in June 2010 voters once more passed a proposition that changed California's primary-election system.

Proposition 14 mandates a form of a blanket primary system known as the "top-two vote getters" or "jungle primary" system. This primary system only applies to state legislative and U.S. congressional elections as well as to the election of statewide officials such as governor and attorney general. (This system does not apply to candidates running for U.S. president, county central committees, or local offices. Presidential primaries continue to use closed or semi-closed primaries.) All registered voters, even those stating no party preference, receive a ballot listing all candidates from all qualified political parties. The two candidates who win the most votes for each office then participate in a runoff in November's general election. An interesting feature of this new primary election system is the possibility that the top two candidates can belong to the same political party.

The June 5, 2012, primary election was the first statewide election held under this new system, and the results were quite interesting. As a result of this new primary system, the November 2012 election saw 29 same-party runoffs for Congress, the state Assembly, and state Senate. This trend continued for the June 2014 and 2016 primaries. The June 2014 primary produced 24 same-party runoffs, and the June 2016 primary resulted in 28 same-party contests. The June 2016 primary made history as it produced the first same-party runoff for a statewide office, the U.S. Senate seat replacing long-term senator Barbara Boxer. Kamala Harris, California's Democratic attorney general, faced off against Democratic House member Loretta Sanchez in the November 2016 election. History repeated itself again in the June 2018 U.S. Senate primary, in which two Democrats were the top two vote getters: long-serving incumbent Diane Feinstein and Democrat Kevin de León. The June 2018 primary garnered national attention as Democrats hoping to win control of the House of Representatives worried that their chances would be greatly diminished because of our top-two primary system. California was home to seven House seats held by vulnerable Republicans, and the Democratic Party needed to flip those seats in their quest to win majority status in the House (we will discuss these contests in more depth later in this chapter).

For statewide races only, this new primary system also allows candidates to designate whether they have a political party preference and how it should be stated on the ballot. According to California law, "a candidate for nomination to a voter-nominated office shall have his or her party preference, or lack of party preference, stated on the ballot, but the party preference designation is selected solely by the candidate." This means that candidates can state the party with which they identify or they can state that they don't have a party preference. In this age of voter frustration directed at party politics and legislative gridlock, electing to have the ballot state "Party Preference: None" appears to be a strategy adopted by some candidates. This is what happened in a race for a hotly contested congressional seat in Ventura County in 2012. The redrawing of the state's congressional district boundaries created a new swing district in the area. A swing district is one in which there are near equal numbers of Republican and Democratic voters and a significant number of independent voters—who often decide the winner. This new district consisted of 41 percent Democrats, 35 percent Republicans, and 19 percent independent voters. There were four Democrats, one Republican, and one independent running in this primary. The "independent" candidate was actually a Republican who switched her party registration to "no party preference" just before filing her papers to run, hoping to win the support of enough independent and moderate voters to be one of the top two winners. A number of candidates have used this strategy, hoping voters won't remember or even know that they have been party loyalists before the campaign. Unfortunately for this candidate, the only Republican on the ballot and the better-known Democrat captured the top two positions and competed against each other in the November general election.

Will this new primary system have the intended result of encouraging more moderate candidates to run in primaries and ensuring their success? Louisiana and Washington operate under similar primary systems, and analyses of their election outcomes found that these states have not seen more moderate candidates elected. It has been found that Democrats in the state legislature have become slightly more moderate, but no similar ideological change has been found among Republican state lawmakers or among Democrats and Republicans in California's congressional delegation.[13] However, some argue that blanket primaries can boost voter turnout by 3 to 6 percent because they attract voters with no party preference. The June 2014 primary election in California did not meet these expectations. Neither did the June 2016 primary, whose exceptionally high turnout of 48 percent (with many voting for the first time) was largely a result of an exciting presidential primary and not the blanket primary. Although the June 2018 primary did see a substantial increase over the June 2014 turnout rate, it was only about 3 percent higher than the typical primary turnout prior to the adoption of the top-two system. One possible explanation for this higher turnout was the national attention focused on a number of California races as well as voters being more engaged and mobilized in this anti-Trump state.

Presidential Primaries: Maximizing California's Clout?

Until 2000 California held its presidential primaries in June of election years and was one of the last states to cast its votes for the parties' nominees. States holding earlier primaries and caucuses often determined the presidential nominees before Californians had a chance to go to the polls. To have more influence in the nomination process, California changed its presidential primary election date to March for the 2000 and 2004 presidential primaries.

Many believed it fitting that the most populous state should have an early primary date. However, this earlier primary date did not give California voters more clout in the presidential nomination process, because other states moved their primaries to even earlier dates. Hence, for the 2008 presidential primaries California changed the date once again, to February 5, the earliest permissible date under national party rules.

Many political analysts and journalists heralded the early February presidential primary date. But did this move really have the intended effect, as reflected in a hopeful 2007 *Los Angeles Times* article titled "Earlier Primary Gives California a Major Voice"? Many who had argued for the 2008 presidential primary in early February believed that candidates would have to campaign early and hard in the Golden State and win support from a racially and ethnically diverse population, especially the growing number of Latino voters. To win voters' support, the candidates would need to address issues important to Californians, and all this would result in California's greater prominence in presidential campaign politics. Or so the theory went.

One of the unanticipated consequences of California's adoption of an early primary date was that a number of states with long-standing early primaries set their election dates even earlier, not wanting to be overshadowed by the most populous state in the nation. Twenty-three other states also moved their primaries to February 5, resulting in something akin to a national primary. California's dream of being in the electoral limelight quickly faded.

Another consequence of the early February presidential primary was additional cost for the state, as the primaries for statewide offices continued to be held in June. The June 2008 primary election for statewide offices cost the state and counties $100 million and resulted in a historically low voting turnout rate of less than 25 percent of the registered voters. Including the November 2008 general election, California voters were asked to vote in three elections in less than 10 months. California's presidential primary went again back to the June date. However, the June 2012 California primary (which included primaries for presidential and statewide candidates) saw a record low turnout of only 22 percent of registered voters. Some believe that the frequent date changes for primary elections confuse voters and thereby contribute to California's less than spectacular voting turnout rates. We witnessed a slight improvement in June 2016, with 33 percent of registered voters casting ballots in the primary, and again in 2018, with a 37 percent turnout rate. To further confuse voters, California's 2020 presidential primary will be on March 3.

Initiative Campaigns: Direct Democracy or Tool of Special Interests?

One legacy of California's early-twentieth-century Progressive reform movement is the **ballot initiative** process. Californians can completely bypass the state legislature and their elected representatives and place proposed policies on the ballot for direct vote by the people. As the name suggests, the electorate *initiates* initiatives. Most people think of the initiative process as direct democracy in action—concerned citizens circulating petitions to qualify their issue for the ballot and then holding an election for the public to state its preference for or against the proposed policy. In reality, only a small number of ballot initiatives emerge as a result of grassroots efforts. Initiatives are largely a political tool used by special-interest groups to achieve their policy goals. Depending on the issue, interest groups sometimes find it politically expedient to bypass the legislature altogether, believing they have a better chance of achieving their policy goals if they take the issue directly to the voters.

For example, many members of the California legislature would find it politically unwise to introduce legislation to legalize marijuana, abolish the death penalty, or raise taxes. Positions on these issues are sure to outrage some voters, making re-election more difficult. That is why these types of issues find their way onto our ballots as initiatives or referendums. Likewise, legislation that would curb the power of special interests, interests that make sizable campaign contributions to legislators, also are unlikely to be dealt with by our elected representatives. Recently, some local ballot measures have passed that reduce retirement benefits for public employees. If an elected official introduced this type of proposal, he or she would be targeted for re-election defeat by unions representing public employees. Therefore, for many of these types of issues, interest groups realize that the most productive route is to go directly to the voters via the initiative process. In addition, citizen groups have found the initiative process to be the only avenue for policy change in the areas of legislative term limits, nonpartisan redistricting, and the blanket primary system. These changes would never have been proposed or approved by legislators, whose power and that of their political party would be curbed.

Since 1912, the first year initiatives were permitted, nearly 400 statewide initiatives have appeared on the California ballot. These ballot initiatives have dealt with a wide range of issues, such as legalization of marijuana, campaign-finance reform, same-sex marriage, taxation policy, legalization of gambling casinos, the establishment of a state lottery, environmental regulations, affirmative action policy, the criminal justice system, and labor issues. Of these hundreds of initiatives, only about one-third have been approved by the voters. In the past three decades, there has been a dramatic surge in the number of initiatives that have been proposed and that have qualified for the ballot. Many surmise that the reason for this increase is that special interests have become more sophisticated in their use of the initiative process to achieve their policy goals.

QUALIFYING FOR THE BALLOT For initiatives creating new laws (statutes) to qualify for the ballot, the state requires signatures of registered voters equal to 5 percent of the number of people who voted in the previous governor's race. For propositions aiming to amend the state constitution, the state requires 8 percent—about 600,000 for initiatives and 1 million for constitutional amendments. Signatures are gathered on petitions, which are then submitted to the secretary of state's office for verification. Collecting hundreds of thousands of signatures of registered voters is a daunting task. Rarely is this a grassroots movement in which ordinary citizens fan out across the state, knock on doors, and stand in front of supermarkets, asking strangers to support their initiative by signing a petition. More common is the hiring of professional signature gatherers, such as political consulting firms that hire people to go to college campuses, supermarkets, malls, and other places where voters congregate. Typically they are paid an average of $1.50 for every signature they acquire. However, the November 2018 election, with 11 ballot measures and many big-money donors, saw the average price of a signature rise to $6. All total, to qualify for the November 2018 ballot, campaigns spent over $20.5 million just on signature-gathering activities.[14]

CAMPAIGNING To wage a successful campaign either in support of or in opposition to a more controversial initiative, one needs ample political resources, particularly money. Not only must a statewide initiative campaign hire political consultants, but it must also plan and implement a sustainable media campaign. Such campaigns are very costly because of California's size and expensive media markets. Therefore, it is not surprising that the more high-profile and controversial initiative campaigns cost tens of millions of dollars. In 2008 slightly over $80 million was spent on the highly controversial initiative Proposition 8, a constitutional amendment to eliminate same-sex marriage in California. Proposition 8 was put on the ballot in response to the state Supreme Court's May 2008 ruling (in a 4-to-3 decision) declaring that the state constitution protects a fundamental "right to marry" that extends equally to same-sex couples. Both sides of the issue collected near equal contributions, with the majority of the contributions in support of Proposition 8 coming from members of the Mormon Church throughout the United States.[15] As expensive as Proposition 8 was, it did not break the record for the most expensive initiative campaign. In 2006 both sides combined spent more than $150 million on Proposition 87, the alternative energy initiative, which was soundly defeated by a 55 percent vote. Breaking that spending record was a series of initiatives in 2008 (Propositions 94–97) that sought to expand the number of Native American casinos in the state. According to a recent report by the *Washington Post*, the two sides combined spent over $170 million on those campaigns.[16] This was, by far, the most expensive proposition campaign not only in California history but in U.S. history.

It should be noted that spending more money than the opposing side does not always guarantee victory. Case in point: Proponents of Proposition 34, an initiative to repeal the death penalty on the November 2012 ballot, spent over $8 million on the yes campaign, whereas the opposition spent only a paltry $400,000 to defeat the measure.

Political savvy is another important resource. The chances of winning an initiative campaign increase if one understands how the game is played. For example, the naming of the proposition can increase its chance of passage. In the November 1996 election, Proposition 209, officially titled "Prohibition against Discrimination or Preferential Treatment by State and Other Public Entities," appeared on the ballot. Its supporters referred to the proposition as the "California Civil Rights Initiative." Considering these titles alone, it would be difficult to imagine this proposition failing; in these progressive times, it is fair to say that most voters are opposed to discrimination and are supportive of civil rights. In reality, however, Proposition 209 was not what most would consider a civil rights statute. The proposition proposed to eliminate affirmative action programs in California for women and minorities in public employment, education (college admissions, tutoring, and outreach programs), and contracting. But the clever naming worked: Proposition 209 passed and is now state law.

CRITICISMS OF DIRECT DEMOCRACY Critics of the initiative process believe that too many complicated issues are presented to the voters as ballot propositions. In some recent elections, voters have had to vote for candidates for federal, state, county, and city elective offices as well as cast their votes for more than a dozen important state propositions and numerous county and city measures. Case in point—the November 2016 election had 17 ballot propositions, and the Official California Voter Information Guide was 224 pages, the longest ever. It was estimated that it would take about 14 hours to read the guide. Not surprisingly, few voters will spend this amount of time educating themselves on the ballot propositions. David Redlawsk, co-author of *How Voters Decide: Information Processing in Election Campaigns*, describes the situation as follows: "People want to do what we would call a good job—that is make what they think is the right decision—but they want to do it essentially with the least amount of effort necessary."[17]

Some argue that many of the issues that appear as ballot initiatives are best suited for debate and deliberation by our elected representatives and should not be represented by misleading television ads aimed at the public. Sometimes the propositions are very confusing in name and in substance, and some question whether we are asking too much of the electorate to wade through all this information. Another problem with the initiative process is that the constitutionality of many propositions approved by the voters is later challenged. It takes years for the courts to render a decision, and it is not uncommon for the courts to declare the law based on the passage of the proposition to be unconstitutional, null, and void. Not only does this complicate the process, it also frustrates the public to see the courts invalidate its will.

The legislature understands some of the problems associated with the initiative and has created state commissions to investigate and reform the process. Some of these suggested reforms aim to accomplish the following: prohibit the use of paid signature gatherers, which only well-funded interest groups can afford; increase the number of signatures required, with the goal of reducing the number of initiatives; restrict the types of issues that can appear as ballot initiatives; and review the constitutionality of initiatives prior to placing them on the ballot. In September 2014 the legislature enacted two bills that reform the initiative process. One bill provides for a 30-day public review period that commences when the initiative is first proposed. Reformers hope that public input during this time will result in constructive modifications to propositions before they appear on the ballot, and that such input may motivate supporters of the proposed initiative to work with lawmakers to find a legislative solution to the issue. The other bill requires that the secretary of state post online and continuously update the top 10 donors contributing to both sides of an initiative. This provision creates more transparency by revealing exactly who is contributing big money in support of or in opposition to an initiative.

The 2003 Gubernatorial Recall Election: A Perfect Political Storm

On October 7, 2003, Governor Gray Davis made history. Only 11 months after he successfully won his re-election bid, he was recalled from office. He was the first and only governor in the state of California and the second governor in the nation's history to be recalled. The recall movement and election of Arnold Schwarzenegger were in every sense dramatic, historic, and stunning.

Davis was re-elected in November 2002, thanks in part to a very weak challenger, even though just before the election a majority of voters disapproved of his overall performance as governor.[18] Voters held Governor Davis responsible for the 2000–01 energy crisis, during which Californians were forced to reduce their energy consumption and pay more for their electricity while experiencing or being threatened by blackouts. News reports focused on this issue for many months, which had a negative impact on Davis's popularity. Compounding the problem was a dramatic decrease in state revenues. The governor had to announce that the state was short $23.6 billion and that the 2003–04 budget shortfall would rise to nearly $35 billion. The state legislature could not produce a budget on time, and voters were very uneasy about the economic future of the state. Davis entered his second term as a wounded, unpopular governor, viewed as distant, too beholden to special interests, and ineffectual.

Darrell Issa, a multimillionaire Republican member of Congress from the San Diego area, was a dominant force in the movement to recall Davis. He injected nearly $2 million into the recall effort and had hopes of running for governor if the recall succeeded. Nearly 1.5 million voter signatures were collected on recall petitions, meeting the state requirement for an October 2003 recall election. Unfortunately for Representative Issa's hopes of capturing the governorship, a well-known, charismatic, moderate Republican anti-politician, anti-establishment actor/businessman appeared on the scene: Arnold Schwarzenegger. In the summer of 2003 Schwarzenegger announced his candidacy and immediately became the front-runner among Republican candidates, making national and international headlines with his decision to run.[19] Politically, it was a perfect storm: a weak and unpopular governor, an unhappy electorate, and an internationally known celebrity. On the day of the election, 9.4 million Californians cast ballots, 11 percent more than the turnout in Davis's

2002 re-election. Fifty-five percent voted to remove Davis from office. Schwarzenegger was elected governor in his place with 48.6 percent of the votes cast. Schwarzenegger's adoption of moderate positions—pro-choice on abortion, moderate on the environment, and cooperative with the Democratically controlled state legislature—placed him in sync with voters, resulting in his re-election victory in 2006.

The 2008 Election: Demographic and Ideological Shifts

The 2008 election was somewhat unusual, even by California standards. A very popular, young, charismatic candidate, Barack Obama, topped the ticket as the Democratic candidate for the presidency, winning 61 percent of the popular vote compared to John McCain's 37 percent, the biggest margin in the state of California since 1964.

The *Los Angeles Times*, in an article aptly titled "State's Shifting Political Landscape," described the election results:

> Those unpredictable decisions by voters, however, were accompaniments to the election's main theme: the demographic and ideological shifts that have delivered the state into Democratic hands and demonstrated anew the tough road ahead for the Republican minority.[20]

The Democratic Party was hopeful that it could continue to win the support and allegiance of the overwhelming number of voters who had cast their votes for Obama, including 83 percent of first-time voters. Seventy-six percent of those 18–29 years of age voted for Obama compared to only 48 percent of those 65 and older. However, some analysts were not confident that future elections would see high percentages of young voters turning out to vote or substantial increases in support for the Democratic Party.

By November 2, 2010, the evidence was in. The lead headline from Scott Fahey's Elections 2010 blog from Southern California Public Radio read, "Low youth voter turnout hurts Democrats." As he described it, "In California, one of every five voters in 2008 was between the ages of 18 and 29, compared with about 1 in 10 on Tuesday." California reflected the overall national trend with fewer young, liberal, and black voters casting votes in the November 2010 general election.

The 2010 General Election

While the nation witnessed a historic "shellacking" of the Democratic Party, as President Obama called it, with an unprecedented loss of Democrat-held seats in Congress, Californians voted to the beat of a different drummer. All of the Democratic candidates running for statewide elective office won, and nearly all of them won by respectable margins. The *Los Angeles Times*, in an analysis of the vote based on exit poll data, concluded that the strength of the Latino vote was a key factor in the success of Democratic candidates. Latino voters made up 22 percent of the California voter pool, a record tally that sunk the election hopes of many Republicans.

THE GOVERNOR'S RACE The costliest statewide race in the nation's history pitted novice politician and billionaire Meg Whitman against political insider Jerry Brown. Whitman spent a record-breaking $160 million on her general election campaign (see Table 4.3 on p. 112), with over $140 million from her own personal wealth. Of this total, she poured nearly $110 million into TV and radio advertising.

Californians quickly became aware of her candidacy, and voters easily recognized her name. In contrast, Jerry Brown, who had served two terms as governor (1975–83), had been mayor of Oakland (1999–2007), and most recently had served as state attorney general, spent only $25 million on his campaign. In the end, Brown won by a very comfortable margin, 54 percent to 41 percent. Furthermore, Brown's cost per vote was only $1.24, whereas Whitman spent a whopping $51.82 per vote!

THE U.S. SENATE RACE Barbara Boxer, a liberal Democrat running for her fourth term in the U.S. Senate, had a tough re-election challenge, the toughest of her political career. Boxer, a career politician, ran against outsider and novice campaigner Carly Fiorina, a Republican and former CEO of Hewlett-Packard (HP). Typically, incumbents such as Boxer, running for re-election in a state where their political party dominates, have a relatively easy time keeping their seat. The situation was different this time around. California's economy was in shambles, Boxer's popularity had been declining, and Fiorina was a formidable opponent. In the end, Boxer prevailed, winning re-election with 52 percent of the vote compared to Fiorina's 43 percent. Many pundits believe that Fiorina's failure to moderate her position on social issues (she was ardently antiabortion and anti-illegal immigration), along with Boxer's stinging ads highlighting the layoff of 30,000 HP workers under Fiorina's stewardship, was responsible for Fiorina's loss.

PROPOSITION 20: REDISTRICTING CONGRESSIONAL DISTRICTS VS. PROPOSITION 27: ELIMINATING THE STATE REDISTRICTING COMMISSION Propositions 20 and 27 were actually competing initiatives. Proposition 20 is an extension of Proposition 11, which passed in November 2008. Proposition 11 created the 14-member Citizens Redistricting Commission that would be in charge of drawing the boundaries of state Assembly and state Senate districts after each U.S. Census. November 2010's Proposition 20 asked voters to remove the authority for congressional redistricting from the legislature and give this power to the newly created Citizens Redistricting Commission. The commission would then be responsible for drawing congressional district lines as well as continuing to exercise the power to draw state Assembly and state Senate district boundaries. The competing initiative, Proposition 27, on the other hand, would have eliminated the Citizens Redistricting Commission and returned to the legislature the power to draw state district boundaries (essentially repealing Proposition 11). California voters soundly endorsed the Citizens Redistricting Commission (defeating Proposition 27 with a 59 percent vote against it) and gave the Commission the power to determine congressional districts as well (Proposition 20 passed with a 61 percent vote in favor).

PROPOSITION 25: SIMPLE MAJORITY VOTE TO PASS BUDGET Proposition 25 changed the legislative vote requirement to pass the budget from two-thirds to a simple majority. In addition, all members of the legislature must permanently forfeit reimbursement for salary and expenses for every day the budget is late. At the time that Proposition 25 was introduced, California had not passed a state budget by the mandatory June 15 deadline in 23 years. Budget negotiations in 2010 extended 100 days past the deadline, just close enough to Election Day for it to be fresh in voters' minds. Californians passed Proposition 25 with a 55 percent affirmative vote. Supporters of this initiative were labor unions (especially teachers who received layoff notices when the budget was not passed on time), the League of Women Voters, groups representing retirees, and others who were able to devote resources to the "Yes on Prop 25" campaign. Since passage of this proposition, the state budget has been passed on time.

The 2012 Primary Election

The June 2012 primary was an interesting one. Usually, the major contest in the primary during a presidential election year is between the candidates competing for their party's nomination for the presidential race. But, as typically happens when states hold their primary late in the political season, Mitt Romney already had won enough delegates to secure his party's nomination, and President Obama had no Democratic challenger and was, by default, his party's nominee. Perhaps this explains why only one in three registered voters participated in this election, with one of the lowest turnout rates in Los Angeles County, at less than 22 percent. As mandated by the passage of Proposition 14, this was the first statewide blanket primary using the new top-two candidates system. It was also the first election since the adoption of the newly drawn congressional and state legislative districts. The ballot looked different, all voters regardless of party affiliation were given the same ballot, the results were calculated differently, and some candidates found themselves running in new or very different districts. A very interesting election, indeed.

The 2012 General Election: More Demographic and Ideological Shifts

THE PRESIDENTIAL RACE The outcome of the November 2012 presidential election looked similar to that of the 2008 presidential election, with young and minority voters favoring President Obama and older and white voters supporting Romney. Statewide, Obama won 59 percent of the vote, slightly less than the 61 percent he won in 2008. He received 71 percent of the votes cast by 18- to 29-year-old Californians, which is close to the 76 percent he received in 2008. Of those 65 years of age and older, 48 percent voted for Obama, the same percentage as did in 2008. Other notable demographic results were based on race, marital status, and place of residence. While only 45 percent of whites supported Obama, 79 percent of Asian Americans and 72 percent of Latinos voted for him. Marital status also made a difference, with Obama receiving 67 percent of the votes of unmarried Californians and 51 percent of the votes of married voters. Voters living in urban areas chose to re-elect the president by 65 percent compared to rural voters at 50 percent.

The 2012 election was interesting in terms of voter turnout rates. Although 5 percent fewer Californians voted in 2012 than in 2008, more young voters turned out to vote in 2012. The youth vote accounted for 20 percent of all votes cast in 2008 and 28 percent of all votes in 2012. That is a 40 percent increase in turnout among 18- to 29-year-old California voters. Nationwide, there was only a slight increase in the youth vote, which grew from 17 percent in 2008 to 19 percent in 2012. What accounted for this dramatic increase in the turnout of young California voters?

According to political scientist Peter Levine, California's new online voter registration system (described later in this chapter), made available shortly before the 2012 election, registered nearly 700,000 new voters, many of whom were young people.[21] Also, Proposition 30 (the initiative to fund higher education) was a salient issue for young voters. If the measure did not pass, college students would face another round of tuition increases, crowded classes, and cuts in enrollment to the California State University and University of California systems. This combination of an accessible online voter registration system and an important initiative impacting higher education motivated young voters.

CONGRESSIONAL RACES As mandated by the U.S. Constitution, all House members serve two-year terms in office. California has 53 House members, and in the November 2012 election, 11 new members were elected, the most in 20 years. Democrats won 38 of the 53 seats, and the number of seats held by Latinos increased. These changes were a result of the recent remapping of House districts and changing demographics. A number of incumbent House members retired when their districts were redrawn after the 2010 U.S. Census, and some found themselves in competitive districts where their re-election was not assured. Prior to the 2012 election, only one House seat had changed between the parties during the last five congressional elections. In 2012, Democratic candidates won four more House seats than they had in 2010. A second factor related to the strong showing by Democratic candidates is the growing number and clout of Latino voters, especially in Southern California. As reported in the *Los Angeles Times*, "Voters in Riverside and San Bernardino counties elected three Democrats to Congress— two Latinos and a gay Asian American—after having sent only two Democrats to Washington in the last four decades."[22]

CALIFORNIA LEGISLATIVE RACES The *Los Angeles Times* headline on November 8, 2012, read, "Blue reign in Sacramento: Democrats' historic gains position them for unchecked power." Prior to the November 6 election, Democrats had controlled both the state Assembly and the state Senate. Amazingly, this election not only allowed the Democratic Party to maintain its majority status, it also gave it *supermajority* status. Having a supermajority means there are enough Democratic votes in each chamber to raise taxes without needing any votes from Republicans. The last time a party had supermajority power in California was in 1933 when the Republicans were in charge. The Democrats last had this power in 1883. This supermajority status was short-lived, however—three Democratic state senators were suspended in March 2014 after being indicted on felony criminal charges.

PROPOSITIONS There were 11 measures on the November 2012 ballot. Voters were asked to weigh in on a number of issues ranging from increased taxes to funding for educational programs to the repeal of the death penalty. A record-breaking amount of money was spent on these campaigns. George Skelton, a *Los Angeles Times* columnist, wrote, "It's almost unfathomable that $372 million was spent to promote or attack the 11 measures. To put it in perspective, that amount of money could pay for the annual tuitions of 31,000 undergrads at the University of California. The top 20 donors provided 69 percent of all initiative funding."[23] What follows is a description of some of the more high-profile measures:

- **Proposition 30: Taxes to Fund Education versus Proposition 38: Tax to Fund Education and Early Childhood Programs** These two competing propositions dealt with ways to raise revenue to fund education. Proposition 30, backed by the governor, would temporarily raise the state sales tax for 4 years and increase taxes on the wealthy for 7 years. Proposition 38 would raise taxes on earnings for all Californians for 12 years. Since these were competing measures, if both passed, the one receiving the most votes would prevail. Proposition 30 passed with 55 percent of the vote. Proposition 38 received only 28 percent of the vote even though its sponsor, Molly Munger, spent $44 million of her own money on the measure. In addition, an outside political group from Arizona spent over $11 million to defeat both Propositions 30 and 38.

- **Proposition 34: Death Penalty**   This initiative statute would repeal the death penalty and replace it with life in prison without possibility of parole. Those currently on death row would have their sentences commuted to life imprisonment. Proponents of this measure spent over $8 million. Opponents spent a small fraction of that amount. The measure was defeated with a 52 percent "no" vote.

- **Proposition 36: Three Strikes Law: Repeat Felony Offenders**   This measure would revise the existing three strikes law to impose life sentences only when the offender is convicted of a new violent felony. Those previously convicted under this law for nonviolent felonies may have their sentences reviewed. The measure easily passed with 69 percent of the vote.

- **Proposition 37: Genetically Engineered Foods Labeling**   This proposition would require the labeling of food that is made from plants or animals containing genetically altered material. Agroscience opponents, including DuPont, Dow Agro, and Monsanto, spent over $15 million to defeat this measure. The proposition failed, receiving only 48 percent of the vote.

The 2014 Election

Nationally, the contest between Democrats and Republicans over control of the U.S. Senate was the most important issue of the 2014 midterm elections. If the Republican Party gained six Senate seats, they would then control both chambers of Congress. The Democratic Party hoped to maintain control of the Senate but faced an uphill battle in a number of important U.S. Senate contests. The Republican Party prevailed, and both chambers of Congress were controlled by the Republican Party. In California, however, 2014 was a rather subdued election year, evidenced by the fact that fewer than three in 10 voters participated in this election. California's two U.S. senators were not up for re-election, the governor's race was not very competitive, and only a few ballot initiatives engaged in media campaigns.

THE GOVERNOR'S RACE Governor Jerry Brown, a popular incumbent, was re-elected by a comfortable margin. His opponent, Neel Kashkari, never stood much of a chance to win. Unlike Brown's 2010 challenger, Meg Whitman (who raised over $176 million), Kashkari was virtually unknown to the public and was seriously underfunded. Six weeks prior to the election his campaign had less than $700,000 to spend compared to Governor Brown's nearly $24 million. Brown agreed to only one 60-minute televised debate, which did not enjoy a large audience and did little to boost Kashkari's popularity. Kashkari's weeklong stint as an undercover homeless person in Fresno also failed to generate support for his campaign. Kashkari even gave away $25 cash cards to the first 100 people who showed up at one of his campaign events (most likely violating the state's election code that prohibits candidates from giving gifts to win votes). Brown beat Kashkari 54 percent to 41 percent and was re-elected to serve a historic fourth and final term as governor.

PROPOSITIONS Six propositions appeared on the ballot, comparatively few by California standards. Below is a description of the initiatives that passed:

- **Propositions 1 and 2: Water Bond and State Budget** These two measures were publicized as companion initiatives ("Save Water, Save Money") and had virtually no opposition. These propositions dealt with the water crisis in California and ensured stricter enforcement of the state's "rainy day" surplus money fund. Both propositions passed overwhelmingly with 67 percent and 69 percent of the vote respectively.

- **Proposition 47: Criminal Sentences; Misdemeanor Penalties** As described earlier in this chapter, crimes such as drug possession, shoplifting, petty theft, and forgery would qualify as misdemeanor, not felony, crimes under this measure. The result would be lesser penalties for those with no prior convictions for serious, violent crimes. As reported in the *Los Angeles Times*, it is believed that 20 percent of criminals would face more lenient sentences and more than 7,000 current inmates could petition the courts to reduce their sentences.[24] Most law enforcement organizations were opposed to this measure, arguing that thousands of dangerous criminals would be released from prison and that our criminal justice system would be overwhelmed with petitions for reduced sentences. However, pre-election polling found the public to be overwhelmingly in favor of this measure. The proposition passed with 59 percent of the vote.

The 2016 Primary Election

Many believed that California would finally have a June presidential primary that mattered. California's impact, however, was not as great as had been anticipated. All but one of the Republican candidates vying for the presidential nomination had dropped out prior to the June primary: Donald Trump was the last man standing on the Republican side and won the California Republican primary with over 75 percent of the vote. On the Democratic side, in the Clinton versus Sanders contest, Clinton had surged far enough ahead of Sanders in the delegate count that her nomination was a foregone conclusion prior to the California primary. Her victory in the California Democratic primary (winning nearly 56 percent of the vote to Sanders 43 percent) technically put her in the position where she could officially declare that she was her party's presidential nominee.

One positive consequence of this primary was that it engaged the public. As previously mentioned, the 2016 presidential primary motivated people to register to vote. From May 2012 to May 2016 California voter registration numbers had increased by over 760,000 people, with 650,000 people registering in the few weeks prior to the June 2016 primary.

The contest to fill retiring Democratic U.S. senator Barbara Boxer's seat saw two Democrats win the top-two primary, out of a field of 34 candidates. Kamala Harris, the twice-elected California attorney general, trounced Loretta Sanchez, a 20-year House member, in the primary. Harris, a daughter of Jamaican and Indian immigrants, and Sanchez, a daughter of Mexican immigrants, ensured that the next U.S. senator from California would be a woman of color.

The 2016 General Election

THE PRESIDENTIAL RACE The outcome of the November 2016 presidential race was a stunner. Virtually all the polls and predictions had Hillary Clinton winning the presidency. Surprisingly, on election night as the state by state results were coming in, it gradually became apparent that Clinton was losing the electoral college vote. Donald Trump exceeded the necessary 270 electoral college votes needed to win the presidency, in the end winning over 300 electoral college votes. Clinton, however, won the popular vote count by more than two million votes. To say this was an upset victory would be an understatement: the nation was shocked. Young people across the country protested in the streets (a number of the larger protests were in California). It was calculated that if 1 out of every 100 Trump voters had shifted their vote to Clinton, she would have won the presidency with 307 electoral college votes. That's how close of an election it was. California, not surprisingly, voted overwhelming for Clinton by a nearly 2-to-1 margin (62 percent Clinton; 33 percent Trump). Statewide, Clinton beat Obama's margin over Romney in 2012 by 6 percentage points. This was the widest margin in a presidential election in the past 80 years. In fact, southern California's Orange County, birthplace of the reactionary John Birch Society and historic Republican stronghold, voted for a Democratic candidate for the first time in 88 years. Clearly, California was out of step with the rest of the nation.

In the 2012 presidential election, Obama won 71 percent of the 18- to 29-year-old vote. Clinton fell slightly short of that number, winning 66 percent of the youth vote. Those 45 to 64 years of age had the highest turnout of any age group, contributing 38 percent of the total vote count in the state. This age group voted for Trump at a higher percentage (39 percent) than any other age group. Minority voters were overwhelming in favor of Clinton but fell short of their support of Obama in 2012. Seventy percent of Asian Americans, 71 percent of Latinos, and 88 percent of African American voters supported Clinton. White voters voted for Clinton at a lower rate: 50 percent of white men and 57 percent of white women voted for Clinton. Similar to the national trend, whites with no college degree were more likely to vote for Trump. In California this group supported Trump at 59 percent, compared to 67 percent of this group nationally. Religion was another differentiating factor. Protestants were more likely to vote for Trump than any other religious group (51 percent). Slight regional differences were noted in this election. The areas that were the most supportive of Clinton were the Bay Area (79 percent), coastal communities (67 percent), and Los Angeles (71 percent). Trump drew support from inland and central California (45 percent) and parts of southern California (45 percent).[25]

Nationwide, voting turnout rates were the lowest in about 20 years. Of those eligible to vote, only about 57 percent went to the polls. In California even fewer eligible voters participated (approximately 50 percent), with the exception of Latino voters, who flocked to the polls. This group mobilized in California most likely due to Trump's anti-immigrant positions. The Latino vote comprised nearly one-third of all votes cast, an increase of nearly 10 percent from the 2012 election. African American turnout was slightly below the 2012 turnout. White turnout fell by about 7 percent, and Asian American turnout remained about the same. The youth vote declined by about 7 percent from 2012 and mirrored the national youth turnout, where 18- to 29-year-olds made up about 20 percent of all those voting.

CONGRESSIONAL RACES In 2016, California sent its first new senator in 24 years to Washington. Kamala Harris, California's attorney general, won the seat vacated by Senator Barbara Boxer. Harris also made history as the first African American to represent California in the U.S. Senate as well as the second African American woman ever to be elected to the Senate. In our new top-two primary system, Harris ran against another Democrat, Representative Loretta Sanchez. Overshadowed by the more media-driven presidential race, this race received scant attention and was not competitive. Harris easily beat Sanchez, winning 63 percent of the vote.

California's House delegation saw few changes in the 2016 election. No seats switched party, and California sent 39 Democrats and 14 Republicans to the House of Representatives. A handful of Republican incumbents narrowly won re-election. One of the most watched contests was between six-term Republican House member Darryl Issa, representing a district that straddles Orange and San Diego counties, and newcomer retired colonel Doug Applegate. Issa had fended off challengers before with double-digit leads, but Applegate made this contest highly competitive. Issa eked out a win by a very slim margin.

CALIFORNIA LEGISLATIVE RACES The Democratic Party again had firm control over both the state Assembly and the state Senate. Three Republican Assembly incumbents lost their seats to Democrats. Two Democratic Assembly incumbents lost their seats to fellow Democratic challengers (remember, we now have a top-two vote-getter primary system that makes it possible for the top two candidates running against each other in the general election to be from the same political party). Democrats had a supermajority in the state Assembly with 55 seats; Republicans had 25 Assembly seats. Incumbent state senators all won their re-election bids. The Democrats also won a supermajority in the state Senate and had 27 seats to the Republicans' 13 seats.

PROPOSITIONS There were 17 measures on the November 2016 ballot, the largest number of initiatives on a ballot since March 2000. Voters were asked to consider issues such as legalization of marijuana (again), repeal of the death penalty (again), background checks on purchases of ammunition, a ban on plastic grocery bags, caps on health care costs, and workplace rules for adult movie actors, to name a few. Let's look at some of the more high-profile, controversial initiatives:

- **Proposition 58: Repeal English-Only Education** This proposition repealed Proposition 227, the initiative passed in 1998 that made California public schools English-only. Proposition 58 requires school administrators to solicit input from parents in developing language acquisition programs and allows schools to offer dual immersion language programs. This proposition had overwhelming support and passed with more than 72 percent of the vote. Proposition 227 passed in 1998 with more than 60 percent of the vote. The dramatic reversal in 20 years most likely reflects the demographic changes in the state and the growing Latino population and its strength at the ballot box.

- **Proposition 61: Drug Price Standards** This initiative would require that the state of California pay no more than prices paid by the U.S. Department of Veterans Affairs for prescription drugs. Over $125 million was spent on this campaign, with most of the money coming from major drug companies hoping to defeat this measure. Most experts agreed this was a poorly crafted measure that would not bring about the desired outcome of lower prescription drug costs. The measure failed with a 54 percent "no" vote.

- **Proposition 62: Repeal the Death Penalty and Proposition 66: Death Penalty Procedures**   These were competing initiatives. Proposition 62 sought to end the death penalty in California. Prisoners already on death row would have their sentences commuted to life in prison with no chance of parole. Proposition 66 was an opposing measure that would retain the death penalty and speed up the appeals process, mandating that all appeals be completed within five years of the death penalty sentence. Proposition 62 failed with 54 percent of voters not wanting to repeal the death penalty. Proposition 66 passed by a slim majority of 51 percent. It is interesting to note that Los Angeles County and virtually all of the northern California coastal counties voted to repeal the death penalty and voted against speeding up the appeals process, whereas most of the inland counties voted against repeal and for the expedited appeals process.

- **Proposition 63: Background Checks for Ammunition Purchases and Ban on Large-Capacity Magazines**   This measure requires individuals to have a permit to purchase ammunition, closes the loophole on allowing exemptions to the ban on large-capacity magazines, strengthens enforcement prohibiting felons from owning firearms, and makes the theft of firearms a felony. This initiative passed with a 63 percent vote. Proponents outspent opponents by a 5-to-1 margin. Surprisingly, the National Rifle Association, which opposed this measure, spent less than $100,000 on efforts to defeat it. And again we see a regional split, with most inland counties voting against this measure and coastal and near-coastal counties supporting it.

- **Proposition 64: Legalization of Marijuana**   California, along with Massachusetts, Maine, and Nevada, voted to legalize the recreational use of marijuana. In addition, Arkansas, Florida, North Dakota, and Montana all passed initiatives to make medical marijuana legal. Proposition 64 passed with 56 percent of the vote. Many of the counties voting against this measure are solidly Republican (as indicated in Figure 4.4 on page 88).

- **Proposition 65: Disposable Bag Sales Revenue to Wildlife Conservation Fund and Proposition 67: Plastic Bag Ban**   These two competing measures dealt with the legislative ban on plastic bags (Senate Bill 270). Proposition 65 was supported by the plastic bag industry and, if passed, would essentially kill Senate Bill 270. Proposition 67 would ratify SB (Senate Bill) 270, which outlaws single-use plastic bags and mandates that stores make available recyclable bags for a minimum cost of 10 cents. Revenue from the sale of these bags would be used to cover their costs and to educate consumers about sustainability. Proposition 65 failed to pass with a 55 percent "no" vote while SB 270 was ratified with 52 percent of the vote.

The 2018 Election

California was home to seven Republican House seats that the Democratic Party had targeted as vulnerable, and they needed to flip those seats in their quest to gain control of the House of Representatives. Democrats worried that their chances of winning these House seats might be diminished because of our top-two primary. There was a possibility that in some of the highly competitive House districts the top two candidates receiving the most votes would end up being two Republicans who would compete in November's election, thereby making it impossible for Democrats to win those seats.

How could this happen: two Republican candidates running against each other in November 2018? The problem was that too many Democratic candidates had entered these races. Some races had a total of 16 or more candidates on the ballot! The concern was that Democratic voters would split their votes amongst their party's numerous candidates, and that Republican voters would not splinter their votes (five of the seven targeted districts had an incumbent Republican on the ballot with few if any Republican challengers). In the end, all congressional primaries resulted in both a Democratic and a Republican candidate competing in the November 2018 general election. However, as mentioned earlier, the competition for the U.S. Senate resulted in two Democrats winning the top-two primary: Dianne Feinstein, the incumbent, and her fellow Democratic challenger, Kevin de León. It is interesting to note that there were 31 candidates running against the incumbent Feinstein.

The November 2018 midterm election was historic. Nationwide, an estimated 113 million people went to the polls, breaking the record for the most number of people voting in a non-presidential election in U.S. history. Over 49 percent of eligible voters participated in this midterm election, the largest percentage in a midterm election in over 100 years. In California, a whopping 62.5 million people cast votes, a 20 percent increase over the 2014 midterm election. Analysts believe one reason for these historically high turnout rates was voters' displeasure with President Trump. As political scientist Michael McDonald, head of the University of Florida's Elections Project, describes it:

> In a typical midterm election, where the President's party is overseeing an economy that is on sound footing, you would not expect high turnout. So clearly, something has changed here in our politics. The only logical explanation for the thing that has changed is Donald Trump.[26]

And as with June's primary election, California was in the spotlight once again. Democrats needed to flip 23 seats in the U.S. House of Representatives to gain control of that chamber. Gaining control of at least one chamber of Congress would result in a divided government where there would be a check on the Republican Party's power over the legislative and executive branches of government. The Democratic Party had identified seven Republican House seats located in California that they needed to flip in their quest to win majority status in the House. In the end, Democrats won control of the House, winning 40 seats nationwide previously held by Republicans. And, all of the seven targeted House races in California were won by Democratic candidates, providing nearly one-third of the needed 23 seats.

CONGRESSIONAL RACES It would be an understatement to say that the 2018 midterm congressional election in California was historic. As described above, voting turnout rates were exceptionally high. Over 12 million ballots were cast in California. However, it was the House of Representatives contests that were the focus of national attention. Control of the House depended on a number of House seats in California flipping from Republican control to Democratic control. This was not an easy feat as many of these House seats were in congressional districts that historically voted Republican. Case in point was four Republican-held House seats in Orange County, one of the most Republican counties in California. Former president Ronald Reagan once quipped "Orange County is where all good Republicans go to die." It is the home of one of the most right-wing conservative groups, the John Birch Society, and the birthplace of Richard Nixon and home to his presidential library. This previously reliable Republican stronghold saw all four of these targeted seats turn from Republican to Democratic control, leaving Orange County with no Republican House members, a first since the 1930s. Stuart Spencer, a veteran Republican strategist, commented "this election is one hell of a wake-up call for the Republican Party in California."[27] Of California's 53 House seats, only seven are now held by Republicans. This is the lowest number in the California House delegation since 1883.

As mentioned earlier, as a result of our top-two primary system, the U.S. Senate race pitted two Democrats against each other: long-term incumbent Senator Dianne Feinstein versus state senator Kevin de León. Feinstein, representing the moderate wing of the Democratic Party, did not receive the endorsement of the California Democratic Party, who instead supported the candidacy of the more left-leaning de León. However, Feinstein was endorsed by Governor Jerry Brown, Los Angeles mayor Eric Garcetti, and the *Los Angeles Times*. The 85-year-old Feinstein campaigned on her experience and seniority in the Senate, outspent her rival, and won her re-election bid with 54 percent of the vote.

THE GOVERNOR'S RACE Jerry Brown, the popular two-term Democratic governor, was prohibited by state law from running for office again. The 2018 governor's race saw Democratic Lieutenant Governor Gavin Newsom run against Republican John Cox, a San Diego businessman. In California, Republican candidates in statewide races typically need to run as moderates in order to win enough independent voters to propel them to victory. Cox was not a centrist Republican and lost the governor's race to Newsom, winning only 38 percent of the vote.

CALIFORNIA LEGISLATIVE RACES The blue wave extended to the California state house races. Democrats won enough seats in the state Assembly and the state Senate to maintain their supermajority status in both chambers. A supermajority (two-thirds votes) is needed to pass tax increases and to place constitutional amendments on the ballot. Democrats won enough seats to accomplish this without Republican support. In the state Assembly Democrats won 59 seats, nearly three-quarters of the 80 seats open. Republicans hold a paltry 21 seats in this chamber. This is the largest Democratic advantage in 40 years. The state Senate will now have 29 Democrats and only 11 Republicans serving, the largest Democratic advantage since 1962 (with one exception in 2012).

PROPOSITIONS There were 11 propositions on the ballot, three of which were bond measures. Voters were asked to weigh in on issues such as housing programs for the mentally ill, repeal of the state fuel tax, regulation of kidney dialysis treatment centers, change to daylight savings time, rent control, and the humane treatment of farm animals.

Propositions 6 and 8 were two of the more high-profile propositions. Proposition 6: Repeal of the Gas Tax, which was discussed earlier (see p. 92), ultimately failed. Proposition 8: Regulate Kidney Dialysis Treatment Charges was the most expensive proposition in 2018, and it also failed. This law would require dialysis clinics to issue refunds to patients or insurance companies for revenue above 115 percent of the costs of direct patient care and health care improvements. More than $130 million was spent by both sides. The "No" on Proposition 8 side raised over $111 million while the supporters raised only $18 million with most of the funds contributed by the Service Employees International Union (SEIU), who sponsored this ballot initiative. The SEIU, a labor union, had an ongoing conflict with the state's two largest dialysis companies concerning alleged retaliation against workers at these clinics trying to unionize. The proposition was defeated 60 percent to 40 percent.

Campaigning in California

California politics presents many challenges to those seeking elective office or the passage of a ballot measure. First, the immense size of the state means that groups hoping to pass or defeat statewide propositions, candidates running for statewide office, and candidates vying for the U.S. Senate or the presidency must plan campaigns that reach voters throughout the entire state. California has 13 distinct media markets, making it very expensive to communicate to its 39 million residents about politics. Second, California's population is very diverse, with many ethnicities, racial groups, cultures, professions, occupations, and interests represented. Successful campaigns must find ways to effectively communicate their platform and messages to all of the state's 19 million registered voters. And third, California has passed a number of political campaign reform acts in an attempt to regulate campaign spending and to provide public information on contributions and expenditures. These laws have proved beneficial to some and not as helpful to others.

Whatever the challenges of campaigning in California, one thing is certain: California's campaign politics are watched by the nation. We are a campaign trendsetter.

Money and Politics: California Style

As the record-breaking spending in the campaigns of 2010 demonstrated, campaigning in California requires money, and lots of it. In fact, California is one of the most expensive states in which to conduct a political campaign. Table 4.3 illustrates how the candidates in the 2010 governor's race spent nearly $200 million, making it the most expensive governor's race in U.S. history.

Running for the California legislature is also very expensive. Citing a Pew Center on the States study, blogger and researcher D. P. Osorio notes that California is the costliest state in which to win a state Senate seat ($938,522). The least expensive state is North Dakota where it costs $5,713; in Arizona it costs $36,696; in Wisconsin, $140,287; and in North Carolina, $234,031.[28] The prohibitive cost of campaigning in California limits those who can realistically run for office, another factor contributing to the state's governance challenges. Incumbents far outspend challengers, and incumbents' spending has increased over time while challengers' spending has not. On average, challengers spend only a fraction of what incumbents spend. This discrepancy helps to explain the high re-election rates of those elected to the California legislature. Some competitive races for the California legislature cost in excess of $1 million.

The following are some reasons that California campaigns are so expensive:

MEDIA-DOMINATED CAMPAIGNS Because of the state's size and its 13 different **media markets**, candidates must run **media-dominated campaigns**, spending

TABLE 4.3 ● Spending in California's Gubernatorial Election: How the Money Was Spent, 2010

Expenditure	Whitman ($)	Brown ($)
Television and radio advertising	$106,930,505.28	$21,259,408.00
Campaign consultants	11,693,547.95	167,200.00
Campaign literature and mailings	10,582,303.93	2,532,801.36
Campaign workers' salaries	5,918,110.80	157,870.01
Radio airtime and production costs	5,472,228.17	0
TV or cable airtime and production costs	4,139,919.07	182,103.12
Information technology costs (Internet, email)	3,177,977.76	23,345.51
Office expenses	2,321,340.46	132,023.40
Meetings and appearances	1,772,342.56	0
Polling and survey research	1,410,893.36	93,728.30
Staff/spouse travel, lodging, and meals	1,260,616.12	2,618.30
Fund-raising events	1,241,158.66	70,626.38
Candidate travel, lodging, and meals	950,890.17	12,071.76
Professional services (legal, accounting)	880,044.13	39,310.00
Postage, delivery, and messenger services	668,059.56	2,117.00
Campaign paraphernalia/miscellaneous	633,946.72	65,129.65
Phone banks	549,904.75	0
Contribution	252,500.00	0
Print ads	153,440.00	0
Voter registration	66,710.00	0
Civic donations	16,383.00	0
Returned contributions	0	99,364.14
Candidate filing/ballot fees	0	3,579.74
TOTAL	**160,092,822.45**	**24,843,296.67**

SOURCE: Lance Williams, "Meg Whitman Spending: Where did $160 Million Go?" *Huffington Post*, November 2, 2010, www.huffingtonpost.com/2010/11/02/meg-whitman-spending-wher_n_777644.html (accessed 11/2/10).

enormous amounts of money producing political ads and buying the broadcast time to air them. During the 2003 gubernatorial recall election, it cost approximately $2 million a week to run political ads statewide.[29] In the 2006 governor's race, Schwarzenegger's campaign alone spent $9 million on TV ads in the short time span between July 1 and September 30. As is shown in Table 4.3, an astounding $128 million was spent in the November 2010 governor's race just on TV, cable, and radio airtime and production. This cost is in addition to the $57 million spent on media during the primary campaign. As one media consultant described it, "There's a lot to be said for traditional politicking, kissing babies and shaking hands, but you have to get on TV to reach voters."[30]

POLITICAL CONSULTANTS Professional campaign managers and various **political consultants**—media consultants, pollsters, fund-raisers, direct-mail experts, and voter mobilization professionals—cost money. Because of California's love for direct democracy, especially the initiative process, many well-known political consultants have established offices in California. There is money to be made in California politics, and candidates and supporters of ballot initiatives know that to win elections you must hire the costly services of top-notch political consultants.

WEAK POLITICAL PARTIES California has comparatively **weak political parties**. The Progressive reform movement of Governor Hiram Johnson (served 1911–17) implemented many rules that reduced the organizational strength and clout of political parties within the state, as described earlier. Because of California's weak party system, the party organizations are minimally involved in organizing and conducting the campaigns of candidates running for office. In addition, California has a relatively large number of registered voters who decline to affiliate with any political party and consider themselves politically independent. These unaffiliated, independent voters compose nearly one-quarter of all registered voters. The combination of weak party structure and less party attachment means that candidates themselves have to work harder—raise and spend more money—to reach these voters.

Campaign-Finance Reform in California

To create more transparency in the electoral process and to make public the flow of money in political campaigns, several **campaign-finance reform** laws have been enacted in California over the past 100 years. Brief descriptions of the most recent laws follow.

1974: POLITICAL REFORM ACT In 1974 a group of reform-minded Californians crafted a statewide proposition that would require the most detailed campaign-finance reporting in the nation. Proposition 9 appeared on the ballot during the Watergate scandal and passed with an overwhelming majority of votes. This act created the Political Reform Division within the office of the secretary of state to administer and oversee key provisions of the law. A new independent state agency, the Fair Political Practices Commission, was also created for the purposes of interpreting and enforcing the act.

1988: PROPOSITION 73 In 1988, California voters overwhelmingly passed Proposition 73, which limited contributions to legislative and statewide candidates to $1,000 per donor, including individuals, labor unions, and corporations. A federal judge struck it down in 1990.

1996: PROPOSITION 208 Voters approved Proposition 208 by a 61 percent vote in 1996. Contributions to candidates from individuals, political parties, committees, corporations, unions, and political action committees (PACs) were limited. Spending limits also were imposed on candidates, although these were voluntary. Candidates who abide by the spending limits are allowed to collect larger contributions, whereas candidates who do not abide by them have lower contribution limits. Proposition 208 was being challenged in the courts when Proposition 34 was proposed and passed.

2000: PROPOSITION 34 Proposition 34 was placed on the ballot by the legislature. Spending limits were substantially increased, as were contribution limits. For example, under Proposition 208, individuals were permitted to contribute $1,000 to gubernatorial candidates—$500 if the candidate decided not to abide by the voluntary spending limits. Proposition 34 increased individual contributions

While Latinos in California currently vote at a significantly lower rate than whites, the Latino population is poised to exert great influence over California's electoral outcomes as it increases in size and clout.

to $21,200. Many reform-minded organizations that had supported Proposition 208, such as the League of Women Voters and Common Cause, were opposed to Proposition 34. They saw Proposition 34 as an attempt by the legislature to replace the more stringent Proposition 208 that was then under review in the courts. Nevertheless, in November 2000, Proposition 34 passed with close to 60 percent of the popular vote and has replaced the provisions of Proposition 208.

Although it could be argued that Proposition 34 has resulted in less control of campaign financing, California does receive high marks when it comes to laws requiring public disclosure of campaign contributions and expenditures. The Campaign Disclosure Project conducted by UCLA in 2008 studied the campaign disclosure laws in all 50 states and ranked the states accordingly. California received a grade of A for its disclosure laws and ranked second in the nation; Washington State ranked first.

Voting in California

Of California's 39 million residents, slightly more than 25 million are eligible to vote. Seventy-eight percent of those eligible (nearly 20 million) are registered. Contrary to some beliefs, registering to vote does not put one at higher risk of being selected for jury duty, nor does one receive more income tax scrutiny. To register to vote in the state of California, you must meet the following criteria:

- You will be 18 years of age on or before Election Day.
- You are a citizen of the United States.
- You are a resident of California.
- You are not in prison or on parole for a felony conviction.
- You have not been judged by a court to be mentally incompetent to register and to vote.

How You Can Register to Vote

The law mandates that you must register to vote at least 15 days before an election. In California, 16- and 17-year-olds are allowed to preregister to vote, and will be automatically registered at age 18. Since this law was passed in September 2016, more than one-quarter of a million young people have preregistered to vote! Here are the options for doing so:

- **Obtain a voter registration form** from any U.S. post office or library. Forms are usually available on counters. Fill out the preaddressed, stamped form and mail it in.

- **Visit a branch of the California Department of Motor Vehicles.** The National Voter Registration Act of 1993 (also known as "**Motor Voter**") permits persons conducting business at a DMV office to register to vote or to update their voter registration information while at the office. Since 1995 more than 12.5 million people have registered or reregistered in conformance with this law. California passed a new voter registration law, effective January 1, 2016. Now, at the DMV office, individuals will be asked if they are eligible to vote and, if so, their information will automatically be transmitted to the secretary of state's office where citizenship will be verified and names added to the voter registration rolls. An individual may opt out of this automatic registration.

- **Register online.** Go to the secretary of state's website and use the new online voter registration system (registertovote.ca.gov). The process is very simple and can be completed entirely online if you have a California driver's license or identification card. Because voter registration applications must be signed by the individual, the online system retrieves your signature from your driver's license or ID card and electronically transfers it to your online registration application. This new system has proven to be extremely popular: of the record 1.4 million newly registered voters for 2012, over half of them registered online. As of October 2018, California, along with 36 other states and the District of Columbia, offers electronic voter registration.

You will need to reregister to vote if:

- you move,
- you change your name, or
- you change your political party affiliation.

Who Votes in California?

There are demographic differences between those adults who are likely to vote and those who vote infrequently or who are not registered to vote. Table 4.4 also clearly illustrates this. Of the individuals who are very likely to vote, 59 percent are white, 21 percent are Latino, 11 percent are Asian American, and 6 percent are African American. Likely voters live in urban areas, are older, are college educated, are U.S. born, and earn higher incomes. Over the decades, the composition of the eligible voting population has changed and now there are more minority voters.

TABLE 4.4 ● California's Likely Voters, 2018

	Percentage of registered voters likely to vote in California's next statewide election (%)
Race/Ethnicity	
White	59%
Latino	21
Asian	11
Black	6
Other/Multirace	3
Region	
Los Angeles County	26
San Francisco Bay Area	23
Orange/San Diego Counties	17
Central Valley	16
Inland Empire	9
Other	9
Age	
18 to 34	18
35 to 54	34
55 and older	48
Education	
No college	19
Some college	42
College graduate	39
Nativity	
U.S.-born	84
Immigrant	16

SOURCE: Eight PPIC Statewide Surveys from September 2017 to July 2018, including 13,669 adults and 7,999 likely voters. California Secretary of State, Report of Registration, May 2018. US Census Bureau, 2012-16 American Community Survey.

But overall the same pattern has held: whites vote at a higher rate. Three factors help explain this discrepancy:

- **Eligibility** A significant proportion of the Latino and Asian populations are not eligible to vote because they are not citizens.

- **Youth** The Latino and Asian populations are both younger, and younger people are much less likely to vote than are older people.

- **Education** The probability of voting increases significantly for those with college or advanced degrees.

Research shows that if you control for these three factors, Latinos vote at rates comparable to whites.[31]

The 2016 presidential election saw a decline in voter turnout nationally. According to an analysis by political website FiveThirtyEight, a smaller percentage of eligible voters participated in the 2016 presidential election than in the previous two elections.[32] Only about 57 percent of voters went to the polls, down from about 59 percent in 2012 and nearly 62 percent in 2008.

As Figure 4.5 illustrates, California fits in with this national trend. Fifty-six percent of eligible voters turned out in 2012, and about 54 percent voted in 2016. It is interesting to note that, nationwide, the decline in turnout was more prevalent in states that voted for Clinton, as evidenced in California. Although overall turnout declined in California, Latino turnout in the 2016 election substantially increased from previous years. Over 30 percent of voters self-identified as Latino compared to the 2012 election when that number was 22 percent. Latino voters were probably mobilized to vote in 2016 because of the anti-Latino, anti-immigrant campaign of Donald Trump. Midterm elections typically have low voter turnout, but the 2018 midterms broke voting turnout records. In California, there was about a 50 percent increase in early voting and requests for absentee ballots among Latinos compared to the 2014 midterms. (See the "Who Are Californians?" feature for a breakdown of California's voting population in 2018.)

THE EVER-EXPANDING GROUP OF VOTERS: VOTING BY MAIL California now has very liberal vote-by-mail laws. Before 1978 voters could only receive a mail ballot if they signed a sworn statement affirming that they would be away

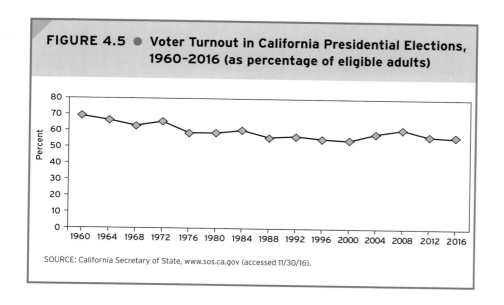

FIGURE 4.5 ● Voter Turnout in California Presidential Elections, 1960–2016 (as percentage of eligible adults)

SOURCE: California Secretary of State, www.sos.ca.gov (accessed 11/30/16).

Who Votes in California?

Gender

■ Male ■ Female

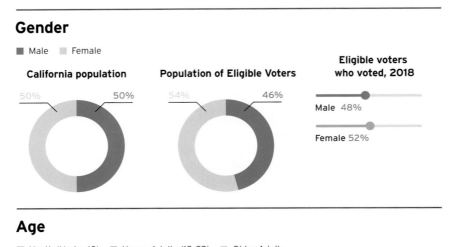

California population

50% | 50%

Population of Eligible Voters

54% | 46%

Eligible voters who voted, 2018

Male 48%

Female 52%

Age

■ Youth (Under 18) ■ Young Adults (18-29) ■ Older Adults

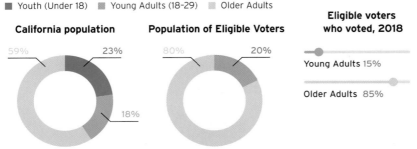

California population

59% | 23%

18%

Population of Eligible Voters

80% | 20%

Eligible voters who voted, 2018

Young Adults 15%

Older Adults 85%

Race*

■ White ■ Latino ■ African American ■ Asian American

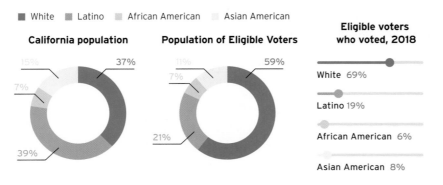

California population

15% | 37%

7%

39%

Population of Eligible Voters

11% | 59%

7%

21%

Eligible voters who voted, 2018

White 69%

Latino 19%

African American 6%

Asian American 8%

* Percentages do not sum to 100 because some people identify with another race or as multiracial.

SOURCES: U.S. Census Bureau, Quick Facts: California, https://www.census.gov/quickfacts/ca (accessed 10/2/18); Public Policy Institute of California, California's Likely Voters, http://www.ppic.org/publication/californias-likely-voters/ (accessed 10/2/18); State of California Department of Finance, Projections,http://www.dof.ca.gov/ Forecasting/Demographics/projections/ (accessed 10/2/18). CNN Exit Polls, www.cnn.com/elections/2018/exit-polls/ California/governor (accessed 11/12/18).

The active voting population in California is not reflective of general population demographics. Compared to their proportion of the population, white non-Latinos (Anglos) and older voters were overrepresented among active voters in the 2018 midterm election. Despite the large size of the Latino population, they are a relatively small share of the electorate. Latinos have long been considered the "sleeping giant" of California politics, because they have yet to fully participate at a level proportional to their size.

forcriticalanalysis

1. What do you think might account for the differences in turnout rates among different groups in California? Why is turnout among whites and African Americans so much higher than among Latinos and Asians? Why is turnout among older voters higher than among young voters?

2. Looking ahead, what impact will the shifting electorate have on California politics, when the percentage of Latinos in the population increases and percentage of whites decreases, as discussed in Chapter 1?

from their home precincts on Election Day or that they were infirm or bedridden and physically unable to cast a vote in person. All this changed in 1978 when California eliminated the requirement that voters present a valid excuse in order to vote absentee. Now, mail ballots are available to any voter who wants one. You are permitted to request a mail ballot for a particular election, or you may request permanent vote-by-mail status, meaning that a mail ballot is sent automatically to your home before each election.

From 1962 to 1978 the percentage of those voting by mail in primary and general elections averaged slightly under 4 percent of all votes cast. After the change in the law, voting by mail increased substantially. Of the over 11 million votes cast in November 2016, over 5 million were cast by mail ballots. Compared to the rest of the country, California's approach is fairly distinctive: 29 states allow voting by mail without an approved excuse, but only 3 other states allow for permanent voting by mail.

EARLY VOTING There is a special type of voter in California: the early voter. In fact, in the November 2016 general election, nearly 60 percent of all voters were early voters. There are several ways in which Californians can vote early (casting votes before official Election Day).

Most early voters voluntarily request **vote-by-mail ballots**. Virtually all of these voters are classified as "permanent vote-by-mail" voters, which means they have requested to automatically receive a vote-by-mail ballot for every election. Otherwise, one needs to request such a ballot for each election. These ballots must be received by the county registrar's office no later than Election Day, often making it necessary to mail in the completed ballot at least a few days before this deadline. In fact, a number of voters fill out and mail their ballots weeks before Election Day because state law permits voting as early as 29 days before an election. A number of sparsely populated rural precincts in California, where staffing a traditional polling place makes little sense, have moved entirely to mail-in ballots for all voters. And in an attempt to lighten the volume of voters on Election Day, some counties have permitted "early voting," in which voters can go to various publicized locations (such as shopping malls, registrars' offices, and civic centers) to cast their votes as early as 29 days before an election.

In 2016 California passed the California Voter's Choice Act, which allows counties to provide more flexibility and convenience to voters. For those counties opting in, mail ballots will automatically be mailed to all registered voters, in-person early voting will be expanded, and voters can vote at any vote center throughout their county (rather than having to vote only in their precinct). In 2018, 14 counties were permitted to conduct elections under the Voter's Choice Act; by 2020 all remaining counties will be permitted to conduct Voter's Choice Act elections.

Nationally, states' approach to early voting is varied: early voting that requires no special excuse is permitted in 37 states.

Many view these developments as positive changes, in the belief that making voting more convenient will increase participation in this important civic activity. However, as with many reforms, there are unintended consequences. One major consequence is that early voting has had a direct impact on campaign strategy. Traditionally, political campaigns approach the weekend before the election as their last opportunity to communicate with voters. Candidates spend an enormous amount of money in the last days of their campaigns trying to convince people to vote for them or their initiative (or at least not to vote for their opponent or opposing side) by bombarding them with TV ads and messages. By this point in the election cycle, however, nearly half of California voters have most likely already voted by mail or at an early-voting location. Therefore, candidates must now spend money earlier in the campaign cycle in order to reach these early voters before they cast their votes. As an example, state senator Tom McClintock lost a race for state controller by less than one-half of a percentage point because he did not have enough money to buy TV ads until the final days of the campaign. Many absentee voters had already mailed in their ballots and did not see his campaign ads until after they had cast their vote. Earlier campaigning means more expensive campaigning in a state that is already prohibitively expensive.

HOW YOU CAN VOTE BY MAIL To apply for a mail ballot, you may use the application form contained in the sample ballot mailed to your home before the election, or you may apply in writing to your county elections official. Ballots can be returned by mail or in person to a polling place or elections office within your county on Election Day.

What Reforms Are Needed?

It is fascinating to observe electoral politics in California. We live in a state where ballot initiatives are frequently used to make law, bypassing our duly elected representatives and the deliberative process of the legislature. In recent elections voters have been asked to weigh in on important policy matters such as same-sex marriage, abortion and parental notification, renewable energy, legalization of marijuana, the state budget process, tax issues, and the process by which state and congressional district boundaries are determined. Many people question whether the initiative process is the best way to make public policy.

Although the recall, referendum, and initiative originally were established as Progressive reforms, during the past few decades these tools of direct democracy have been taken over by special-interest groups. Some believe that reforms are needed to make it more difficult to recall an elected official or to bypass the legislative branch through the initiative process. Suggested reforms have included the prohibition of paid signature gatherers, a judicial review of the proposed initiative before placement on the ballot, and a higher requirement for the number of signatures needed to qualify a recall or initiative for the ballot. For a recall to qualify for the ballot, California law currently requires the number of signatures to equal 12 percent of the votes cast in the last gubernatorial election. Other states require 25 to 40 percent. While progress has been made with the reforms recently signed into law, many serious issues with the initiative process remain.

Candidates and initiative campaigns spend enormous amounts of money in hopes of electoral victory. Proposition 34, the campaign-finance initiative passed in 2000, substantially increased spending and contribution limits. California's limits on contributions to gubernatorial candidates are far more liberal than federal limits on contributions to presidential candidates. In fact, Californians can contribute more than 10 times the amount to gubernatorial candidates than they are permitted to contribute to presidential candidates ($25,900 versus $2,500). Many fear that these high limits will lead to spiraling campaign costs in a state where it is already expensive to campaign. The amounts of money spent in the 2010 governor's race seems to indicate that these fears are becoming reality.

Study Guide

FOR FURTHER READING

Barabak, M. "California's Not Goofy, It's Really Big. That's Why Counting the Vote Takes So Long." *Los Angeles Times*, November 9, 2018. www.latimes.com/politics/la-me-pol-midterm-california-ballots-20181109-story.html#nws=mcnewsletter. Accessed 11/30/18.

Blume, H. "Push for Young Minority Voters Reaches into High School." *Los Angeles Times*, October 24, 2018. www.latimes.com/local/education/la-me-edu-youth-voter-registration-20181024-story.html. Accessed 11/30/18.

Cain, B. "The California Recall." Interview, Brookings Institution, October 8, 2003.

Cain, Bruce E., and Elisabeth R. Gerber. *Voting at the Political Fault Line: California's Experiment with the Blanket Primary*. Berkeley: University of California Press, 2002.

California Fair Political Practices Commission. "Proposition 34." www.fppc.ca.gov. Accessed 12/03/14.

California Secretary of State's History of Political Reform Division. www.sos.ca.gov/campaign-lobbying/history-political-reform-division/. Accessed 9/26/16.

Cohen, Micah. "Over the Decades, How States Have Shifted." FiveThirtyEight, October 15, 2012. www.fivethirtyeight.com/features/over-the-decades-how-states-have-shifted/. Accessed 9/26/16.

Douzet, Frédérick, Thad Kousser, and Kenneth P. Miller, eds. *The New Political Geography of California*. Berkeley: Berkeley Public Policy Press, 2008.

Lubenow, Gerald C., ed. *California Votes: The 2002 Governor's Race and the Recall That Made History*. Berkeley: Berkeley Public Policy Press, 2003.

Marinucci, C. "RIP California GOP: Republicans Lash Out After Midterm Election Debacle." *Politico*, November 18, 2018. www.politico.com/story/2018/11/17/rip-california-gop-republicans-lash-out-after-midterm-election-debacle-1000481. Accessed 11/30/18.

Meyers, John. "California's Major Political Parties Feared the Top Two Primaries But Emerged as Powerful as Before." *Los Angeles Times*, June 6, 2018. www.latimes.com/politics/la-pol-ca-california-primary-rules-election-analysis-20180606-story.html. Accessed 9/17/18.

Meyers, John. "GOP on verge of being third choice of state voters. No-party voters nearly pass GOP." *Los Angeles Times*, May 11, 2018. enewspaper.latimes.com/infinity/article_share.aspx?guid=4aaa86a9-5fea-431d-9afb-72436bb8caa5. Accessed 9/17/18.

Peterson, Pete. "Why Californians Don't Vote." *Business Insider*. www.businessinsider.com/why-californians-dont-vote-2014-6. Accessed 6/24/14.

Pastor, Manuel. *State of Resistance: What California's Dizzying Descent and Remarkable Resurgence Means for America's Future*. New York: The New Press, 2018.

Rarick, E. *California Votes: The 2010 Governor's Race*. Berkeley: Institute of Governmental Studies, 2012.

Rasky, Susan. Introduction to "An Antipolitician, Anti-establishment Groundswell Elected the Candidate of Change." In *California Votes: The 2002 Governor's Race and the Recall That Made History*, edited by G. Lubenow. Berkeley: Berkeley Public Policy Press, 2003.

UCLA School of Law, Center for Governmental Studies, and the California Voter Foundation. "Grading State Disclosure 2008: A Comprehensive, Comparative Study of Candidate Campaign Finance Disclosure Laws and Practices in the 50 States." 2008. campaigndisc.calvoter.org/gradingstate/index.html. Accessed 9/17/18.

Warren, M. "Can the News for Republicans in California Get Any Worse?" *The Weekly Standard*, November 26, 2018. www.weeklystandard.com/michael-warren/midterms-postmortem-the-gop-cant-even-win-in-orange-county-california. Accessed 11/30/18.

ON THE WEB

Baldassare, Mark, Dean Bonner, David Kordus, and Lunna Lopes. "PPIC Statewide Survey: Californians and Their Government." www.ppic.org/main/publication.asp?i=1218. Accessed 11/11/2016.

California Elections and Voter Information. www.sos.ca.gov/elections. Accessed 11/11/16. The California secretary of state offers a comprehensive guide to California elections, including information on how to register to vote.

California General Election Results. http://vote.sos.ca.gov. Accessed 12/3/14. Detailed breakdowns of California election results.

The California Voter Foundation. http://calvoter.org. Accessed 7/25/12.

Fair Political Practices Commission. www.fppc.ca.gov. Accessed 12/3/14.

Join California. www.joincalifornia.com. Accessed 12/3/14.

Los Angeles Times. "Did Your Neighborhood Vote to Elect Donald Trump?" www.latimes.com/projects/la-pol-ca-california-neighborhood-election-results. Accessed 11/12/16.

SUMMARY

I. Introduction.
  A. California as an epicenter of anti-Trump movement.
    1. California challenges federal laws and Trump's executive orders.
    2. Expected role for California as a political, social, economic trendsetter.

II. Political parties.
  A. An important function of parties is to mobilize voters at election time.
  B. The Progressives' (1890s–1920s) impact on parties was sizable.
    1. They disliked corrupt parties and passed legislation to weaken the power of parties.
    2. They created many nonpartisan elective offices.
    3. They introduced direct primary elections to select the party candidate who will run for office against candidates of opposing parties in the general election.
  C. California has two dominant political parties: the Democratic Party and the Republican Party.
    1. California is considered a very Democratic state.
  D. Third parties struggle to compete.
    1. There are six certified minor parties.
    2. Third parties can impact the political agenda by raising issues the major parties ignore.

III. Party affiliation of California voters varies by region and demographics.
  A. The Democratic Party represents a plurality of voters.
  B. Historic shift from Republican Party to Democratic Party largely due to anti-immigration positions of Republican candidates (Prop. 187) and changing demographics.
  C. There has been an increase in the number of independents ("no party preference").
  D. Demographics and party affiliation.
    1. Whites tend to vote Republican; Latinos tend to vote Democratic.
    2. Younger and middle-aged voters compose the highest percentage of independents.
    3. Women tend to prefer the Democratic Party, as do non–U.S.-born citizens.
  E. The blue and red in California. Similar to the nation overall, areas of California are either distinctly Democratic or Republican.
    1. Coastal and urban areas tend to be Democratic.
    2. Inland and rural areas tend to be Republican.

IV. Elections in California.
  A. There have been many changes in the primary system.

1. California operated under a *closed* primary system until Proposition 198 in 1996.
2. Then a *blanket* primary system was in place from 1998 to 2000. In *California Democratic Party v. Jones* (2002), the California Supreme Court ruled this form of the *blanket* primary unconstitutional.
3. A *modified closed* primary system was adopted from 2002 to 2010. "Decline to state" voters (also known as "no party preference") were permitted to vote in party primaries if the party granted permission.
4. Proposition 14, passed in 2010, replaced the *modified closed* primary system with another version of the *blanket* primary.

  B. Presidential primaries.
    1. California has changed the date of its presidential primaries in order to allow voters to have more of an impact in the selection process.
    2. The 2008 presidential primary was moved to an early February date. Unfortunately, the increase in clout for the state was unrealized.
    3. In 2012, it was moved back to June. In 2020, the primary is scheduled for early March.

  C. Initiative campaigns.
    1. Typically, initiatives are tools of special-interest groups or grassroots movements. Such groups find it easier to bypass the state legislature and take their issue directly to the people. Often, initiatives deal with controversial issues that legislators would rather avoid.
    2. From 1912 to 2018 there were approximately 400 ballot initiatives.
    3. How to qualify an initiative for ballot.
       a) Nearly 600,000 signatures of registered voters are needed for an initiative to qualify for the ballot, and nearly 1 million are needed to place a constitutional amendment on the ballot.
       b) For an initiative to be successful requires millions of dollars and highly paid political professionals. As an example, the cost of collecting petition signatures for the 17 ballot propositions in the November 2016 elections exceeded $45 million.
    4. Criticisms of direct democracy.
       a) Critics say that issues presented as ballot propositions are often too complicated or confusing and should be decided through legislative deliberation rather than a popular vote.

b) Recent reforms have provided for a 30-day public review process for all proposed initiatives as well as more transparency regarding donations to initiative campaigns.

D. The 2003 gubernatorial recall election of Gray Davis.

1. Only 11 months after he won his re-election bid, Davis was recalled from office. He was the first and only governor in the state of California and the second governor in the nation's history to be recalled.

2. Voters held Governor Davis responsible for the 2000–01 energy crisis and for the fiscal struggles of the state.

3. Arnold Schwarzenegger, an actor and a moderate Republican, was elected governor.

E. The 2008 election: ideological and demographic shift to Democratic side.

1. Obama won 61 percent of the popular vote compared to John McCain's 37 percent, the biggest margin in California since 1964.

2. Young people voted in historic numbers, solidifying the Democratic Party's dominance in the state.

F. The 2010 election was the most expensive governor's race in history.

1. Brown, the former governor, beat a wealthy billionaire, Meg Whitman.

2. Initiatives passed that have an important impact on state budget process and political representation and party politics.

G. The 2012 election: results similar to 2008 but more of a Democratic shift.

1. The Democratic Party gained supermajority status in the state legislature (lost it in 2014).

2. Young voters' turnout increased, but overall turnout declined.

3. California adopted a new online voter registration system.

4. Proposition 30 passed, increasing the state sales tax and taxes on the wealthy to fund education.

H. The 2014 election: a noncompetitive governor's race.

1. Incumbent Jerry Brown easily beat underfunded challenger Neel Kashkari.

2. For the more controversial ballot measures (Propositions 45, 46, and 48), the well-funded "no" campaigns were successful because the proponents were absent from the airwaves.

I. The 2016 election: Democratic Party remains strong.

1. Decline in Republican Party registration and increase in number of "no party preference" voter registrations.

2. Hillary Clinton won California by a 2–1 margin but lost the presidential contest.

3. Kamala Harris elected as first African American U.S. senator from California and second ever female African American elected to Senate.

4. Democratic Party won supermajority in state Assembly and state Senate.

5. Proposition 58 repealed English-only in public schools. Proposition 62 to repeal death penalty failed while Proposition 66 to expedite death penalty appeals passed. Proposition 64 legalized marijuana. Proposition 67 banned plastic shopping bags.

6. Overall voter turnout declined, but Latino turnout surged from 22 percent in 2012 to 33 percent in 2016.

7. Voting by mail continued to be very popular.

J. The 2018 Election:

1. There were historic voting turnout rates for a midterm election.

2. California congressional races attracted national attention as Democrats targeted vulnerable seats to win a majority in the House of Representatives.

3. Democrats won all targeted House seats leaving Orange County (historically conservative stronghold) with no Republican House members.

4. Democrats maintained their supermajority status in both the state Assembly and the state Senate.

V. Running for elective office in the largest state is expensive.

A. The size of the state requires candidates to spend a lot of money on campaigns. California often attracts wealthy candidates with personal fortunes.

B. Because of the size of the state, candidates need to spend a lot of money on TV ads in order to reach voters. Statewide campaigns are very expensive because of the need to broadcast political ads throughout the state.

C. Numerous state laws have been passed to reform political campaigns and to minimize the influence of big money and create transparency.

1. 1974: Proposition 9, Political Reform Act created the Political Reform Division and established the Fair Political Practices Commission.

2. 1988: Proposition 73 passed, limiting campaign contributions, but was later declared unconstitutional in 1990.

3. 1996: Proposition 208 passed, limiting campaign contributions.

4. 2000: Proposition 34 passed, increasing spending and contribution limits and invalidating Proposition 208.

5. 2008: in a study of 50 states California gets an A for campaign-finance disclosure laws.

VI. Voting in California.
   A. With a population of 39 million, there are 19 million registered voters in the state. Since September 2016, more than 250,000 16- to 17-year-olds have preregistered to vote.
   B. How to register to vote:
      1. Obtain a voter registration form from any post office or library.
      2. Visit the California DMV.
      3. Register online.
   C. Who votes?
      1. Whites are overrepresented in the voting population; Latinos and Asians are underrepresented; African Americans vote in equal proportion to their percentage of population.
      2. About 60 percent of all registered voters cast their votes by mail.
      3. California Voter's Choice Act of 2016 makes voting more flexible and convenient.
VII. Reforms may be necessary.
   A. Is the initiative process the best way to make policy?
   B. Need for campaign-finance reform to limit contributions and candidate spending.

PRACTICE QUIZ

1. In the 2016 general election, 18- to 29-year-olds voted at a lower rate than they did in 2012.
   a) true
   b) false

2. In running for the state legislature, incumbents and challengers spend nearly the same amount of money on their political campaigns.
   a) true
   b) false

3. Political campaigns are so expensive in California because
   a) campaigns need to hire political consultants.
   b) campaigns need to spend a substantial amount of money on media advertising.
   c) political parties are not very involved in the planning and running of campaigns.
   d) all of the above

4. Special-interest groups often use the initiative process to achieve their policy objectives.
   a) true
   b) false

5. Which of the following is *not* true about Proposition 34, which deals with campaign finance?
   a) The League of Women Voters and Common Cause supported Proposition 34.
   b) Proposition 34 increased allowable individual contributions to candidates to $21,200.
   c) Proposition 34 has resulted in less control of campaign financing.
   d) Proposition 34 replaced the stricter campaign-finance law enacted through Proposition 208.

6. Of California's 39 million people, approximately how many are registered to vote?
   a) 30 million
   b) 25 million
   c) 5 million
   d) 20 million

7. Democrats are the plurality party in California.
   a) true
   b) false

8. The number of voters who decline to state a party affiliation at the time they register is declining.
   a) true
   b) false

9. Most of the Democratic counties encompass major urban areas, whereas most of the Republican counties are more rural in nature.
   a) true
   b) false

10. California presently operates under which of the following primary election systems?
   a) open primary
   b) blanket primary
   c) modified closed primary
   d) fully closed primary

CRITICAL-THINKING QUESTIONS

1. How might the cost of campaigning be reduced in California? Because incumbents spend much more money than challengers do, what reforms might level the playing field of campaign politics?
2. What do you think have been the successes and failures of campaign-finance laws in California? Do you think that additional reforms are needed? Why or why not?
3. How do you think the increase in unaffiliated voters and the increase in mail voters will affect campaigns and elections in the future?
4. Why do you think so many states follow California's lead in the areas of ballot propositions and recall efforts? Do you think this is a good or bad development? Explain why.

KEY TERMS

ballot initiative (p. 96)
blanket primary system (p. 93)
campaign-finance reform (p. 113)
closed primary system (p. 93)
general election (p. 81)
media-dominated campaigns (p. 111)
media markets (p. 111)

modified closed primary system (p. 93)
Motor Voter (p. 115)
no party preference (p. 84)
office block ballot (p. 81)
open primary system (p. 93)
political consultants (p. 112)

political culture (p. 89)
political party affiliation (p. 84)
primary elections (p. 81)
vote-by-mail ballots (p. 119)
weak political parties (p. 113)
winner-take-all system (p. 80)

5 The California Legislature

WHAT CALIFORNIA GOVERNMENT DOES AND WHY IT MATTERS

Californians give little if any thought to their legislature. We have a general sense that it is made up of a group of elected individuals who write laws, but beyond that our knowledge is limited.

Our lack of knowledge is related to the minimal media coverage that legislatures receive. The media find it difficult to cover institutions that have multiple members who are doing many different things and have no single voice. They find it much easier to focus on a chief executive who has a press office that provides news-ready stories. Moreover, media coverage of state politics is minimal. Prior to the election of Governor Arnold Schwarzenegger, no Los Angeles television station had a Sacramento bureau. But even the interest in a movie-star governor did not carry over to the legislature, and since the arrival of Governor Jerry Brown, who made only a minimal effort to feed the news establishment, media interest in Sacramento has sharply declined. The last Los Angeles TV news bureau in Sacramento closed in 2013.

Accompanying our lack of knowledge is the general belief that the legislature does not work well. According to Public Policy Institute of California (PPIC) polls, a low was reached in 2010 when only 14 percent of Californians approved of the job that the state legislature was doing (72 percent disapproved). Among likely voters only 9 percent approved. Our dissatisfaction with the legislative process stems in part from a lack of understanding of how it works, but it has several other sources as well.

First, Americans dislike and distrust politics in general. They also like harmony and are turned off by conflict between the governor and the legislature and between parties. Since the legislature is the most transparent and thus most observable political arena, conflict here is more obvious.

Second, the dysfunction that so often characterizes state government negatively affects attitudes toward the legislature. While the legislature is not the principal cause of this dysfunction, term limits and voting rules have, at times, led to gridlock and to elevated partisan conflict, which makes it difficult for the legislature to function well.

Third, while voters want their legislators to work together, these same citizens want their individual interests forcefully represented against competing ones. We have conflicting expectations of legislatures, and legislators' attempts to balance these expectations often contribute to our dissatisfaction. "Laws are like sausages; it is better not to see them being made." This quote, often attributed to the nineteenth-century German statesman Otto von Bismarck, has a point in suggesting that, like in the making of sausages, respect for the making of laws decreases with our awareness of how they are made.

Finally, the occasional bad behavior of individual legislators brings the entire institution into disrepute. During the spring of 2014 three Democratic senators facing criminal charges were suspended by their colleagues. And in 2017-18, after the WeSaidEnough movement focused attention on sexual harassment in the state capitol, three legislators resigned under pressure. These events were followed by dips in the public's evaluation of the legislature. However, according to PPIC polls, the trend in public opinion since 2010 has been toward increased approval of the legislature, to the point where since July of 2018 more Californians approve than disapprove of the job it is doing. A Fall 2016 Field Poll found 50 percent of voters approved of the legislature, the highest in 28 years. (A July 2018 PPIC poll of all adults showed a favorable view of the legislature by an 8 percent margin.)[1]

Several factors have contributed to the legislature's improved reputation: redistricting by a nonpartisan commission, new primary election rules, removal of the two-thirds vote requirement to pass budgets, and changes in term limits. (Each of these factors will be discussed later in this chapter.) But perhaps most important, in 2010 a Democrat was elected governor, and in subsequent elections the Democrats gained a two-thirds majority in each legislative house, greatly reducing both gridlock and conflict. The legislature became more harmonious not because Democrats and Republicans began to work together but rather because Republicans became marginalized. At the same time, the public's approval rating of the U.S. Congress—where power is closely divided and gridlock is common—dropped to a historic low of 9 percent in November 2013 and has generally been in the teens since then.[2]

In spite of Californians' distrust of and lack of interest in their legislature, the influence it has on our lives is significant. In the 2017-18 session alone, the legislature considered (and in some cases passed) legislation dealing with internet privacy, affordable housing, gasoline taxes, bail bonds, gender identification, net neutrality, community college tuition, housing for the homeless, and climate change. The range of issues could hardly be greater. In addition, the legislature funds all state government agencies, including parks, the highway patrol, and universities.

Legislatures, although poorly understood, play a critical role in our government. The framers of the U.S. Constitution, fearing a powerful executive, gave Congress the most significant and most explicit powers, including control over taxation and spending and the authority to write all laws. Today the president gets the most media attention, and some congressional powers have gravitated to the executive branch; Congress, however, remains a very powerful body.

Most state legislatures, including California's, have been modeled on the U.S. Congress in structure, process, and function. California has a **bicameral** (two-house) legislature consisting of the 40-member Senate (sometimes called the upper house) and the 80-member Assembly. As in the U.S. Congress, members of both houses represent geographically determined districts and are elected in winner-take-all elections. As in Congress, bills become law by being approved by both houses and signed by the chief executive. The bulk of the work of each house is done in committees. Each house is organized by party, and party leaders determine committee membership. Despite these similarities, significant differences—such as the role of seniority in committee assignments—do exist. These differences will be addressed in more detail later in the chapter.

The recent history of the California legislature has been remarkable in its extremes. In the 1960s, under the leadership of Assembly Speaker Jesse Unruh, the legislature was transformed from an often corrupt, amateur body into a well-paid, well-staffed professional organization regarded by many as the best state legislature in the country. Then in 1990 California voters passed **Proposition 140**, imposing **term limits** on legislators. Although this did not change the basic structure of the legislature, it did change the collective knowledge, effectiveness, and power of the legislature by reducing the time that legislators were permitted to serve to 14 years, and by reducing the size of the staff that makes legislative work possible.

In 2012 term limits were slightly modified when voters passed Proposition 28, which further reduced the time that legislators could serve to 12 years. However, unlike Proposition 140, which limited members to 6 years in the Assembly and 8 in the Senate, Proposition 28 allowed for all 12 years to be served in one house. The principal result, in time, should be to increase the effectiveness of the Assembly by giving members and leaders more time to become knowledgeable in their jobs and thus become more competent players in the policy game.

Functions

Legislatures have two principal functions: **representation** and policy making. The tensions between these functions make it difficult for a legislature to perform as effectively as citizens might wish.

Representation

The legislature is the principal representative institution in our society, although the executive branch and interest groups also lay claim to this function. It is the duty of legislators (also called members, representatives, assemblypersons, or senators) to represent the voters and other residents (collectively known as **constituents**) within their districts, as well as to represent the dominant district interests. This is easier said than done. In the first place, the term *representation* has many meanings. Here we will simplify it to mean that our representative is our counterpart in Sacramento and that he or she will do what we would do if we were there, especially when it comes to influencing legislation or voting. Of course, there are many more constituents than there are legislators, and rarely do all people see things the same way. Some are wealthy and educated; others, destitute. Some see government as the means to solve society's problems; others see it as the main problem.

Furthermore, representatives face many different and difficult issues: same-sex marriage versus traditional marriage, lower taxes versus improved services, new highways versus neighborhood preservation, higher spending on prisons versus lower college tuition. How one approaches these issues depends in part on the way in which one understands the goal of representation: Is it to give constituents what they want or what they need?

Political scientists talk about two poles of representation style: the delegate who tries to find out what constituents want and then act according to their wishes, and the trustee who believes that he or she has been chosen to act based on his or her own best judgment. Delegates most often try to provide what constituents want, whereas trustees are more inclined to provide for their districts' needs *as they perceive them*. Both types of representation are difficult to achieve in practice. It is often impossible to know what constituents want because they do not communicate with their representatives very well, if at all. It is no easier to determine district needs, which are often diverse, conflicting, and influenced by ideology or other subjective factors.

In theory, a representative should act based on the wants and needs of each member of his or her district equally. But in practice, certain groups wield more influence than others. For instance, some legislators identify closely with a particular group—such as women, small business owners, or immigrants—and they view themselves as representatives of that group. In addition, some groups are better organized and funded than others and are particularly adept at gaining the representative's attention. These would include chambers of commerce, large employers, labor unions, and environmental organizations. Large campaign contributors do not give their donations without expecting something in return, so the legislator is unable to ignore them. Ultimately, it is the constituents who have the vote, and this should force representatives to pay attention to the needs of the entire district. However, even this principle has been weakened in recent years by big money and term limits. Rarely do voters have a realistic chance of keeping favored representatives in power or "throwing the rascals out."

In addition to representing our policy views, representatives try to look out for us when we have specific problems with government, whether it's not getting a disability check, being treated unfairly by an inspector, worrying that a new highway will be built through our property, or opposing the sale of liquor near our kids' school. This ombudsman function is called *constituency service* or *casework*, and it involves intervening with the bureaucracy to resolve specific problems. Representatives also try to get favorable treatment for economic interests in their districts—when a restaurant owner wants a liquor license that he or she believes is

It is easy to stay on top of what is happening in the legislature on the internet. Both houses have web pages. The Senate page is www.sen.ca.gov; the Assembly page is www.assembly.ca.gov. From these sites you can find out about the legislative process and about the status of individual bills. You can also find out how to stay in touch with your legislators. If you type in your address, the site will tell you who your legislators are and how you can contact them. Another useful site is that of the legislative counsel: http://leginfo.legislature.ca.gov.

State legislators are surprisingly accessible, especially in the district. If you have an issue for which you want to contact your legislator, be informed, call for an appointment, and be brief and forthright. Information is helpful, and a good anecdote is always useful! Thoughtful letters are also helpful. Email is used too much, and staff can recognize form mail as soon as it is opened.

Of course, working through a lobby is also effective, and you may belong to an organization that lobbies. Environmental groups, unions, and student organizations are just a few of the many organizations that write, track, and try to influence legislation in their area of concern. Many of these organizations maintain websites discussing the status of legislation in which they have a stake.

being unfairly denied, for instance, or when a construction company wants to build more buildings at the local state university. Representatives will also take stands on issues that are largely symbolic but still important to their constituents, such as flag burning or prayer in schools.

Another important part of representation is being available to constituents. People want to see their representative, and representatives accordingly spend much of their time in their districts attending functions, speaking to groups about the activities of government, distributing commendations and certificates, and listening to constituents. Individual constituents as well as leaders of organized groups also visit with their representatives in Sacramento. See Box 5.1 for information on contacting your state representatives.

Policy Making

Representatives come together to make policy, most obviously through the complex process of making laws, which involves writing bills, holding committee hearings, conducting legislative debates, and adding amendments. These steps will be described in more detail later in the chapter.

Policy making also involves ensuring that legislation is carried out by the bureaucracy as the legislature intended and looking out for potential problems in the implementation of policy. This function, called **oversight**, is carried out through a variety of means, including staff follow-up on constituents' concerns, legislative hearings, budgetary hearings, and confirmation hearings. Legislators do not have much appetite for holding hearings that might make a governor of their own party uncomfortable, but any scandal involving a public agency almost automatically triggers such hearings. In recent years the state legislature has held hearings on construction flaws in the new Bay Bridge, progress of the high-speed rail project, private (ex parte) meetings between coastal commissioners and developers, sexual harassment, and the unnecessarily cumbersome college transfer process. Congressional oversight hearings at the federal level gain far more attention, sometimes due to divided government, but more recently because the strong ideological stances of some of the political appointees in government departments often conflict with congressional expectations. While these hearings most often have a valid administrative or legislative purpose, they are also used to embarrass or damage the members of the opposite party. If they can do both, so much the better. Perhaps the most notable recent examples have been the hearings on Hillary Clinton's role in Benghazi and on her email servers, which were, at the very least, difficult to deal with in her presidential campaign and likely contributed to her loss.

Members and Districts

Unlike Congress, in which each state has two seats in the Senate regardless of population, both houses of the California legislature are apportioned by population. The state is divided into 80 Assembly districts and 40 state Senate districts. In each of these districts a single representative is elected by local voters, which means that these representatives will give serious attention to local interests. As former Speaker of the U.S. House of Representatives Tip O'Neill once said, "All politics is local." Our legislative system is designed to favor local interests (and interests with money), and for representatives, these local interests often take precedence over statewide interests.

State Senator Richard Pan (D-Sacramento) meeting with constituents after his bill requiring nearly all schoolchildren to be vaccinated was signed by Governor Jerry Brown.

Legislators have offices in both Sacramento and in their districts. Mail, email, and phone messages are answered from both places. When representatives are in their districts, they listen to the concerns of their constituents and tell them about government activities, policy, and politics (e.g., they try to explain what life is like in the capital). In Sacramento they interact with those constituents who travel to the capital as well as with representatives of interest groups. In addition, they work on framing policy, primarily in committees. Legislators often spend Monday through midday Thursday in Sacramento and return to their districts for the remainder of the week; however, this varies with the time of the year, and special events often bring them back to their districts. It is essential to keep a high profile in the district to discourage potential election opponents. Being accused of ignoring one's district could be fatal in an election. Since minority party members often have little say in policy making, they may emphasize their availability to constituents to demonstrate that they have value in Sacramento.

Elections

Every member of the California Senate and Assembly must be elected by voters from a single geographic district. Most members with previous elective experience have served on school boards, city councils, or county boards of supervisors. Many are self-selected. Others are tapped to run for office by party leaders or interests who see them as viable candidates and friendly to their policies. Assembly members serve two-year terms while senators serve for four years.

Legislative elections are **winner-take-all** elections, which means that minor or third parties are generally excluded from the legislature even if they have substantial support statewide. Without a majority of votes in any single district, they cannot place a representative in Sacramento.

The process by which candidates are elected changed significantly in 2010 with the passage of Proposition 14. Prior to 2010, the primary elections were structured to select one candidate from each party to run in the general election. Candidates ran as Republicans, Democrats, or as representatives of a third party in separate contests against members of their own party only. Voters could choose one of those contests in which to vote. The winners faced off against each other in the general election in November. In districts where the voters were overwhelmingly of one party—typical of many California districts—the real contest was in the primary, and election was all but assured to the candidate of the majority party. Many believed that this resulted in the election of extremist legislators who were beholden only to the majority of the voters in their party, not to the majority of the voters in their district.

Proposition 14 instituted a single blanket primary, or top-two primary, in which all candidates run and all voters take part. Voters in the primary or preliminary election vote for the candidate of their choice for each office from a single list of all candidates, and the top two candidates go on to the November election regardless of party. Candidates need not state their party identification on the ballot. The expectation is that, even if both of the winning candidates are in the same party, the more moderate candidate will win the general election by appealing to voters in the minority parties (see Chapter 4). It is not uncommon for there to be more than two dozen contests (out of more than 150 legislative races) in which the top two candidates belong to the same party. In 2018 there were 13 in the state legislature and four for congressional seats. Even the race for the U.S. Senate was between two Democrats, as it was in 2016.

If there are only two candidates in the preliminary election, they will have to run against each other for a second time in the general election. While this may seem redundant, the electorate in November is almost always larger (and therefore less Republican) than in June, which can affect the outcome of the election. In 2012 the 65th Assembly District in Orange County provided an excellent example of an incumbent challenged by a single opponent—in this case, a Republican challenged by a Democrat. When they ran against each other in June, the Republican incumbent won with over 58 percent of the vote. In the runoff in November, the Democratic challenger won with about 52 percent of the vote, helping the Democrats gain a two-thirds majority in the Assembly. Contributing to this victory was a significant increase in voter turnout: about 50,000 people voted in June while over 120,000 voted in November. The new incumbent lost to a different Republican two years later when only 77,000 people voted and regained the seat in 2016 when there were over 140,000 voters.

Two other key features of California politics have a significant influence on who gets elected. First, the large size of each district means that campaigns are expensive and fund-raising is necessary. Second, the manner in which district boundaries are drawn influences the role of political parties and the strength of incumbents.

Fund-raising

Campaigns can easily cost millions of dollars (see Chapter 4), and campaign expenditures are likely to be much higher in the future because of the Supreme Court ruling in *Citizens United* (see Chapter 3), which rejected corporate spending limits, and because the California Citizens Redistricting Commission has created more competitive legislative districts. Fund-raising is one of the most significant obstacles to winning an election. The nature of California and the size of the districts make election victories unlikely through old-fashioned precinct work. Use of TV and radio advertising is also impractical in the larger media markets because of cost. Most candidates have campaign consultants and engage in polling, which help them come up with strategies for targeted distribution of literature, internet advertising, and social media outreach.

Districting

Because of the relatively small size of the state legislature, its districts are among the largest in the country. Senate districts have over 950,000 constituents, and Assembly districts over 475,000. (For comparison, U.S. House districts in California have approximately 715,000 constituents.) Historically, district lines were drawn by the legislature, often leading to charges of **gerrymandering**. This term dates to the early 1800s, when Massachusetts governor Elbridge Gerry oversaw a redistricting that benefited his party and resulted in district lines that resembled, in a famous cartoon of the day, a salamander. To *gerrymander* means to draw district lines in a manner that favors one party over another, generally by packing most of the opponent's voters into a few districts and spreading the remainder thinly over the remaining districts. To date, the courts have generally accepted this practice, saying only that districts must be equal in population and must not be drawn to diminish the voting strength of any minority.

Redistricting is done following each census and until 2012 had to pass both houses and be signed by the governor, like any other piece of legislation. However, after the 2000 census, despite Democratic control of both houses and the governor's office, the party did not create more gerrymandered Democratic districts. Instead, endeavoring (successfully) to avoid a lawsuit, they approved a set of maps known as the "incumbency protection plan," which maintained safe seats for both parties. Thus, the power of voters to hold their legislators accountable was diminished, as incumbents throughout the state were unlikely to lose a future election.

Therefore, before 2012 most action took place in the primaries, though incumbents rarely faced a serious challenge there either following the advent of term limits in 1992. Knowing that an incumbent assemblyperson would be out of office in no more than four years, the astute challenger waited for that vacancy to occur rather than engaging in an expensive, divisive challenge. Term limits had the unintended consequence of inhibiting voters from "throwing the rascals out," and thus the legislature was more immune from direct electoral challenge than ever before.

Since 2012 the situation that created safe districts with highly partisan incumbents has significantly changed. As a result of their continued frustration with the legislature, the voters approved two measures—Proposition 11 in November 2008 (followed by Proposition 20 in 2010) and Proposition 14 in June 2010—that have had an impact on who gets elected to the legislature.

The consequences of Proposition 14, the top-two primary law described above, have been overwhelmingly overshadowed by those of Propositions 11 and 20, both redistricting initiatives that unexpectedly resulted in a two-thirds Democratic majority in both houses. Proposition 11 took the task of drawing legislative districts away from the legislature and replaced it with a 15-person Citizens Redistricting Commission. This commission created districts with a closer partisan balance.

The expectation was that Proposition 11 would result in fewer safe seats and in the election of moderate legislators more willing to engage in bipartisan compromise. It will take several election cycles before these results can be assessed because the large Democratic majorities currently in the state legislature make bipartisan compromise largely unnecessary. However, some observers believe that the smaller Republican minority is less moderate and less inclined to compromise while the larger Democratic majority is more moderate—not a surprising result as the minority shrinks towards its base while the majority becomes larger and more inclusive of different viewpoints.

The Democratic two-thirds supermajority has wavered in recent years. In 2014 it was lost after three state senators were suspended. It was recouped in 2017, only to disappear again after the recall election discussed below. In 2018 the supermajority was regained, allowing Democrats to carry out business with little regard for their Republican colleagues. Thus, gridlock has been reduced, and the public's regard for the legislature has become correspondingly more favorable.

Still, the large majority of Democrats have not proven to be radical. They did raise taxes, but those taxes were narrowly focused on the transportation infrastructure (still, it resulted in a successful recall election of a single state senator and a defeated ballot initiative to repeal the taxes, both discussed below). Yet most actions have been moderate and have not resulted in drastic or excessive new laws or regulations. This is partially because the legislature has had to work with a moderate and fiscally conservative Democratic governor who would probably veto such measures. More important, many of these new Democratic legislators are from marginal seats that have many Republican voters (such as the 65th Assembly District in Orange County and the 32nd Assembly District in Bakersfield) and are reluctant to take bold actions that might endanger their chances of re-election.

In addition, when contests in the general election are between two Democrats, big corporations (such as Chevron Oil) often spend large sums of money backing the candidate who is more supportive of their interests. While these candidates may or may not be moderates, they are definitely supportive of the corporations that have funded them.

There are enough business-oriented Democrats to form a loosely structured caucus that has designated leaders, as well as a PAC, and that holds fund-raisers. Membership is not published but is probably around 20, more or less, depending on the issue. As the Democratic tent has grown bigger, the new members are most often from more conservative districts, and big business with big money has taken advantage of the top-two primaries to aggressively support friendly Democratic candidates. One Assembly member, Cheryl Brown (D-San Bernardino), who was key to helping gut climate control bills in 2015, received over $1 million from Chevron in independent spending supporting her 2016 primary campaign, leading her opponents to label her "Chevron Cheryl." Brown was ultimately defeated in November 2016 in a race that cost $6.1 million in independent spending, mostly from the oil companies.

If the Democrats in the Assembly have 52 members, as was the case in 2015 (in 2018 there were 55 Democrats), then it takes only 12 "moderates" to join 28 Republicans to defeat legislation, as they did in 2015. In 2016, at the end of the two-year session, the governor and the Democratic leadership through intense politicking were able to pass meaningful climate control legislation with the minimum number of needed votes, over the opposition of the oil companies. Although the governor and the Democratic leadership made a comeback, overcoming the opposition in 2016 to pass strong climate change legislation was a struggle. Business-oriented Democrats have demonstrated that they are an important third force in the legislature. A new chapter in California politics has begun, and no one knows exactly how it will be written.[3]

Organization

The process of policy making is complex, involving many steps and many actors. Over time, both the Senate and Assembly have, for reasons both practical and political, adopted principles of organization that structure how the legislature works.

Leadership

The leader of the Assembly is the **speaker**, and he or she has a remarkable array of powers (although these were diminished by the 6-year term limit on members of the Assembly). In an attempt to increase the power of the speaker by lengthening his or her time in the position, in 2003 and 2009 the Democrats elected a first-term legislator to the speakership. In 2014 they elected a member, Toni Atkins, in her second term (well regarded, she is now the president pro tempore of the

Assembly speaker Anthony Rendon, center, was elected to the position in only his second term, but new rules on term limits may allow him to serve longer than any speaker in recent history and offer some stability to a legislature lacking experience and institutional memory.

state Senate). In 2016 she was replaced by another member in his second term, Anthony Rendon. Rendon, however, was elected to the legislature under new rules that allow him to serve 12 years in the Assembly. If he serves as speaker for the remainder of his allotted time—until 2024—he will have been one of the longest-serving speakers in recent history. This is a game changer that should increase the speaker's effectiveness and thus the effectiveness of the legislature.

The Assembly speaker's powers are considerably more extensive than those of the Speaker of the U.S. House of Representatives. Beginning with control over assigning parking spaces and offices, these powers include almost complete control over establishing committees, assigning members to serve on them, and, if the speaker chooses, removing members from these committees. Because the bulk of legislative work is done in committees, members depend on the speaker to provide them with a meaningful role in the legislature. The speaker can also assign floor leadership of high-profile or popular bills to legislators of his or her choice, enhancing their reputations both inside and outside the Assembly.

When the full Assembly meets, the speaker acts as presiding officer and thereby controls the debate; when not presiding, he or she designates the person who does. The speaker also appoints the majority floor leader, who assists in running legislative sessions. It is difficult to overstate the speaker's power, which can move bills, help supporters, and hurt opponents. Speakers can raise money as well, which in turn allows them to solidify support. Members find it advantageous to cooperate with the speaker. The speaker is elected by the entire membership of the Assembly, but in most cases the outcome is determined in advance by the majority party caucus, which consists of all of the members of the majority party meeting together. Only when the majority is split does the full Assembly vote become significant.

The minority caucus elects the Assembly minority leader, who is the public voice of the minority party and who works with the speaker to determine minority party assignments on committees. The speaker, however, has the final say.

The other important element of the leadership is the **Assembly Rules Committee**, which is made up of nine members, four elected by each party's caucus, plus a chair appointed by the speaker. The committee's responsibilities include hiring staff, assigning bills to committees, and reviewing legislative rules. Rarely does this committee operate independently of the speaker's wishes.

The organization of the Senate is similar to that of the Assembly, but the Senate leader, the **president pro tempore** (sometimes shortened to president pro tem), does not have the absolute power of the Assembly speaker. Many of the speaker's powers in the Assembly rest with the Rules Committee in the Senate. Yet for a time the president pro tempore—most notably John Burton—was the most influential legislator in Sacramento, largely because of the impact of term limits. Prior to 2012 senators often served 6 years in the Assembly first, and their time in the Senate could last up to 8 years. Senate leaders could accrue 10 to 12 years of experience in Sacramento before assuming leadership roles. In contrast, Assembly leaders might have had only two or three years of experience. John Burton, who was the last of his breed, had far more experience than that, including experience in the U.S. Congress.

This pattern is now changing thanks to the passage of Proposition 28 in June 2012. Legislators elected in 2012 and after may now serve no more than 12 years in the state legislature, but those years can be spent entirely in one house or in a combination of both houses. Thus, Speaker Rendon may remain in his position for up to 8 years, potentially having greater influence than his immediate predecessors did. Senators will no longer be able to serve 14 years, which will level the playing field and provide members and leaders of the Assembly the opportunity to attain the same level of experience.

Committees

The bulk of legislative work is done in **committees**. Committees allow for greater specialization, greater expertise of those involved, and greater attention to detail. In 2017–18 there were 32 standing or permanent committees in the Assembly and 22 in the Senate (see Table 5.1). Each member sits on several standing committees. In addition to standing committees, there are many select committees that exist to study specific issues and joint committees to look at issues that concern both houses. Members may serve on a dozen or more of these less important committees.

Committees are at the heart of groups of players often referred to as **issue networks**. These networks consist of committee members and **staff**, senior members of the respective executive branch agency, and interest groups concerned with issues in a committee's jurisdiction. The bulk of policy details are worked out in these networks. Lobbyists and bureaucrats involved in issue networks tend to be specialists who spend their entire careers in a single subject area. It would be unusual for someone who has spent a career in transportation to move to education. Previously, legislators would spend their careers in specific issue areas as well. Term limits have changed that, or rather have shortened the length of careers. While policy is still worked out within these networks, the power to shape the policy has shifted to those who have greater permanency, experience, and expertise—namely, lobbyists and bureaucrats. The less experienced and less knowledgeable legislator is now

TABLE 5.1 ● Standing Committees of the California Legislature, 2017–18

State Senate

Agriculture
Appropriations
Banking and Financial Institutions
Budget and Fiscal Review
Business, Professions and Economic Development
Education
Elections and Constitutional Amendments
Energy, Utilities, and Communications
Environmental Quality
Governance and Finance
Governmental Organization

Health
Human Services
Insurance
Judiciary
Labor and Industrial Relations
Natural Resources and Water
Public Employment and Retirement
Public Safety
Rules
Transportation and Housing
Veterans Affairs

Assembly

Accountability and Administrative Review
Aging and Long-Term Care
Agriculture
Appropriations
Arts, Entertainment, Sports, Tourism, and
    Internet Media
Banking and Finance
Budget
Business and Professions
Communications and Conveyance
Education
Elections and Redistricting
Environmental Safety and Toxic Materials
Governmental Organization
Health
Higher Education
Housing and Community Development

Human Services
Insurance
Jobs, Economic Development, and the Economy
Judiciary
Labor and Employment
Local Government
Natural Resources
Privacy and Consumer Protection
Public Employees, Retirement and Social
    Security
Public Safety
Revenue and Taxation
Rules
Transportation
Utilities and Commerce
Veterans Affairs
Water, Parks, and Wildlife

more dependent than before on these individuals for policy details. Experienced staff can help, but since the severe staff reductions required by Proposition 140 in 1990, staff members are often no more experienced than legislators.

Staff

Without staff, the legislature cannot effectively do its job. Staff members are crucial in both the policy-making and the representative functions of the legislature. All legislators have staff in both their Sacramento and district offices to help with constituency contacts, including handling casework, scheduling appearances, and answering mail and phone calls from constituents. In addition, committees have staff, called consultants, to help with the policy work of that committee, and consultants are also critical components of the issue networks. Some of the best consultants will take their hard-earned experience and move on to become lobbyists, where the pay is often far higher and the job more secure. Each legislator is allotted an office budget for staffing. Legislators are permitted additional staff depending on whether they occupy a committee leadership role and on the generosity of the party leadership. In addition, the house leaders and caucuses have staff that may number more than 150 for the majority party. This staff helps with bill analysis for individual members and public relations for both individual members and the party.

There are over 2,000 legislative aides. It is not unusual for majority legislators to have 13 or 14 staff members. Minority members may have only 4 or 5. While most aides are modestly paid, some—especially highly-valued committee consultants—make over $150,000 a year. The total personnel budget for legislative workers in 2015 was $216 million. The median salary for staff members is about $55–65,000. These aides often work alongside members of the prestigious Assembly and Senate Fellows program as well as many college interns.

There are three important and well-regarded groups of staff who are nonpartisan and who work for the entire legislature. The first is the Legislative Analyst's Office, which analyzes budget proposals and the fiscal impact of ballot propositions. The second is the Legislative Counsel, which helps write bills, analyze ballot propositions, and provide legal advice. The third is the State Auditor's Office, which handles management and fiscal audits of the executive branch.

Before Proposition 140 passed in 1990, the staff of the California legislature was considered the best in the nation. However, that proposition required a staff cut of 40 percent and resulted in layoffs and the departure of many of the most experienced staffers, especially the highly-paid experts on which the committees relied. Staff is still a significant factor in the legislature, and over the years it has inched back toward its previous size and influence.

Legislative Process

There are three types of items that may pass the legislature: bills, which if successful become laws; constitutional amendments, which require a two-thirds vote of both houses and a referendum by the voters; and resolutions, which are largely symbolic expressions of opinion. The remainder of this section is concerned primarily with bills.

Bills are introduced only by legislators, even if the content was originally proposed by someone as politically important as the governor. Indeed, bills are often written by someone other than the person who introduces them. Many bills may be written by, or in conjunction with, lobbyists; and the nonpartisan Legislative Counsel's office may help in drafting language. An individual senator may introduce no more than 40 bills in a two-year session, whereas Assembly members may introduce 50 bills. Legislators may have a variety of motives for introducing a bill, such as impressing constituents or paying off a political favor, and most go nowhere. In the 2017–18 legislative session, 2,511 bills were introduced in the Senate and 2,264 in the Assembly for a total of 4,775. Of these, 2,214 reached the governor's desk. He signed 1,895 of them and vetoed 319, including some that were strongly supported by his allies. In his 16 years as governor, Brown signed nearly 20,000 bills into law.

Once a bill is introduced, the rules committee of the appropriate house assigns the bill to a standing committee or even two committees, depending on its content.

There may be a political or strategic component to this assignment. The bill is also numbered and printed. Committees cannot act on a bill until it has been in print for 30 days to allow comment from interested parties. Committees hold hearings, scrutinize the language to make sure that it clearly and accurately states what members intend, add amendments, and pass or reject bills. An absolute majority of the committee must vote favorably to report a bill out. If a bill is reported out of committee, it may go to the floor for discussion by the entire house; or bills with major fiscal impact may end up in the "suspense file" of the appropriations committee of either house to die, be amended, or be advanced without public vote and without explanation. These committees substantially reduce the number of bills reaching the floor and may significantly change others. In the closing weeks of a legislative session, these committees may report out hundreds of bills in a single day, which adds to the end-of-session logjam. Once a bill reaches the floor, amendments may be added and require only a majority vote. Bill passage requires an absolute majority (41 in the Assembly, 21 in the Senate). Once a bill has passed one house, it goes to the other house for similar consideration. Bills must pass both houses with identical language before they are forwarded to the governor for his signature. If the governor vetoes a bill, a two-thirds vote in each house is required to override the veto. This rarely happens.

Most bills pass through each house with different wording. In this case one house may acquiesce to the wording of the other house, or a conference committee will be established to work out the differences. A conference committee is a joint committee consisting of three members from each body. Assembly members are appointed by the speaker, and Senate members are appointed by the Senate Rules Committee. They suggest compromise language that must pass both houses. If this attempt fails, two additional attempts may be made before the bill is put to rest. See Figure 5.1 for an illustration of how a bill becomes a law in the California legislature.

SHORTCUTS The process described above is the textbook approach, but much legislation is able to bypass some of these steps, especially near the end of a legislative session when bills tumble over one another and deals are made in back rooms in a rush to adjourn. (In the last weeks of the 2015–16 session the legislature dealt with over 1,500 bills.) Many bills reappear as amendments to other bills, attracting even less public attention than they would have in the normal process. At this time, the influence of party leaders is greater because they are able to grease the skids for compromises and logrolling. **Logrolling** is vote trading, the process by which members exchange votes: "You vote for my bill, and I will vote for yours." Another common end-of-session legislative tactic is to hijack a bill and then **"gut and amend"** it. An issue that may have been presumed dead suddenly reappears, without warning, in a procedurally alive bill that previously dealt with an entirely different topic. In an editorial denouncing the practice, the *Sacramento Bee* describes how "gut and amend" works:

> A bill on air pollution morphs into a bill on immigration. A bill on college tuition becomes a bill on shark fins. In the last three weeks of the 2011 session, legislators gutted and amended 48 bills, passing 22 of them. Gov. Jerry Brown signed 19 of them.[4]

Efforts to reform this procedure in the legislature by requiring bills to be in print for several days before coming up for a vote never gained traction; so in 2016 wealthy Republican Charles Munger solely funded a successful ballot proposition

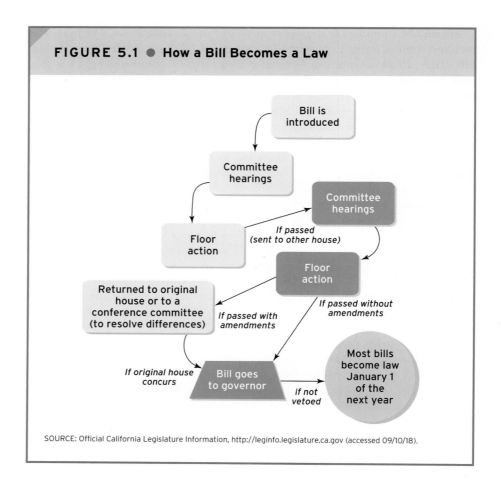

FIGURE 5.1 ● How a Bill Becomes a Law

Bill is introduced

Committee hearings

Floor action

If passed (sent to other house)

Committee hearings

Floor action

If passed without amendments

If passed with amendments

Returned to original house or to a conference committee (to resolve differences)

If original house concurs

Bill goes to governor

If not vetoed

Most bills become law January 1 of the next year

SOURCE: Official California Legislature Information, http://leginfo.legislature.ca.gov (accessed 09/10/18).

that prohibits the legislature from passing a bill until it has been in print and published on the internet for 72 hours (Proposition 54). Attempts have been made to lessen the impact of this initiative by defining "bill" narrowly and by limiting "passing" to mean only the final vote in the legislature before the bill goes to the governor, not earlier votes.

End-of-session periods in Sacramento reflect quintessential American politics: a system that favors insiders, corporations, and those with big money. While this goes on throughout the year, these backroom strategies work best when time is compressed and the media and other outsiders cannot follow what is going on or cannot do anything about it.

At the end of the session there is intense pressure to get things done. As noted earlier, 2,214 bills passed in 2017–18, and many others were in play. Insiders and lobbyists focus their attention on a single bill or a small number of bills that are important to their clients. Large corporations and other interest groups hire full-time lobbyists and lawyers, sometimes a full platoon of them, to follow their important bills, develop strategy, and take the necessary actions to ensure the desired outcome, all of which can be written off as business expenses.

These insiders work out deals behind the proverbial closed doors, and provisions to bills are added and removed at the last minute. Often the junior members voting on the floor have no idea of what they are voting on. Before the legislature was term-limited, members were extremely well-versed about their policy interests and had long memories about what tricks lobbyists and other legislators had pulled in previous sessions. This meant that it was more difficult to make unnoticed changes in legislation to benefit a special interest. Institutional memory is much more limited now among legislators. Experience, knowledge, and skills rest disproportionately with lobbyists and agency representatives.

Differences from U.S. Congress

While the California legislature is modeled closely on the national legislature, there are important differences that, collectively, make the California legislature a weaker body.

Term Limits

Unlike members of Congress, who can serve as long as they are re-elected, California legislators are limited to a total of 12 years, which can be served in one or both houses. Term limits enacted by the passage of Proposition 140 in 1990 limited members to three 2-year terms in the Assembly and two 4-year terms in the Senate for a maximum total of 14 years. Proposition 28 in 2012 instituted the current 12-year limit.

There were numerous reasons for the success of Proposition 140. First, it was a reaction to the highly effective Assembly Speaker Willie Brown, a flamboyant African American politician from San Francisco who was immensely unpopular with conservative voters. Second, it was an effect of public aversion to **gridlock** and divided government (generated by partisan conflict between the Republican governor and the Democratic legislature). Third, voters were protesting against the large fund-raising efforts of incumbents. Fourth, it was a reflection of the national trend against entrenched incumbents. Finally, it was the product of a belief among some Republicans that term limits could overthrow the Democratic majority. However, these term limits did not end divided government, gridlock, or large fund-raising (campaign-related spending has vastly increased), and they only briefly suspended the Democratic majority and in only one house, the 1994 Assembly. The proposition did reduce the ability of the legislature to act effectively. It is still too early to know if Proposition 28 will ultimately make the legislature more effective.

Item Veto

In Washington, D.C., the president has to sign or reject bills passed by Congress in their entirety. The president cannot approve parts that he or she likes and reject those that he or she dislikes. In California, as in most states, the governor has a **line-item veto** on appropriations, including those in the budget. This power allows the governor to reduce or eliminate a specific spending item, although he or she cannot increase items. This means that the legislature cannot force the governor's hand by including an item that the governor opposes in a large spending bill that he or she mostly supports. In 2016, for the first time in over 40 years, the governor did not use the line-item veto when signing the budget. A line-item veto can be overridden by an absolute two-thirds vote in both houses.

Apportionment and District Size

Both houses of the California legislature are apportioned by population, called **apportionment**; in Congress, the Constitution allots two senators to each state, regardless of size. California has a population about equal to the populations of the 22 smallest states combined. While these states have 44 senators between them, California has the same number of senators as the smallest of these states, Wyoming. In fact, there are four states that have fewer residents than are in each of California's 53 congressional districts.

Because California is so populous (about 39 million people) and because its legislature is relatively small, its legislative districts are among the largest in the nation. Senate districts have over 950,000 constituents, while Assembly districts contain over 475,000 residents. Compare this to New Hampshire, with a population of about 1.3 million and with 400 members in its lower house, which results in one representative for about every 3,000 residents. While New Hampshire's representatives are very accessible and elections are not expensive, most representatives do not wield much influence in their very large chamber. California senators, unlike any other U.S. legislative body, represent more constituents than members of Congress and more than the U.S. senators of seven states. This means that they are considerably less accessible than their counterparts in other states and that their elections are considerably more expensive.

The fact that both legislative houses are apportioned by population has led some informed observers to suggest that a unicameral legislature of 120 members would make more sense. This would result in smaller districts and increased accessibility to legislators.

Media Visibility

In Washington, D.C., the media interpret the national government's actions by focusing on the president, who consequently dominates the news. The comments of members of Congress are generally used to give more depth to a presidential story. Most often, these are party leaders, committee chairs, or the occasional legislator who has managed to make a name for himself or herself on a given issue.

The same is true in California's capital, but the statewide media, especially television, rarely cover news in Sacramento. Only the four party leaders receive air time, and because they hold their positions for so few years, the public has difficulty keeping track of who they are. The former Speaker of the U.S. House of Representatives from 2015–18, Paul Ryan, was practically a household name, but California Assembly Speaker Anthony Rendon is not. Consequently, most of what happens in Sacramento occurs out of the spotlight.

Court Appointments

Some of the greatest legislative battles in Congress have occurred during the Senate's hearings to confirm judicial appointments, especially to the Supreme Court. In contrast, many judges in California are elected. Those who are appointed by the governor are approved by the Commission on Judicial Appointments. The Senate does get to approve many other gubernatorial appointments to executive positions and regulatory boards and commissions, including the governing boards of both the California State University and the University of California. In both the U.S.

Senate and the California Senate, legislators have rejected recent nominees over policy differences.

Filibusters

In the U.S. Senate, a body that is not apportioned on the basis of one person, one vote, 41 members (potentially representing slightly more than 33 million people—about 10 percent of the country's population) can block the passage of most legislation through use of the filibuster. California has no such provision. Indeed, in most cases the majority rules. The principal exceptions are tax increases and constitutional amendments, which require a two-thirds vote.

Initiatives

Unlike the U.S. Constitution, the California Constitution provides several means of taking issues directly to the voters. Of these, the most significant is the initiative. The initiative is important in the legislative context because those who are thwarted in their attempts to get legislation passed can always threaten to take it—or an even more extreme version of it—to the voters. This tactic is often used to persuade legislators to vote for measures that they would otherwise oppose, and it significantly weakens the legislature (see discussion on the soda tax initiative later in this chapter).

Seniority

In the U.S. Congress, seniority is used as an informal rule in appointing members to committees and in choosing each committee's majority and minority leaders; once members are appointed to their committee positions, they are almost never removed. In the California legislature, both the appointment and removal power resides with the Assembly speaker and Senate majority leadership. Seniority plays a much smaller role (with term limits, seniority is of course limited). Both the speaker and the Senate majority leadership in recent years have removed members of both parties from committee leadership roles for disagreeing with them over various issues and because of financial and sexual harassment scandals.

Challenges Facing the California Legislature

When voters pay attention to the legislature, complaints and criticism of its actions often result. At times these objections are on target, at times not. State government tends to be perceived as dysfunctional, and the legislature is an easy target. It is easy to be repulsed by the contentious process of arriving at legislative agreements. Moreover, individual members often run for the legislature by running against it, emphasizing the legislature's shortcomings and foibles in order to play up their own importance as an agent of change.

Scandal also gets the public's attention. In 2014 three senators were suspended for misbehavior ranging from lying about living in their district to international gunrunning. Another was fined for misuse of campaign funds. A fifth was removed from his committee positions as a result of claims of domestic violence. During the 2017–18 session over 140 women working in or around the capitol went public about incidents of sexual harassment that they had experienced or witnessed from legislators, staff, or lobbyists. As a result, two Assembly members and one senator resigned under pressure. All were replaced by women.

The misbehavior of any one of the 120 legislators is often generalized to reflect badly on the whole institution. To have several legislators in the news at the same time for improper behavior is especially damaging, and these latest scandals may have contributed to the marginal decline in the legislature's approval rating. While the Senate had the authority to suspend the three senators in 2014, it did not have the authority to cut off pay and benefits. As a consequence, Proposition 50, which would allow a house of the legislature to suspend a member's pay and privileges with a two-thirds vote, was passed in June 2016. The threat of these powers has since been used in forcing the resignation of at least one legislator.

Among the most common criticisms of the legislature are the following:

Money

In the California legislature, as is the case throughout American politics, money carries a great deal of clout. Elections are expensive, and the money for elections comes from many sources, including the candidate's personal wealth, small contributions from many individuals, and larger contributions from business, unions, and other special interests. Large contributions are generally given to ensure support for a particular interest. Although legislators claim that their vote cannot be bought and that contributors are buying access and nothing else, that claim is difficult to support. Moreover, simply having access that the ordinary voter does not have is a significant advantage for these contributors. We have the best legislature that money can buy, and short of moving to public financing of campaigns—an idea rejected by the voters in June 2010—those who have money will always have an advantage over those who do not. With increasing social inequality and more money available to big industries and a few very wealthy individuals (and less available to the rest of us), and with the Supreme Court having loosened the restrictions on campaign spending, this advantage is growing.

Money is usually distributed to legislators who support the position of a given interest or to those who might be swayed by an offer of monetary support. It also goes to party leaders, who then distribute it to other legislators or candidates to solidify their support both within their party and against the other party. Indeed, the amassing of a large war chest contributed to the distrust and dislike of Speaker Willie Brown and led to the passing of Proposition 140, setting term limits. However, term-limited legislators, having little background in fund-raising, have become more dependent than their predecessors on large donations from special interests. Jesse Unruh once said, "If you can't take their money, eat their food, drink their booze . . . and then vote against them, you don't belong here."[5] On this basis, there are probably more legislators now than before that "don't belong here."

Term Limits (and Insufficient Knowledge and Expertise)

When Proposition 140 was passed in 1990, many believed that term limits would remove a remote professional class of legislators and bring in a new breed with closer ties to their districts. The ballot argument said that term limits "would remove the grip that vested interests have over the legislature" and create a "government of citizens representing their fellow citizens."[6] The expectations for this proposition were too high, and the results were unfortunate.

Legislative politics works best as an ongoing game among a relatively stable group of experienced players. Many of the aphorisms about politics, such as "Politics makes strange bedfellows" and "Don't burn your bridges" are based on ongoing relationships played out over a period of years. With a short, fixed term limit, the players change too rapidly for legislators to learn whom they can trust, with whom they can work, and whom they should avoid. This knowledge could facilitate cooperation across party lines as legislators come to learn that not all good is on their side of the aisle and that not all evil is on the other side. But in a short six years, legislators cannot learn that well; the players change too rapidly. The people who can work out effective compromises seldom emerge, and even if capable negotiators materialized, they would not know with whom to work.

Nor can effective leadership emerge with term limits as short as six years. In recent years, to give leaders more time in office, Assembly Democrats have often chosen freshmen legislators as committee chairs and as speaker. But a freshman legislator, no matter how talented, cannot effectively lead a large collegial body.

Nor in six short years is there time to develop expertise in process or subject matter, which are the ordinary skills of a good legislator. This dilemma was summed up by a lobbyist:

> I feel sorry for the first-term members who faced the energy crisis. They don't know who's smart; they don't know who knows what they're doing; they don't know the policy; they don't know the politics. And they are faced with a crisis.[7]

Real power has shifted from the legislature to the permanent establishment—the bureaucracy and interest groups. Members in these institutions may spend a career in Sacramento outlasting three or four generations of Assembly members. Much as they were dissatisfied with the legislature, it is doubtful that the voters wanted to shift power to either of those two groups. In June 2012 voters made a change in term limits, which on balance may have shifted *some* power back to the legislature. Proposition 28 reduced the time a legislator could serve in Sacramento from 14 years (6 in the Assembly and 8 in the Senate) to 12 years, but now those years can all be served in one house. When this change is fully played out, it will give each house more stability and should result in more experienced leaders. Senators may be a little less experienced than they were previously, but whatever is lost in that body will be gained by the much greater experience that Assembly members will achieve before being forced to leave.

The result could be a more knowledgeable and effective legislature that is at least marginally better able to deal with lobbyists and bureaucrats. But we have not yet reached this point. Only those legislators elected in 2012 and after operate under the new term limits, and change is not likely to be significant until sometime after 2018. Speaker Rendon, the first speaker chosen under the new limits, may serve for up to eight years in that position. In the previous eight years there were three different speakers.

If there has been a positive aspect to term limits, it is the increased diversity in the legislature. The percentage of Latino legislators rose from 6 percent in 1990 to 25 percent in 2009, before declining to 19 percent in 2015. In 2017 the percentage of Latinos rose slightly to 22.5 percent. In the 2017–18 session the Assembly membership was 54 percent nonwhite minority. The percentage of women in the legislature increased from 17.5 percent in 1990 to 32 percent in 2008 before dropping to 21.6 percent in 2017 (see "Who Are Californians?" on p. 149). Toni Atkins, the speaker of the Assembly prior to Anthony Rendon, was the first openly lesbian politician to hold that office (in 2018 she was elected president pro tempore of the state Senate). Her immediate predecessor as speaker was John Pérez, an openly gay Latino, and before that by Karen Bass, an African American woman. Women and members of nonwhite ethnic groups regularly occupy positions in the Democratic leadership of both houses.[8]

Partisanship

Many believe that **partisanship** has increased in the legislature in recent years. This trend has often been attributed to safe districts, in which representatives who couldn't lose in a general election were elected by their party's—often extremist—majority. In these safe districts the general election is determined by the primary election outcome and results in representatives who are more extreme than average voters. According to the common interpretation, safe districts have resulted in increased partisanship and legislators who are less willing to compromise.

As usual, the issue is more complex than this, although the new, more competitive general elections that began in 2010 may have resulted in the election of more moderates—at least in the Democratic Party. The problem with partisanship is not that there are strong partisans in the legislature—this has always been so. It is that in recent years the quality of public discourse has become less civil, and the participants have come to have less regard for their opponents and less willingness to work with them. Part of this incivility is a reflection of the increasing homogeneity and polarization of the national parties and their leaders (epitomized by the in-your-face style of the president). Term limits may play a role as well. Recognizing that they will not have to live with and deal with their opponents for years into the future, legislators make less effort to develop civil working relationships with them.

But legislators should be partisan. We elect representatives on a partisan basis. If we vote for Republicans rather than Democrats, then the Republicans should deliver on their partisan promises. Even those who rail against partisanship still want their interests to be forcefully proposed and protected.

Some of the greatest legislatures in the world, such as the British Parliament, are fiercely partisan and yet manage to govern. The difference is that in those bodies, the majority is permitted to rule. In our system, which permits a minority veto on taxation, bipartisan cooperation is essential; when it is not forthcoming, the system functions badly. If the California legislature appears to function better in recent years, it is not because of a reduction in partisanship; rather it's because the Democrats' overwhelming majority makes cross-party cooperation less necessary. Proposition 25, passed in 2010, which removed the requirement for a two-thirds vote on the annual budget, also reduced the need for cross-party cooperation.

Gridlock, Minority Rule, and Lack of Accountability

While California does not have the filibuster that thwarts majority rule in the U.S. Senate, it does have two major checks on effective majority governance. The first is that the legislature and the governor are elected separately and may represent different parties. The second is that a **two-thirds vote** is required to raise taxes, necessitating, in the absence of an overwhelming one-party majority, that the two parties work together to produce realistic fiscal policy.

How Diverse Is the State Legislature?

California's demographic changes are changing the electorate and the state legislature. White Californians now make up less than half of the representatives in the State Assembly (46 percent), but still make up the vast majority of the State Senate (78 percent). Women account for just under 21 percent of the state legislature, which is the lowest percentage since 1991–92.

How does this compare to the population of California? Look at the infographics below. The United States Census Bureau survey in 2017 found the population of California to be 37 percent white, 39 percent of Latino descent, 6 percent black or African American, and 15 percent Asian. What groups are overrepresented? Which groups are underrepresented?

By Race

	1	2	3
● White	37%	46%	78%
● Latino	39%	28%	12%
● Black or African American	6%	10%	5%
● Asian-Pacific Islander	15%	14%	5%
● Multi-Racial	2%	2%	0%

Key

1. Total population
2. Assembly distribution*
3. Senate distribution*

By Gender

	1	2	3
● Male	49.7%	79%	77%
● Female	50.3%	21%	23%

*Note: The Legislature of California has 40 state Senators and 80 Assembly members.

SOURCES: "Demographics in the California Legislature," California Research Bureau: California State Library, www.library.ca.gov/Content/pdf/crb/reports/LegDemographicsNov16.pdf (accessed 07/27/2018); United States Census Bureau, "Quick Facts: California, 2017", https://www.census.gov/quickfacts/fact/table/ca/PST045217 (accessed 07/27/2018).

forcriticalanalysis

1. Thinking back to the projected population growth by demographic group in the Chapter 1, Who Are Californians? feature, what changes would you expect to see in terms of diversity in the state legislature in the next ten years?

2. In addition to the demographic trends outlined in this feature, what political issues—both at the state and national level—do you think will influence the composition of the state legislature in the future?

Perhaps no other provision of governance has contributed more to the dysfunctional state of California and to the **lack of accountability** that characterizes the legislature than the two-thirds vote needed to raise taxes. Californians may elect a majority in the legislature and even a governor of the same party, but unless that party controls two-thirds of each house, it cannot control fiscal policy. Voters blame the majority party for gridlock when in fact control rests with the minority party, a political dynamic known as **minority rule**. This provision is even more restrictive than the filibuster, which can only work with 41 percent of the U.S. Senate actively backing it; California fiscal policy is held hostage to a one-third minority sitting on its collective hands, ensuring gridlock. As Peter Schrag describes it:

> More than any other structural flaw, it [the two-thirds rule] diffused accountability and brought on much of the budgetary gridlock that California became notorious for in the 1980s and early 1990s.[9]

This structural flaw has been in place for several decades, and in recent years the minority party has relied on it to refuse to compromise on the most critical issue before the state: the need for adequate and stable sources of revenue. The power of the minority to block taxation measures and the unwillingness of Republicans to vote for any tax increase can lead to harmful gridlock. If this has been less noticeable in recent years, it is partly because of the passage of Proposition 30 in 2012, which temporarily increased taxes and revenues, and partly because of an improving economy. Together, these have reduced the need for new or increased taxes. While the provisions of Proposition 30 expire in 2018, Proposition 55 on the November 2016 ballot extended these tax provisions for 12 years. But at some point, the economy will turn sour and, if anything, the Republicans have hardened their opposition to any tax increase (see discussion below on the 2018 tax repeal initiative). Gridlock will return.

Even Governor Jerry Brown, a political moderate, a skilled negotiator, and one of the most experienced individuals to serve as governor of California, was at first unable to find negotiating partners in the legislature's minority leadership. If he were governing amid the political culture of the 1970s, when he first served, he would have been very successful. According to a long-time associate of the governor, Jodie Evans, "He is aghast. He reports on some of his conversations like he couldn't believe the narrowness or lack of comprehending by public officials. . . . He said, 'Some of my old tools are not going to work.'"[10] Brown himself said that the Republicans have a "perverse fidelity to each point in the Republican gospel."[11] These points are reinforced in the party caucuses.

The Republicans, of course, saw it differently. Senator Bob Dutton stated, "He's all talk and no go. He throws a few scraps out there . . . let's demonize the Republicans, and that's supposed to fix a problem?"[12] *Los Angeles Times* columnist George Skelton wrote, "The entire legislative system has been corrupted by Democrats' fear of angering labor unions and Republicans' subservience to a few antitax opportunists and entertainers."[13] But while the governor has shown a willingness to oppose the unions (an important Democratic constituency) on pensions and organizing child care workers, the Republicans seem unwilling to agree to increasing revenues, going so far as to place a repeal initiative on the ballot in 2018 when taxes were raised for transportation infrastructure improvements—a widely recognized need.

Change began in 2010 when enacting budgets with a simple majority vote became permitted. Budgetary gridlock tapered off further after the Democrats' overwhelming electoral victory in 2012 and the passage that same year of Proposition 30, which raised taxes and lessened the need for further immediate tax increases. These changes together greatly lessened the need for Republican cooperation on legislative action. Although the Democrats temporarily lost their two-thirds margin in the Senate in 2014, their overwhelming majorities still allowed them to largely ignore the minority. However, when Governor Brown decided to put a "rainy day fund" constitutional measure on the ballot for November of 2014 (ACA 4), he needed and—in a rare demonstration of bipartisanship—gained Republican support. Brown also secured bipartisan support for a $7.5 billion water bond for the same election. Both measures passed by healthy margins.

Initiatives

A further complication to effective policy making in California is the initiative, which is often used to bypass the legislative process. If an interest group has the money and believes that it can get an initiative proposition with a populist appeal on the ballot, then it has little incentive to submit legislation for careful consideration by committees in each house of the legislature or to engage in legislative bargaining. Taking a page from the interest groups' playbook, Governor Brown in 2016 threatened to place an initiative on the ballot if adequate progress was not made on climate change legislation. In spite of his ultimate success in passing that legislation, the possibility of an initiative to achieve far-reaching climate control regulations remains.

Moreover, initiatives have passed that have weakened the legislature or weakened the legislature's ability to make responsible policy. Proposition 140, which instituted term limits, greatly weakened the ability of the legislature to function effectively by ensuring that there were rarely any experienced legislators in Sacramento. Propositions 13 (1978) and 98 (1988) each limited legislators' ability to make responsible fiscal policy, the first by limiting the use of a stable tax tool (property taxes), the second by locking up a huge chunk of the available funds for a single purpose—education.

In 2014 modest changes were made to the initiative process through the passage of SB (Senate Bill) 1253, which provided a public review period for initiatives (see Chapter 4). Of most significance to the legislative process is the bill's provision that after 25 percent of the needed signatures for an initiative proposition are obtained, the Senate and Assembly must hold a joint hearing on the issue. These hearings could possibly result in compromise legislation that would make the initiative unnecessary. The process envisioned by SB 1253 worked in 2016 to help get a minimum pay bill enacted after labor unions had started the initiative process. However, it was not until June of 2018 that the real potential of this legislation was demonstrated. On June 28, facing a deadline for removing initiatives from the fall ballot, four issues were in play, all of which had qualified for the ballot and most of which had substantial corporate money behind them: rent control, lead paint cleanup, internet privacy, and soda taxes.

No deal was reached on rent control, and the issue went on the ballot, where it failed. The paint issue, in which paint companies wanted a subsidy to clean up lead paint, also fell short of a deal, but the measure was pulled (legislators threatened drastic action if it passed), and legislators promised to keep trying to seek a solution. A compromise was worked out between the supporters and opponents of internet privacy, which resulted in a bill that was less objectionable to the opponents than was the initiative.

The most controversial of the four issues was the one on taxing soft drinks. The industry wanted legislation to prevent local governments from raising taxes on soft drinks, something the legislature did not favor. To move the legislature to action, the industry qualified an initiative, a constitutional amendment, that would prevent local governments from raising any taxes without a public, extra-majoritarian vote, an almost impossible achievement. Faced with that draconian possibility, the legislature passed and the governor signed a bill banning local governments from raising soda taxes until 2030.

While some saw this flurry of activity resulting in legislative compromise and the removal of three issues from the 2018 fall ballot as evidence of a successful reform, others saw chaos, frenzy, and extortion.[14] Few, however, could disagree with Speaker Rendon's understatement that "it can spur the Legislature to act on issues that challenge us."[15] We will probably see many more propositions in the future: in 2016 there were 17 (resulting in a voter information guide of over 200 pages), and in 2018 there were 11. Already in a reaction to the soda tax deal, major health care groups announced they would pursue a soda tax initiative in 2020, which would put in the constitution the right of local governments to impose soda taxes.[16] Live by the sword, die by the sword. It is often easier to sway a majority of the voters than a majority of the legislature, and there are increasingly large amounts of money available to do just that.

Californians have done a lot of damage to effective legislative governance through the initiative process. Voters feel dissatisfied with the legislature and consequently, though not intentionally, pass propositions that result in the legislature working less effectively. That makes voters more dissatisfied, and they vote for more propositions. Since 2008 there has been a modest reversal in this trend, and at the moment the state government is functioning more effectively.

The 2017–18 Session of the Legislature

In 2017–18 the legislature faced a unique set of issues: it became a key player in resisting federal policies that were at odds with California culture and policy; it passed a gas tax increase that subsequently resulted in an unsuccessful referendum on the law itself on the November ballot and a successful recall election against one member who voted for it; and it faced a massive protest by many women working in the legislature and other Sacramento organizations against a culture of rampant sexual harassment.

CONFRONTATION WITH THE FEDERAL GOVERNMENT With the election of 2016 the Republican Party took complete control of the federal government. This was not the traditional, elite, business-oriented Republican Party, but one led by Donald Trump drawing on the most populist elements of the party. As defined by Trump, the party emphasizes opposition to immigration—legal and illegal—and the rolling back of much of the progressive policies of the past 85 years. This runs counter to the culture and policies of California, which remain in that progressive tradition. Among the areas of conflict, in addition to immigration, are climate change and reducing greenhouse gasses, protecting national parks and monuments, supporting the Affordable Care Act, opposing vote suppression, and more.

Along with the governor and the attorney general (and many private groups including the ACLU, Planned Parenthood, Common Cause, and the Environmental Defense Fund) the legislature is a key player in these battles that have led the state to be viewed as a center of anti-Trumpism (Trump received less than a third of the vote in California in the 2016 election). Perhaps the one battle that has gained the most attention has been that over California's status as a so-called sanctuary state. In 2017 alone the legislature passed (and the governor signed) bills that would prohibit the police from detaining crime victims or witnesses on immigration violations (AB [Assembly Bill] 493); require colleges and universities that offer Cal Grants to create policies that safeguard their campuses from immigration officials (AB 21); prohibit landlords from reporting tenants' immigration status (AB 291); and limit assistance with federal immigration enforcement and prohibit detaining immigrants for federal immigration enforcement (unless they have committed violent crimes, are repeat offenders, or committed one of 800 other crimes) (SB 54, The California Values Act).

These laws do not make the state a sanctuary state in the traditional meaning of the word but rather spell out noncooperation with the federal government within the constitutional structure of federalism. These battles, which began in 2017–18, are sure to intensify, especially with the restructuring of the already conservative U.S. Supreme Court.

GAS TAX, RECALL, AND AN INITIATIVE In the 2016 election, Democratic state Senate candidate Josh Newman won a close election (by fewer than 2,500 votes) in a traditionally Republican district, helping to give Democrats a two-thirds majority in both houses. Taking advantage of those large numbers—and using a lot of good old-fashioned political horse trading—the Democrats, with one defection and one Republican vote from a termed-out member, passed a narrowly focused tax increase (mostly on fuel and automobile registration) to improve the badly deteriorated and outdated transportation infrastructure in the state—a widely recognized need.

Subsequently, a Republican-funded campaign spearheaded by a talk radio host and a former San Diego councilman was launched against Newman, saying (erroneously) that he cast the critical vote for the tax increase. In fact, that honor would more accurately go to the termed-out Republican Anthony Cannella, who in return for his vote got important transportation projects for his district.

Cynically, the proponents called this the "gazelle strategy," an attack on the weakest member of the group. Newman's "crime" had been to vote as a Democrat along with 81 other Democrats, thereby gaining a narrow victory for the tax. The point of the recall was to eliminate the two-thirds Democratic majority and to send a message to all legislators, Republicans and Democrats alike, that voting for tax increases is risky even in a liberal state. With fewer than half the number of voters that voted in the general election turning out, Newman was recalled by a margin of about 58–42 percent. Though the two-thirds majority was regained in 2018, the recall's message—we can take you out in a low-turnout recall—is unlikely to be forgotten.

In addition, the Republican Party successfully placed an initiative issue on the 2018 November ballot repealing the infrastructure tax and prohibiting the legislature from enacting any future gas tax without a vote of the electorate. Again cynically, proponents of this effort—funded in large part by the national Republican establishment—stated that this was largely a means to draw Republican voters to the polls in November with the hopes of preserving the seats of several endangered Republican U.S. Representatives.[17] The initiative failed by 13 points.

SEXUAL HARASSMENT The state legislature has many different employers (each legislator hires his/her own staff) who hire a mix of experienced and inexperienced workers (most without civil service protection). Many of the latter are young interns or staff members in their first jobs. There are also lobbyists with lots of money and booze who throw receptions nightly. And many of the legislators and lobbyists are far from home and families. These conditions can contribute to a culture of sexual harassment.

While the #MeToo movement did not start in Sacramento, it got a huge boost when in October of 2017 a group called WeSaidEnough, consisting of over 140 women with jobs in the state capitol or related to government (including legislators, senior staff, and lobbyists), sent a letter to the *Los Angeles Times* detailing the sexual harassment they had experienced or witnessed. Theirs was the ". . . first open statement by women working in politics calling for an end to the pervasive culture of harassment and assault within a Capitol community."[18]

The impact was immediate and reached to political centers far beyond Sacramento. Hundreds of media articles were written, many interviews were given, and dozens of bills were introduced into the legislature. Ultimately Governor Brown signed at least four into law, including those that would expand anti-harassment provisions in state law and limit non-disclosure agreements. Under some pressure two Assembly members (Raul Bocanegra and Matt Dababneh) and one senator (Tony Mendoza) resigned, ultimately to be replaced by women. Another legislator, Sebastian Ridley-Thomas, facing harassment charges, resigned for "health" reasons and was also replaced by a woman. Assemblywoman Cristina Garcia was stripped of her committee assignments after accusations of groping. And another legislator, John Moorlach was reprimanded for putting women in headlocks and giving them "noogies." A subcommittee chaired by Assemblywoman Laura Friedman on Sexual Harassment Prevention and Response was established under the Joint Committee on Rules, and in June of 2018 it recommended, among other actions, that a special investigative unit be set up in the Legislative Counsel's office and that a panel of five outside experts be established to examine the findings of that unit.[19]

This is only a start, and what we have heard to date is probably only the tip of the iceberg. Policies, however far-reaching and while essential, are not enough. Assemblywoman Friedman has said, "This is about culture change. It's not about voting on a set of policies and saying that you're done."[20] The change required is huge, and it will not happen overnight.

California Legislature: Where Are We Now?

The legislature serves two principal functions: policy making and representation. The different requirements of these two functions create tensions. Legislators are also pressured by the needs versus the wants of their districts; state versus local interests; and the demands of interest groups, campaign contributors, party leaders, and the governor. California is a large state with many competing wants and needs. Legislative districts are among the largest anywhere. These factors turn policy making into a complex and often unseemly process, a process moved by humans who will always be imperfect. Even before term limits were imposed, the once highly regarded legislature passed some bad legislation and left problems unaddressed.

Yet the legislature could work better than it does, and it is valid to ask if the legislature is the creator or the victim of this impaired system. In large part, problems of inefficacy have been generated by outside forces. Term limits, big money for campaigns and elections, and the two-thirds vote requirement for passing tax legislation are the most notable outside factors. The declining level of civility in the legislature is a reflection of the impact of term limits and of the increasing political polarization in the nation. But individuals are responsible for their own behavior. Regardless of outside forces, individual legislators of goodwill could make a difference.

Since 2008 a series of changes have taken place (mostly via the initiative process, ironically) that appear to have strengthened the legislative process and reduced gridlock, at least for the time being.

- **Proposition 11 (November 2008), Proposition 20 (November 2010), and Proposition 27 (November 2010, defeated)** Proposition 11 took redistricting of the legislature away from the legislature and put it in the hands of a Citizens' Redistricting Commission. It passed by only 50.9 percent of the vote. It was strengthened by the passage (by 61 percent) of Proposition 20, which extended the jurisdiction of the commission to congressional districts, and by the corresponding defeat (by 59.5 percent) of Proposition 27, which would have eliminated the commission. As a result of the commission's redistricting, which took effect in 2012, districts became more evenly balanced, and Democrats gained a two-thirds margin in both legislative houses.

- **Proposition 14 (June 2010)** Proposition 14 created the top-two primary system, with the expectation that more moderate legislators would be elected. It is too early to tell if that result was accomplished, and whatever impact this has is overshadowed by the impact of Propositions 11, 20, and 27. But in the first election following this change, in 19 districts two members of the same party ended up winning the primary election and running against each other in the general election. In 2018, thirteen of the same party—all Democrats—ran against each other for state legislative seats. This kind of primary system offers an opportunity for minority party members to help select the more moderate of the opposing candidates. It also provides an opportunity for big businesses to put a lot of money behind the candidate who is most friendly to their goals, which has resulted in the rise of "business-friendly" Democrats in the legislature.

- **Proposition 25 (November 2010)** The requirement for a two-thirds majority to pass the annual budget was eliminated by this measure, which has ended the ability of the minority—whose involvement in this fiscal measure was required every year—to block this required legislation. Thus, the influence of the minority in the legislative process has been substantially reduced.

- **Proposition 28 (June 2012)** This proposition reduced the term limits in the legislature from 14 to 12 years, but it allowed members to serve all that time in a single house. This allows legislators the opportunity to gain more experience, especially in the Assembly, and presumably to achieve greater knowledge and effectiveness. However, it is too early to make a judgment of whether that is actually happening.

- **Proposition 30 (November 2012)** Proposition 30 temporarily increased taxes, giving the state greater fiscal stability and reducing the need for the minority party's help in passing tax legislation. Proposition 55 in 2016 extended the tax provisions for 12 years.

The two-thirds Democratic majority did not reappear until 2017. During this off-year election—as is usually the case—Republicans were more likely to vote than Democrats, resulting in some marginal districts switching to Republicans.

It is too early to make a long-term assessment of the impacts of these propositions on the legislature. The current trend is promising, and on the positive side, both houses currently have experienced leaders. But the power of big money and the threat of dominating interests are always there to skew the process.

While the skilled moderate leadership of Governor Brown has been an important factor in creating the current favorable situation, there is about to be a sea change in California politics. For eight years the Democrats have ruled the state under an experienced, highly respected—if not much loved—governor. Those who may have had doubts about the overwhelming Democratic membership of the legislature could still look to the governor as "the adult in the room" who would keep the legislature in line and not let it spend too much money or veer too far to the left.[21] Or at least that was the image. The new governor, Gavin Newsom, does not have that gravitas or stature, and the public may begin to view the legislature and the Sacramento governing structure with a more skeptical eye. The legislature's approval rating tends to follow that of the governor, and if his is low, that of the legislature will likewise decline.

In addition, American politics tends to have a self-correcting nature. The Democrats have been in control with huge majorities, and yet many problems remain unsolved, most notably the creation of a stable financial base. Other unsolved problems include: the homeless, a lack of affordable housing, crime, traffic, water, air, and many more. Moreover, many feel that the Democrats, using their exceptional majorities, have overreached themselves with policies such as the gas tax increase and laws protecting illegal immigrants.

The attitude of the public towards the government is affected by how people feel about life in general. The current favorable economic climate will predictably cycle downwards. Major disasters are inevitable. The Democrats have had a reasonably favorable climate in which to work (created in no small part by having changed a budget deficit of $27 billion when Governor Brown came into office to a surplus of about $6 billion when he left). At some point it will end, and the Democrats will face a more hostile public that will be demanding change.

Given the challenging national mood, the diverse nature of the state, and an electorate that is itself divided, positive change cannot be ensured. Moreover, the public has little understanding of legislative functions or processes, making further positive change through the initiative process unlikely. In the past, ill-advised measures such as a part-time legislature have often been suggested. As the cartoonist Walt Kelly's character Pogo said, "We have met the enemy and he is us."

But not always. We should be thankful for the current hiatus in gridlock that has permitted the legislature to address many of the issues that face our state.

Study Guide

FOR FURTHER READING

Cain, Bruce E., and Roger G. Noll, eds. *Constitutional Reform in California: Making State Government More Effective and Responsive*. Berkeley: Institute of Governmental Studies Press, 1995.

California Journal and State Net. *Roster and Government Guide*. Sacramento: California Journal, 2004.

de Sá, Karen. "How Our Laws in California Are Really Made." *San Jose Mercury News*, July 10, 2010. www.mercurynews.com/politics-government/ci_15452125. Accessed 8/15/16.

Institute of Governmental Affairs. "IGS Goes to Sacramento to Assess Ten Years of Term Limits." *Public Affairs Reports* 42, no. 3 (Fall 2001).

Mathews, Joe, and Mark Paul. *California Crackup: How Reform Broke the Golden State and How We Can Fix It*. Berkeley: University of California Press, 2010.

Muir, William K., Jr. *Legislature: California's School for Politics*. Chicago: University of Chicago Press, 1982.

Schrag, Peter. *California: America's High-Stakes Experiment*. Berkeley: University of California Press, 2006.

———. *Paradise Lost: California's Experience, America's Future*. New York: New Press, 1998.

Wilson, E. Dotson. *California's Legislature*. Sacramento: Office of the Chief Clerk, California State Assembly, 2016.

ON THE WEB

California Choices. http://californiachoices.org. Accessed 8/16/16.

California Legislative Analyst's Office. www.lao.ca.gov/. Accessed 8/16/16. The LAO is a nonpartisan fiscal and policy adviser to the legislature.

California State Assembly. http://assembly.ca.gov/. Accessed 8/16/16.

California State Assembly Democratic Caucus. www.asmdc.org. Accessed 8/16/16.

California State Assembly Republican Caucus. http://asmrc.org. Accessed 8/16/16.

California State Senate. http://senate.ca.gov/. Accessed 8/16/16.

CALmatters. https://calmatters.org/. Accessed 8/16/16.

Legislative Counsel. www.leginfo.legislature.ca.gov/. Accessed 8/16/16. The Legislative Counsel of California's official site, maintained by law.

Los Angeles Times. "Essential Politics." www.latimes.com/politics/essential/la-pol-sac-essential-politics-updates-1471460386-htmlstory.html. Accessed 8/16/16. A daily news feed on California government and politics.

Rough & Tumble. www.rtumble.com. Accessed 8/16/16. Daily summary of California news.

Sacramento Bee. www.sacbee.com/news/politics-government/. Accessed 8/16/16.

Senate Democrats. http://democrats.senate.ca.gov/. Accessed 8/16/16.

Senate Republicans. http://cssrc.us/. Accessed 8/16/16.

University of California, Berkeley, Institute of Governmental Studies Library. http://igs.berkeley.edu/library. Accessed 8/16/16.

SUMMARY

I. Legislatures are not well understood, but they are critical to a democratic form of government. Indeed, a working legislature is practically the definition of a democratic government.

II. The California legislature is, for the most part, modeled on the U.S. Congress.
   A. It is bicameral.
   B. Members are elected from single-member, geographically based districts.
   C. Unlike the U.S. Congress, both houses of the California legislature are apportioned by population.

III. Legislators must both represent their constituents and make policy.
   A. These two items are not always compatible.
   B. In representing their districts, members must decide whether to follow the wants or the needs of their constituents and whether to follow directions from the district or use their own best judgment.
   C. Poor communication from constituents makes these actions difficult.
   D. Legislators have offices both in Sacramento and in their districts.

IV. Members of both the California Senate and Assembly are elected through a blanket or top-two primary followed by a general election. Two key features of California politics influence who gets elected:
   A. Candidates must engage in extensive fund-raising to increase their chances of getting elected.
   B. Redistricting, which follows each census, has a significant impact on who is elected. For example, redistricting by a Citizens Redistricting Commission in 2012 resulted in a Democratic supermajority in the legislature.

V. The leader of the Assembly is the speaker; the leader of the Senate is the president pro tempore.
   A. Each leader is elected by all of the members in that body, but the majority party caucus usually determines the outcome.
   B. The speaker controls most of the resources and is very powerful.
   C. The speaker and the president pro tempore are term-limited.
   D. The president pro tempore shares powers with the Senate Rules Committee.

VI. The bulk of legislative work is done in committees.
   A. Bills are read and amended here.
   B. Issue networks are made up of a group of individuals—lobbyists, staffers, members, and bureaucrats—who make and control policy in a given substantive area.

VII. Professional staff members make the legislature possible.
   A. Some of them work in districts, some in members' offices, some for committees, and some for the leadership.
   B. The best-paid staff members are usually subject-matter experts working for committees.

VIII. The legislative process has several steps.
   A. Bills are first introduced by members and sent to committees.
   B. Bills must pass the floors of both houses (with identical wording) before they are sent to the governor for his or her signature.
   C. If the governor vetoes a bill, it takes a two-thirds vote in each house to override it.

D. Tax bills also require a two-thirds vote, giving the minority party important power in the legislature and making it difficult for the majority party to govern.

IX. The state legislature is different from the U.S. Congress in several ways.
   A. Members are term-limited.
   B. The governor has line-item veto power (he can cut or eliminate any item in a budget bill, while still approving the entire bill).
   C. Both houses are apportioned by population.
   D. Very little media attention is given to the California legislature.
   E. The legislature does not have a role in judicial appointments.
   F. The legislature does not have a filibuster, unlike the U.S. Senate. However, the two-thirds requirement for increasing taxes has a similar effect in thwarting the majority.
   G. California also has the initiative process, which allows the legislative process to be bypassed, most often by special-interest groups with deep pockets.

X. The effectiveness of the California legislature is limited
   A. by the power of big money;
   B. by term limits and members' lack of experience;
   C. by intense partisanship;
   D. by the two-thirds-vote rule on taxes, which limits the majority party's decision-making ability and makes accountability difficult; and
   E. by the initiative, which is often used to bypass the legislative process.

XI. Propositions passed since 2008 have reduced gridlock and made the legislature more effective by increasing the size of the majority party and by eliminating the two-thirds vote required for the budget.
   A. Propositions 11 and 20 took districting away from the legislature.
   B. Proposition 14 created the top-two primary system.
   C. Proposition 25 removed the two-thirds-vote requirement for passing budgets.
   D. Proposition 28 increased the amount of time that legislators can serve in one house.
   E. Proposition 30 temporarily increased taxes, and therefore state revenues.

PRACTICE QUIZ

1. A line-item veto allows
   a) the governor to reject any single item in an appropriations or budget bill.
   b) the speaker or the president pro tempore to pull any single item from the agenda.
   c) a single member to block a single piece of legislation by signing a written objection.
   d) a petition by a group of 10 legislators to block any single piece of legislation.

2. Proposition 140
   a) limits the time that legislators can serve in Sacramento.
   b) limits the power of the legislature to raise property taxes.
   c) sets aside 40 percent of the budget for education purposes.
   d) requires the speaker to assign staff to the minority party.

3. The legislature is composed of
   a) 80 members in the Senate and 40 in the Assembly.
   b) 120 members in a single body.
   c) 60 members in each body.
   d) 80 members in the Assembly and 40 in the Senate.

4. A two-thirds vote is needed to pass
   a) appropriation bills.
   b) budget bills.
   c) tax bills.
   d) all of the above

5. Partisanship in the legislature
   a) has declined because of apportionment.
   b) has declined because of the blanket primary now in effect.
   c) has led to greater ease in getting budgets improved.
   d) has increased in recent years.

6. The powers of the speaker of the California Assembly include all of the following *except*
   a) the power to assign parking spaces.
   b) the power to assign office space.
   c) the power to assign members to committees but not to remove them during the current term.
   d) the power to assign a member to a committee against both the member's wishes and the wishes and needs of his or her constituency.

7. Proposition 140 resulted in all of the following *except*
   a) an increase in office budgets.
   b) the establishment of term limits.
   c) a reduction of committee staff and personal staff.
   d) layoffs of some of the most knowledgeable staff experts from committees.

8. The legislative process is biased in favor of
   a) issues favored by the public.
   b) the status quo.
   c) change that interest groups favor.
   d) legislation proposed by the governor, who can introduce a limited number of bills directly to both houses, bypassing some of the steps of the legislative process.

9. California has some of the largest legislative districts in the nation. This means that
   a) elections in California tend to be expensive.
   b) citizen access to legislators is unusually good because legislators need to face the voters so often.
   c) legislators appear in the media more often because they represent so many people.
   d) California has an unusually large number of legislators.

10. Term limits have resulted in which of the following:
    a) an increase in expertise among legislators, who have only a few years to make a name for themselves.
    b) an increase in citizen legislators, people with little or no political experience who are able to run because seats are open.
    c) an increase in staff members, who are needed to help legislators lacking experience.
    d) a decline in the knowledge needed to pass good-quality legislation.

CRITICAL-THINKING QUESTIONS

1. Should a legislator vote for what his or her constituents want or what his or her constituents need?
2. Who should apportion the legislature?
3. What criteria should be used to apportion a legislature?
4. Should a legislator take orders from constituents or use his or her own best judgment, even if it is unpopular?
5. How much access should lobbyists have to legislators?
6. When should a legislature have rules that allow a minority to block legislation?

KEY TERMS

apportionment (p. 144)
Assembly Rules Committee (p. 138)
bicameral (p. 129)
committees (p. 138)
constituents (p. 130)
gerrymandering (p. 134)
gridlock (p. 143)
"gut and amend" (p. 141)

issue networks (p. 138)
lack of accountability (p. 150)
line-item veto (p. 143)
logrolling (p. 141)
minority rule (p. 150)
oversight (p. 131)
partisanship (p. 148)
president pro tempore (p. 138)

Proposition 140 (p. 129)
representation (p. 129)
speaker (p. 136)
staff (p. 138)
term limits (p. 129)
two-thirds vote (p. 148)
winner-take-all (p. 133)

6

The Governor and the Executive Branch

WHAT CALIFORNIA GOVERNMENT DOES AND WHY IT MATTERS

Consider the following activities that recently took place in the executive branch of our state government:

- Governor Brown's administration initiated an investigation of Caltrans after receiving reports of shoddy work on a segment of the Bay Bridge and learning that Caltrans had transferred or ended the contracts of the "whistle-blowing" project managers.

- In June 2018 Governor Brown signed a budget creating a $13.8 billion cash reserve, the largest in state history, a result of the increase in taxes approved by the voters in 2012 and extended in 2016.

- After President Trump withdrew from the Paris climate accord in 2017, Governor Brown traveled to China to discuss global warming with President Xi Jinping. In 2018 Governor Brown signed an executive order to boost the state's supply of zero-emission vehicles and charging and refueling stations.

- Caltrans decided to replace high-occupancy vehicle lanes with toll lanes on an Orange County freeway over the objections of local governments and agencies.

- Attorney General Xavier Becerra sued the Trump administration after it was announced in March 2018 that the 2020 Census would include a question on citizenship status. Becerra argued that this would make noncitizens reluctant to participate, generating an undercount that would allow the federal government to direct resources away from California, which has the largest immigrant population of any state.

- In August 2018 Attorney General Becerra led an 18-state coalition seeking legal protections against potential deportation for hundreds of thousands of people in the United States who hold Temporary Protected Status (TPS), including individuals from El Salvador, Haiti, Nicaragua, and Sudan.

If you think you know little about the executive branch of California, you are not alone. The media rarely pay much attention to state government, and in 2013 the last out-of-town TV bureau in Sacramento closed. California government operates largely out of the public view. The governor's reputation is based mainly on his interactions with the legislature, which are often public and may be contentious—and therefore newsworthy. Barring major scandal, the governor's actions as the executive head of a huge bureaucracy are off the press's radar. Few reporters would be able to locate Caltrans or the Natural Resources Agency either physically or on an organization chart. Most of California's 500,000-plus state employees are known to the public only as friends and neighbors.[1] Other members of California's plural executive tend only to make headlines when their actions relate to President Trump—as when Attorney General Xavier Becerra filed various lawsuits in 2017 and 2018 to block the president's policies on immigration, the U.S. Census, and other issues.

When Governor Brown came into office in 2011, it was not uncommon to hear that the state was ungovernable. Now, government is said to be working well, and many credit Brown's widely acknowledged political skills with helping to increase the state's productivity. However, the government's recent successes are a result not only of Brown's abilities but also of the overwhelming Democratic majorities in the California legislature and unified Democratic control of other executive branch positions.

Recent changes in the state constitution that have made it possible to pass budgets on a majority vote have made a difference as well. When Brown had to deal with a larger Republican minority in the legislature, he was less successful. Governor Gavin Newsom, who took over as governor in 2019, similarly presides over a unified Democratically controlled legislature and a uniformly Democratic executive branch. While political conflicts always exist, the party is relatively unified and currently focused more on opposing the Trump administration than on intra-party disagreements. While Trump's approval rating in the state is below 30 percent, both the governor and legislature have recently enjoyed approval from strong majorities of the California public.

The Invisible Governor?

While the governor is the most visible political figure in the state, his visibility pales in comparison to that of the president of the United States. There are a number of reasons for this lack of visibility. We depend on the media for most of what we know about our government, and for the most part the media in California are not interested in state politics or governance. The media, after all, are a business, responding to the desires of their consumers and advertisers. For many Californians, and thus for the media, Sacramento does not capture much attention; it is a long way from the major population centers of the state, and what happens there just does not captivate an audience the way a good car chase does. The media have found that their business model works best by focusing on well-known or riveting personalities. For California, this generally means a focus more on U.S. Senators Dianne Feinstein and Kamala Harris, and, except in election seasons, less so on state politicians such as Governor Gavin Newsom or Attorney General Xavier Becerra. Media-wise, what happens in Sacramento stays in Sacramento.

The governor's job is divided analytically into two roles: **head of government** and **head of state**, mirroring the dual roles held by the president of the United States. As the leader of the California state government, the governor's role is to govern—that is, to develop policy and get it passed through the legislature and implemented via the bureaucracy. The governor's approach to these various tasks is often divisive. For example, when Governor Jerry Brown signed a bill into law in October 2017 making California a sanctuary state, critics reiterated their concerns that the measure was a danger to public safety and would cause the Trump administration to withhold federal funds from the state. Governor Brown's lobbying on behalf of the California high-speed rail project, even in the face of massive price overruns and multi-year delays, contributed to growing opposition over time.

In contrast, the governor's role as head of state—attending groundbreaking ceremonies, lighting the capitol Christmas tree, attending memorial ceremonies—are less visible. Often the events are so insignificant that not many people care. Few dignitaries of note visit Sacramento, and the media simply do not warm to filming the governor talking to teachers or highway patrol officers. Because he was a showman able to generate his own buzz, Governor Arnold Schwarzenegger made as

In 2018, Californians elected former lieutenant governor Gavin Newsom as governor of the state. Throughout his campaign, he emphasized California values that were being challenged in Washington, among them immigration rights, civil rights, and environmental protections.

much as he could of the head-of-state role; Governor Brown simply had no interest in it. Instead, that role was filled more by other members of the California executive branch, such as Attorney General Becerra and Alex Padilla, the California secretary of state. Governor Newsom has a stronger history of seeking the media limelight; his administration is likely to bring more overt attempts to highlight his role as head of state.

Also, as with the presidency, the governor's role is one of limited power. In fact, the state's plural executive and the federal government's sovereignty over state government mean that the governor of California is significantly weaker than the public might expect. The governor does not run the state of California any more than the president runs the United States. Our nation's founders feared a strong executive, having experienced such rule under a king and under capricious colonial governors. Consequently, they created a system in which the powers of all institutions were strictly limited, and in which the powers of the executive were secondary to those of the legislature. The California state government mirrors the federal government's system of separation of powers and limits on the **formal powers** of the executive branch.

As with the president, people have many incomplete, incorrect, and conflicting views about the governor. Political scientists Tom Cronin and Michael Genovese compiled a list of what they call the paradoxes of the presidency:

- We want the president to be an effective politician while being above politics.

- We want the president to be a common person and an extraordinary person at the same time.

- We want the president to be powerful but not too powerful.[2]

In sum, we want the president to be all things at all times, and, of course, this is not possible.

The governor is not burdened with as much symbolic baggage as the president, yet many misperceptions carry over to this office as well. These misperceptions are amplified by the fact that people think they understand the office. After all, it is an executive office, a position with which all of us who work in organizations have some familiarity. But the governorship is a *political* executive office, in an organization that often does not have a single, identifiable chain of command and which does not respond well, if at all, to direct orders.

Our greatest misperception is exaggerating the amount of power wielded by the governor. The governor does not control the legislature and has trouble making policy without the cooperation, or at least acquiescence, of legislators who may have little reason to support the governor. The governor can win legislative cooperation only through persuasion—perhaps hardball persuasion, but persuasion nonetheless. The governor is one of multiple independently elected members of the plural executive and does not control the attorney general, secretary of state, or other executive officers—individuals with their own constituencies, their own political ambitions, and their own policy goals. Although all of these executives are currently Democrats, sometimes the plural executive has included officials from opposition political parties, which further limits the governor's influence.

Within the bureaucracy of the executive branch, it is possible for the governor to exert influence more directly. But the executive branch is large, employing hundreds of thousands of people who in many cases are very remote from the governor. How does the governor get a Caltrans engineer in San Diego or a park ranger in Marin County to follow his wishes? Some organizations, such as the University of California, are governed by boards that can be influenced only by appointments, budgetary threats, or strongly voiced public opinion. The lack of formal powers and direct accountability mean that gubernatorial power is less reliant on formal powers than on political skills and an ability to bargain, a long political memory, and friends and allies in important positions. A good economy, an absence of natural disasters, and luck can also be important.

Arnold Schwarzenegger came into office in 2003 on a wave of popularity that initially gave him a substantial amount of informal power. By sheer dint of personality and the threat to go to the public with initiatives, he managed a series of impressive victories in the early days of his tenure. His success did not last, however. He overreached, and he antagonized the members of his own party with his moderate positions on many issues. His attempt to pass four initiatives in a special—and costly—election in November 2005 was a disaster. Near the end of his time in office, his approval ratings had reached a low of 23 percent in a Public Policy Institute of California (PPIC) poll.[3]

Schwarzenegger's successor, Jerry Brown, was the polar opposite of Arnold Schwarzenegger. Due in part to his previous stints as governor from 1975 to 1983 and his long career of public service, he came into office in 2011 as one of the most knowledgeable governors that California has ever had. He loved the details of policy making, knew the intricacies of governing, and did not crave or need the limelight. He knew how to bargain and make deals. In 2011 he was faced with a bad economy, huge revenue shortfalls, and an opposition party that would not bargain on revenue issues. But things turned around with the emergence of favorable political and economic situations. Republican opposition became less important after new redistricting and primary laws provided the Democrats with overwhelming majorities in both houses of the legislature. Along with the improved economy and the passage of tax-raising Proposition 30—thanks in large part to the governor's political acumen and skills—and the earlier elimination of the two-thirds vote requirement for approving budgets, governing suddenly became much easier. In a PPIC poll during May of 2018, 48 percent of California adults approved of the job he was doing.[4]

In November 2018, Californians elected Lieutenant Governor Gavin Newsom to succeed Jerry Brown. Unlike Brown, Newsom enjoys being in the media spotlight and is working to move California to the left and away from Brown's policies of fiscal conservatism. While he came into office with a strong victory and robust approval ratings, it remains to be seen if his style will be effective at generating significant policy changes and how those public approval ratings will change as his administration moves from promises to action.

Formal Powers of the Governor

The formal powers of the governor, while limited, are still significant. The governor has powers—the most important of which is the **line-item veto**—that are denied to the president. The true value of these powers, however, is as vantage points from which the governor bases his or her **informal powers**, or powers to persuade. (See Box 6.1 for a summary of the governor's formal and informal powers.) A governor who expects to use only formal powers to govern will not accomplish much. Those powers must be leveraged to persuade other political actors to support the governor's goals. For example, in 2017, to get Republican support for his cap-and-trade bill, Governor Brown agreed to a proposal from the state Assembly's Republican minority leader, Chad Mayes, to a vote in the legislature in 2024 on how to spend the cap-and-trade revenues. In 2018, Governor Brown was seeking Republican support in the legislature for a massive ($52.4 billion) infrastructure bill. In a last-minute meeting with state Senator Anthony Cannella (R-Merced), Brown agreed to add $500 million to the bill for a commuter rail and expressway connecting Merced to the Bay Area; in exchange, Cannella voted for the governor's bill.[5]

The state constitution vests supreme executive power in the governor, a phrase that conveys both more and less than it seems. Less, because the governor's office is an office of limited powers in which nothing is supreme. More, because executives often push established constitutional limits. However, given a supportive legislature that views most executive requests positively—as is true currently—most of the executive's goals can be reached.

Appointments

Making appointments is one of the governor's most significant powers. The governor appoints four distinct groups of individuals: **personal staff**, heads of major administrative divisions, some judges, and members of a number of **boards and commissions**. Some of these appointments require confirmation by other bodies, while others do not. Some appointees work at the governor's pleasure, while others serve for fixed terms. Some answer directly to the governor, while others are several steps removed or protected from executive intervention. Over the course of an administration, a governor can make more than 2,500 appointments, including about 500 positions that will be filled at the start of the term.

The governor's personal staff consists of about 100 individuals who craft policy recommendations, work with the legislature, or handle all the details to make the governor's life run smoothly, including providing structure, and packaging and presenting him or her to the public. Governors hire, fire, and move these individuals about at will. No confirmation is required.

Next closest to the governor are the members of the **cabinet**. The governor determines who will serve in the cabinet and what role, if any, the cabinet will play in policy development. The heads of the **superagencies** of state government (large organizations similar to federal departments, which contain a number of related bureaus and agencies) are in the cabinet, as are the director of finance and others whose presence the governor finds useful and appropriate. These positions require confirmation by the Senate, but the governor has the ability to remove them at will.

The governor also appoints the heads of the major bureaus or departments, which are mostly located within the superagencies. These individuals have the responsibility of overseeing the organizations and the more than 230,000 state employees (not including employees of California's public universities) that do the real work of government.

In addition, the governor appoints members to more than 325 boards and commissions, important and unimportant, visible and invisible. Once appointed, individuals do not have to answer to the governor, although the governor can apply political pressure, including threatening to cut the budget of the institution that the individuals administer.

Stating that "the state's bureaucracy is a labyrinth of disjointed boards, commissions, agencies and departments,"[6] Governor Brown in 2012 proposed a restructuring and consolidation of agencies, having eliminated 25 boards and commissions the previous year. There was no political payoff in this. Few outside of the government would notice. Not surprisingly, little came of this proposal.

Independent Executive Actions

The governor's powers are constitutionally restricted by the legislature, but in some cases he or she is able to act independently of it. Independent executive actions are permitted by the constitution or under laws passed by the legislature. They are most significant in times of an emergency.

Few laws passed by the legislature are self-implementing; most require positive action on the part of the administration. This process of implementation involves clarification of the law (e.g., what does the language used by the legislature imply?) and the assembling of finances and an administrative structure to allow action to take place. All of this requires prioritization and fund requests by the governor's appointees or the governor. This allows the governor considerable influence; using the line-item veto or failing to request adequate funds, for example, can effectively kill a program. Governor Brown has used these powers several times, in one instance eliminating both the California Postsecondary Education Commission and the duplicative office of the secretary of education, neither of which he found useful.

The governor also has the power to issue executive orders. This can be fairly noncontroversial orders, such as declaring a state of emergency due to a wildfire, but can also be used to make public policy, such as when Governor Brown in January 2018 ordered the creation of more zero-emission vehicle charging stations and worked to get more zero-emission vehicles on California's roads.[7]

Commander in Chief

The governor is the commander in chief of the California National Guard. This role is of little significance until times of civil disorder or natural disaster, when the governor has the power to call out the guard, though not to direct its actions. In April 2018, in response to an order from President Donald Trump that National Guard troops be sent to control the U.S.–Mexico border, Governor Jerry Brown ordered the mobilization of 400 members of the California National Guard to fight transnational criminal gangs, human traffickers, and illegal firearm and drug smugglers, but declined to order them to aid in enforcing federal immigration law.[8]

Organizing and Managing the Executive Branch

The governor is empowered to organize and manage the executive branch. *Organize* means that he or she can make a number of administrative appointments. *Manage* means that many of these appointees must report to the governor, at least indirectly, and the governor can remove them from office. Again, the limits of this power should be recognized.

First, the functions of the state government are not boundless. Much of the money that it collects is passed on to local government and school districts to spend.

Second, the rest of the elected executive branch, most notably the attorney general, limits the governor's actions, and some state employees report to these elected officials—over 4,500 report to the attorney general alone.

Third, some of the appointments made by the governor are to boards that can, and do, act independently of the governor. These appointments may be for fixed terms. The best known of these independent boards is the Regents of the University of California. This 26-member board consists of 7 ex officio members (members, including the governor, who sit on the board because they occupy another office), one student, and 18 members appointed by the governor for 12-year terms—terms that are longer than the governor's. Control over this board, if the governor wishes to exert it, is possible only through new appointments, the loyalty of previously appointed members, persuasion (including threats to cut the budget), and, in extreme cases, working with the legislature to restructure the body.

Fourth, the governor must make appointments to agencies about which he or she knows little, often appointing individuals about whom he knows little. Information coming out of these agencies is limited; hence, the governor is often in the dark about what is happening until something goes terribly wrong and it appears in the press.

The controversy over Caltrans' management of the rebuilding of the eastern span of the Bay Bridge mentioned earlier provides a case in point. In 2006, Caltrans, perhaps the most visible of California's government agencies, hired a Chinese company with limited bridge-building experience to build key elements of the new span. According to the *Sacramento Bee*, numerous flaws and cost overruns followed, leading to questions of whether the bridge will meet its planned 150-year lifespan. The governor's public stance was that "stuff happens" (or words to that effect), but his administration initiated investigations, legislative and external, into the entire operation and culture of Caltrans. Were it not for aggressive reporting on the issue by California newspapers in the north of the state, the governor might never have acted to address long-standing issues within Caltrans.[9]

Intense public scrutiny over actions (or inactions) by the California Public Utilities Commission (CPUC) also led to a flurry of activity by the governor and the legislature (the governor appoints all five members of the CPUC). The handling of the Aliso Canyon (Porter Ranch) gas leak, the San Bruno gas pipeline explosion, and the closure of the San Onofre nuclear power plant with public utility customers picking up most of the cost were all major scandals. In the latter case, the chair of the CPUC—a former Edison president—had an ex parte (secret) meeting with top Edison executives in Warsaw during which a settlement favorable to the utility was discussed. Subsequently, Edison donated $25 million to a program at UCLA favored by the chair. This meeting remained secret until the state Justice Department raided the chair's home on another matter.

In September 2016, Governor Brown signed a set of five reform bills aimed at increasing transparency and accountability at the CPUC. Commissioners must now disclose and report ex parte communications with utility executives and other interested parties in rate-setting cases. The new laws also required more information to be made publicly available, established the position of safety advocate, and authorized the attorney general's office to bring enforcement actions in Superior Court against commission employees who violate ex parte rules.[10]

Also, ex parte meetings between developers and members of the California Coastal Commission (the governor shares appointments to the 12-member board with the legislature) and the firing of its well-regarded executive director by more development friendly commissioners drew intense public scrutiny that led to proposed—but as of yet unsuccessful—legislation that would limit such meetings.[11] The issue remains alive in the courts and media. Not only will the governor and the legislature ultimately have to deal with the ex parte issue, it will also be a factor in future appointments to the commission.

Budget

Perhaps the governor's most significant power is that of preparing the budget, coupled with the power to exercise a line-item veto of budget provisions. At the federal level, the president presents Congress with a budget proposal—but it is only a proposal; the House of Representatives has constitutional authority over fiscal matters. The California Constitution gives the power of preparing the budget to the governor. This means that all budget requests from executive branch agencies must pass through the governor. It is at this point that the governor has life-or-death power over a program and can have a critical impact on the policy that a program implements. The actual work on this process of preparing the budget is done by the Department of Finance.

The budget is prepared and sent to the legislature by January 10, with revisions following later in the spring (called the May Revise) as the financial picture becomes clearer. The governor then lobbies for his or her budget, negotiating with members of the legislature as they make final changes. Until the 2011–12 budget, a supermajority of two-thirds was required to approve a budget, and impasses and late budgets were common while marginal votes were rounded up. Now only a simple majority in both houses of the legislature is needed, and budgets come in on time.

Although a supermajority vote is no longer needed to pass a budget, it is still required to raise new revenues. Because budgets may not have adequate revenues, in the absence of a supermajority the support of the minority party can be important, requiring expensive trade-offs with recalcitrant legislators who withhold their support until they receive an offer they cannot refuse. There are, in effect, five major players in the budget game: the governor and the leaders of both parties in both houses of the legislature. Because of his or her role at both ends of the budgetary process, and because one person needs to broker the deal, the governor usually has the key role. But even the governor can be held hostage by stubborn legislators. Although in recent years Republican legislators have been adamant in opposing any and all tax increases, the passage of the tax-raising Proposition 30 along with the improving economy has marginalized their influence. While neither the Republican Schwarzenegger nor the Democrat Brown were able to persuade the two parties to work together to shape revenue legislation, the Democratic majorities in the legislature make bipartisan cooperation largely unnecessary at present. Proposition 30 expired in 2018, but an extension on the 2016 ballot (Proposition 55) successfully extended the tax provisions for 12 years.

Veto and Line-Item Veto

The second most significant power of the governor is the **veto**. Just as in Congress, all bills passed by the legislature can be vetoed by the governor. The legislature passes about 1,000 bills each year, and since 1967 the governor has vetoed 13 percent of them on average. Veto rates vary considerably, however; Governor Schwarzenegger holds the record for the highest veto rate—over 35 percent in 2008—while Governor Brown holds the record for the lowest veto rate—less than 2 percent in 1982, a record he attributed to his behind-the-scenes work to change or kill proposals he doesn't like.[12] The veto can be overridden by a two-thirds majority of each house of the legislature, but that has happened only seven times since 1946 (and four of those were against Jerry Brown in the 1970s). The most recent veto override attempt was on a 2012 bill that would have permitted local governments to take over the management of some state parks to keep them open during the fiscal crisis.

Equally important, and unlike the president, the governor has a line-item veto, which permits him or her to reduce or delete any appropriation in a spending bill. Consequently, legislators cannot force the governor to accept funding for a program that he or she does not like by burying it inside a large spending bill that the governor must sign. The governor cannot add items, but the ability to reduce or eliminate the favorite programs of legislators is a powerful tool. It is a key item in the governor's box of bargaining tools, and one that no other player has (although it is impossible to tell how often governors use it).

In recent years line-item vetoes have been minor, often correcting technical errors. However, they have also been used to kill programs that the governor feels are unnecessary or ineffective, such as Brown's 2011 veto of funding for the California Postsecondary Education Commission, a body that provided policy advice to the governor on the three branches of higher education. In the state budget for 2014–15, Governor Brown used the line-item veto only 10 times for cuts totaling $37.9 million (out of a budget of $156 billion).[13] Large majorities in the legislative houses that support the governor make the line-item veto less necessary, and in 2016, for the first time in over three decades, the line-item veto was not used.

Legislative Powers

Much of the governor's success depends on having the ability to persuade the legislature to go along with specific programs. This is a difficult task because legislators owe little to the governor, who does not help elect them. Legislators represent smaller and different constituencies and often look out for local rather than statewide issues. They are on different career paths with different time constraints. Because they are term limited, they are relatively inexperienced in bargaining and do not have a long-term commitment to the Sacramento governing process. Their next jobs may be in the private sector, perhaps as lobbyists. If so, they may be more interested in pleasing potential employers (special interests) than in cooperating with the governor.

The governor's ability to persuade legislators depends on political skill as well as on many factors beyond his or her control, including the partisan makeup of the legislature and the political and economic environment. Although much of this influence depends on informal and other formal powers, the governor does have several specific powers that are directed primarily toward influencing the legislature. These include preparing the budget, vetoing bills or provisions of bills, and making legislative recommendations.

Rather than twisting arms to get legislators to support his programs, Governor Brown was in the enviable—and nearly unique—position of having to persuade the Democratic legislature not to overreach and antagonize the electorate by passing too much legislation, spending too much money, or attempting to raise taxes.[14] However on some issues, especially the complex one of climate control, he did at times run into resistance from a group of moderate or business-friendly—some say petroleum-friendly—Democrats, especially in the Assembly. In 2015 they were able to gut his climate control bill, which would have reduced oil use by 50 percent by the year 2030; but in 2016 through astute politicking, the governor and the Democratic leadership made a successful comeback, persuading 17 Assembly members to change their votes (some agreed to the change only when the outcome was not in doubt) from the previous year.[15] As *Los Angeles Times* columnist George Skelton has pointed out, "Dominant Democrats in Sacramento hang together more often than not. . . ."[16] Still, this group is an emerging third force in the legislature.

Legislative Recommendations

At the beginning of a legislative session, as required by the constitution, the governor presents a State of the State address to the legislature. This speech may be short or long, general or specific. It is normally not covered in detail by the media, unlike the president's State of the Union address. Whether or not the State of the State address contains the governor's legislative program, most governors have such a program, which addresses the state's problems as they see them and which they hope to get passed through the legislature.

The governor cannot introduce legislation but has allies who will introduce specific proposals. As the most prominent political figure in the state, the governor is in a position to press for action on these proposals. Success once again depends on a variety of factors, including political skills. Because of his star power, Governor Schwarzenegger had greater access to the public through the media and, more than most governors, could bring outside pressure to bear on the legislature through public appearances. But Schwarzenegger's governorship is widely considered to have been filled with wasted opportunities, partly because of his support for ill-advised initiatives. Jerry Brown preferred to work on the inside, using his significant personal political skills. But he too needed public support for tax increases, and his successful public appearances to lobby for Proposition 30 may have had more impact simply because previously they had been so rare. Former state librarian Kevin Starr feels that the governor's reputation is enhanced by "everything he chooses not to say"—by staying, for the most part, out of the press.[17]

Judicial Powers

The governor has the power to grant pardons and commute or shorten sentences for state crimes. He or she can also reverse parole decisions or delay a death sentence. While these are significant powers, governors tend to use them with extreme care and caution, because appearing "soft on crime" can have serious political consequences. Among other judicial powers of the governor is the power to nominate justices to the Supreme Court and appellate courts, as well as the power to appoint other judges if positions are opened by retirement or resignation.

Public Roles of the Governor

While the governor's role as head of state does not provide as much access to the public as the president enjoys, the governor still is occasionally seen cutting a ribbon, bestowing an honor upon some citizen, leading an international trade delegation or, most often, signing a bill into law. These and other ceremonial and symbolic appearances may have little policy content, but they keep the governor in the public eye. Because of his—and the state's—longtime leadership on global warming, Jerry Brown received notable attention in Paris when he attended the important 2015 UN Conference on Climate Control.

While far less visible than the president, governors do not underestimate these appearances, which remind people that the governor is on the job and cares about their concerns, and that, in case of a disaster, the governor and the resources of the state will be available.

Occasionally issues arise of such overwhelming importance—the budget crises are prime examples—that the media are willing to give the governor significant air time. On other occasions the governor can stage policy-related events such as showing up at a school to emphasize his or her education policies (or to mask opposition to certain education policies). Finally, disasters such as earthquakes, droughts, and fires require the governor to be publicly active, and during these crises the media will broadcast every statement he or she makes.

The governor also moves into the public spotlight during elections, and not only when campaigning for re-election. California governors often think they have a chance to become president, in that governors of far less populous or attention-getting states have been elected. However, only one governor of the state, Ronald Reagan, has successfully moved on to the presidency. Nevertheless, when governors sense a chance for the presidency they try to get into the national media as much as possible. Jerry Brown ran for president twice during his first two terms in office (and once afterward), to the detriment of his performance as governor. Speculation that Gavin Newsom has his eyes on the presidency has circulated for years, leading him to vow during the 2018 campaign that he would not run for president in 2020 or 2024, having learned from Brown's mistakes.

Governors also campaign for political allies, including candidates for president or loyal legislators, although their influence in the latter cases is probably marginal at best. Additionally, they may take an active role in an initiative or referendum campaign, either to bolster the chances of an initiative that they support or to gain more public attention. In spite of his mixed success in this arena, Governor Schwarzenegger continued to be involved right through the elections of 2010, endorsing the successful Proposition 14 in June of that year and leading the successful effort in November to defeat Proposition 23, which would have suspended an air pollution control law (AB (Assembly Bill) 32). Governor Brown's campaign for Proposition 30, which greatly enhanced his political reputation and helped put the state on a firmer financial footing, provides a critically important recent example. In 2014 Governor Brown also campaigned vigorously and successfully for Proposition 1, the water bond, and Proposition 2, the Rainy Day Budget Stabilization Fund Act. In 2016 Brown campaigned successfully against Proposition 53, which would require a public vote on public works projects of over $2 billion before bonds could be issued. This would make some of Brown's projects—especially the Delta tunnels—difficult to implement. The governor's extensive fundraising appearances may also receive public attention, which is useful because it shows the opposition that the governor has a formidable war chest and convinces the party faithful that the governor is out there stumping on their behalf.

Gavin Newsom as Governor

Gavin Newsom was elected governor in November 2018, easily defeating his Republican Challenger John Cox. The true battle was earlier that year, in June 2018, when Newsom and Cox were chosen in the state's unique Top Two Vote Getter (TTVG) system to continue to the November election. Polls taken before the June primary suggested that two Democrats might instead be the finalists, as was the case for many other elected offices that year. In fact, Newsom faced criticism in the primary season for his campaign advertisements, which seemed to encourage turnout in favor of Cox and to the detriment of challenger Antonio Villaraigosa—former mayor of Los Angeles, and who would likely have presented a tougher head-on challenge in the November run-off.

Newsom began his political career in 1997, when he was appointed to fill a vacancy on the San Francisco Board of Supervisors. After winning several re-election campaigns, he successfully ran for Mayor of San Francisco in 2003. Just a month into his term in 2004, he rose to national prominence when he directed the city-county clerk to begin issuing marriage licenses to same-sex couples, in violation of state law. While those marriages were later annulled by the California Supreme Court, the move cemented his popularity in the city.

In early 2009 he launched a run for governor of California but consistently lagged behind front-runner Jerry Brown. He dropped out later that year and instead filed paperwork to run for Lieutenant Governor, winning that election in November 2010 and re-election in 2014. In 2017 Newsom again launched a gubernatorial bid (as Jerry Brown would now be termed out of office). This time he was a consistent favorite in the polls; he won the multicandidate June primary with a comfortable 33.8 percent of the vote (John Cox won 26.2 percent), and in November he won the general election with 61.6 percent of the vote to Cox's 38.4 percent.

As Lieutenant Governor, Newsom served under his predecessor, Jerry Brown. Jerry Brown was the son of Pat Brown, one of California's most popular governors, who in the 1960s helped develop the education system and infrastructure that made California the envy of the nation. In 1974, seven years after his father left office, Jerry Brown was elected governor for two consecutive terms.

During his first term as governor, in the 1970s, Brown was given the nickname "Governor Moonbeam," a moniker reflecting his youth, idealism, and eccentricity. His advocacy of fiscal restraints (which reflected his personal lifestyle) did not go over well in a state that still remembered his father, who had presided over an era of seemingly unlimited promise.

After his first two terms of office ended in 1983, Brown, still in his early 40s, was adrift. During the next 16 years he studied Buddhism, ran for president (again), and chaired the California Democratic Party. In 1999 he reestablished his career as an elected official by starting at the local level as mayor of the economically troubled city of Oakland (1999–2007), and he held the position of attorney general from 2007 to 2011. In the 2010 governor's race, voters had the opportunity to select between Brown, an experienced if unpredictable Democratic politician, and Meg Whitman, a billionaire Republican internet entrepreneur. The voters chose political experience over business acumen. Whitman had little political experience but a lot of money, and her self-financed campaign (see Chapter 4) was the most expensive in California history. Brown spent far less and won by emphasizing his political experience and ability to work with the opposition Republicans.

Jerry Brown's predecessor in office, Arnold Schwarzenegger, was elected in the October 2003 recall of Governor Gray Davis. Davis was recalled partly because of the state's inadequate response to a manipulated energy crisis, legislative budgetary stalemates, fund-raising scandals, and his own remoteness. Hoping for change, the voters turned to the inexperienced but flamboyant movie actor who stood out in a weak field of possible replacements.

Most of Schwarzenegger's years in office were characterized by extreme state budget deficits that the governor and legislature were unable to close on a long-term basis. There were annual standoffs lasting for months with Republicans unwilling to raise taxes and revenues under any circumstances (a two-thirds vote was needed for a budget or for tax increases). In the end, the Schwarzenegger governorship failed to resolve the crises in California politics. Schwarzenegger's failures as a political outsider likely contributed to the decision by California voters in 2010 to elect an experienced politician, Jerry Brown, rather than yet another outsider candidate.

The 2012 election resulted in the passage of the tax-raising Proposition 30 and in overwhelming Democratic majorities in both legislative houses. Along with an improved economy and the elimination of the supermajority vote requirement for passing a budget, these results set a far more positive tone for state politics. Overnight, gridlock became a thing of the past; rather than encouraging the legislature to act, Governor Brown had to caution Democrats about overreaching—advice they appeared to take to heart. Journalists who a few years before had viewed California as a disaster area began talking about Jerry Brown's "political reboot," "turnaround," and "revenge."[18]

But California's problems, especially its fiscal problems, have not disappeared. While Brown engineered a change from a $25 billion budget deficit when he took office to a $14.8 billion surplus projected for 2019–20, the Proposition 30 tax increase is temporary. Although Proposition 55 in 2016 extended the tax provisions for 12 years, substantial long-term debts remain, along with vexing issues concerning water, transportation, income inequality, climate change, and infrastructure deficiencies. Because the California Constitution still requires a two-thirds vote on tax measures, the minority party has a veto so long as the majority does not enjoy a supermajority; without the minority's support, approving the increased revenues needed for significant infrastructure repairs or creating an adequate and stable source of revenue will not happen. Moreover, there are times when a coalition of Republicans and moderate Democrats will thwart attempts to pass environmental legislation or to regulate businesses and developers, as they did in 2015 when, in response to heavy lobbying by oil companies, they killed a provision that would have reduced gasoline use by 50 percent by 2030. Governors also face ongoing battles with well-funded private industry. For example, in 2018, Governor Brown reluctantly agreed to a law banning new local taxes on sodas and sugary drinks for 12 years in order to get beverage industry backers to pull away from a proposed ballot initiative that would have made it harder for local governments to raise taxes of any kind.

See the "Who Are Californians?" feature on p. 177 for more information on how California's governorship compares to other states' governorships.

Structure of the Executive Branch

The executive branch of California has several significant divisions: the governor's personal staff; the appointed cabinet and other department heads; the other elected officials of the executive branch (the plural executive); the appointed boards and commissions; and the more than 500,000 state employees (including those in state universities), who are divided into more than 85 agencies and 30 educational institutions. Not all of these agencies and employees are under the control of the governor. Figure 6.1 provides a graphic representation of the executive branch.

Personal Staff

Closest to the governor is the personal staff. The members of this staff include schedulers, speechwriters, and press officers. In addition, some staff members oversee the appointment process and the general development of policy, and act as liaisons with the legislature. They structure the governor's day, develop statements for the press and the public, arrange relations with various groups, and set up appearances throughout the state. Members of this staff tend to be young and transient and are expendable. Their positions depend on staying in the governor's good graces.

Governor Brown, preferring a flatter administrative structure, did not appoint a chief of staff. His principal (unpaid) aide, with the title "special counsel," was his wife, Anne Gust Brown, a former lawyer with Gap, Inc. She was credited with having strong political and personal skills and with softening many of the rough edges that Brown demonstrated during his first stint as governor in the 1970s. She was even suggested as a possible successor to Governor Brown.[19]

The Cabinet and Agency Heads

The governor uses the cabinet as he or she sees fit. It has no official policy function as a body but can be used to help formulate policy. The cabinet is often more

FIGURE 6.1 ● Executive Branch of the California State Government

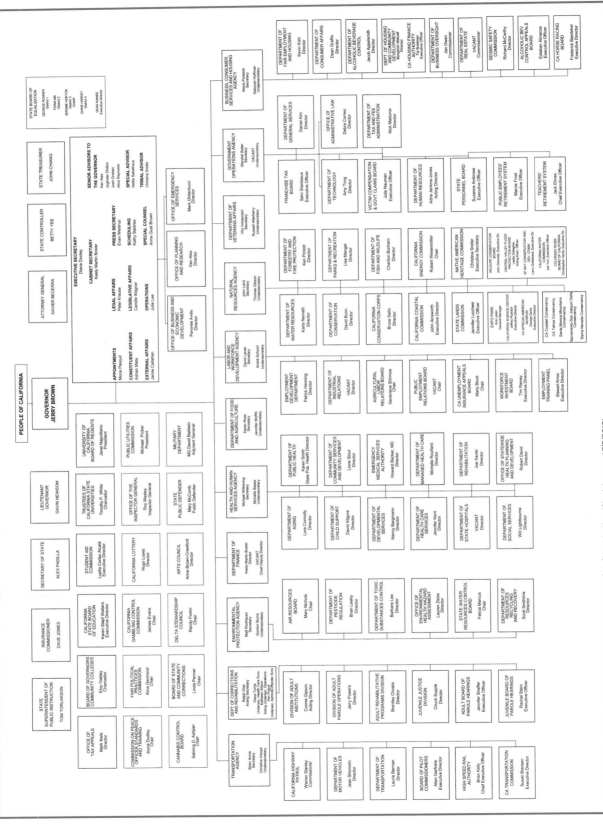

SOURCE: California Online Directory, https://cold.govops.ca.gov/File/OrganizationalChart (accessed 7/5/2018).

How Does California's Governorship Compare?

The powers of the governorship vary considerably from state to state. In California, governors can serve a total of two four-year terms. They have full budget-making power as well as the power to veto line items in appropriations bills. How do the powers of California's governor compare to the powers of governorships in other states?

	Can serve unlimited terms	Budget making power	Line-item veto?
AK		✓	✓ (light)
AL		✓*	✓
AR		✓ (light)	✓ (light)
AZ		✓*	✓ (light)
▶ CA		✓*	✓ (light)
CO		✓ (light)	✓ (light)
CT	✓	✓ (light)	✓
DE		✓*	✓
FL		✓ (light)	✓ (light)
GA		✓	✓ (light)
HI		✓ (light)	✓ (light)
IA	✓	✓ (light)	✓ (light)
ID	✓	✓ (light)	✓
IL	✓	✓ (light)	✓
IN		✓	✓ (light)
KS		✓	✓ (light)
KY		✓*	✓ (light)
LA		✓ (light)	✓ (light)
MA	✓	✓	✓
MD		✓	✓
ME		✓ (light)	✓ (light)
MI		✓	✓ (light)
MN	✓	✓ (light)	✓ (light)
MO		✓*	✓ (light)
MS		✓ (light)	✓ (light)

	Can serve unlimited terms	Budget making power	Line-item veto?
MT		✓	✓ (light)
NC		✓ (light)	✓ (light)
ND	✓	✓	✓ (light)
NE		✓ (light)	✓ (light)
NH	✓	✓*	✓ (light)
NJ		✓*	✓ (light)
NM		✓	✓ (light)
NV		✓	✓ (light)
NY	✓	✓ (light)	✓
OH		✓	✓ (light)
OK		✓ (light)	✓ (light)
OR		✓ (light)	✓ (light)
PA		✓	✓ (light)
RI		✓ (light)	✓ (light)
SC		✓ (light)	✓ (light)
SD		✓	✓ (light)
TN		✓ (light)	✓ (light)
TX	✓	✓ (light)	✓ (light)
UT	✓	✓ (light)	✓ (light)
VA		✓	✓ (light)
VT	✓	✓	✓ (light)
WA	✓	✓	✓
WI	✓	✓*	✓ (light)
WV		✓	✓ (light)
WY		✓ (light)	✓ (light)

Key

Can serve unlimited terms
✓ Yes

Budget making power
✓ Full   ✓ Shared

Line-item veto?
✓ Yes   ✓ Appropriations bills only

*Governor proposes budget; legislature amends; governor then signs or vetoes.

SOURCE: The Council of State Governments, http://knowledgecenter.csg.org/kc/content/book-states-2017-chapter-4-state-executive-branch (Accessed 10/22/18).

forcriticalanalysis

1. What are the advantages or disadvantages of having term limits? What effect might a term limit have on a governor's actions?

2. What are the advantages or disadvantages of having a governor with full versus shared budget-making power? What about the ability to veto line items?

a symbolic body than an integral structure of governing. The executive branch is divided into seven superagencies, and the heads of these agencies, called secretaries, are generally in the cabinet. These are State and Consumer Services; Youth and Adult Corrections; Environmental Protection; Health and Human Services; Labor and Workforce Development; Business, Transportation, and Housing; and Resources. These superagencies contain most of the executive branch's agencies. It is the individual agencies, not the umbrella superagencies, that carry out functions, and they may act independently of the superagency secretaries. The governor appoints these agency heads, although he or she often does not have a free choice. Someone with expertise in the area needs to be appointed, and sometimes the qualifications are spelled out in law. These agencies and superagencies are called *line agencies*, the term used to describe organizations that have their own statutory authority to carry out functions and provide services.

In addition, the governor has several staff advisory agencies, including the Department of Finance, the Office of Planning and Research, and the Department of Personnel Administration. Perhaps the most important of these is the Department of Finance, which prepares the governor's budget.

The Plural Elected Executive

One of the most notable features of California government is the number of statewide *elected* administrative offices. There are seven of these positions, plus the Board of Equalization, which oversees the administration of property, sales, and excise taxes (see Box 6.2). This means there are eight elected independent bases of power that do not report to the governor or need to adhere to gubernatorial wishes. This differs from other states that have a single elected leader who appoints lesser state executives. While California government's distribution of power may limit the governor's freedom to make or implement policy, most of these elected positions do not deal with substantial policy issues. The attorney general is usually the governor's only real policy competitor. A vacancy in most of the plural executive offices, such as the attorney general, is filled by the governor, subject to the approval within 90 days of both houses of the legislature.

Let's take a closer look at each of these seven elected administrative offices.

THE LIEUTENANT GOVERNOR The lieutenant governor sits on many of California's regulatory commissions and executive agencies, and takes up the role of acting governor if the sitting governor dies, resigns, or is otherwise unable to fulfill the duties of the office or is out of the state. Since he or she is occasionally from a different party, this provides occasions for great mischief. In 1979, while Governor Jerry Brown was traveling, lieutenant governor Mike Card signed bills, issued vetoes and executive actions, and even created commissions and made judicial appointments, leading to a battle in the state Supreme Court over the limit of those powers.[20]

The lieutenant governor can also preside over the Senate, breaking tie votes. Perhaps more than others, this position captures the imagination of those who would restructure government, either by eliminating the office or by linking the election of the lieutenant governor to that of the governor, as is the case in other states, such as Illinois. The lieutenant governor serves on several important boards, including the governing boards of both the University of California and the California State

BOX 6.2 ● The Plural Executive

In addition to the selected duties listed below, all these officeholders sit ex officio on various state boards.

Governor: Organizes the executive branch, prepares the budget and legislation, signs or vetoes bills.

Lieutenant Governor: Replaces the governor if he or she is out of the state, incapacitated, or leaves office for any reason.

Attorney General: Enforces laws, oversees and assists district attorneys.

Secretary of State: Holds elections and oversees the records and archives of the state.

Treasurer: Manages state money, including investments and bond sales.

Insurance Commissioner: Regulates insurance companies.

Controller: Monitors collection of taxes, provides fiscal controls for receipts and payments.

Superintendent of Public Instruction: Administers the state role in public education, sits on the state board of education.

Board of Equalization: Oversees the assessment and administration of property taxes, the collection and distribution of sales taxes, and the collection of excise taxes. The controller is a member of this body.

University system, and the State Lands Commission. The current lieutenant governor, first elected in 2018, is Democrat Eleni Kounalakis. Kounalakis is the first woman to be elected to the position in California history. In 2009–2010, Mona Pasquil served briefly as acting Lieutenant Governor when John Garamendi was elected to the U.S. House of Representatives. Prior to her candidacy, Kounalakis worked in her family's housing development firm and as U.S. ambassador to Hungary under President Barack Obama.

THE ATTORNEY GENERAL The attorney general (AG) oversees the Department of Justice, which employs more than 4,500 people and is responsible for ensuring that the laws are enforced. The attorney general is free to determine which areas and which issues will receive the most attention and resources and has oversight responsibilities for local district attorneys and county sheriffs. The AG is legal counsel to the state and defends the state in lawsuits. There is no obligation to cooperate with the governor, and the AG is often viewed as a rival. In 2004 Governor Schwarzenegger ordered the attorney general to intercede with the state supreme court to stop gay marriages in San Francisco. The governor had no statutory basis for giving such an order, and although the attorney general ultimately followed the order, it was done on the AG's own authority. This office is very powerful, second only to the governor of California, and incumbents often see themselves as leading candidates for governor. Although few have successfully made this transition, Jerry Brown used this office to launch his successful campaign for governor in 2010. The attorney general's office is able to set its own agenda, which may run counter to the governor's agenda. It can also use its substantial powers to counter or even embarrass the governor.

The most recently elected attorney general is Xavier Becerra (appointed in 2017 and re-elected in 2018). He is the first Latino attorney general, the child of immigrants from Mexico. Prior to serving as attorney general, Becerra served in the U.S. House of Representatives from 1993 to 2017, representing downtown Los Angeles. Becerra grabbed headlines in 2017 and 2018 with a series of 44 lawsuits filed against the Trump administration, including legal action involving environmental protection, health care, reproductive rights, education, transgender military troops, immigration, and the 2020 U.S. Census. Becerra's predecessor, Kamala Harris, first elected in 2010, was the state's first female African American state attorney general, as well as the nation's first Asian American state attorney general. Harris was elected to the U.S. Senate in 2016.

THE SECRETARY OF STATE The secretary of state is the chief elections officer, responsible for maintaining a database of registered voters, for overseeing all federal and state elections in the state, and for disclosure of campaign and lobbyist financial information. The secretary of state is also responsible for corporate filings

In 2018, Alex Padilla was re-elected as secretary of state. His campaign focused on his accomplishments during his first term, which included increasing voter registration and turnout, as well as protecting voter rights.

and other filings related to businesses operating in the state, for registries including the Safe at Home confidential address program, and for safeguarding the state archives. The current secretary of state, Alex Padilla, was first elected in 2014 and re-elected in 2018. The son of Mexican immigrants, Padilla has served in public office since 1999, when at age 26 he was elected to the Los Angeles City Council.

THE CONTROLLER The controller is the chief fiscal officer of California, responsible for accountability and disbursement of the state's financial resources. The controller also safeguards many types of property until claimed by the rightful owners, independently audits government agencies that spend state funds, and administers the payroll system for state government employees and California State University employees. The controller serves on 70 boards and commissions with authority, ranging from state public land management to crime victim compensation, and is a member of numerous financing authorities and fiscal and financial oversight entities including the Franchise Tax Board and Board of Equalization. The current controller, Betty Yee, was first elected in 2014 and re-elected in 2018. She is the daughter of Chinese immigrants and is the first woman of color to hold the position. Prior to running for controller, Yee served on the Board of Equalization from 2004 to 2015.

THE TREASURER The treasurer manages the state's money after it comes in and before it is spent. He or she manages the investment of money and the sale of bonds. The current Treasurer, Fiona Ma, was elected in 2018. The child of Chinese immigrants, Ma won her first election in 2002, when she was elected to the San Francisco Board of Supervisors. She then served in the California State Assembly from 2006 to 2012 and on the Board of Equalization from 2015 to 2019.

THE SUPERINTENDENT OF PUBLIC INSTRUCTION The superintendent is the chief administrator of the Department of Education. Unlike the other elected statewide officers, the superintendent is elected on a nonpartisan basis. Education administration is a confusing policy area: the superintendent shares power with an appointed board of education. This arrangement ensures controversy and was even more confusing before Governor Brown eliminated the parallel position of the appointed secretary of education in 2011. The current superintendent, Afro-Latino Tony Thurmond, was first elected in 2018.

THE INSURANCE COMMISSIONER The insurance commissioner's office was made elective by Proposition 103 in 1988, making it the newest plural executive in the state. It is the only position of the plural executive created by an initiative. The commissioner regulates the insurance industry, and Proposition 103 passed because the public felt that the appointed commissioner was not doing his job. It is not clear that making this an elective post has improved matters, because most of the contributions to the campaigns for this position come from the insurance industry. The state's current insurance commissioner, Ricardo Lara, was first elected in 2018 and is the state's first openly gay statewide office holder.

In addition to these positions, voters elect by district four members to the Board of Equalization (BOE), which is chaired by the state controller. Created with the 1879 Constitution, the BOE is the only elected tax collection agency in the nation, and until 2017 was responsible for administering more than 30 tax and fee programs, and for hearing appeals to assessments and other tax decisions. In 2017 the agency came under fire for inappropriate behavior regarding tax assessment appeals and misallocation of funds. A set of legislative reforms signed by Governor Jerry Brown in June 2017 stripped the BOE of much of its power and moved it to two new unelected entities: the Department of Tax and Fee Administration (to handle most tax and fee programs) and the Office of Tax Appeals. Of the 4,800 BOE employees, 4,400 were transferred to the new organizations, leaving a much smaller BOE retaining only the few tax administration responsibilities originally given to it in the state constitution.

Agencies and the Bureaucracy

Most of the work of California state government is carried out by more than 200,000 state employees (not counting employees in higher education) housed in over 85 agencies. Most of these agencies are located within the seven superagencies, and most are invisible to the general public, which tends to sustain the impression that state government runs by itself. A few agencies, such as the California Highway Patrol and Caltrans, are well known if not well understood. Others, such as the Office of Small Business Development or the Department of Aging, rarely make it into the news or the public consciousness. Few Californians could name anyone in the executive branch up to and including department heads; few governors could name more than a handful. Many of these individuals are professional experts on policy subjects who are quietly doing their jobs.

Most California employees have civil service protection. Many are also represented by unions. A few of these unions, notably the CCPOA (discussed in Chapter 3), are very powerful and politically well connected to the point where the wishes and desires of the unions are more likely to become state policy than are, for instance, the wishes and desires of the governor, the head of the relevant administrative agency, or the administration of the department in which the employee works.

There are more than 325 state boards and commissions. Positions on these boards are mostly filled by the governor and subject to the approval of another body, most often a legislative body (some are appointed by the legislature; some are ex officio). These boards and commissions include the Air Resources Board, the Public Utilities Commission, the California Coastal Commission, and the Gambling Control Commission. Probably the most visible are the Board of Regents of the University of California and the Trustees of the California State University, which together are responsible for more than 100,000 employees. On the other hand, boards such as the Board of Chiropractic Examiners and the Apprenticeship Council are probably known only to those with a direct interest in that area. Most members of these boards and commissions serve for fixed terms, some as long as 12 years, and, once appointed, do not have to respond to the governor's wishes.

The California bureaucracy does not enjoy a particularly positive reputation with the public, in part in response to various news stories revealing unethical and illegal behavior by various state employees. For example, a 2009 internal investigation found that Stockton Caltrans employees were operating a porn-exchange ring using government computers. Recent reports from the state auditor have documented other misconduct by state employees, including misuse of state vehicles, unauthorized disclosure of confidential information, and wrongly received excess pay and leave time. In 2015 the auditor shared details about a Caltrans engineer who played dozens of rounds of golf during work hours.[21] There is also concern over looming retirement costs for state employees. The California Public Employees' Retirement System (CalPERS) and the California State Teachers' Retirement System (CalSTRS) do not have enough funds to pay for the retirement benefits they have promised. Increasing spending on public employee pensions and medical benefits over the next few years is expected to put enormous pressure on city budgets, requiring either increased taxes, reduced services, or negotiated changes to existing compensation packages.

California Executive Branch: Where Are We Now?

In recent years several tentative steps have been taken toward tackling the biggest long-term structural problems facing the state and providing the governor with a greater capacity to lead. First, Proposition 25 removed the two-thirds vote requirement to pass a budget. Although this loses some of its force because revenues cannot be similarly raised, its impact has been greater than expected. Even in the absence of a supermajority in the legislature, Governor Brown was able to largely ignore Republican legislators and work out legislative deals with the more accommodating Democrats. (This may come back to haunt the Democrats if someday the Republicans should control all parts of the state government and have the ability to cut programs at will.)

Second, Proposition 11, approved in November 2008, took the power to draw the state legislative districts away from the legislature and gave it to a citizens' commission. This commission created new districts that have a closer partisan balance and that initially pitted some incumbents of the same party against one another. The hope was to gain a legislature that was willing to cooperate and compromise both internally and with the governor. The result of Proposition 11 was different than expected, however: the overwhelming Democratic majorities that resulted made cooperation and compromise between parties largely unnecessary.

Along similar lines, Proposition 14, approved in June 2010, created a system of preliminary and final elections for the party primary (see Chapter 4). Again, the ambition was to create a less partisan legislature. As a result of these two measures, the reduced number of Republicans appear to be no less conservative than before, but the policies of the heavily Democratic legislature have not been as extreme as some feared. Even during the supermajority period following the 2012 election, for instance, there was no push to raise taxes, as might have been expected. Five years later, however, Democrats used their majorities to pass a significant increase to state gasoline taxes. The bill, approved in April 2017, passed without any Republican support in the state Assembly and with only one Republican yes vote in the state Senate. The gas tax went on to survive an attempted repeal by statewide initiative on the November 2018 ballot, which voters rejected by a 55–45 percent margin. The Democrats are held in check in part by having to work with a moderate governor who would veto extreme bills, as well as by some Democrats who were elected from marginal districts or who are backed by big business money and who are more likely to share some values with Republicans. While these changes have resulted, unfortunately, in a marginalized minority party, they have also given rise to an executive (and legislative) branch that is more effective, productive, and popular with the electorate.

However, nothing has been done to fix the distortions caused by Proposition 13 (the 1978 proposition that limited property tax increases) and the series of other initiatives that have locked in certain parts of the budget and have made it close to impossible to create a stable and adequate revenue stream for the state. California's revenues are far more volatile than those of other states, and Californians' willingness to govern by initiative remains undaunted. Given this situation, it is difficult to see how the state's revenue problems will be solved in the near future. And while the government seems to be functioning smoothly at the moment, there are many unfunded needs in the state—infrastructure, the homeless, and the costs of education, among others—that are not being addressed.

Study Guide

FOR FURTHER READING

Cain, Bruce E., and Roger G. Noll, eds. *Constitutional Reform in California: Making State Government More Effective and Responsive.* Berkeley: Institute of Governmental Studies Press, 1995.

California Performance Review. *Prescription for Change, Report of the California Performance Review.* Vols. I–IV. California Performance Review, 2004. https://www.ucop.edu/acadinit/mastplan/cpr/Commission_Perspective.pdf. Accessed 8/31/18.

Gerston, Larry N., and Terry Christensen. *Recall! California's Political Earthquake.* Armonk, NY: M. E. Sharpe, 2004.

Lubenow, Gerald C., ed. *Governing California: Politics, Government, and Public Policy in the Golden State.* 2nd ed. Berkeley: Institute of Governmental Studies Press, University of California, 2006.

Mathews, Joe. *The People's Machine: Arnold Schwarzenegger and the Rise of Blockbuster Democracy.* New York: Public Affairs Press, 2006.

Schrag, Peter. *California: America's High-Stakes Experiment.* Berkeley: University of California Press, 2006.

———. *Paradise Lost: California's Experience, America's Future.* New York: New Press, 1998.

Simmons, Charlene Wear. *To Faithfully Execute the Law: California Executive Branch Agencies 1959–2003.* Sacramento: California Research Bureau, California State Library, 2004.

ON THE WEB

Around The Capitol. www.aroundthecapitol.com. Accessed 8/25/16. Includes a daily blog, *The Nooner*.

California Choices. www.californiachoices.org. Accessed 8/25/16.

California Department of Finance. www.dof.ca.gov. Accessed 8/25/16.

California State Library. www.library.ca.gov. Accessed 8/25/16.

CALmatters. https://calmatters.org. Accessed 8/25/16.

Governor of California. www.gov.ca.gov/home.php. Accessed 8/25/16. The official site of the Office of the Governor, where you can find background information and up-to-date news and even send an email to the governor.

Public Policy Institute of California. www.ppic.org. Accessed 8/25/16.

Rough & Tumble. www.rtumble.com. Accessed 8/25/16. A daily summary of California news.

University of California, Berkeley, Institute of Governmental Studies Library. http://igs.berkeley.edu/library. Accessed 8/25/16.

SUMMARY

I. The office of the governor is modeled on that of the U.S. president, but there are significant differences between the two offices, mostly having to do with visibility.

II. Each job has two analytical roles.
   A. Head of state, which is largely ceremonial, symbolizing the unity of the state or country. In this role, the governor or president makes public appearances doing activities that bring people together. The president, in this role, is on TV almost every evening. The governor has less opportunity to play this role, and even when he does, the state TV stations seem uninterested.
   B. Head of government, which involves making policy and trying to get it passed by the legislature and implemented by the executive branch. This role is partisan and divisive. It is also an almost invisible role, especially on the implementation side.

III. The formal powers of the office are greater for the governor than for the president.
   A. The governor's formal powers include making appointments and organizing the executive branch; conducting independent executive actions that are permitted by law; being commander in chief; proposing the budget; making legislative recommendations; and exercising the veto, including the line-item veto.
   B. The governor has powers similar to those of the president in domestic policy but also can use the line-item veto, which gives the governor more control over the political process of constructing the budget.
   C. California has an initiative process that a popular governor can use to pressure the legislature into action.

IV. The governor's public roles as head of state include cutting ribbons, signing bills, and leading the response to natural disasters. Non–head-of-state public roles include campaigning and fund-raising as well as advocating for initiatives.

V. Like the presidency, the office of governor is one of limited powers, which are restricted by the legislature, the judiciary, the plural elected executive, and the permanent executive branch.

VI. The structure of the state government includes the following:
   A. The governor's personal staff.
   B. The governor's cabinet, which includes the heads of major departments (superagencies).
   C. The plural elected executive, which includes the lieutenant governor, the attorney general, the secretary of state, the controller, the treasurer, the superintendent of public education, the insurance commissioner, and the State Board of Equalization.
   D. The 85 or more agencies that comprise the major departments.
   E. More than 325 boards and commissions, including the Public Utilities Commission and the Regents of the University of California.

VII. California employs the equivalent of more than 300,000 full-time employees to staff the government, including more than 100,000 in higher education, who are not under the direct control of the governor.

PRACTICE QUIZ

1. Which of the following is *not* part of the plural executive?
   a) the chancellor of the California State University
   b) the secretary of state
   c) the attorney general
   d) the controller

2. Which of these powers does the governor have that the president does *not* have?
   a) legislative veto
   b) line-item veto
   c) power to appoint the secretary of state
   d) power to appoint judges

3. Which of the following activities of the governor would be considered part of his or her role as head of government?
   a) proposing a budget
   b) vetoing legislation
   c) proposing new air quality standards
   d) all of the above

4. Which of the following groups of employees are under administrative control and report ultimately to the governor?
   a) legislative aides
   b) supreme court clerks
   c) highway patrol
   d) professors at California State University, Fullerton

5. How many state boards and commissions are there?
   a) fewer than 50
   b) between 50 and 150
   c) between 150 and 300
   d) more than 300

6. The California governor is "invisible" under normal conditions for all of the following reasons *except*:
   a) California's governors appear in events where they are visible to the public, but for the most part there is little public interest in those events.
   b) For almost every recent governor, there has been little media interest in Sacramento.
   c) The governor splits his or her power with other state executives, who are also trying to attract the media.
   d) The governor's star power is only of interest to those who like superhero movies.

7. The governor manages the executive branch, but this power is limited by all of the following *except*:
   a) There are many appointees of the governor, many of whom belong to agencies the governor doesn't know much about.
   b) Some of California government is outside the governor's power to supervise, such as the University of California and California State University.

c) The boards and commissions whose members the governor appoints are mostly, except in extreme cases, outside of his or her power.

d) The attorney general must approve appointments to many boards and commissions, and that appointment approval is difficult for the governor to obtain.

8. The line-item veto allows the governor to adjust any appropriations item up or down, including reducing it to zero.
   a) true
   b) false

9. All of the following are true of the governor's appointments to the cabinet *except*:
   a) Most cabinet appointments are routine, usually given to the governor's political supporters and campaign contributors.

b) The cabinet as a whole has no official policy function, unless the governor wants to give it a role.

c) Some cabinet and subcabinet positions require an appointment of someone with qualifications that are spelled out in law.

d) The superagency heads are usually considered part of the governor's cabinet.

10. The job of the lieutenant governor, one columnist wrote not entirely in jest, consists of getting up in the morning, checking that the governor is still alive, and then making arrangements for lunch!
   a) This statement is probably true.
   b) This statement is probably false.

CRITICAL-THINKING QUESTIONS

1. Is the state government too large?
2. Does the plural elected executive contribute to effective or efficient government?
3. What is the value of having independent boards such as the Regents of the University of California that employ large numbers of people?

4. Which is more important for governing: the formal or informal powers of the governor? Think about this question in terms of "necessary" versus "sufficient" powers.

KEY TERMS

boards and commissions (p. 166)
cabinet (p. 167)
formal powers (p. 164)
head of government (p. 163)

head of state (p. 163)
informal powers (p. 165)
line-item veto (p. 165)
personal staff (p. 166)

superagencies (p. 167)
veto (p. 170)

7 The California Judiciary

WHAT THE CALIFORNIA JUDICIARY DOES AND WHY IT MATTERS

State courts are an integral and necessary component of state government. They ensure that a state's citizenry is guaranteed due process of law and that the other branches and levels of government within the state uphold state statutes, codes, and the provisions in the state constitution. Therefore, judges play a much larger role than simply punishing criminals or imposing fines on a polluting company. Courts make decisions that are often political and sometimes controversial, with the potential to affect more individuals than just those directly involved in the cases. Court rulings can have far-reaching consequences that not only ignite political debate but that also have an iterative effect. This is especially true in California, a state that witnesses a high rate of litigation and where politics can be very contentious. And while some cases that come before the California courts gain a significant amount of statewide and national media attention, many cases that remain under the radar still have an impact on citizens' daily lives.

California court decisions on immigration policy, for example, have the potential to influence national debates on immigration reform and are particularly salient in a state with a high population of undocumented immigrants. Questions of state policy regarding undocumented immigrants who entered the United States as children were tested in the case of Sergio Garcia, who came with his family to California only months after his first birthday. Garcia and his family moved back to Mexico when he was nine years old, but they returned to the United States eight years later, in 1994. This time, Garcia's father attained lawful permanent resident status for himself and filed a petition seeking the same for his family. But, because of limits on the number of visas distributed each year, Garcia graduated from high school, college, and law school while still undocumented. After obtaining his law degree, Mr. Garcia passed the California Bar Examination and applied for admission to the bar, at which point his undocumented status came under scrutiny from the Committee of Bar Examiners. The committee asked the California Supreme Court to determine whether state law or public policy banned Garcia's admittance. The court ruled that it did not, and it held that the intent of the legislature and the governor clearly indicated that Garcia's status should not be an impediment to his application. Garcia's case effectively illustrates the complexity of contemporary immigration issues in the United States. It also serves as a good example of what it means to be an undocumented person versus a person with legal immigration status.

Immigration and immigrants are very important to California. Immigration is a political topic that receives considerable media attention. It is also a political topic that often gets vetted through the courts. Recently, and as discussed in Chapter 4, California has become actively involved in a number of lawsuits challenging the federal government and President Trump's administration's policies. The *Los Angeles Times* reported on July 22, 2018, that "California has sued the Trump administration 38 times."[1] While these cases involve a range of policy issues, it is very important to note that immigration is a key area of conflict between California and the current administration. The state is at odds with federal positions on undocumented children and seeks to continue to protect them. California sought a preliminary injunction (an injunction is a court order telling an official to either stop or start doing a specific act) to prevent undocumented children from being deported.

The California case regarding these children centers on family separation/reunification policies, which have been well-documented in the media in 2018. A federal judge in San Diego had earlier ruled that the separation policy was invalid. The state has also been at odds with the Trump administration's position on sanctuary cities. On July 5, 2018, a federal judge ruled that the Trump administration could not compel local government officials to enforce immigration policies. The judge did state, however, that California could not prohibit private employers from working with immigration agents.[2] Another controversy included a suit against the Trump administration's plan to build a wall on the U.S.-Mexico border. In a lawsuit, California Attorney General Xavier Becerra challenged the construction of the wall, claiming that it violated California environmental protection laws. The state, however, lost.

It is important to note that these immigration issues, though they involve the state, are federal controversies that have been decided by federal courts or are pending in federal courts. They are significant illustrations of federalism and how a state and the national government can use the courts when their policy preferences conflict. We will focus primarily on California state courts for the remainder of this chapter, including a discussion of how California courts and federalism are involved in the case of medical marijuana.

Organizers of this Los Angeles rally in 2017 called for an immediate stop to the Immigration and Customs Enforcement (ICE) raids, demonstrating how the policies of the Trump administration have been at odds with California's values. California has used the courts during these conflicts.

Structure of the California Judicial System

To understand the role that courts play in California politics, consider the following: from 2015 through 2016, approximately 6,200,000 cases were filed in California **superior courts** (trial courts of general jurisdiction).[3] Of these, almost 80 percent were criminal in nature (crimes against the state or society; for instance, failing to pay state taxes or stealing a car), and the remaining 20 percent were civil cases (disputes between individuals). Each one of these 6.2 million cases had to be handled individually in one way or another by the appropriate state court until it was resolved. To put this into context, let's consider the number of people living in the state. According to the U.S. Census Bureau, as of July 2018 California's population was estimated at almost 40 million (39.78 million), which puts the case-to-person ratio at 1 to 6. While this is obviously a very significant statistic, it is worth noting that the California court system actually witnessed a 9 percent decline in case filings from the previous two years.

To adjudicate both criminal cases and civil cases, the state's courts comprise three levels: superior courts (trial courts), California Courts of Appeal, and the California Supreme Court.

The Lower Courts

Superior courts adjudicate cases that involve violations of state and local criminal and civil law. These are the trial courts of California. We often refer to these courts as "courts of first instance" because this is the first time that a case is heard in a court of law. When cases come before the superior courts, a jury or judge reviews the facts of the case and determines guilt or innocence in a criminal proceeding. If it is a civil case, the jury or judge determines which side presents the best case and awards damages accordingly. There are 58 state trial courts (one in each county), with approximately 2,000 judicial officers presiding. This number includes judges, commissioners, and referees. The superior courts are the busiest courts of the state court system.

The California Courts of Appeal are intermediate courts with **appellate jurisdiction**; those who lose their cases at the superior court can appeal first to the California Courts of Appeal. The purpose of this intermediate appellate court is to review the trial or the superior court records for error. The California Courts of Appeal are divided into six districts across the state. Ninety-seven justices preside over these courts, and the judges sit on three-judge panels to review cases.[4]

The Supreme Court

The California Supreme Court is the highest court in the state. Like the California Courts of Appeal, it is an appellate court that reviews decisions for reversible error, submitted by losing parties in the lower courts. When a party to a case is unhappy with the ruling of the California Courts of Appeal, the next step is to appeal to the California Supreme Court. In California, the supreme court has what is known as **judicial discretion**. Discretion allows the justices on the state supreme court to decide which cases they wish to review. Therefore, appeals filed with the California Supreme Court are not automatically reviewed. This is the only court in California with discretionary authority. Discretion is valuable because it provides the high court with a tool to moderate its workload. However, this discretion is not absolute: all death-penalty sentences are automatically appealed and go directly to the California Supreme Court for review (see Figure 7.1). The supreme court

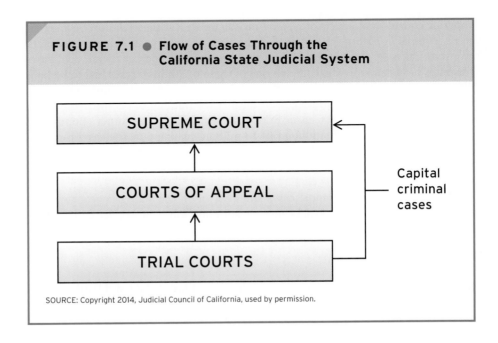

FIGURE 7.1 ● **Flow of Cases Through the California State Judicial System**

SUPREME COURT

COURTS OF APPEAL

TRIAL COURTS

Capital criminal cases

SOURCE: Copyright 2014, Judicial Council of California, used by permission.

Tani Gorre Cantil-Sakauye, chief justice, appointed by Governor Arnold
 Schwarzenegger in 2010
Ming W. Chin, appointed by Governor Pete Wilson in 1996
Carol A. Corrigan, appointed by Governor Arnold Schwarzenegger in 2005
Goodwin H. Liu, appointed by Governor Edmund G. Brown in 2011
Mariano-Florentino Cuéllar, appointed by Governor Edmund G. Brown in 2014
Leondra R. Kruger, appointed by Governor Edmund G. Brown in 2014

is also required to hear disciplinary cases involving judges or attorneys. The court includes one chief justice and six associate justices (see Table 7.1). Currently, the court has one seat vacant. Kathryn Werdegar retired from the bench in 2017. Governor Brown did not announce an appointment to fill her seat. Judges from other courts have been filling in to help with the workload. Four out of the seven justices must agree in order for a party to win the case.

While the supreme court may seem remote, it often makes decisions that have an impact on Californians' daily lives. For example, on July 26, 2018, the California Supreme Court announced its ruling in *Troester v. Starbucks*. The issue in this case centered on whether or not employers were obligated to pay employees for work they performed off the clock. In a unanimous ruling, the California Supreme Court stated that "California labor law 'contemplates that employees will be paid for all work performed.'"[5] While the opinion of the court stressed that employers were not required to pay employees for off the clock work that was performed from time to time, they did determine that if employees regularly performed work off the clock, they were to be compensated. Why is this decision so important? First, because people should be paid for their work. Consider how many people live and work in the state who are paid hourly wages, then think about how ten minutes or more each day could add up in wages over a week or month. Second, it's important because of what the California Supreme Court did: a *state* court of last resort set a precedent that other states may follow. Finally, the decision is important because it demonstrates that state courts can offer more protections than the federal government or United States Supreme Court may require. Over sixty years ago the United States Supreme Court ruled that employers were not required to pay employees wages if employees had to work a few minutes off the clock. States could, however, decide to compel employers to pay for time worked off the clock if they chose.[6] As those of us who teach law and courts often tell our students, "The United States Supreme Court sets the floor, and states set the ceiling." In this instance, the state of California has raised the ceiling.

When individual citizens or groups of citizens believe that private entities or government has trampled on state law or on their civil liberties or civil rights, they turn to the courts. The judges serving on California's courts must decide if the state's laws or the rights of Californians have been violated.

Jurisdiction

Both criminal and **civil courts** in California are limited as to the cases and controversies they handle because of jurisdiction. Jurisdiction refers to the kind of law handled by a court. For example, there are criminal courts that deal with violations of state and local laws, and there are civil courts that hear cases involving disputes between individuals or classes of individuals. Civil courts may rule on cases involving breach of contract, tort liability, and wrongful-death suits, to name a few. Jurisdiction also refers to geographic boundaries. There are 58 superior court divisions in California, with at least one superior court in each county. Cases are assigned to these courts depending on where the parties in civil suits reside or where alleged crimes have been committed in criminal cases.

It is easier for an individual to go to criminal court (just drive over the speed limit and get caught) than to civil court. Civil courts have rules about the types of cases they can hear. In civil disputes, parties must also have what is known as "standing to sue." To bring a case to court, an individual must suffer personal and real injury. Typically, an individual cannot sue on behalf of someone else. As well as requiring standing to sue, California courts, like the federal courts, will not handle collusive suits. Collusive suits are lawsuits in which both parties want a similar or the same outcome. Our legal system is an adversarial one, in which it is presumed that parties want opposite outcomes, and when one party wins, the other loses.

Both civil and criminal courts have rules that guide how they proceed. Civil cases are typically classified by the dollar amounts that plaintiffs (the party or parties initiating the case) are seeking. In California, a plaintiff who is not represented by an attorney and is seeking a dollar amount of $10,000 or less is filing a "small claim" and goes to small claims court. Cases in which plaintiffs are seeking more than $10,000 but no more than $25,000 are called "limited civil filings." Finally, cases in which plaintiffs are seeking more than $25,000 in damages are called "unlimited civil cases." In 2015–16 almost 50 percent of the civil actions filed were limited civil cases (individuals suing other individuals for more than $10,000 but less than $25,000).

Criminal cases are also divided into different classifications: felonies, misdemeanors, and infractions. Felonies are serious crimes. The punishment if a person is convicted of a felony is incarceration in state prison or, if it is a capital offense, the death penalty. Examples of felonies in California include murder, rape, burglary, and robbery. Misdemeanors are far less serious crimes, and the punishment for committing a misdemeanor ranges from county jail time (up to one year) and/or a fine. Prosecutors do have discretion in this state to charge people who may have been arrested for committing a misdemeanor with a felony. Cases where prosecutors may choose to do this are called "wobblers," and they typically involve something like the use of a weapon during the act of committing the misdemeanor offense. Finally, we have infractions. Infractions are typically offenses that come with citations or tickets. Traffic violations are a form of infraction. Other infractions in California include possession of less than one ounce of marijuana and fishing without a license. Here too, prosecutors can use their discretion to raise an infraction to a misdemeanor. An example of an infraction "wobbler" would be if a person had a number of other outstanding traffic violations or a record of other criminal activity at the time they received their ticket. Infractions constitute an overwhelming amount of the California criminal court system's workload. For example, in 2015–16, 80 percent of criminal cases were infractions. By contrast, misdemeanors accounted for 17 percent, while felonies only made up 4 percent of criminal court filings.[7]

Access to the Court

The California Constitution and its statutes provide rights to the people of California regarding access to the courts. For example, Californians have:

- the right to sue for money owed and for other relief,
- the right to defend oneself against a lawsuit,
- the right to be presumed innocent if charged with a crime,
- the right to defend oneself against all criminal charges,
- the right to a public and speedy trial by jury if charged with a misdemeanor or a felony, and
- the right to an attorney at public expense if one is charged with a felony or misdemeanor and cannot afford an attorney.

These rights apply to citizens and noncitizens of the state alike. However, they do not mitigate concerns about quality of legal representation for indigent persons. The lack of resources in some local court jurisdictions, especially in smaller localities, and the impact of the current budget crisis on the state's judiciary as a whole will affect access to the courts.

Federalism and the California Courts: The Case of Medical Marijuana

The California court system must occasionally negotiate discrepancies between federal law and state law in a particular policy area. For example, California's laws permitting medicinal marijuana use are at odds with federal laws that classify marijuana as a controlled substance. In 1996, through use of the initiative, voters in California approved Proposition 215, the Compassionate Use Act (CUA). This act provides for the medical use of marijuana for seriously ill persons. It requires that a physician recommend that a patient's health would benefit from using marijuana to alleviate symptoms of serious illness. In addition, the act also shields patients and their caregivers from criminal prosecution for cultivating or possessing marijuana for use approved under the act.

More recently, voters approved Proposition 64, the California Marijuana Legalization Initiative, which allows persons 21 years or older to use and grow marijuana for personal use. The sale and taxation of marijuana went into effect in January 2018. The passing of Proposition 64 expanded the legalization of marijuana and may lead to future conflict between the federal government and the state. The Department of Justice under the Trump administration has made statements that it would revert to enforcing federal law involving the regulation of controlled substances, including enforcing it in states that permit medical and recreational use of marijuana. As you read below the accounts of the conflict over this controversial issue, think about the significance of Proposition 64 with respect to growing one's own marijuana and the facts and ruling in the U.S. Supreme Court case, *Gonzales v. Raich*.

Confusion ensued shortly after the CUA was implemented. First, there were many (successful) attempts at expanding the scope of the law. And second, the state law came directly into conflict with federal law, which makes the cultivation, possession, sale, and consumption of marijuana illegal.

Seven years after the CUA was passed, Governor Gray Davis signed Senate Bill 420, the Medical Marijuana Program Act (MMPA), into law. The MMPA was designed to flesh out the parameters of the CUA. Among other things, the MMPA sought to create collective cooperatives in the state where marijuana could be cultivated and sold to qualified patients and caregivers. The cooperatives would be regulated by state and local agencies, and the patients and caregivers would be issued identification cards that would help law enforcement more easily determine whether persons were covered by the CUA and, therefore, not subject to criminal prosecution under state law. The MMPA also allows for persons who can be classified as cooperatives, caregivers, or patients to raise a defense if they are charged with violating state laws involving the cultivation, possession, sale, or consumption of medical marijuana.

The MMPA had immediate implications regarding federalism. Although both the CUA and the MMPA are technically "good law" (meaning they are still current and enforceable), the national government has made various attempts to exercise preemption—a practice in which the government claims to have authority over a particular policy area when it comes to legislation, thus preempting state and local regulations. In 2005, for example, the U.S. Supreme Court reviewed the case *Gonzales v. Raich*. At issue was whether Congress's power to regulate the manufacture and possession of marijuana under the Controlled Substances Act (21 U.S.C. § 801) allowed the national government to preempt California's laws governing the medicinal use of marijuana. The Supreme Court ruled in a 6–3 decision that the Commerce Power gives Congress the authority to regulate and to punish the manufacture and cultivation of marijuana despite California law allowing for compassionate use. The dissenting Supreme Court justices argued that to preempt these laws was a violation of federalism and that, because the issue involved purely local or *intrastate*, rather than interstate, commerce, the state law should prevail.

Since this ruling in 2005, many local California governments have seized the opportunity to create new zoning ordinances to limit the expansion of marijuana dispensaries. In fact, one tactic commonly used by local governments to close down dispensaries involves calling the U.S. attorney's office. The U.S. attorney has the authority to order these shops to discontinue their operations under the threat of having their property forfeited or seized, as well as other criminal sanctions under federal law.

Despite the U.S. Supreme Court's ruling in *Gonzales v. Raich*, California courts have continued to try medical marijuana cases according to state law. For example, a 2009 case, *People v. Colvin*, involved a co-owner (William Frank Colvin) of two nonprofit medical marijuana dispensaries: Holistic I (in Santa Monica) and Holistic 2 (in Hollywood). The dispensaries are registered with the city of Los Angeles and have been incorporated for several years. In addition, they are often reviewed by local law enforcement to ensure that they meet the requirements and restrictions of the MMPA. Like other similar dispensaries, and in compliance with the MMPA, Holistic 1 and Holistic 2 grow some of their marijuana on-site but also belong to a cooperative that includes growers in Los Angeles and Humboldt. In March 2009, Colvin was less than a block from Holistic 2 en route to Holistic 1. He was stopped by police, taken into custody, and charged with violating state laws for possession of cocaine, sale or transportation of marijuana, and possession of marijuana. He was carrying an identification card for medicinal use and showed it to the arresting officer at the time. He also presented evidence to the trial court that he was registered to run the Holistic dispensaries.

The trial court judge agreed that Colvin's dispensaries seemed to be in compliance with both the CUA and the MMPA, which are still California law despite the *Raich* decision. Colvin's attorneys argued that he was only transporting the marijuana (one pound) from one dispensary to another. However, the trial court judge disagreed and ruled that the MMPA did not cover the transportation of marijuana. Colvin was found guilty of all three charges, placed on probation, and given community service. Colvin appealed this conviction, and the court of appeal determined that the transportation of marijuana from one dispensary to another fell within the scope of the MMPA, reversing the trial court's decision with respect to two of Colvin's convictions (transportation and possession; the cocaine conviction was not appealed).

However, both parties to a case have the right to appeal, and the state appealed the decision of the court of appeal. The California Supreme Court had to determine whether it would take the case and rule on its merits or if it would choose not to hear the case and allow the court of appeal decision to stand (remain in effect). In May 2012 the California Supreme Court denied review, noting that medicinal marijuana remains an issue that has important implications for local, state, and federal law. It also cited the many cases dealing with this policy issue that continue to be filed in the courts. This is an interesting case study in the principle of federalism, particularly in those circumstances in which state and national law clearly conflict over a very controversial issue.[8]

In January 2014 the U.S. Court of Appeals for the Ninth Circuit disposed of a number of cases involving medical marijuana use. In their "unpublished" memorandum, the court wrote that states have no special protection from federal law when it comes to use, including medicinal, of marijuana.[9] One month later, the Ninth Circuit disposed of the case *Sacramento Nonprofit Collective v. Holder*. Here, the plaintiffs argued that because nine western states permit the use of marijuana for medicinal purposes, it should be recognized as a fundamental right. The court chose to dismiss the case in favor of the federal government. In fact, it dismissed with prejudice: the plaintiffs in this legal action are prohibited from ever bringing the case back to the court.

In a federal system, like ours, what may seem to be the end of a story isn't necessarily so. In October 2015, Governor Brown signed the California Medical Marijuana Regulation Safety Act (MMRSA) into law. This new law puts into place several state regulations of medical marijuana that had not existed in the past. Various state and local level agencies are given oversight authority with respect to the cultivation of medical marijuana, the operations of dispensaries, and the licensing and practices of prescribing physicians.[10] Given all of the state and federal court cases involving this issue, it might seem as if California were picking a fight with the federal government. This is not the case. In December 2014, Congress passed the "Consolidated and Further Continuing Appropriations Act of 2015," which includes Section 538 that basically prohibits the U.S. Department of Justice from spending any funds to interfere with California's laws regarding medical marijuana, including cultivation, dispensing, and possession.[11]

Judicial Selection

California's court system is the largest in the nation. Serving on the bench requires (1) qualifications and (2) having been selected to serve. The qualifications for

The members of the California State Supreme Court are (from left to right) Mariano-Florentino Cuéllar, Kathryn M. Werdegar (retired August 2017), Carol A. Corrigan, Chief Justice Tani Gorre Cantil-Sakauye, Goodwin H. Liu, Ming W. Chin, and Leondra R. Kruger.

judges are the same for all three court levels. In California, potential judges must have at least 10 years of experience practicing law in the state of California or service as a judge of a court of record.

The selection process for judges to serve on the California Supreme Court and California Courts of Appeal is the same. Judges are initially nominated by the governor to serve on the appellate bench and are then approved by the Commission on Judicial Appointments. The Commission on Judicial Appointments consists of the chief justice of the supreme court, the attorney general, and a presiding judge on the California Courts of Appeal. In addition, all nominees for California's appellate courts are reviewed by the State Bar of California's Commission on Judicial Nominees Evaluation. This body evaluates the nominees by conducting thorough background checks on their qualifications as judges and as citizens. The governor may use the commission's decision as a source of information when making his or her selections but is not bound by the commission's findings. After a judge's appointment is confirmed, the judge holds office until the next **retention election**. To remain on the appellate courts in California, judges must win their retention elections. These elections are noncompetitive; the voters are simply asked whether the judge should remain on the appellate bench. If a judge does not receive a majority of affirmative votes, he or she is removed and the governor will appoint a new judge.

Likewise, judges serving on California's superior courts must face their nonpartisan retention elections. However, their electoral process is different from the retention elections of sitting supreme court and courts of appeal judges. While appellate court judges run uncontested, simply against their own records, judges serving on California's superior courts can be challenged in their retention races. In addition, superior courts may have open seat races from time to time. These occur when a judge decides to retire close to an election. Finally, if an incumbent is up for retention and has no challengers, he or she may simply be declared re-elected; thus, no retention election is held.

Governors take advantage of opportunities to appoint judges to the courts by placing qualified jurists on the bench whose political beliefs most closely resemble their own. From time to time, a governor may be quite transparent about his or her preferences for those serving on the state supreme court. In the 1980s former governor George Deukmejian spoke out to the press and public about his desire to put more conservatives on the state supreme court because the liberals serving on the bench at the time were making decisions he vehemently disliked.

In addition, governors may have other political goals for the bench. They may, for example, seek to place more women and minorities on the supreme court so that it is more representative of the state's diverse population. Today's supreme court is diverse in regard to gender, race, and ethnicity; as of 2018 four of the justices are women, and five identify as persons of color or of more than one race. (See the "Who Are Californians?" feature on p. 198 for more on the diversity of California's justices.)

However, the court is not so diverse ideologically. Three of the six justices seated on the court were appointed by Republican governors. Generally, Republicans are more conservative than Democrats on issues of ideological preference, such as civil rights or civil liberties. For example, a liberal judge is more likely than a conservative judge to uphold laws that involve regulating business. This expectation, that ideology or party identification translates into differences in judicial decision making, is even more important when we consider issues such as same-sex marriage/LGBTQ rights, affirmative action, voting rights, freedom of expression, and capital punishment. Because the decisions of the California Supreme Court are binding on all persons residing in the state, the composition and dominating political ideology of the state's high court can be very important.

We may start to see some ideological shifts in the court. Since 2011, Governor Brown, a Democrat, has had the opportunity to appoint three justices, who will likely be more liberal than their predecessors. He has also demonstrated a commitment to diversifying the high court through his appointments. For example, in 2014 the governor announced his nomination of Mariano-Florentino Cuéllar to replace Justice Marvin R. Baxter, and the California Commission on Judicial Appointments unanimously confirmed the nomination. Cuéllar, who took office on January 5, 2015, is the first Latino immigrant appointed to the California Supreme Court.[12] Governor Brown has brought additional diversity to the bench by appointing an African American attorney, Leondra Kruger, who replaced Justice Joyce L. Kennard. Ms. Kruger was previously a deputy attorney general in President Obama's administration. Kruger is the first African American to hold a seat on the court since 2005.[13]

Judicial Elections

Unlike the federal judiciary, which consists of appointed judges who serve life terms with good behavior, many states, including California, have some form of election system for selecting their judges. Federal judges are appointed to allow for **judicial independence**. Theoretically, appointed judges are less likely to be influenced by politics in their decision making because they do not have to rely on the electorate to maintain their positions on the bench. Most states, however, have adopted some kind of election system for selecting or retaining their judges in order to secure **judicial accountability**. Elections allow voters to select members of the courts and to remove them for decisions contrary to the public's preferences.

Justices Corrigan and Kruger were on the November 6, 2018, ballot seeking retention. Both were re-elected. Justices Werdegar (retired), Liu, and Cuéllar faced elections in November 2014, and all successfully retained their seats on the bench. Over 70 percent of California voters supported Werdegar's retention, while Liu and Cuéllar received approximately 67 percent of all votes. Although the voters rarely pay much attention to competitive judicial races or retention elections, there have been instances when judges have lost their seats on the bench because of voters' perceptions about judicial rulings. For example, in the November 1986 election, six justices serving on the California Supreme Court were seeking retention. Governor George

Who Are California's Judges?

Since 2006, the Judicial Council of California has produced an annual report with information about the demographic characteristics of the state's justices and judges. Over time, increasing proportions of the judiciary have been women and people of color, although the proportions do not yet reflect the general population. The ethnoracial composition of the California bar (lawyers who are qualified to practice law in California) is heavily white, at 80.3 percent and just 5.9 percent Asian, 4.6 percent Latino, and 1.9 percent black; the bar is 40.6 percent female.

Justices and Judges in California, 2018

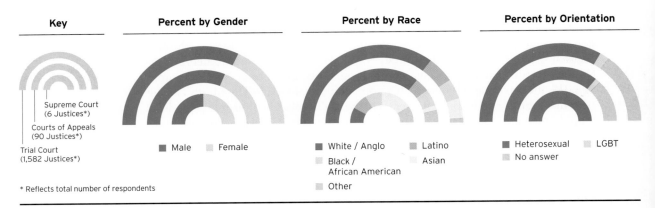

Key

Supreme Court
(6 Justices*)

Courts of Appeals
(90 Justices*)

Trial Court
(1,582 Justices*)

* Reflects total number of respondents

Percent by Gender

■ Male   ■ Female

Percent by Race

■ White / Anglo   ■ Latino
■ Black /   ■ Asian
  African American
■ Other

Percent by Orientation

■ Heterosexual   ■ LGBT
■ No answer

Gubernatorial Appointments, 1975–Present

■ Female
■ Latino
■ Black / African American
  Asian
■ Democratic governor

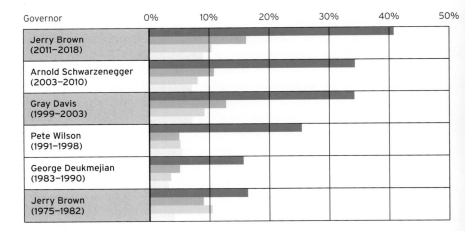

SOURCES: "Demographic Data Provided by Justices and Judges Relative to Gender, Race/Ethnicity, and Gender Identity/Sexual Orientation," As of December 31, 2017, http://www.courts.ca.gov/documents/2018-JO-Demographic-Data.pdf (accessed 7/30/2018); The State Bar of California, "2017 Demographic Survey," http://www.calbar.ca.gov/Portals/0/documents/reports/ORIA/Survey-2017.pdf (accessed 7/30/18); and "Governor Brown Releases 2017 Judicial Appointment Data," Office of Governor Edmund G. Brown Jr., https://www.gov.ca.gov/2018/03/01/governor-brown-releases-2017-judicial-appointment-data/ (accessed 7/30/18).

forcriticalanalysis

1. Is it important for the judiciary to reflect the diversity of the California population? Why or why not?

2. Besides gender, ethnicity, race, and sexual orientation/gender identity, what other dimensions of diversity are important to consider and why?

Deukmejian spoke out against the retention of three of the six judges for their rulings on death-penalty cases and was especially critical of Rose Bird, the chief justice of the California Supreme Court at the time. While she served on the court, Bird participated in 61 death-penalty cases and voted every time to vacate the death sentence—an especially notable choice during a time of widespread public support among Californians for the death penalty. In fact, her appointment as chief justice occurred the same year that the death penalty was reinstated by a legislative override of a gubernatorial veto. One year later (1978), an initiative was adopted that expanded the number of special circumstances allowed for death-penalty cases. While she had many supporters, her decision making went against the tide of moneyed interests and those supportive of capital punishment.[14]

Governor Deukmejian warned Bird and two associate justices, Cruz Reynoso and Joseph Grodin, that he would oppose their retention elections if they did not change their rulings in death-penalty appeals and uphold the death-penalty sentences. Numerous interest groups and political action committees joined the governor's campaign against Rose Bird and her two colleagues. Political advertisements against the retention of Bird, Grodin, and Reynoso aired on radio and television. In response, Chief Justice Rose Bird produced a television ad explaining her decision-making record. Her explanations did not satisfy voters, however, and on November 4, 1996, Bird, Grodin, and Reynoso lost their seats on the California Supreme Court. Shortly thereafter, Governor Deukmejian appointed three justices to replace them, including Malcolm Lucas, who was nicknamed "Maximum Malcolm" for his rulings that sentenced convicted criminals to the maximum penalties, including death.

Despite their low visibility, judicial elections have many political scientists and jurists concerned, particularly over the amount of money being spent by candidates in them. A 1995 study of contested elections in Los Angeles County Superior Court reported that campaign spending by trial court judges had risen a great deal in the years between 1976 and 1994. In 1976 the median cost of a judicial campaign for a Los Angeles County Superior Court seat was approximately $3,000. By 1994 the median had skyrocketed to $70,000. Meanwhile, incumbents running for re-election spent, on average, $20,000 more than the median challenger, or $90,000. Compare that to the $1,000 median campaign expenditure of an incumbent in 1976.

The Civil Justice Association of California (CJAC), a group of citizens, taxpayers, and professionals, reviewed campaign contributions to the California judiciary from 1997 to 2000 and found the following:

- From 1997 to 2000, contributions to candidates in contested superior court elections totaled over $3 million for four counties.

- In a single race in Sacramento County, over $1 million was raised.

- Attorneys are the largest contributors to most judicial races.

- Two supreme court justices seeking retention in 1998—in uncontested elections—received contributions of $887,000 and $710,000.

The escalation of campaign spending in judicial elections is controversial because it usually requires judicial candidates to seek funding support from outside sources. Like candidates seeking election to state legislative or executive offices, judges now receive and even solicit financial support from organized interests. This phenomenon has even spilled over into retention elections for the state supreme court, even though these elections are noncompetitive. Judges must solicit campaign contributions to retain their seats on the bench. Contributors often include trial lawyers associations and other special interests. This connection has raised concern: financial contributions by interest groups to a judge's campaign increase the potential for influence over judicial decision making. The original intent by lawmakers in instituting elections for judicial candidates was to ensure judicial accountability to voters, not to the narrow preferences of an organized interest group. This concern has mobilized a national movement for reform. One of the most active reform advocates is former associate justice of the U.S. Supreme Court Sandra Day O'Connor. Retired justice O'Connor has been a vocal critic of state judicial elections because of the amounts that judicial candidates are soliciting and spending and because of the public perception that money buys influence.

Most people consider the judiciary to be the least political of all branches of government, yet the increased spending in competitive and noncompetitive elections for judgeships compromises this assumption. Even judges are expressing concern. In 2001 an opinion survey, "Justice at Stake Campaign," revealed that 53 percent of California judges are dissatisfied with the current climate of judicial campaigning in the state. Over 80 percent of the judges surveyed believed that voters knew little about candidates for the bench and were electing judges based on criteria other than qualifications for office. The majority of judges polled agreed that reform of campaign financing for judicial elections is necessary and that public financing of these elections would be an appropriate alternative.

In response to stories in the media—including a series of articles published in the *Los Angeles Times*—and the concerns of the public, judges, public officials, and others, the Judicial Campaign Task Force for Impartial Courts was established in 2007. It consists of 14 members appointed by former California Supreme Court chief justice Ronald M. George, and it investigates several issues, including the structure of California judicial elections as well as the filing, reporting, and accessibility of judicial campaign contributions and spending. The findings of this commission to date were reported in a 408-page volume in December 2009.[15] Many problems with respect to judicial campaigns and elections were documented, most notably the amount of money spent by candidates for judicial elections and, ironically, the poor quality or low level of information disseminated by judicial candidates to the public. In 2012 the commission released an update on the implementation of these 2009 recommendations. The following reforms have so far been successfully implemented:

- Judicial candidates are prohibited from making statements that commit or appear to commit them with respect to cases, controversies, or issues that could come before the courts.

- Judicial candidates may not knowingly misrepresent certain facts, including the identity, qualifications, or present position of themselves or an opponent.

- Any contributions to or expenditures of $100 or more by judicial candidates must be itemized.

- Judicial candidates for superior court may file a candidate statement to be included in the voter's pamphlet. These statements are very expensive, however, and the cost is prohibitive for most candidates.

There is one further caveat that should be mentioned. Whenever limits or rules are placed on campaign spending, the rights of freedom of expression and freedom of association guaranteed by both the California and U.S. constitutions may be abridged. Campaigning for political office is guaranteed by the right to speak freely, and in today's political contests, it is becoming increasingly expensive. It is almost impossible to impose limits on campaign spending. Therefore, judges running for retention on the California Supreme Court or running to serve on the state's trial courts must exercise their own restraint—not an easy task if your opponent or opposing forces are spending a lot of money to keep you off the bench. Added to this are concerns about the impact of the U.S. Supreme Court's 2010 ruling in *Citizens United v. FEC*. This decision allowed corporations and unions substantial freedom to spend money during elections through "independent expenditures." As long as corporations and unions do not coordinate their campaign advertising expenditures with candidates, they can spend practically without limits. In a 2011 report, "Spending in Judicial Elections: State Trends in the Wake of *Citizens United*," researchers suggested that California judicial politics may not be as influenced by this ruling as judicial elections in other states. The authors noted that the unions and corporations were already influential in the state's campaigns and elections.[16] Retention elections for the high court are uncontested and, therefore, spending remains relatively low. Moreover, most vacancies on all other state courts, including trial, are filled by gubernatorial appointment. Finally, campaign spending in trial court races is likely suppressed (compared with other states) because judicial incumbents are automatically re-elected if they are unopposed.

Removing Judges from the Bench

As we have already discussed in this chapter, voters may remove judges from the bench during an election. In addition, there are other means for removing judges in the case of public concern regarding judicial misconduct or judicial competency:

- **Impeachment**   California's judges may be impeached by the Assembly and convicted by a two-thirds majority of the state Senate.

- **Recall election**   Like the governor, California judges are subject to recall election petitioned by voters.

- **Regulatory commission investigation**   The Commission on Judicial Performance may, after investigation of complaints regarding misconduct or incapacity, punish, censure, or remove a judge from office.

Contemporary Issues in the Judiciary

Change in the Court

The new justices appointed by Governor Brown influenced the court's patterns of decision making. The California Supreme Court had a conservative majority for a significant period of time, and Governor Brown appointed justices who are more liberal than their predecessors. This shifted the ideological direction of the state high court from a conservative majority to a liberal one.

Legislative Redistricting

Every term, judges serving on the California bench across all court levels (trial, intermediate appellate, and supreme) are confronted with cases that require them to make political decisions or decisions that have political consequences. One example of this is political redistricting. The redrawing of electoral districts is always a political process. Political parties seek either to maintain or to increase their odds of getting candidates re-elected through the redrawing of district lines. It is common for redistricting plans to end up contested in the courts by political parties, elected officials, candidates seeking political office, or organized special interests.

Since the 1980s the California courts have been involved in many cases and controversies regarding redistricting. Perhaps the most controversial occurred in 2005 when Governor Schwarzenegger and others proposed an initiative, Proposition 77, which would reform redistricting procedures in the state. Rather than having legislators redraw district lines after each census, the responsibility would be given to a panel of three retired judges (selected by legislative officials). This ballot measure was contested in the California Courts of Appeal before it even appeared on the ballot. Those opposed to the measure argued that judges should not have the power to redraw or create new political districts. Although there was some success with procedural challenges to the initiative in the courts of appeal, attempts to block the initiative from the ballot finally failed, and in November 2005 the voters vetoed the measure by a margin of approximately 19 percent, prohibiting retired judges from redrawing the state's electoral district lines.

Judicial Review and the Statewide Initiative

Another issue of concern regarding the judiciary in California is the relationship between direct democracy and judicial review. California is one of 26 states that allow citizens to propose and enact their own legislation through the initiative. Like any piece of legislation coming out of the state legislature, the initiative is subject to judicial interpretation and review. When the initiative is used to enact controversial policies—such as anti–affirmative action laws, a temporary tax to fund education, the decriminalization of marijuana, or term limits for elected officials—it is usually debated in the press and often contested in the courts. In fact, the constitutional validity of each of the initiatives mentioned above has been challenged in at least one court of law. The outcomes of these court cases have been varied. But most central to the controversy is the ability of state court judges, like judges on federal courts, to conduct judicial review. Judicial review is the power of a judge, on a state or federal court, to determine whether or not a law, agency policy, or some action of government is valid. When judges invalidate or overturn laws and policies they are often referred to as activists. We have already covered examples of judicial review in the beginning of this chapter when we briefly explored the legal battles between California and the Trump administration. We also witness judicial review in our discussion of California's policies on the use of marijuana. Judicial review and the statewide initiative puts this power in a starker contrast. When state judges have the power to overturn laws enacted by the people as well as laws composed by state legislators, the tension between lawmaking and law reviewing is heightened.

Is this tension all that important? Many scholars and many voters would argue that it is. In fact, the common opinion among the electorate in California is that the initiative as an alternative policy-making tool has become an exercise in futility, precisely because of legal intervention. The consensus among California voters is that once an initiative passes at the ballot box, it ends up in a court of law. In truth, courts are reactive bodies. Judges must wait until a case comes to their courtrooms to make a legal decision. So why do so many initiatives end up in the California courts? The answer is simply *politics*. California is a very diverse state, and our diversity can be measured in a number of ways. We are diverse in race and ethnicity, we are diverse in culture, we are diverse economically, we are even diverse in terrain and climate. Given so many dimensions of diversity, there is no dearth of conflict in our state regarding which political problems are important and which solutions to these problems should be adopted. Hence, California courts also function as an arena for the continuation of political debate.

For example, the United States Supreme Court's landmark ruling in *Obergefell v. Hodges* determined that the Fourteenth Amendment requires states to permit same-sex couples to obtain marriage licenses and to recognize the marriages of same-sex couples from other states. Although this case did not originate in California, the issue of same-sex marriage has been a subject of California politics for over a decade. It began in February 2004, when the county and city of San Francisco began to issue marriage licenses to same-sex couples. The following month, the California Supreme Court issued an injunction ordering San Francisco to stop issuing these licenses. Several pending cases regarding same-sex marriage were consolidated and some traveled through the courts separately. Groups organized in support of and in opposition to same-sex marriage as the cases percolated up to the California Supreme Court.

In May 2008 the California high court ruled in favor of gay and lesbian couples, finding that denying them the right to civil marriage violated the state constitution. Meanwhile, opponents to same-sex marriage drafted an initiative, "Prop. 8," which was adopted by 52 percent of the voters. Proposition 8 amended the California Constitution to exclude same-sex marriage. All of these events, which occurred over a relatively short period of time, were part of the broader national debate regarding rights of same-sex couples to legally marry.

Legal challenges to Proposition 8 were brought very quickly. A federal district court found Proposition 8 unconstitutional. There were subsequent appeals, and the case went all the way to the United States Supreme Court in *Hollingsworth v. Perry*. At issue was whether or not Proposition 8 violated the United States Constitution's Fourteenth Amendment rights to due process and equal protection. The Supreme Court did not decide these constitutional questions, however, because they determined that the petitioners, Hollingsworth and others, did not have standing and therefore couldn't bring this suit before the Court. The effect of the Supreme Court's ruling, even though it did not answer the questions on the merits, left lower-court decisions in place. Same-sex couples had the right to marry in California. Two years later this right was extended to gay and lesbian couples in all states in the *Obergefell* decision.

Caseload

While the caseload for all court levels in California has recently begun to decline after increasing over a period of several years, it remains very high when compared with other state court caseloads. And while the superior courts and appellate courts have managed this load fairly efficiently, there are legitimate concerns about the system's ability to continue to do so, given the state's continued fiscal crisis. As noted earlier, from 2015 to 2016 approximately 6.2 million cases were filed in California superior courts (trial courts of general jurisdiction).[17] There are many reasons for the high caseloads in the state court system. Following are a few examples: California, like many other states, has modified its laws to allow juveniles to be tried as adults in some criminal cases. Although the intent of this law may have been to let juveniles know that California has little tolerance for certain types of crime, regardless of the defendant's age, the effect has been to shift cases from the courts of judges who deal exclusively with juveniles to the already overburdened courts handling crimes involving adults. In addition, victims' rights legislation, which has elevated some misdemeanors (nonserious crimes) to felonies (serious crimes), increases not only the severity of the penalties for the accused but also the workload for the courts. California's three strikes law, originally enacted to punish repeat offenders, has had a similar impact. Keep in mind that these are just a few reasons for the high number of court cases in California.

To be sure, most of the cases filed in California's civil courts will be resolved through negotiation between the parties and their attorneys. For example, in 2015–16 almost 80 percent of unlimited jurisdiction civil cases were resolved without trial, while 92 percent of limited jurisdiction civil cases were disposed of before trial.[18] However, the courts must still process the paperwork and deal with the other administrative issues that each civil case may involve.

Similarly, most of the cases in the state's criminal courts will be resolved through plea bargaining, despite what we see in film or on television. Full court trials for the prosecution of high-profile crimes, like that of Conrad Murray, the personal physician found guilty in 2011 of involuntary manslaughter of his patient, singer Michael Jackson, are rare. A plea bargain is the norm. Even so, the courts are still involved in the process. Even if a criminal case never goes beyond the formal filing of charges against a defendant, judges are part of a plea bargain. As a referee, the judge's job is to determine if the plea bargain is appropriate and if the defendant entered into the plea bargain knowingly. If the judge decides that the terms of the plea bargain are inappropriate, that the defendant's ability to comprehend the terms of the plea was compromised, or that the plea was not entered into voluntarily, then a new plea may have to be negotiated, or the case may actually go to trial. Regardless, a single case in the criminal courts involves many people, from clerks to administrators and, of course, a judge.

Despite this incredible workload, California's criminal courts typically resolve cases involving felonies within 12 months (85 percent were resolved in 2015–16). Civil cases are also resolved fairly quickly; on average, 75 percent of civil cases filed in a given year are resolved within 12 months. Most recently, California superior courts reported disposing of 95 percent all civil cases within the 2015–16 fiscal year.

While these are impressive figures, problems remain. The lack of resources in some local court jurisdictions, especially in smaller localities, and the impact of the current budget crisis on the state's judiciary as a whole affect access to the courts and can compromise the quality of legal representation for indigent persons.

California Courts: Where Are We Now?

A number of issues currently confront California's courts. As discussed earlier, chief among these issues is the court system's ability to manage its caseload as the state continues to face a tenuous fiscal situation. Courts are subject to constraints similar to those that affect state agencies. It is fairly easy to argue that the greatest of these constraints, aside from jurisdiction, is the state's economy and budget. In recent years, the court system in California has found itself constrained by the extraordinary challenges of the state's budget. Chapter 8 discusses the budgetary process and its political implications in greater detail, but here we can examine the impact of this budgetary crisis on the courts.

Taken at face value, a discussion about budgets and courts may not appear all that interesting. However, when Governor Brown signed the budget on June 27, 2012, it included $6 billion of automatic cuts—hundreds of millions to the court system—severely affecting both day-to-day operations and future construction plans. It is important to note that these cuts come on top of other actions that have been taken to reduce the size of court administration throughout the state. Because most courts are located at the local level, counties and municipalities have taken the brunt of these budget cuts. Responses to the ramifications of these cuts have included threatened strikes by state court administrative personnel and the elimination of some innovative, albeit controversial, programs at the local level. One such program focuses on nonviolent misdemeanor crimes by juvenile offenders in the Los Angeles area. This program is part of a relatively recent legal movement known as "problem-solving justice," or the good courts movement. It served as an alternative to traditional, more punitive, forms of addressing juvenile low-level crime. The nontraditional court served more than 100,000 children each year, but it has been shut down by the county because of budget cuts.[19]

In addition, Chief Justice Tani Gorre Cantil-Sakauye has had to respond to some criticisms by organized interests and other parties about wasteful spending on projects and the growth of the state's Administrative Office of the Courts (AOC). The Alliance of California Judges, established in 2009, has been pressuring the chief justice and the judicial council to respond to past and present budget cuts more proactively and to pay closer attention to wasteful spending, predicting (accurately) that, like his predecessors, Governor Brown would include more cuts to the state courts' budgets in the new fiscal year. More specifically, this organization targeted the now defunct electronic Court Case Management System. According to the *Courthouse News Service*, "Even as trial courts were closing, the [Judicial] Council voted repeatedly, with only one or two dissenting votes, to continue pouring hundreds of millions into that now failed IT project. That money came primarily from trial court funds." The same article claims that over half a billion dollars was spent before the Court Management Case System was terminated.[20]

On top of this, Chief Justice Cantil-Sakauye released a report "prepared by a committee of state judges" in late May 2012 criticizing the AOC for understating the number of its employees and for paying "hundreds" of its personnel six-figure salaries. The report noted that this growth in both size and salaries paid was taking place during a hiring freeze. The investigation concluded, among other things, that the AOC had circumvented the hiring freeze and had violated some of its own personnel rules; it recommended significant cuts to the staff and organizational consolidation to allow for more oversight and, presumably, more efficiency.[21]

Additionally, reforming judicial campaigns in the state is also a critical agenda item. Some attempts at reform, such as campaign finance reporting, have been implemented and have not been found unconstitutional. However, when voters amended the state constitution in 1986 to prohibit political parties from endorsing judges who run in nonpartisan elections, the California Supreme Court found the initiative unconstitutional because it violated Californians' rights to freedom of expression and freedom of association. Obviously, judges have a lot of say when it comes to these reforms, and it is up to the individual judge to decide how much is too much when it comes to campaign spending.

Finally, there is the vacancy that remains on the court since Justice Werdegar's 2017 retirement. The court has been able to manage its workload by having judges from the lower appellate courts sit in. As of March 2018, 56 judges from California's intermediate courts of appeals served as "pro tem justices" (pro tem means temporarily) on the high court. Before leaving office Governor Brown did not announce an appointment to this vacant seat.[22]

Study Guide

FOR FURTHER READING

Bonneau, Chris W., and Damon Cann. "Campaign Spending, Diminishing Marginal Returns, and Campaign Finance Restrictions in Judicial Elections." *Journal of Politics* 73 (October 2011): 1267–80.

Bonneau, Chris W., and Melinda Gann Hall. *In Defense of Judicial Elections*. New York: Routledge Press, 2009. This book is a critique of previous empirical studies of judicial elections. Bonneau and Hall argue that elections as a selection method for judges are actually beneficial to democratic society.

California Courts. "Guide to California Courts." www.courtinfo.ca.gov/courts. Accessed 9/27/12.

Civil Justice Association of California. "Campaign Contributions to the California Judiciary 1997–2000." http://cjac.org/assets/finalrept2000.pdf. Accessed 8/16/12.

Hall, Melinda Gann, and Chris W. Bonneau. "Attack Advertising, the *White* Decision, and Voter Participation in State Supreme Court Elections." *Political Research Quarterly* 66 (March 2013): 115–26.

The National Center for State Courts (NCSC). www.judicialselection.us. Accessed 10/3/16.

Streb, Matthew J., ed. *Running for Judge: The Rising Political, Financial and Legal Stakes of Judicial Elections*. New York: New York University Press, 2007. This book is a collection of contemporary research conducted by professors who study state courts and judicial elections. Each chapter examines current issues and controversies that are confronted by state courts and state court judges.

Streb, Matthew J., and Brian Frederick. "When Money Can't Encourage Participation: Campaign Spending and Rolloff in Low-Visibility Judicial Elections." *Political Behavior* 33 (2011): 665–84.

ON THE WEB

California Courts. www.courts.ca.gov. Accessed 11/27/18. This is the official website of the California court system.

The California Supreme Court Historical Society (CSCHS). http://cschs.org. Accessed 11/27/18. CSCHS catalogs and archives information about the history of the California Supreme Court.

Institute for the Advancement of the American Legal System. http://iaals.du.edu/. Accessed 11/27/18.

The National Center for State Courts (NCSC). www.ncsc.org. Accessed 11/27/18. NCSC is an organization that provides services for court administrators, practitioners, and others interested in state courts. The website includes information, data sets, and articles about state courts and court-related topics.

SCOTUSblog (Supreme Court of the United States blog). www.scotusblog.com. Accessed 7/30/18. SCOTUSblog is a website that provides legal analysis of pending and decided cases of the United States Supreme Court. It also includes hyperlinks to case materials such as litigant briefs, amicus briefs, oral argument, and opinions.

SUMMARY

I. Structure of the California courts.
   A. Court rulings, such as the recent rulings on undocumented immigrants, can affect all Californians.
   B. Superior courts are the trial courts of the California court system. They are courts of "first instance" and triers of fact. The California Courts of Appeal are intermediate appellate courts. They are divided into six districts across the state. All cases except for death-penalty cases are first appealed to the California Courts of Appeal.
   C. The supreme court is the highest court in the state. It is composed of seven justices and, like the courts of appeal, is an appellate court—that is, it reviews cases that were first heard in lower state courts such as the courts of appeal or a superior court.
   D. Jurisdiction limits the types of cases that civil courts and criminal courts can hear. Criminal courts deal with violations of state and local laws, and civil courts hear cases involving disputes between individuals or classes of individuals.
   E. Access to California courts is widely available. However, there is concern about the cost of litigation and legal representation.
   F. Federalism and California courts.
      1. Legal challenges to Proposition 215, the Compassionate Use Act (CUA), illustrate the tension between state and federal government. California permits the use of medical marijuana under certain conditions, but the federal government does not. There have been frequent attempts by federal law enforcement to close marijuana dispensaries that are operating legally under the CUA.
      2. Some local governments are adopting ordinances to regulate or even prohibit dispensaries from operating in their communities. At times, local governments will call on federal law enforcement to assist them in closing dispensaries.
      3. The California courts currently have a number of cases across all levels examining this policy.

II. Judicial selection.
   A. Methods of selection for the California courts include nonpartisan elections for superior court and merit selection for appellate courts.
   B. The California courts are diverse in terms of gender, race, and ideology. Governor Brown has appointed three justices to the court: Goodwin Liu, Mariano-Florentino Cuéllar, and Leondra Kruger. These appointments may give him the opportunity to shape the decision making of the California Supreme Court for years to come.
   C. There are two competing theories regarding judicial selection—appointment and election. Those who favor judicial independence argue that appointment is a better method for selecting judges because it insulates judges from politics. Conversely, those who favor accountability argue that election as a method of selection is essential in a democracy and that judicial elections allow citizens to hold judges accountable for their decision making, similar to the way other elected officials are held accountable for their actions in office.
   D. Controversies about judicial campaigning and campaign finance have led to some high-profile jurists (for example, retired U.S. Supreme Court associate justice Sandra Day O'Connor) and others to call for reforms. The most radical reforms proposed would eliminate judicial elections entirely. The increasing cost of judicial campaigns, which are low-saliency and low-turnout elections, have many members of the bar and legal community concerned.
   E. Methods of removal from the bench include recall elections and impeachment. In addition, because all judges in California face some sort of election (direct or retention), voters may choose to vote for another judicial candidate or they may choose to vote against retaining an appellate court judge.

III. Contemporary issues in the judiciary.
   A. Governor Brown's appointments of Goodwin Liu, Mariano-Florentino Cuéllar, and Leondra Kruger to the bench has shaped and influenced the court's decision making.
   B. Justice Werdegar's seat on the bench remains vacant.
   C. Judges serving across all court levels are confronted with cases that require them to make political decisions and often exercise the power of judicial review.
   D. State judges have the power to overturn laws enacted by the people through the initiative as well as laws composed by state legislators. There is a very strong likelihood that contested initiatives will end up in the courts, and the courts serve as an arena for continued political debate.
   E. California courts have a very high caseload, though they remain fairly efficient and are able to dispose of a significant percentage of their criminal and civil caseload at all court levels.

PRACTICE QUIZ

1. All death-penalty sentences are automatically appealed directly to the California Supreme Court for review.
   a) true
   b) false

2. The California Supreme Court is similar to the U.S. Supreme Court in that it has nine justices.
   a) true
   b) false

3. Most civil cases in California are resolved before going to trial.
   a) true
   b) false

4. Voters in California are highly informed about the candidates running in judicial elections.
   a) true
   b) false

5. Initiatives passed in California are not subject to either judicial interpretation or judicial review.
   a) true
   b) false

6. In recent years, campaign spending in judicial elections
   a) has increased.
   b) has decreased.
   c) has remained the same.
   d) cannot be determined.

7. Chief Justice Rose Bird and associate justices Cruz Reynoso and Joseph Grodin were voted out by citizens who were angry about the judges' decisions concerning
   a) same-sex marriage.
   b) the death penalty.
   c) Proposition 13.
   d) term limits.

8. Judges selected by the governor to serve on the supreme court and the courts of appeal in California must be approved by
   a) the state legislature.
   b) the attorney general.
   c) the Commission on Judicial Appointments.
   d) none of the above

9. Superior courts in California adjudicate which of the following types of actions?
   a) civil and criminal cases
   b) only civil cases
   c) only criminal cases
   d) only appeals

10. One method of removing judges in the state of California is
    a) removal by the governor.
    b) censure by the state legislature.
    c) agreement between the speaker of the Assembly and the attorney general.
    d) a recall election.

CRITICAL-THINKING QUESTIONS

1. Given the concern on the part of lawmakers and the public over the role of money in judicial elections, what kinds of reforms might be implemented that would still allow for accountability? Is it possible to keep money and special interests out of judicial elections?

2. What factors do you believe are responsible for the tremendous criminal caseload in the California superior courts?

3. Is judicial independence important for state court judges?

4. What kinds of checks have been placed on the California judiciary? How do the other branches and political actors hold the state courts accountable?

KEY TERMS

appellate jurisdiction (p. 190)
civil courts (p. 192)
judicial accountability (p. 197)

judicial discretion (p. 190)
judicial independence (p. 197)

retention election (p. 196)
superior courts (p. 189)

8 The State Budget and Budgetary Limitations

WHAT CALIFORNIA GOVERNMENT DOES AND WHY IT MATTERS

Why does student tuition keep rising? The answer is simple: higher education is a major category of the state budget, the third or fourth largest in most years, and charts circulating among politicians in Sacramento made it look as if California students until recently paid relatively low tuition and fees by national standards. The charts came from the Legislative Analyst's Office and the California Postsecondary Education Commission (CPEC), a research agency created by the legislature to be independent of the three systems of higher education. Everyone involved in higher education policy saw these charts: the governor's department of finance; the legislative committees and their staff; the bureaucracy; and two of this book's authors, who were members of the California State University (CSU) statewide academic senate for several years. After seeing these charts, legislators on the hunt for an extra several hundred million dollars to cut from the budget felt justified in saying, "Well, the students are paying relatively little by U.S. standards; just increase the university's fees to cover the difference."

And that was the process that occurred, year after year, for about a decade. Meanwhile, the inequalities have increased. University of California (UC) students pay for more than half their education cost; California Community College (CCC) students cover 15 percent. The Legislative Analyst's Office found that "UC's tuition and fees are higher than all but 10 of the 65 largest public research universities in other states. By contrast, tuition and fees at the CSU are lower than all but 42 universities among a group of 244 masters-level public universities in other states. CCC tuition and fees are the lowest in the country. . . ."[1] As the legislative analyst has stated several times, the "state currently does not have a tuition policy." Instead, when economic times are good, tuition and fees are frozen, but when the inevitable downturn comes, fees and tuition rise sharply. What kind of budget process produces such inequalities over time?

Ultimately, over the four years from 2008 to 2012, higher education lost $2.8 billion in funding (about 22 percent of its total), and by 2018, despite limited increases granted by the governor, the CSU had 19 percent less money to spend than it had in 2007–08.[2] Similar statements can be written about the University of California.

Figure 8.1 contrasts state spending on higher education with state spending on prisons and corrections. Forty years ago the state spent almost 18 percent of the state general fund on higher education and less than 4 percent on corrections. By 2008–09, the shares were almost equal at 11.1 percent on higher education and 10.7 percent on corrections. Since then, higher education spending has increased a bit and corrections spending has fallen, in part because the state has shifted inmates from state prisons to locally funded jails.

Students aren't the only citizens heavily affected by California's budget woes. With a budget of over $169 billion, plus almost $100 billion in federal funds, California represents one of the largest economies in the world. Its *deficit* in recent years has been larger than the entire budgets of all but the 10 largest states. Over

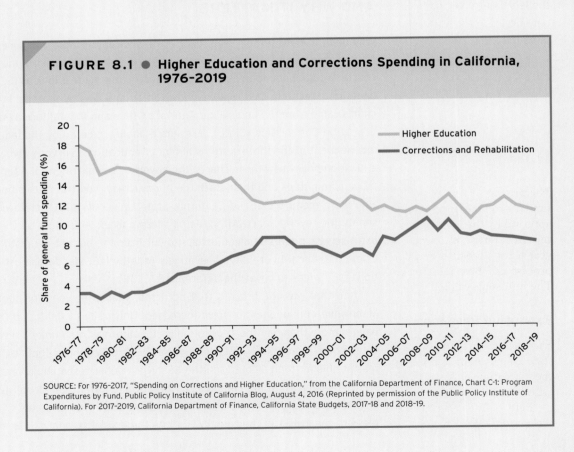

FIGURE 8.1 ● **Higher Education and Corrections Spending in California, 1976–2019**

SOURCE: For 1976–2017, "Spending on Corrections and Higher Education," from the California Department of Finance, Chart C-1: Program Expenditures by Fund. Public Policy Institute of California Blog, August 4, 2016 (Reprinted by permission of the Public Policy Institute of California). For 2017–2019, California Department of Finance, California State Budgets, 2017–18 and 2018–19.

2.5 million workers in California (1 out of 6) work for the federal, state, or local governments, and a number of other workers are indirectly funded by the public sector.[3]

It is therefore unsurprising that the process to approve a budget that controls the livelihood of so many people is controversial. The public itself is split—most Californians are opposed to spending cuts in public programs as well as to increases in taxes or fees. They are also distrustful of state government and disapprove of the job their politicians are doing. One political party in the state legislature—the Republicans—won't increase taxes under any circumstances; indeed, some Republicans consider the entire budget so illegitimate that they won't vote for it under any realistic set of circumstances (one legislator didn't vote for a budget for over a decade). In 2002 the legislature came within one vote of increasing the sales tax, but that vote was impossible to obtain. The amount and intensity of political controversy over the state budget, a document that embodies the values and decisions of the citizens, its legislature, and its leaders, is truly remarkable.

Passing the budget is at the center, both in difficulty and in scope, of what the state government does each year. Since the passage of Proposition 13 in 1978, the state government has received less revenue than it would have otherwise, and that revenue has become more volatile, rising and falling with the economy. The state constitution mandates that the legislature pass the budget by June 15. Since 1990 the legislature has met this deadline in only 12 of 29 years. Two of those were budget surplus years, when it is always easier to pass a budget. Eight others occurred after the passage of Proposition 25 in 2010. Proposition 25 requires only a majority vote to pass the budget and penalizes legislators by cutting their salaries when the budget is overdue.

How Is the Budget Formed?

The process of forming a budget has four steps. Most governments today follow a similar process—proposal by the executive branch, enactment by the legislature, approval by the governor, and implementation by the executive branch. Note that the preparation, enactment, and implementation of the budget for a single fiscal year takes almost three calendar years. See Box 8.1 for a summary of the budget process and Box 8.2 for the constitutional requirements for California's budget. The four steps of the budget process are discussed in detail below.

Executive Proposal

Each fall, state agencies send their budget proposals to the governor through the state **Department of Finance**. The governor formulates a proposal and sends it to the legislature in January. In late spring, he or she revises the proposal in what is called the **May revise**.

Before 1922, agencies proposed their budgets directly to the legislature; there was no **unified budget** proposed by the governor or anyone else. Instead, "budgeting

BOX 8.1 ● California's Budget Process

CALENDAR YEAR 1

JULY–SEPTEMBER

- Agencies prepare requests and make proposals.
- Requests sent to Department of Finance.

OCTOBER–DECEMBER

- Department of Finance reviews requests and consults governor.

CALENDAR YEAR 2

JANUARY–MARCH

- California Constitution requires governor to send a balanced budget to the legislature by January 10.
- Governor's budget proposal is introduced in both houses as identical budget bills.
- Legislative Analyst's Office prepares extensive analysis.
- Budget hearings held in both houses.

APRIL–JUNE

- May: Governor sends revised and updated projections of revenues and expenditures to legislature (the May revise).
- June 15: California Constitution requires legislature to pass (by a majority vote) a balanced budget by this date. As of 2010, all members of the legislature permanently forfeit salary and expenses every day until the budget is passed.
- Governor signs budget, using line-item veto, if desired, to lower any appropriation items. Legislature can override by a two-thirds vote.

JULY–SEPTEMBER

- July 1: California's fiscal year begins. This is the first quarter. (The federal fiscal year, in contrast, begins October 1.)

OCTOBER–DECEMBER

- Second quarter of California's fiscal year.

CALENDAR YEAR 3

JANUARY–MARCH

- Third quarter of California's fiscal year.

APRIL–JUNE

- Fourth quarter of California's fiscal year.

was the domain of interest groups, department heads, and ranking committee members."[4] In 1911, upon finding little or no justification for the amounts contained in the appropriations bills sent to him, Progressive governor Hiram Johnson created the Board of Control to advise him on the fiscal justification for each appropriation.

In 1922, California adopted its own version of new federal legislation that had been passed the previous year, thus *unifying* the budget process. The legislation called for a consolidated administration proposal in the form of a **governor's budget** that must be balanced, contain justifications for the amounts proposed, and be accompanied by bills introduced by legislative leaders in each house, thus providing a starting point for the negotiations and decisions each year. The existence of a governor's budget was an improvement over the situation before 1900, when "government structures . . . hid more than they revealed to the public."[5]

Legislative Adoption

The legislature adopts a balanced budget based on the governor's proposal. As of 2011 both the Assembly and the state Senate must adopt the budget by a majority of the entire membership. The Assembly and Senate budget committees and their subcommittees hold hearings on the budget bills, during which they receive testimony and input from individuals and groups, including the affected departments and agencies, the Department of Finance, the **Legislative Analyst's Office**, committee staff, and interest groups.

The Legislative Analyst's Office provides nonpartisan and independent review of the entire budget, including alternative ways to accomplish the same goals and objectives. The reviews are so nonpartisan that former legislative analyst Elizabeth

Hill was called the "Budget Nun" because of her "incorruptible" fiscal reports. Respected columnist George Skelton of the *Los Angeles Times* said about the reports that "They're the bible. The one source of truth. . . . She's the most influential non-elected official in the Capitol."[6] The current legislative analyst, Mac Taylor, was appointed in 2008 and has 30–plus years of experience in the Legislative Analyst's Office.

Before 2011 a **Budget Conference Committee** was appointed to work out the differences between the Assembly and Senate budget bills. Since the passage of Proposition 25 in 2010, however, a majority vote is now the sole requirement to pass the budget; the endless compromising with the Republican Party that used to occupy Sacramento through the summers of the 1990s and 2000s is over. The "Big 5" group, consisting of the governor, Assembly speaker, Senate president pro tempore, and Assembly and Senate minority leaders, used to be instrumental in soliciting a few Republican votes to pass the budget under the old two-thirds requirement. Their influence in the budget process is now largely irrelevant, or at least it has been in the first few years under the new system. From 2011 to 2018 the budget was passed by June 15, the official deadline in Proposition 25; if legislators miss this deadline they lose their salaries for every day that the budget is late.

Raising a tax, however, still requires a two-thirds vote of both the Assembly and the state Senate (or the approval of the majority of the voters through an initiative). While the Democrats achieved majorities of over two-thirds in both the Assembly and Senate in 2012, the voters approved Jerry Brown's initiative proposal on the November 2012 ballot, Proposition 30, to raise the state sales and income taxes in the same year. Because of this new source of revenue, Governor Brown strongly urged the legislature not to pass any additional tax increases in 2013. The two-thirds supermajority disappeared in early 2014 after three Democratic state senators were suspended for their involvement in various scandals. In 2017 the Democratic party again had a two-thirds majority in the Assembly and state Senate and passed an increase in the gas tax and related fees to repair roads and bridges and accomplish other transportation-related tasks. Proposition 6 on the November 2018 ballot was a referendum on the increases, and it failed by a vote of 43 percent to 57 percent.

Gubernatorial Action

The governor may use the **line-item veto** to lower any line-item appropriation in the budget, including lowering it to zero. The legislature may override the governor's veto by a two-thirds majority in each of the two houses and replace the lowered number with its own amount, although doing so is rare. Because of the line-item veto, the final budget is usually very close to the governor's May revise proposal.

Implementation

Agencies implement the budget as passed, with the fiscal year beginning July 1. The Department of Finance states explicitly that agencies and departments are expected to operate within their budgets and comply with any provisions enacted by the legislature: There is some flexibility in implementation, but, compared to other states, the governor's flexibility is limited, as we shall see.

Other Groups Involved in the Budget Process

In addition to the governor and legislature, the agencies mentioned earlier—the Department of Finance on the executive side and the Legislative Analyst's Office on the legislative side—are closely involved in the budget process, as are two other groups:

- The courts have sometimes ruled on the constitutionality of particular budget actions, particularly on proposed administrative actions to be taken when the legislature has been late submitting a budget. They have also had to decide on the constitutionality of various budget provisions, such as the limits on property taxes established by Proposition 13 in 1978.

- **Moody's, Fitch Ratings, and Standard & Poor's** rate the ability of the states to repay their bonds. A "bond" is a loan in which the investor is lending the government a certain amount of money for a certain length of time at a certain rate of interest. The rating is one of several factors that influence the cost of selling a bond issue. The lower the credit rating, the higher the interest rate that must be paid to induce investors to purchase the bonds. In 2003, Moody's rating of California's bonds was the lowest rating given for any state, but since then California's credit rating has risen. Standard & Poor's raised California's credit rating in 2015, reflecting the budget discipline imposed by Governor Jerry Brown during his administration. However, 27 of the 39 states rated in 2018 still have a higher credit rating than California's. The 2018 ratings have come up to the AA level, meaning the state's bonds are of high quality but with more fluctuation or long-term risk than bonds at the AAA level. Of more significance perhaps was Moody's test in early 2016 of the four most populous states and their ability to withstand a potential recession in the next two years. Of the four (Texas, Florida, New York, and California), California was the least able because of revenue volatility and inadequate reserves.[7]

What Is in the Budget?

Every state budget contains the following information:

- economic assumptions—how the economy should respond during the forthcoming fiscal year, and what that response means for revenues and expenditures

- revenues expected in the various categories

- expenditures broken down by department and program

Revenues

The **general fund** includes all state revenues that are *not* **federal funds**, special funds, or bond funds. (See Box 8.3 for more on federal funds.) The state budget is usually assumed to consist of either just the general fund or the general fund plus special funds and bond funds. The general fund receives over 90 percent of its

The 2018-19 budget included $106 billion in federal funds, almost three-fourths of which was intended for use in the health and human services category. Most of this was for Medi-Cal, California's Medicaid program (medical care for the poor). About $7 billion of the total was for labor and workforce development, mostly federal funds to supplement the Unemployment Insurance program. Another large portion was for education. None of the $106 billion included the additional $290 billion the federal government spent in California on wages and benefits for California-based federal employees, Social Security payments, Medicare payments to doctors, hospitals, and other providers (for those 65 and over, and some of those with disabilities), procurement contracts (defense and others), grants to universities and nonprofits, and so forth.[a]

Federal dollars are important to states during economic downturns, when states often cut back their budgets to meet balanced budget requirements. Federal money for unemployment insurance and stimulus packages typically increases substantially during recessions. Federal money received in California increased from $52.9 billion in 2006-07, just before the great recession of 2008-09, to $91.5 billion in 2010-11, according to the California Budget Project.[b]

Reports from the state controller's office indicate that cities in California received about 4 percent of their total income in 2016 from federal funds, and counties received some 16 percent, about $11 billion. Counties receive more because in California they are responsible for administering state and national health and welfare programs.[c]

Does California receive more from the feds than it pays in taxes? In spite of the large amounts discussed above, the answer is "no," because no wealthy state gets back more from the federal government than it pays in taxes. Federal funds, in general, redistribute money from wealthier states to poorer ones.

Many federal programs are based on population counts, and in 2018 the U.S. Census Bureau proposed asking whether respondents of the 2020 Census were citizens, a factor certain to reduce California's population count, since an estimated 2.5 million of California's 40 million citizens are undocumented. The results could affect both California's representation in the U.S. House of Representatives, based on the census, and the funds received from various federal programs.

[a]Legislative Analyst's Office, "Federal Spending in California," Sacramento: Legislative Analyst's Office, 2017.
[b]California Budget Project, "How Are Federal Dollars Spent in California?" https://calbudgetcenter.org/wp-content/uploads/111117_How_Are_Federal_Dollars_Spent_pb.pdf (accessed 7/25/2018).
[c]Controller's Office, State of California, 2014a, "Cities Financial Data," https://cities.bythenumbers.sco.ca.gov/#!/year/default; and Controller's Office, State of California, "Counties Financial Data," https://counties.bythenumbers.sco.ca.gov/#!/year/default (accessed 7/25/18).

$100 billion–plus revenues from the sales tax, the income tax, and corporate taxes and consists of all state money that is not allocated to a special fund or a bond fund. **Special funds** are funds that are allocated for a specific purpose; thus, there is a beverage container recycling fund, a fish and game fund, and almost 500 more, totaling some $58 billion in the 2018–19 budget. As well as a specific use for which the fund is designated, each also has a specific source of income. **Bond funds** come from bonds that are repaid over spans of a few years to a few decades, though some of them substitute for current expenditures.

Looking at all sources of revenue—both general funds and special funds—we see the revenue sources are as follows, according to the 2018–19 enacted budget (see Figure 8.2).

PERSONAL INCOME TAX Figure 8.2 shows that the **personal income tax** provides 50 percent of California's state budget, some $97 billion. California's personal income tax ranges from 0 to 13.3 percent of income, with a substantial credit per child or dependent. The income tax is considered highly **progressive**, with the top 1 percent of taxpayers paying about half of the income tax most years. The wealthiest 10 percent paid 80.4 percent of the income tax in 2012.[8] This is one of the most progressive personal income taxes in the nation. (See the "Who Are Californians?" feature on the next page for more on how California's income tax figures into its total revenue as compared to other states.) Regular income (salaries and wages) does not vary that much from year to year, but **capital gains** income (income from selling stock that has appreciated in value, for example) varies considerably from one year to the next, making revenues from the income tax fluctuate a great deal. Proposition 30 established three new brackets for taxpayers who make more than $305,100 per year: at 11.3, 12.3, and 13.3 percent of income. They make the California state income tax even more progressive. Proposition 55 on the November 2016 ballot extended those "temporary" brackets for 12 years.

SALES TAX Figure 8.2 shows that the **sales tax** provides about 20 percent of California's state budget, almost $39 billion. The baseline state sales tax rate is 7.25 percent. Counties or taxing districts are allowed to add between 0.13 and 0.5 percent per local district for local services. In some areas there is more than one district tax in effect. The average sales tax in California is 8.5 percent. The minimum in any area is 7.5 percent. The maximum is in eight cities at about 10 percent. Economists consider the sales tax **regressive**—that is, as individual or household income increases, the proportion of income paid through the tax decreases because lower-income households spend a higher proportion of their incomes on consumption goods that are taxed compared with higher income households. In California, the state refunds 1.25 percent of its share to the local city and county; this feature

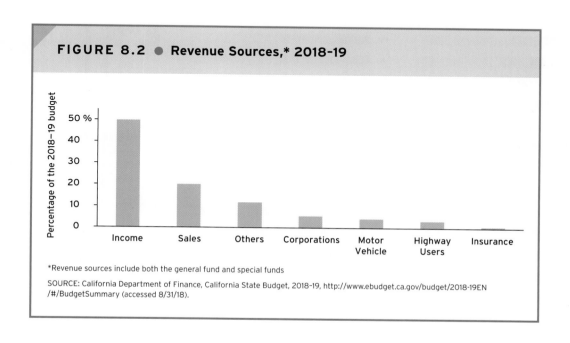

FIGURE 8.2 ● **Revenue Sources,* 2018-19**

*Revenue sources include both the general fund and special funds

SOURCE: California Department of Finance, California State Budget, 2018-19, http://www.ebudget.ca.gov/budget/2018-19EN/#/BudgetSummary (accessed 8/31/18).

Where Does California Get Its Revenue?

There is wide variation in how states fund their programs and activities. Sources of state revenue usually include individual income taxes, sales taxes, property taxes, and corporate taxes; most states also collect a variety of smaller taxes, including gasoline and cigarette taxes. Fifteen states don't levy property taxes at all, while four states (Nevada, Texas, Washington, and Wyoming) don't levy taxes on individual incomes.

Share of State Tax Revenue

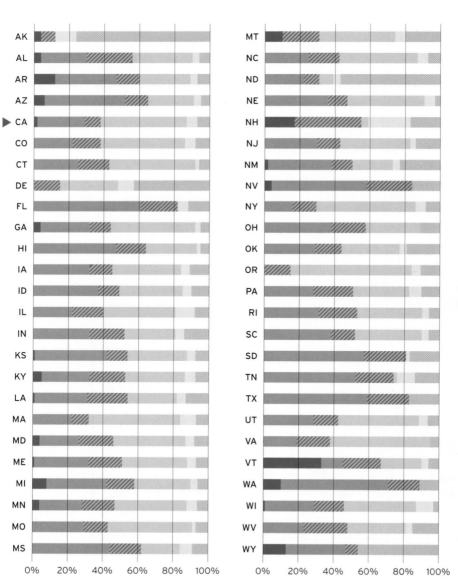

- Property tax
- Sales tax (general)
- Sales tax (selective)
- Individual income tax
- Corporate net income tax
- License tax and other

SOURCE: Ben Casselman and Allison McCann, "Where Your State Gets Its Money," FiveThirtyEight, www.fivethirtyeight.com/features/where-your-state-gets-its-money/ (accessed 8/17/18).

forcriticalanalysis

1. How does the distribution of different types of taxes in California compare to the distribution of taxes in other states? For example, why do you think property tax makes up a smaller share of revenue in California than in New Hampshire?

2. California's largest revenue source, individual income taxes, is structured as a progressive tax: those with larger incomes pay larger percentages. Is this the best system, or would the state be better served by a flat income tax?

has led many cities to search for businesses that are both clean industries and have a high sales volume (thus increasing sales-tax revenue), such as **big-box shopping centers and automobile dealerships**. A "clean industry" is one that produces little air or water pollution. The process has been called the **fiscalization of land use**.

A state sales tax has existed in California since 1933, with the rate raised on average every five years. In 2013, Proposition 30 temporarily raised the state sales tax one-quarter of 1 percent. The increase would have expired in 2016 but was extended by Proposition 55 on the November 2016 ballot.

The sales tax was developed over 75 years ago and is based on an older conception of the economy consisting mostly of goods that are manufactured, bought, and sold. Services make up over half of the modern economy, but these are not taxed in California. In many states, at least some services are taxed. Having a broader base on the sales tax would enable the rate to be lowered from its current high level, but finding a two-thirds majority in the legislature to pass a tax reform act is close to impossible. Even in recent years, when the Democratic Party at some points had a two-thirds majority in both the Assembly and the state Senate, the Democrats were unwilling and not unified enough to modernize the tax code. As a result, every year the proportion of the state revenue total composed of the sales tax goes down slightly. In 2016–17 the sales tax was 23 percent of revenues; in 2018–19 it was 20 percent.

PROPERTY TAX Property tax revenues go to the local level of government, so they are not included in Figure 8.2. All property owners pay California's property tax, limited under Proposition 13 to 1 percent of the assessed value in 1975 or the value of a more recent sale. Once acquired, annual tax increases are limited to 2 percent or the amount of inflation, whichever is smaller. Proposition 13 passed overwhelmingly in 1978 and contains provisions requiring special majorities greater than 50 percent for legislators and voters to raise taxes. Proposition 13 rolled back property taxes in California by more than half, and the state has endeavored to make up the difference ever since. Local property tax revenue available for cities, counties, and school districts has been substantially reduced. As a result, all local government entities are more reliant on the state for revenue, and decision-making power has substantially shifted, in the eyes of virtually all observers, from the local level to the state level.

School districts are an excellent example of the effects of this shift. Whereas California once had some of the best-quality and best-funded schools in the nation, its expenditures per pupil have fallen in comparison to the rest of the nation. Its staff-per-student ratio is now 70 percent of the average for other states. Its student achievement levels lag behind the rest of the nation, and a greater proportion of high-income families send their children to private schools compared to the pre-1978 period. At the same time, teacher salaries are relatively high to accommodate California's cost of living and housing prices, and to attract good-quality recruits to the profession.

Compared to other states, California's overall tax structure depends more on taxes that are volatile, rising and falling with the economy (income tax, sales tax), and less on taxes that don't vary with the economy (property tax) because of Proposition 13's limits. The average state obtains 31 percent of its total state and local tax funds from the property tax, but because of Proposition 13's limits, California obtains only 25 percent.[9] (See Box 8.4 for a more detailed explanation and assessment of Proposition 13.)

California's public schools have suffered since the passage of Proposition 13, which decreased local property tax revenues and effectively transferred the responsibility for funding school districts from the local to the state level. Overcrowded classrooms have been one result of this shift.

CORPORATION TAX The corporation tax is levied on corporate profits and provides about 6 percent of state revenues, some $12 billion. The corporation tax structure is cited favorably by *Governing* magazine in its appraisal of the state's tax system as "tough on the creation of tax-dodge subsidiaries, and the law covers a firm's property and assets, not just its sales."[10] Like the income tax, the corporation tax is mostly paid by corporations earning high profits; the top 1,000 or more pay 70 percent or more of the total.[11]

INDIAN CASINOS Governor Schwarzenegger attempted to increase the amount of revenue received for the general fund from Indian gambling operations in California. In 2005–06 the state received only $27 million for the general fund of the $301 million from the tribal–state gambling compacts negotiated by the governor and ratified by the legislature. In 2008–09 the governor's budget projected $430 million in revenues, but much less was actually received. More recent budgets have no information on Indian gambling revenues, as they are so small as to be insignificant (less than one-tenth of one percent) in a budget of more than $200 billion.

STATE LOTTERY Lottery monies received by the state and allocated to education, approximately $1.6 billion in 2016–17, would be meaningful if the state added them to the education budget. Instead, research shows that in California, as in other states, "lottery funds have merely substituted for normal levels of appropriations, despite the fact that lotteries had been promoted as boosting spending for education," according to the North Carolina Center for Public Policy Research.[12]

Why Do Revenues Vary So Much?

California's budget rises and falls each year, soaring when the economy is healthy and plunging in even the mildest recessions. Here is why:

- Revenues from the sales tax and the personal income tax depend directly on how the state economy performs each year.

BOX 8.4 ● What Exactly Is Proposition 13?

What is it? Proposition 13, passed overwhelmingly by the voters in June 1978, contained the following provisions:

- All property taxes were rolled back to a maximum of 1 percent of the value of the property in 1975–76.

- The value of the property, and thus the tax paid, was allowed to increase by the rate of inflation, but the inflation rate was capped at 2 percent per year.

- When ownership changed, property would be revalued at the current market value.

- No new property taxes could be imposed, either by the state or by local governments.

- Any "special taxes" could be imposed only by a two-thirds margin of the voters in the particular area (the state legislature was already under a two-thirds approval rule for raising taxes, a rule in force since 1933).

- All property taxes collected were to be distributed "according to law," but because no such laws existed, the legislature had to create them.

THE EFFECTS OF PROPOSITION 13

Proposition 13 immediately affected local governments. Before 1978, local governments and agencies each established their own property tax rate, designed to produce sufficient revenues to accomplish the particular function of the agency. Now, each agency's property tax rate was irrelevant; the state would decide "according to law" how much money to apportion to each local jurisdiction. The total property tax collected decreased by over half. The state, however, had a $55 billion surplus, which helped bridge the gap in funds for several years.

The single biggest change set in motion by Proposition 13 is that the state assumed considerable authority over issues formerly handled by local government.[a] Local governments used to set the local tax rate to produce sufficient funds for public services necessary to the locality. Instead, those decisions are now made by the state, and "clearly, the property tax is now really a state tax."[b]

Another consequence stems from the provision that requires a two-thirds vote of the local area to impose or raise a tax. Many localities have seen election results of 60 to 66 percent in favor, just short of the required two-thirds, and have been powerless to initiate local projects, such as acquiring land for parks. Bond issues for the repair and construction of school facilities, however, were authorized by Proposition 39 in 2000 to require the approval of only 55 percent of local voters.

One of the most important consequences is called "the fiscalization of land use"—that is, the tendency of local governments not only to evaluate land use changes in terms of how much money will be brought to the local government but to make decisions on that basis. Because localities receive a share of the state sales tax, land use changes that produce a lot of sales tax revenues are preferred. Many cities favor big-box shopping centers and auto malls over housing developments, and rely increasingly on development fees and other ways to obtain revenue not available through the property tax.

Finally, we have seen the development of many "arcane" financing techniques, those so intricate that no one understands them except the few who developed them. These are also designed to help obtain revenues and replace property taxes.

(continued)

A Legislative Analyst's Office (LAO) study[c] completed in 2016 debunks some common claims about Proposition 13 and provides the best evidence on its current effects. Following the enactment of Proposition 13 and its 1 percent of assessed value property tax limit in 1978, property tax payments fell by 60 percent in California. The LAO study confirms that similar properties purchased at different times pay vastly different property taxes, depending on when the owner purchased the property. Higher-income Californians tend to own more homes and homes of greater value, and they therefore receive the majority of the tax relief dollars provided by Proposition 13. Property turnover has declined considerably since 1978, with Proposition 13 appearing to play some, but not the total, role in this decline.

One of the most significant findings was that homeowners pay only a slightly higher share of property taxes now compared to the period before 1978, and that residential properties do not turn over more than commercial properties. One of the justifications for the proposed split roll reform of Proposition 13, in which commercial properties would be taxed at different and presumably higher rates than residential properties, was that residential properties were thought to be sold and resold at faster rates than commercial properties.

[a]The best description of Proposition 13 and its implications is Jeffrey I. Chapman, "Proposition 13: Some Unintended Consequences," Public Policy Institute of California, www.ppic.org (accessed 7/27/12).
[b]Chapman, "Proposition 13," p. 22.
[c]Legislative Analyst's Office, "Common Claims About Proposition 13," www.lao.ca.gov/Publications/Report/3497 (accessed 7/31/18).

- Compared to other states, the budget relies more on the personal income tax, the capital gains portion of which soars when stock options are cashed out, than on the property tax, which was limited in 1978 by Proposition 13 and is roughly constant every year.

How Well Does the Tax System Function?

The tax system seems to be functioning poorly. Little has changed since *Governing* magazine published "The Way We Tax" in 2003, comparing tax policy in all 50 states. The report gave California one star out of four in the category "Adequacy of Revenue," two out of four in "Fairness to Taxpayers," and two out of four in "Management of System."[13] Only Tennessee received a lower overall rating, and four other states were tied with California.

A more recent study of tax administration, conducted by the Council on State Taxation (COST) and published in December 2013, ranked California's tax administration in 49th place, tied with Louisiana, and graded it a D–. The study cited errors such as permitting the same people to serve on the boards at different levels of tax appeal and allowing officials unqualified in tax administration onto those boards.[14]

Is California Overtaxed?

THE CONSERVATIVE VIEW Conservatives think California is overtaxed. The California Taxpayers Association makes the case that "the extraordinary level of taxation in California can provide more than enough in tax revenue to fund police and fire services, education for our children, and public works projects and health and welfare services for California's poor."[15] Taxes are so high, in their view, that the state is no longer economically competitive with other states. The Washington, D.C.–based Tax Foundation, which calculates the total tax burden, including taxes paid out of state (for vacation property, for example), found California's state and local tax burden for fiscal year 2012 to be the sixth highest in the nation.[16]

THE LIBERAL VIEW Liberals often argue *not* that California's taxes are low, but that they are moderate in comparison with California's income, ranked 15th to 20th among the states. The California Budget & Policy Center, for example, stated in 2014 that California was a "moderate" tax state, ranking 20th among the 50 states "with respect to total 'own source' revenues raised by state and local governments." California ranked 11th in the percentage of state taxes compared with personal income in the state in 2010–11. Personal and corporate income tax collections are relatively high in California, but the tobacco and alcoholic beverage taxes are relatively low.[17]

THE REALITY California is a relatively rich state, but one with significant numbers of relatively poor citizens. Its household and median family incomes are some $8,000 higher than the U.S. averages, but 14.3 percent of Californians are poor by the official statistics, and the Stanford Center on Poverty and Inequality calculates that almost two-fifths of Californians are poor or near-poor. The income and sales tax rates are among the higher tax rates of all American states, although there are numerous exemptions that bring the total tax rate lower.

The critical challenge to California's tax structure is not that taxes are high but that the tax structure is outmoded. It reflects the economy of the 1950s and Proposition 13 decisions made in the 1970s. The property tax collects less money proportionally than other wealthy states because of Proposition 13. The sales tax is based on the purchase of goods (with food exempted), not of services. Lower- and middle-class families with children are largely exempted from the personal income tax. The bottom line is that, like so many areas of the state's governmental structure, California's tax structure needs to be reformed.

Betty Yee, California state controller, established a Council of Economic Advisors on Tax Reform in 2015 to discuss the problems of California's present tax structure. Since Proposition 13 was approved in 1978, policy makers have adopted incremental changes to California's taxes, but no comprehensive restructuring has been adopted. Meanwhile, revenues from the sales tax, the corporation tax, and the property tax have diminished relative to the size of the economy, and the resulting increasing emphasis on the personal income tax has led to greater unpredictability of state tax revenue and increasing challenges for budget policy makers. The commission found that comprehensive reform of the state's tax structure was long overdue and sought in its findings to discuss the underlying principles and tradeoffs that would be necessary in any legislation, without discussing actual proposals.[18]

Without comprehensive tax reform, California will continue to be a battleground for both liberals and conservatives, with conservatives seeking to lower the highest rates, and liberals seeking exemptions for the poor and middle class.

Technology company Google has its global headquarters in Mountain View. Despite talk of California's unfriendly business climate, California ranks second for the number of Fortune 500 companies located in the state, with 53, exceeded only by New York's 54.

Conservative groups rate California's business climate as one of the worst of any state because of the high levels of taxes; the taxation of capital gains at regular tax rates; and the number of regulations and permits affecting citizens' ability to establish, run, and expand a business.[19] Nevertheless, many large corporations are located in California, particularly in Silicon Valley (the area between San Francisco and San Jose) because of the wealth of skilled talent in the area's labor market.

One question is whether California's tax levels hold down the state's economic growth. An analysis of the growth rates of nine states with high personal income taxes compared to the nine states that lack any personal income tax indicates no conclusive relationship. In fact, the states that grow the most seem to be those with high rates of population growth, and several of the non-income-tax states have economic resources (such as oil, which obviates the need for a state income tax) not available to other states.[20] Many observers point to the healthiness of California's recovery from the 2008 recession, especially compared with other states, as evidence that high tax rates do not correlate with low economic growth.

Expenditures

Figure 8.3 depicts the 2018–19 state budget, including the general fund, special funds, and bond funds.

It indicates that the largest spending category is health and human services (HHS), at 32 percent of the budget and some $64 billion. This category includes the state (but not the federal) contribution for Medi-Cal, California's Medicaid program, which provides health coverage for the poor as well as for senior citizens in nursing homes. It also includes the public health system; Healthy Families, California's state children's health insurance program; welfare, including Temporary Assistance for Needy Families; and the state contribution to food stamps and to the Women, Infants, and Children (WIC) supplemental food program, among many others.

The second largest expenditure category in Figure 8.3 is elementary and secondary education, at $57 billion and 28 percent of total expenditures. With the passage of Proposition 13 in 1978, a gradually increasing proportion of the state general fund has been spent on K–12 education. The money in this category supplements property tax revenues for education, collected by each county.

Higher education is the third largest category at $17 billion and 8 percent of total expenditures. Higher education in 2018 includes funding for the community college system (115 campuses, 2.1 million students), the CSU system (23 campuses, 484,000 students), and the UC system (10 campuses, 5 medical centers, 3 national labs, 238,000 students).

Since 1980–81 there has been a downward trend in the proportion of the budget devoted to higher education, as discussed in the beginning of this chapter. In the late 2000s and early 2010s, state funding for higher education was cut severely. A

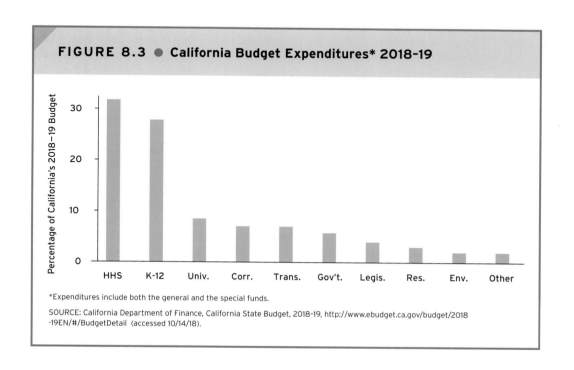

FIGURE 8.3 ● California Budget Expenditures* 2018-19

*Expenditures include both the general and the special funds.

SOURCE: California Department of Finance, California State Budget, 2018-19, http://www.ebudget.ca.gov/budget/2018 -19EN/#/BudgetDetail (accessed 10/14/18).

report from the Public Policy Institute of California demonstrates that funding for higher education composed more than 17 percent of the state budget as recently as 1975, but since then the proportion has declined to between 11 and 13 percent.[21] Another report, from the Center on Budget and Policy Priorities in Washington, D.C., compares spending-per-student cuts and tuition increases in all states from fiscal years 2008 to 2013.[22] All but two of the states cut their expenditures per student during this time period, and California is in the middle of the pack with a 29.5 percent cut. California's tuition increase percentage for the same time period, at 72 percent, is the second largest among the states. Governor Jerry Brown has recently augmented the higher education budgets, partially restoring the millions that were cut from higher education in the 2000s.

The fourth largest category is corrections and rehabilitation, which includes funding for state prisons and youth authorities. At $15 billion and 7 percent of the budget, this category increased steadily from 1980–81 through the mid-1990s as the public demanded the three strikes law and similar measures. It has since leveled off.

The fifth largest category is transportation, at $15 billion and 7 percent of the budget. It includes money for Caltrans, mass transit projects, and subsidizing Amtrak.

The balance of the categories in Figure 8.3 are all 6 percent or less of the budget, including general government administration; the legislative, executive, judicial category; the natural resources category (e.g., state parks); and areas covering state expenditures for the environment. The last category is "other," covering everything else.

Budgetary Limitations

Through the use of initiatives California voters have not only passed bond issues but have also limited what the state government can do in very significant areas. Many of these initiatives, such as Propositions 99, 111, 49, and 71, have placed money into various "special funds," which is why Figure 8.3 includes both the general fund and special funds. Here are a few of the most significant initiatives, by date.[23]

- **Proposition 13 (1978)** cut property taxes to 1 percent of the assessed valuation of the property in 1975 and allows reassessment only when the property is sold. If justified by inflation, the tax can rise a maximum of 2 percent between assessments.

- **Proposition 4 (1979)** limited the state government's growth from one year to the next to the percentage growth in the cost of living and the percentage increase in population. Any excess funds are to be returned to taxpayers. The state must also reimburse local governments for the cost of complying with state mandates. It was proposed by Howard Jarvis's partner, Paul Gann, and called "The Gann Limit."

- **Proposition 98 (1988)** requires that at least 40 percent of the general fund be devoted to K–14 education, including community colleges; annual increases are to be at least equal to the increase in school enrollment and the cost of living.

- **Proposition 99 (1988)** mandated a 25-cent tax on cigarettes, with the proceeds to be spent on antismoking campaigns and medical research.

- **Proposition 111 (1990)** increased the gas tax and trucking fees; the proceeds must be spent on transportation projects.

- **Proposition 218 (1996)** requires voter approval before local tax increases and prohibits property-related fees for general government services.

- **Proposition 49 (2002)**, supported by then potential Republican candidate for governor Arnold Schwarzenegger, requires that several hundred million dollars be spent on after-school programs.

- **Proposition 71 (2004)** authorizes the sale of $3 billion in bonds to fund stem-cell research in the state.

- **Proposition 22 (2010)** banned the state government from balancing the state budget by borrowing or taking money raised by local governments in California. The state had taken some $5 billion the previous fiscal year.

Of these, the two that have had the most effect are Propositions 13 and 98. Proposition 13 has made the state budget more reliant on taxes that vary with the economy and less reliant on sources of income that don't vary with the economy, particularly the property tax. Proposition 98 dictated that a certain proportion of the budget, almost half when higher education is included, must be devoted to one policy area.

Because the initiative requires only a majority vote, it is relatively easy to authorize expenditures through the initiative compared with doing so through the legislature. California has become a state in which it is easy to lower taxes or budget items through the legislature or to authorize expenditures through the initiative, but in which it is increasingly difficult to raise the funds to pay for basic state functions, including higher education and health. Voters in recent public opinion surveys find most items in the budget to be popular (except welfare), but they strongly resist paying extra for any of them.

Recent California Budgets and the Budget Process

In recent years, California lawmakers and the governor have closed the budget gap with the standard techniques used in other states—incremental (small) tax or fee increases; cuts in education, health, and social services (which make up the largest portions of the budget); and borrowing through bond issues that are repaid over a 5- to 10-year period to cover a portion of the yearly deficit. The capital gains tax produced extra funds for the budgets of 2013–14 through 2018–19, making the process easier, although Governor Jerry Brown strongly resisted legislators' push to make agencies that had been cut substantially in the previous decade "whole" again. Governor Brown also insisted that the state begin repaying the funds borrowed during the last decade to close budget gaps.

California Forward, a bipartisan group aimed at fixing some of California's perennial budget process problems, stated in 2008 that

the current budget process is largely a relic of the mid-20th century, with the focus on how much to increase spending (or how much to cut), rather than the value that public services bring to Californians over time. The ongoing and chronic imbalance between revenues and expenditures is one indicator of system failure. Changing how budget process decisions are made could enable public leaders to deal with the more intractable and complex problems involving the revenue system and the state–local relationship.[24]

They identify, as we have, the key problems of budgeting:

> The costs of operating state programs are growing faster than the revenue base that supports them. The revenue system is highly sensitive to changes in the economy, producing significant volatility. The single-year budgeting horizon encourages short-term fixes, rather than long-term solutions. The budget does not take a strategic approach to ensure a return on public investments and there is a lack of public and legislative review of how money is spent.[25]

Many commentators noted the cumulative effect of the fees and caps that have been proposed more and more frequently in recent years.[26] Traditionally, California tried to supply sufficient services for all, on the principle that "if you're eligible, we'll serve you." The community colleges guarantee, for example, that any high school graduate can go to college. That principle has been shifting though. The Schwarzenegger budget for 2004–05 included caps on the number of individuals who could be served in various programs; immigrants in Medi-Cal and the program that supplies drugs for those with HIV/AIDS were both capped at the level of January 1, 2004. Both the CSU and UC have limited admissions in significant ways in the twenty-first century. California's fees for students attending CSU and community colleges used to be among the lowest in the nation, but they have increased substantially in recent years. Measures are often proposed as emergency measures, but few emergency measures have been repealed in the past.

In short, the lowered expectation for services has become particularly apparent in the Arnold Schwarzenegger and Jerry Brown eras but has been in the background for the last two decades or more.

The California Budgetary Process: Where Are We Now?

We retain some optimism about California's fiscal prospects, but we temper it by concurring with Governor Brown's forecast that more recessions will come in the future, and at a time that cannot be forecast. Brown has insisted that California live within the means that the voters have provided. Now that budgets are easier to balance, the governor has insisted that the budget surpluses from the capital gains tax be used to provide the state with a rainy day fund (Proposition 44 on the November 2014 ballot) and to repay some of the bonds that were floated to pay for the deficits of the 2000s under Governor Schwarzenegger. Unfortunately for all of us, tax revenue still retains its tendency to soar in good times and plunge deeply in bad ones. It would be better to reform California's tax system, but this possibility is remote; any meaningful reform would engender substantial opposition.

The biggest fiscal problem facing the state is the voters' willingness to approve propositions (initiatives) that allocate money from the general fund or establish a special fund without having a funding source. Some of these are self-serving; others have more merit. While some initiatives divert money from the general fund by setting up special funds, others simply state that the money for a certain purpose shall be a specific amount to be paid from the general fund; this reduces the funds available for existing programs. Higher education in particular has been hurt by these actions.

Study Guide

FOR FURTHER READING

Barrett, Katherine, Richard Greene, Michele Mariani, and Anya Sostek. "The Way We Tax." *Governing*, February 2003.

California Budget & Policy Center. "2018–19 State Budget Invests in Reserves and an Array of Vital Services, Sets Course for Future Advances." June 2018. https://calbudget center.org/resources/2018-19-state-budget-invests-in -reserves-and-an-array-of-vital-services-sets-course-for -future-advances. Accessed 7/25/18.

———. "An Incomplete Vision: Putting the Governor's Proposed 2014–15 Budget in Context." California Budget & Policy Center, February 2014. https://calbudgetcenter.org /blog/new-from-the-cbp-an-incomplete-vision-putting -the-governors-proposed-2014-15-budget-in-context. Accessed 9/27/18.

———. "Principles and Policy: A Guide to California's Tax System." California Budget & Policy Center, April 2013. https://calbudgetcenter.org/wp-content/uploads/0902 _Californias_Tax_System.pdf. Accessed 9/27/18.

———. "Who Pays Taxes in California?" California Budget & Policy Center, April 2015. https://calbudgetcenter.org/wp -content/uploads/Who-Pays-Taxes-in-CA_Issue-Brief _04.14.2015.pdf. Accessed 9/27/18.

California Taxpayers Association. "Cal-Tax: Taxes Are a Heavy Burden in California." http://digital.library.ucla.edu/web sites/2004_999_003/dynamic/downloads/individual _download_file_link_1_english_10.pdf. Accessed 7/25/18.

Johnson, Hans. "Defunding Higher Education. What Are the Effects on College Enrollment?" Public Policy Institute of California, May 2012. www.ppic.org/main/publication.asp ?i=988. Accessed 7/25/18.

League of Women Voters of California. *Guide to California Government*. 16th ed. Sacramento: League of Women Voters of California, 2015.

Legislative Analyst's Office. "California's Tax System: A Primer." April 2007. https://lao.ca.gov/2007/tax_primer/tax_primer _040907.pdf. Accessed 7/25/18.

———. "Federal Spending in California." January 18, 2017. https://lao.ca.gov/Publications/Report/3531/1. Accessed 7/25/18.

Oliff, Phil, Vincent Palacios, Ingrid Johnson, and Michael Leachman. "Recent Deep State Higher Education Cuts May Harm Students and the Economy for Years to Come." Washington, DC: Center on Budget and Policy Priorities, May 2013.

Public Policy Institute of California. "Just the Facts: California's State Budget: The Enacted 2018–19 Budget." Public Policy Institute of California, July 2018. www.ppic.org. Accessed 7/25/18.

———. "Just the Facts: Proposition 13, 40 Years Later." Public Policy Institute of California, June 2018. www.ppic.org. Accessed 7/25/18.

ON THE WEB

California Budget & Policy Center. http://calbudgetcenter.org. Accessed 7/31/18.

California Forward. www.cafwd.org. Accessed 7/31/18.

Howard Jarvis Taxpayers Association. www.hjta.org. Accessed 7/31/18.

Legislative Analyst's Office. www.lao.ca.gov. Accessed 7/31/18.

Public Policy Institute of California. www.ppic.org. Accessed 7/31/18.

State of California, Department of Finance, Budget Update Site. www.ebudget.ca.gov. Accessed 7/31/18.

State of California, Department of Finance. http://dof.ca.gov /Reports/Demographic_Reports. Accessed 7/31/18. California statistics and demographic information.

SUMMARY

I. How is the budget formulated?
   A. Agencies send their requests to the governor each fall.
   B. The governor sends a balanced budget request to the legislature each January for the fiscal year starting the next July 1.
   C. The legislature adopts a balanced budget by June 15 each year for the fiscal year to start July 1.
      1. In recent years, the volatility of the state's revenues has caused the budget to be substantially readjusted during the fiscal year.
      2. If the budget is not passed by June 15, members of the legislature forfeit their pay and travel reimbursements for each day until it is passed. As a result, budgets have been on time since 2010, when this condition was enacted.
   D. The governor has a line-item veto, allowing him or her to reduce any line-item dollar amount downward, even to zero. However, the governor may not raise any line item.
   E. The legislature is assisted by its own neutral budget office—the Legislative Analyst's Office.
   F. If the Assembly and state Senate versions of the budget differ, a "budget conference committee" will attempt to iron out the differences.
   G. Agencies then implement the approved budget, including specific policy or budget studies to be carried out and presented to the legislature.

II. What is the California budget?
   A. The budget is the governor's and legislature's views of the future.
      1. The future of the state's economy (economic assumptions).
      2. The future income of the state (revenues).
      3. The future spending of the state (expenditures).
   B. The budget is at the center of the state's activities each year.

III. Revenues.
   A. Personal income tax—the largest source of income for the general fund, highly progressive, and subject to extreme volatility because of its dependence on taxes derived from capital gains.
   B. Sales tax—the next largest source of income. Local governments can add a small amount to the state sales tax. A portion of the tax, in addition, is refunded to them. Many localities have added businesses to their communities that produce sales tax, such as big-box shopping centers and automobile dealerships, specifically because of the revenues they then receive from the state.

C. Corporate tax—the third-largest source of revenue. Most corporate taxes are paid by the larger corporations in the state.
   D. Property tax—severely limited by Proposition 13, composes only 22 percent of California's state and local total tax revenues.
   E. The California tax system is volatile compared to the tax systems of other states. It depends on the ups and downs of the economy and produces surges in revenue when the economy booms and precipitous falls when a recession takes place.

IV. Expenditures.
   A. Health and Human Services is the largest budget category, driven by state expenditures for Medi-Cal and other health programs.
   B. Education (K–12) is the second-largest single expenditure and second-largest budget category. Proposition 98 requires that 40 percent of the state general fund be designated for K–12 expenditures.
   C. Higher education is the third-largest budget category; it includes expenditures for the community colleges, the California State University, and the University of California.
   D. The fourth largest category is corrections, followed closely by transportation.

V. Box 8.4 describes Proposition 13 and its restrictions on how property is taxed in California. Among the effects of Proposition 13 was an increased power for the state over local government and the "fiscalization of land use." Conservative groups supporting Proposition 13 strongly resist change, and legislators and interest groups seeking to change it have had little success. A proposal to split the tax roll and place a higher rate on commercial property has faced great opposition from the business community.

VI. Limitations on the budget.
   A. The most substantial limitations have come from initiatives passed by the voters.
   B. Proposition 13, which limits the property tax to 1 percent of the value of one's house, and Proposition 98, which guarantees a certain amount to K–12 education, are the most important of these limitations.
   C. Cumulatively, these budget limitations have limited well over half the general fund and at least half of all expenditures, giving the governor and legislature less flexibility than they would have in other states. This is precisely the intended goal of initiatives—to limit the powers of the governor and legislature. The level of distrust the voters have for the governor and legislature is high in California.

VII. Recent state budgets have been characterized by huge and fluctuating gaps between revenues and expenditures.
  A. These gaps have made it difficult to find the middle ground necessary to obtain a two-thirds vote in the legislature for a budget. But starting in 2011, with only a majority required, the budget has been passed more or less on time. The last six years, 2013–14 to 2018–19, had surpluses because of a surge in income tax (capital gains) revenues. Governor Brown insisted that some of this money be set aside for a rainy day fund, to be used when revenues inevitably turn downward, and that some of the money should repay the bonds used to balance the budget during the 2000s.

VIII. What is the future of budgeting in California?
  A. California seems to have turned a corner, with several budgets in a row passed on time and more or less balanced. The surge in revenues from the capital gains tax is being used to pay back old debt and to create a rainy day fund for the future.
  B. The biggest fiscal problems facing the state continue to be the willingness of the voters to approve propositions (initiatives) that allocate money from the general fund or establish a special fund without having a funding source, and the volatile mix of revenue sources.

PRACTICE QUIZ

1. Both the governor and the legislature are obliged by the California Constitution to pass a balanced budget.
   a) true
   b) false

2. The state of California cannot pass its budget in 2019–20 unless the Assembly and state Senate pass the budget by
   a) 50 percent plus one vote.
   b) 55 percent.
   c) 66.7 percent.
   d) 75 percent.

3. The state of California cannot raise state taxes unless the Assembly and state Senate pass the relevant law by
   a) 50 percent plus one vote.
   b) 55 percent.
   c) 66.7 percent.
   d) 75 percent.

4. Proposition 13 requires
   a) property taxes to be lowered to the level when the property was last sold. Property tax values can rise 2 percent per year.
   b) property taxes to be set at 1975 levels; property is reassessed when it is sold. Property tax values can rise as much as 2 percent per year.
   c) property taxes to be lowered to 1945 levels; property is reassessed when it is sold. The level of the tax can rise 3 percent per year.
   d) Property taxes to be raised to the appropriate level when the properties on both sides of a house or business have been sold—all the property is then reassessed at current values. The level of the tax can rise 2 percent per year if the properties are not sold.

5. Proposition 98 requires education spending to be at least
   a) 50 percent of the entire state budget.
   b) 50 percent of the general fund.
   c) 33.3 percent of the general fund.
   d) 40 percent of the general fund.

6. What is the general fund?
   a) The general fund includes all revenues that are not otherwise allocated into special or bond funds.
   b) The general fund includes all tax revenue.
   c) The general fund includes all state revenue, including special and bond funds.
   d) The general fund includes all state revenue except bond funds, because these are used to construct state facilities and are paid back over a period of several decades.

7. The governor's line-item veto allows
   a) the governor, if desired, to lower any appropriation item.
   b) the governor, in conjunction with an agency, to veto any bill in its entirety.
   c) the governor to "pencil out" any line or sentence in any bill.
   d) the governor to raise or lower any appropriation item, including lowering the item to zero.

8. The governor's line-item veto may be overridden by a 50 percent plus one vote in both houses of the legislature.
   a) true
   b) false

9. The credit rating assigned to the state of California by Moody's, Fitch Ratings, or Standard & Poor's is important because
   a) the credit rating influences the size of California's deficit or surplus in any given fiscal year.
   b) when the credit rating goes down, the interest rate that the state pays to float its bonds goes up.
   c) when the credit rating goes up, the amount of interest the state pays goes down.
   d) all of the above

10. Indian gambling revenues have become a significant source of income for the state of California.
    a) true
    b) false

11. The lottery is a significant source of income for K–12 education.
    a) true
    b) false

CRITICAL-THINKING QUESTIONS

1. How might California's tax system be made more predictable and less dependent on the economy than it is now? How might *Governing* magazine rate your proposed changes?
2. How should the budget process in California be reformed, assuming it should be reformed? What goals are important in reforming the process, and what changes in the process might achieve those goals?
3. Should the governor have more authority in the budget process? What reforms might help with the long-term budget process in California?
4. The other major player in the budget process is the legislature. How might the legislature's consideration of the budget be changed to make California's budget more predictable and timely?
5. How might the tax system be reformed to make it less volatile from year to year?

KEY TERMS

big-box shopping centers and automobile dealerships (p. 219)
bond funds (p. 216)
Budget Conference Committee (p. 214)
capital gains (p. 217)
Department of Finance (p. 211)
federal funds (p. 215)
fiscalization of land use (p. 219)
general fund (p. 215)
governor's budget (p. 213)
Legislative Analyst's Office (p. 213)
line-item veto (p. 214)
May revise (p. 211)
Moody's, Fitch Ratings, and Standard & Poor's (p. 215)
personal income tax (p. 217)
progressive (p. 217)
regressive (p. 217)
sales tax (p. 217)
special funds (p. 216)
unified budget (p. 211)

9 Local Government

WHAT CALIFORNIA'S LOCAL GOVERNMENTS DO AND WHY THEY MATTER

Governing California would be hard to imagine without the more than 5,000 local governments that help run the state. Local officials and workers in cities, counties, school districts, special districts, and regional bodies all play an essential role. The complexity of the state's local government system makes it difficult to generalize about what local governments do. But a short list would include the following:

- General-purpose local governments, such as cities and counties, do everything from putting out fires to cleaning the streets and ensuring that the buses run on time. They protect the health, safety, welfare, and overall quality of life of all who live within their jurisdictions.

- Limited-purpose governments, such as school districts and other special districts, deliver specific public services such as public education, pest abatement, and irrigation to meet particular needs within defined territorial boundaries.

- Regional governments address problems such as air pollution and population growth that affect broad areas across many jurisdictions and that require comprehensive study and planning to solve.

- Many local governments do the actual work involved in implementing state and federal laws, from controlling water quality and producing affordable housing to carrying out duties related to homeland security.

- Most local governments provide citizens with opportunities to learn about public problems, express their opinions, practice hands-on democracy, and collectively exercise some degree of popular control on issues close to home that they really care about.

- Some local governments experiment and innovate to pioneer new ways of better serving citizens or improving the democratic process. Often these local initiatives spread and can have major impacts on how government works at the state and national levels.

California's local governments have been subjected to a severe stress test over the last few years, thanks to both the Great Recession and the political responses to it both inside and outside the system—a system that has evolved over decades to help different levels and facets of local government fit and work together. This chapter offers a description and analysis of the essential parts of that system and discusses its capacity to solve problems and function effectively in serving the public. The goal is to give the reader a basic knowledge and appreciation of California's local governments in all their variety, including what they do and why they matter.

The Legal Framework: Dillon's Rule, Home Rule, and Local Powers of Governance

The U.S. Constitution assigns power and authority to the national and state governments, but it says nothing about local governments. **Counties**, **cities**, **special districts**, and other forms of local government have no inherent rights or powers. What rights and powers they do have are conferred on them by the state constitution or state legislature.

The constitutional doctrine that gives state governments ultimate authority over local governments is known as **Dillon's Rule**. In 1868, Iowa judge John F. Dillon ruled that "municipal corporations" such as counties and cities were mere "creatures of the state" and could exercise only those powers delegated to them by the state.[1] Upheld by the U.S. Supreme Court in 1903 and again in 1923, Dillon's Rule is firmly established, at least in theory, as the basic legal framework for relations between state and local governments. In practice, however, only a few states, including Alabama, Idaho, and Nebraska, demand strict obedience to Dillon's Rule and require local governments to seek their permission in order to act. California, like most states, has passed government codes and **home-rule** laws that allow significant local discretion and autonomy. Within broad limits, county and city residents can select their own form of government, manage their own elections, raise their own revenues, and choose what kinds of functions to perform and at what levels of service.[2]

In California, under the provisions of Article 11, Section 5, of the state constitution and because of various court rulings,[3] most of the more populous cities and counties have adopted home-rule charters. The others are designated as general-law cities and counties that fall more directly under state authority and control.

A more practical restraint on state meddling in local government is based on the maxim that all politics is local. State legislators, after all, are elected by local constituencies to protect their local interests, and legislators won't last long if they forget who brought them to the dance. These political realities have kept state power over local governments in check.[4] Finally, as part of the so-called devolution revolution that began in the 1970s, federal and state authorities have increasingly delegated responsibility to local governments to solve their own problems, using their own money.

In sum, Dillon's Rule is very liberally construed in California. The state's constitutional and legal framework confers broad formal powers of local governance, especially in charter cities and counties. Home rule on paper, however, does not necessarily translate into home rule in reality. In recent years, for example, the state's budget crises, public employee pensions, and other financial stresses have seriously limited the capacity of some local governments to govern effectively and serve the public well. Formal authority minus needed resources weakens home rule and diminishes local autonomy.

County Governments

At the first meeting of the California legislature in 1850, lawmakers divided the state into 27 counties for the purpose of administering state laws. Since then many new counties have been created, mostly by subdivision. The state's current 58 counties have been with us since 1907, when the last addition, Imperial County, was carved out of the old San Diego County (see Figure 9.1). Political movements have arisen from time to time that attempted to split an existing county to make a new one. An 1894 amendment to the state constitution, however, made it virtually impossible to do so by requiring a favorable majority vote in both the entire county affected and the territory of the proposed new county.[5]

California's 58 counties vary greatly in their territory, population, and demographic characteristics.

TERRITORY Just in terms of size, the differences are vast. You could fit 427 areas the size of San Francisco County (at just 47 square miles, the smallest county in California) within the borders of San Bernardino County (the largest county in California, at 20,053 square miles). The differences in physical geography are also striking, ranging from deserts to rain forests, flat farmlands to tall mountains. Some counties are densely urban and covered with cities, whereas others are so rural that coyotes outnumber people.

POPULATION Alpine County's grand total of 1,120 residents could all live comfortably in one San Francisco precinct. Los Angeles County, at the other extreme, is bursting with more than 10 million people, representing over 26 percent of the state's entire population. The lowest-ranking 29 counties combined contain only about 5 percent of the state's total population, while the 5 most populous counties (Los Angeles, Orange, San Diego, San Bernardino, and Riverside) hold about 54 percent of the state's total population.

DEMOGRAPHY If you tour the state's 58 counties, you'll discover vastly different social and economic worlds. The populations of some counties are relatively poor, while those of others are relatively rich. Some counties are mostly white, others are mainly nonwhite. Some are dominated by homeowners, others—for example, San Francisco—by renters.

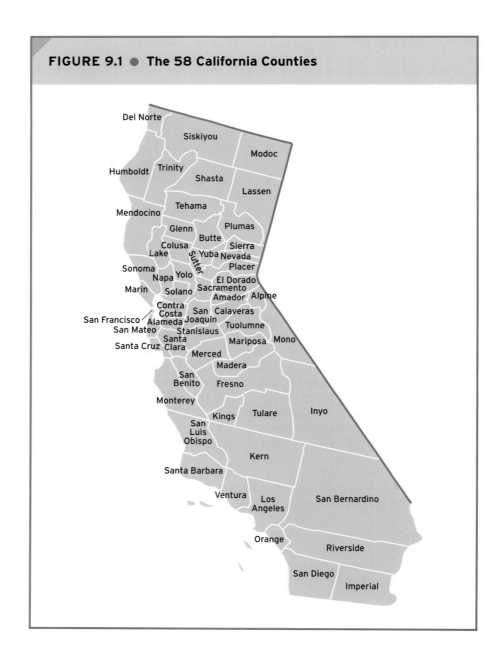

FIGURE 9.1 ● The 58 California Counties

The "Who Are Californians?" feature reports the lowest- and highest-ranking counties on these and other indicators to illustrate the extremes that exist among California's counties.

Legal Framework

The state constitution provides a general legal framework for the governing of most counties, which are known as **general-law counties**. It prescribes the number and functions of elected county officials, how they are selected, and what they may or

Who Lives in California's Counties?

Total Population

- Under 50,000
- 50,000–249,999
- 250,000–499,999
- 500,000–999,999
- 1,000,000 or more

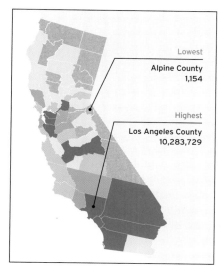

Lowest
Alpine County
1,154

Highest
Los Angeles County
10,283,729

Non-Latino White Population

- Under 30%
- 30–44.9%
- 45–59.9%
- 60–74.9%
- 75% or more

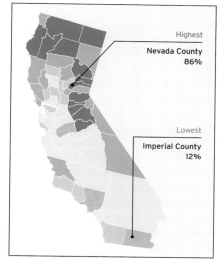

Highest
Nevada County
86%

Lowest
Imperial County
12%

Bachelor's Degree or Higher

- Under 15%
- 15–24.9%
- 25–34.9%
- 35–44.9%
- 45% or more

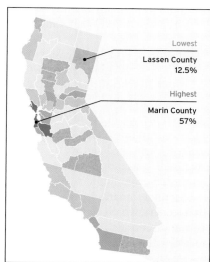

Lowest
Lassen County
12.5%

Highest
Marin County
57%

Median Household Income

- Under $40,000
- $40,000–$49,999
- $50,000–$59,999
- $60,000–$69,999
- $70,000 or more

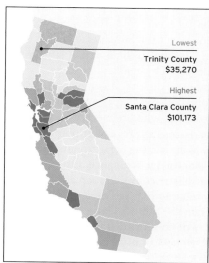

Lowest
Trinity County
$35,270

Highest
Santa Clara County
$101,173

California's 58 counties are extremely diverse in terms of their population size, ethnoracial composition, and economic conditions. Los Angeles, for instance, has the largest population, at nearly 10.3 million residents, and the second smallest white population, at 27 percent. In other ways, Los Angeles falls roughly in the middle: about 38 percent of its residents have a bachelor's degree and the median household income is $58,000.

SOURCES: Population Estimates for Cities, Counties, and the State – January 1, 2017 and 2018, California Department of Finance, http://www.dof.ca.gov/Forecasting/Demographics/Estimates/E-1/ (accessed 09/01/2018); Statistical Atlas, Race and Ethnicity in California, https://statisticalatlas.com/state/California/Race-and-Ethnicity#data-map/county; Statistical Atlas, Educational Attainment in California, https://statisticalatlas.com/state/California/Educational-Attainment#top; Statistical Atlas, Household Income in California, https://statisticalatlas.com/state/California/Household-Income (accessed 10/2/18).

forcriticalanalysis

1. Why are the counties of California so different from one another? Are the four variables considered here related to each other, or to other factors not included here?

2. How do you think this range of ethnoracial diversity, educational attainment, and economic conditions affects California politics? How might this diversity affect local politics vs. state politics?

may not do as they raise revenue, spend money, and deliver services. Fourteen counties have adopted a home-rule charter, which gives voters greater control over the selection of governing bodies and officers, more flexibility in raising taxes and revenues, and broader discretion in organizing to deliver services. All of the state's most populous counties and one small county—Tehama, with 64,000 residents—are now **charter counties**. Voters can adopt a charter for their county government by a majority vote.

Long content to live without a charter, the voters of Orange County adopted one in March 2002. They did so mainly to prevent the governor from filling a vacancy on the county board of supervisors with his own choice of representative, an act within his authority under the general-law provisions.

San Francisco is an unusual case. It is governed under a single charter as a consolidated county and city, an arrangement that is unique in the state but more common in other areas of the country, particularly the Midwest and Upper South. Other consolidated city-county governments include Philadelphia, Pennsylvania; Nashville, Tennessee; and Jacksonville, Florida. County charters vary widely in content and in the range of powers claimed for local control. Anything that goes unmentioned within a charter is governed by the general law.

County Government Organization

In all counties except San Francisco, an elected five-member board of supervisors exercises both legislative and executive authority. Given the extremes in the size of county populations, this yields huge disparities in political representation. For example, each board member in tiny Alpine County represents, on average, only 224 residents. In mammoth Los Angeles County, on the other hand, each board member represents more than 2 million people.

County boards of supervisors, whose members are elected by districts for staggered four-year terms, not only pass laws, called **ordinances**, at the local level, but also control and supervise the departments charged with administering these ordinances. This combination of legislative and executive authority gives county supervisors great power.

In the consolidated city and county government of San Francisco, an elected 11-member board of supervisors has legislative authority. An independently elected mayor has executive authority and some control, shared with many boards and commissions, over the bureaucracy.

In addition to the board of supervisors, other elected or appointed county officers required by general law include a sheriff, who enforces the law in areas outside the cities; a district attorney; and an assessor. A 1998 constitutional amendment consolidated municipal and superior trial courts into a single layer of superior court judges who are elected by county voters. Elections for all county offices are nonpartisan. In terms of appointed positions, charter counties have considerable latitude in creating departments and agencies to serve their needs, either by charter provision or by ordinance. Other offices are required or authorized by state law. Some charter counties, such as Los Angeles County, have appointed a chief executive officer to manage their sprawling bureaucracies under board supervision.

Figure 9.2 shows Placer County's organizational chart, which is very simple and typical of counties with small populations. By way of contrast, Figure 9.3 shows Los Angeles County's organizational chart. The latter illustrates the complexity of

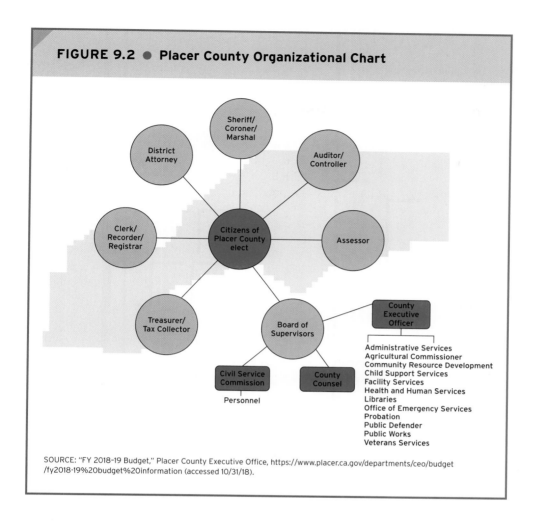

FIGURE 9.2 ● Placer County Organizational Chart

Sheriff/ Coroner/ Marshal

District Attorney

Auditor/ Controller

Clerk/ Recorder/ Registrar

Citizens of Placer County elect

Assessor

Treasurer/ Tax Collector

Board of Supervisors

County Executive Officer

Civil Service Commission

County Counsel

Personnel

Administrative Services
Agricultural Commissioner
Community Resource Development
Child Support Services
Facility Services
Health and Human Services
Libraries
Office of Emergency Services
Probation
Public Defender
Public Works
Veterans Services

SOURCE: "FY 2018-19 Budget," Placer County Executive Office, https://www.placer.ca.gov/departments/ceo/budget /fy2018-19%20budget%20information (accessed 10/31/18).

local government authority and responsibility that can be found in counties with large and diverse populations.

County Government Functions and Responsibilities

County governments have major functions and responsibilities, most of them mandated by state or federal law, especially outside the jurisdictions of cities. County responsibilities include bridges and highways, public safety, public health, employment, parks and recreation, welfare and public assistance, public records, tax collection, general government, court administration, and land use. In the largest counties, the public workforce required to manage these responsibilities and the budget needed to pay for them can be truly massive. In 2018, for example, Los Angeles County had 111,392 employees and an adopted budget of $31.4 billion.[6]

Decisions on land-use policy are perhaps the most important and controversial ones a county board of supervisors can make. If you're ever in the mood to watch a good political fight, attend a county board of supervisors meeting in a place like Napa County or San Diego County. Areas like these still have plenty of open land

FIGURE 9.3 • Los Angeles County Organizational Chart

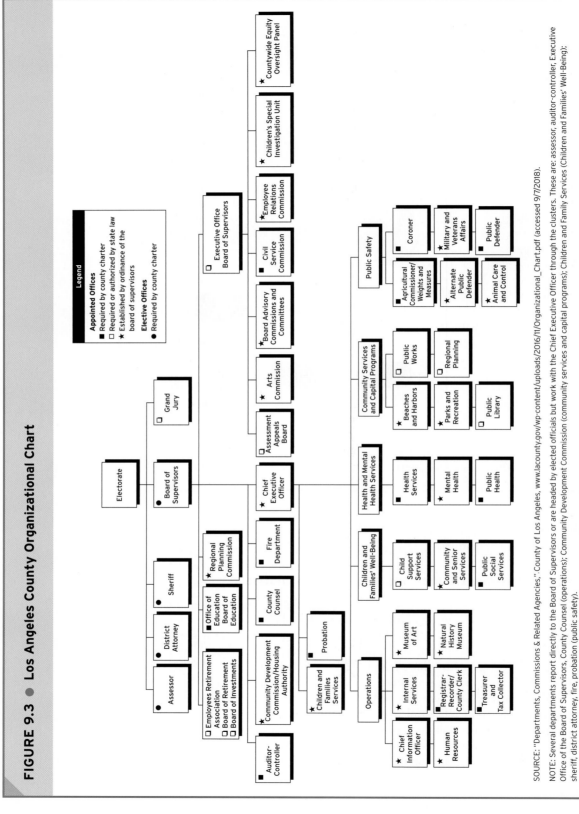

SOURCE: "Departments, Commissions & Related Agencies," County of Los Angeles, www.lacounty.gov/wp-content/uploads/2016/1t/Organizational_Chart.pdf (accessed 9/7/2018).

NOTE: Several departments report directly to the Board of Supervisors or are headed by elected officials but work with the Chief Executive Officer through the clusters. These are: assessor, auditor-controller, Executive Office of the Board of Supervisors, County Counsel (operations); Community Development Commission (community services and capital programs); Children and Family Services (Children and Families' Well-Being); sheriff, district attorney, fire, probation (public safety).

outside the cities and fast-growing populations that fuel a demand for new housing construction, schools, and public infrastructure (sewers, highways, etc.). Landowners and developers typically pressure the county board of supervisors to allow them to build, while conservationists, environmentalists, and other groups mobilize in opposition to push them back. Housing developments are further complicated by the reality that homeowners are usually opposed to new housing in their neighborhoods, whether they are Democrats or Republicans, conservatives or liberals.

For example, on July 31, 2012, the Riverside County Board of Supervisors met to decide whether to "fast-track" approval of Granite Construction's application to build a surface mine known as Liberty Quarry near the small town of Temecula. Fast-tracking would allow the project to skip the county planning commission's standard review and thus expedite the board's final decision. The debate at the crowded public meeting was impassioned on both sides. Orange-shirted opponents faced off against green-shirted supporters. Representatives of the chamber of commerce, labor unions, and other groups backed the proposal, arguing that the quarry would stimulate the local economy and create badly needed jobs. Temecula city officials, environmentalists, and leaders of the Pechanga Band of Luiseño Indians contended that the quarry would pollute the air, wreck the economy, and destroy a nearby sacred tribal site. One supervisor called Liberty Quarry "the most divisive project in county history." The board voted 3-to-2 to fast-track approval, prompting cheers from the green shirts and cries of outrage from the orange shirts. Then, on November 15, 2012, just days before the board was scheduled to give its final approval, leaders of the Pechanga Band announced that they had reached an agreement with Granite Construction to purchase the Liberty Quarry site for $3 million and to pay the firm an additional $17.35 million to cover its project costs. Granite was permitted to build its mine elsewhere, miles from Temecula and the sacred tribal lands. The Pechanga Band promised to preserve the original site as it was.[7]

As California's population continues to grow and spread from the cities into the state's remaining farmlands and rural areas, you can expect to see more land-use battles of this sort erupting in the political arenas of county governments.

Local Agency Formation Commissions

All 58 California counties have a **local agency formation commission (LAFCo)**, whose members are appointed by the county board of supervisors. These commissions play a critical role in resolving conflicts among the many local governments that often compete with one another for power and resources within their county jurisdictions. A county's LAFCo has the following responsibilities:

- reviewing and approving the incorporations of new cities, the formation of new special districts, and any proposed changes of jurisdictional boundaries, including annexations and detachments of territory, **secessions**, consolidations, mergers, and dissolutions

- reviewing and approving contractual service agreements between local governments and between local governments and the private sector

- defining the official spheres of influence for each city and special district

- initiating proposals for consolidation, dissolution, mergers, and reorganizations if such changes seem necessary or desirable

These powerful commissions are especially busy in counties that are rocked by large-scale land-use battles, such as Riverside County, or that teem with masses of people and a multitude of governments, such as Los Angeles County.[8]

City Governments

Legal Framework

Like counties, California's cities derive their powers as municipal corporations from the state constitution and state legislature. Within that legal framework, as of September 2018, the state's 482 incorporated cities fell into three categories: **general-law cities** (361), **charter cities** (120), and the unique case of San Francisco's consolidated city and county.[9] The California Government Code, enacted by the legislature, specifies the general powers and structure of general-law cities. Broader home-rule powers are granted to charter cities, giving citizens more direct control over local affairs. Under these different arrangements, all cities have the power to legislate, as long as their local policies don't conflict with state or federal law. They have the power to raise revenues, levy taxes, charge license and service fees, and borrow. They may also hire personnel as needed; exercise police powers to enforce local, state, and federal laws; and condemn property for public use.

Incorporation and Dissolution

The state grants powers to cities, and in that sense cities are indeed creatures of the state. But cities themselves are created only by the request, and with the consent, of the residents in a given area. In California, this process of **municipal incorporation** is typically initiated by a citizen petition or by a resolution of the county board of supervisors. Landowner petitions are also possible but rare. The following are some of the more important reasons that motivate residents to seek incorporation:

- to limit or accelerate population growth
- to provide more or better-quality services than those provided by the county
- to prevent annexation by a nearby city
- to create a unit of government more responsive to local needs and concerns
- to escape the tax and spending burdens imposed by county government rule

A petition for municipal incorporation must be submitted to the county's LAFCo. The LAFCo panel reviews the proposed plans for the new city, its boundaries, its service provisions, its governing capacity, and its financial viability. The LAFCo also studies the likely financial and other impacts of the proposed incorporation on neighboring local governments, including the county itself. If the petition for incorporation survives this initial review and a later public hearing and possible protests, it moves to an election. If a majority of voters living within the boundaries of the proposed new city approve, a new city is legally born.[10] The rate of incorporation of new cities has fallen dramatically in recent years. Only 9 have incorporated since 1999 and only two in the last decade, raising the total number of cities to 482 in 2018.[11]

The heavy burden of legal obligations and fiduciary responsibilities that come with incorporation can be difficult for municipalities to handle, particularly in times of widespread financial stress. The trials and tribulations of Jurupa Valley, the state's youngest city, illustrate this point. Jurupa Valley, a community of about 100,000 people located in Riverside County, formally became an incorporated, general-law city in July 2011. The community thereby gained home-rule powers and greater local control over land use and service provision within its borders. The summer of 2011 proved an unfortunate time for the city of Jurupa Valley to be born, however, as the governor and state legislators faced yet another budget crisis. Only days after the community's incorporation, the state government diverted all of its vehicle license fee revenues away from local governments to bolster budgets for prisons and other law enforcement programs at the state level. This sudden diversion of funds hurt all California cities, but it hit Jurupa Valley especially hard; city officials had counted on their share of that money, which was several millions of dollars, to make ends meet. On January 16, 2014, after months of cutting staffing and services to the bone while searching in vain for state financial support, Jurupa Valley's city council members voted unanimously to petition Riverside County's LAFCo for municipal dissolution and a return to county rule.

It was the first such petition received by a LAFCo in more than 40 years, and it triggered a legal process of disincorporation that could have taken up to two years to complete.[12] A local reporter warned her readers of some of the implications: "If home rule goes away, decision-making on land-use and other issues like code enforcement, public works and road repairs will revert to Riverside County. Traffic enforcement will be handled by the California Highway Patrol."[13]

This story, however, has a happy ending. On September 22, 2015, with the economy now booming and his budget balanced, Governor Brown signed a bill authored by State Senator Richard Roth (D-Riverside) that restored funding to Jurupa Valley and three other recently born cities in Riverside County. On October 1, Jurupa Valley's city council members joyfully passed a resolution rescinding the earlier dissolution request.[14] Thus did the new city of Jurupa Valley survive its near-death experience.

City Government Functions and Responsibilities

City governments provide a wide range of services and facilities that directly affect the lives of their residents: fire and police protection; street construction and maintenance; sewage and waste disposal; health, social, and recreational programs; and planning and zoning to determine land use that is consistent with the community's needs and values. Most city governments provide water, and some run public transit systems. A few, such as Los Angeles and Sacramento, own and manage municipal electricity or natural gas utilities.

Residents in most cities are content if basic services such as police, fire, and waste management are provided reliably and efficiently, either directly by the municipality itself or, as in many smaller cities, by contracting services from other local governments and the private sector.[15] In some places, however, residents demand more from their city government than just the basics. For example, in some cities, business leaders and entrepreneurs pressure city hall to promote rapid economic growth and development. In other cities, community activists pressure city hall to limit growth and development and to pursue ambitious social agendas on the world stage.

City Government Revenues and Expenditures

As shown in Figure 9.4, the typical city budget in California relies most heavily on current service charges and taxes for most of its revenues. Most of what it spends goes toward public safety, community development and health, public utilities,

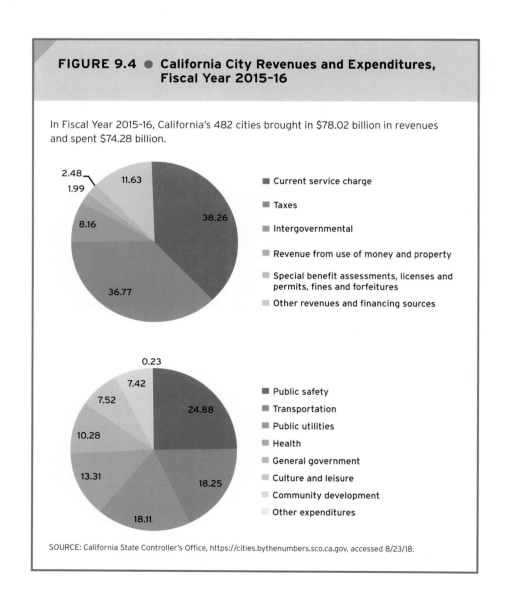

FIGURE 9.4 ● California City Revenues and Expenditures, Fiscal Year 2015-16

In Fiscal Year 2015-16, California's 482 cities brought in $78.02 billion in revenues and spent $74.28 billion.

- Current service charge
- Taxes
- Intergovernmental
- Revenue from use of money and property
- Special benefit assessments, licenses and permits, fines and forfeitures
- Other revenues and financing sources

2.48
1.99
11.63
38.26
8.16
36.77

- Public safety
- Transportation
- Public utilities
- Health
- General government
- Culture and leisure
- Community development
- Other expenditures

0.23
7.42
7.52
24.88
10.28
13.31
18.25
18.11

SOURCE: California State Controller's Office, https://cities.bythenumbers.sco.ca.gov, accessed 8/23/18.

and transportation. We will have more to say about city finances later in this chapter in the context of the state's continuing budget crisis.

Forms of City Government and the Legacy of Progressive Structural Reforms

The overall vision and structural reforms advanced by the Progressives nearly a century ago have had an enduring impact on the form of municipal government in California. Progressive reformers sought to replace the corrupt bosses running partisan, ward-based, big-city political machines with government by reputable civic leaders and nonpartisan experts managing local affairs in the public interest. To implement that vision, the following structural reforms were necessary:

- strong managers and weak mayors
- nonpartisan elections
- at-large council elections
- the tools of direct democracy (the initiative, referendum, and recall)

Other Progressive reforms included civil service (merit-based) systems of municipal employment and, especially in the larger cities, professionally run city planning commissions and departments.[16] Reformers were particularly successful in the southwestern states, where populations were growing fast and new cities were popping up everywhere, isolated from the influence of eastern-style partisanship and urban machine politics.[17] Municipalities that have all or most of these institutional features are known as **reform governments**. Most medium-size American cities and nearly all of California's cities qualify for that label.

COUNCIL-MANAGER PLAN VERSUS MAYOR-COUNCIL SYSTEM Under the council-manager form of government, the voters elect a city council, which in turn appoints a professionally trained city manager to run the administration. The city manager directly controls the bureaucracy and supervises the performance of department heads. The council restricts itself to legislative policy making, while retaining the ultimate authority to fire or replace the appointed manager. Nearly all small- and medium-sized California cities, as well as San Jose and Sacramento, are governed by the **council-manager plan**.[18] Mayors are directly elected in about a third of these cities, but they perform mainly ceremonial duties and have no independent executive powers, such as the veto or budget control. (A partial exception is San Jose, whose mayor has very limited control of the budget and bureaucracy.)

The rest of California's cities are governed by **mayor-council systems**. Most are very small cities that can't afford a professional city manager and have weak mayors of the purely ceremonial type. Most of the state's largest cities, however, have strong mayor-council systems in which the mayor is elected independently of the council and serves as the city's overall chief executive. These are often called strong-mayor systems because the mayor proposes the city's budget, appoints department heads, and has veto power over council legislation. The council (or, in the case of San Francisco, the board of supervisors) is responsible for legislative policy making. Typically, as in Los Angeles and San Francisco, various appointive boards and commissions set overall policy and supervise administration of important city departments such as police and fire, thus limiting the mayor's direct control of the bureaucracy.

In recent years, the voters in some council-manager cities have approved the switch to a strong-mayor system to make local government decision making more accountable, nimble, and responsive to changing political environments. When former governor Jerry Brown ran for mayor of Oakland in 1998, he insisted that the voters support Measure X, which he had helped to draft, that would give the mayor the veto, control over budget preparation, and extensive appointment powers while reducing the then-powerful city manager to an administrator under mayoral authority. Oakland's voters approved the measure by a 3-to-1 margin and elected Brown as the city's new mayor. In 2004, San Diego's voters followed suit, changing one of the nation's largest council-manager systems into a strong-mayor system on a trial-run basis, and voted again in 2010 to make that new system permanent. In contrast, on November 4, 2014, Sacramento's voters soundly rejected (57-to-43 percent) Measure L, a proposed charter amendment that would have changed the city's current council-manager plan to a strong-mayor system. Sacramento and San Jose remain the state's two largest cities still sticking with the council-manager system.

In practice, formal and informal power arrangements vary widely across both the council-manager and mayor-council systems. Personal ambition, political skill, and leadership style are key factors that influence the degree of power accorded to a given mayor or manager to run local government and shape public policy.[19]

NONPARTISAN ELECTIONS California law requires that all local elections be officially **nonpartisan**. The Progressive Era reformers had pushed for nonpartisan elections as a means to insulate the important business of local government from what they saw as the distracting and corrupting influence of partisan politics. In nonpartisan elections, no information about a candidate's political party membership is shown on the ballot. In practice, of course, many local contests are fiercely partisan, even if the voters do not see a "D" or an "R" next to the candidates' names. They can infer partisanship through statements about other elected officials (for example, about President Trump or members of his administration) or from endorsements from local party organizations and other local officials.

AT-LARGE VERSUS DISTRICT COUNCIL ELECTIONS More than 90 percent of California cities conduct at-large council elections, in which voters elect council members citywide rather than by districts or wards.[20] Under the **at-large elections** system, for example, if a number of candidates compete for one of the three vacant seats on the council, all of the city's voters have the opportunity to vote for any three of them, and the top three vote-getters are declared the winners. About 5 percent of cities use the **district elections** method, which divides the city into districts and requires the voters in each district to elect one of the candidates running in that district to represent them on the council. The remaining cities—Oakland is an example—use some hybrid combination of at-large and district elections to elect their councils.

Local governments change their election systems infrequently, if at all, and they usually do so only after being pressured by political reform movements or lawsuits. (As an illustration of how lawsuits can force such change, see the discussion of the California Voting Rights Act on the next page.) In 2000, for example, San Francisco switched from at-large to district elections for electing its board of supervisors in response to voter demand for greater representation of neighborhoods and minority groups, reduced influence of big money on elections, and a wider field of candidates who otherwise could not afford to run citywide campaigns.[21] Of course, the district system by itself doesn't guarantee a more neighborhood-oriented council, less costly campaigns, or political life on a smaller scale. The 15 members of the Los Angeles City Council, for example, are elected by districts. But each council member represents nearly a quarter of a million residents on average and must run expensive campaigns over vast territories to get elected.

The major trend in the past two decades has been a shift to district elections to allow for better representation of historically marginalized groups, especially Latinos. The first city to make the switch, in 1989, was Watsonville. Attorney Joaquin Avila and the Mexican American Legal Defense and Educational Fund sued Watsonville in federal court, arguing that the increasingly-Latino town's at-large system of electing city council members was diluting the Latino vote in violation of the federal Voting Rights Act of 1965 (VRA). The victory made national news, but few cities or counties chose to follow suit. Instead, many were forced to follow Watsonville's lead as various legal groups filed charges of vote dilution. Avila worked to help draft the California Voting Rights Act of 2001 (CVRA), which made it easier to prove minority vote dilution.

The CVRA expanded on the VRA by eliminating the need for minority plaintiffs to identify a particular geographic district in their city in which a minority is sufficiently concentrated to result in a majority of voters. This crucial distinction makes it easier for plaintiffs to claim that at-large elections dilute their votes. CVRA-based lawsuits by minority groups in Modesto, Compton, Anaheim, Escondido, Whittier, Palmdale, and other cities have been successful, and more are coming. Local governments using at-large elections in racially diverse communities have been put on the defensive, and it's not hard to see why. Consider the egregious case of Palmdale, whose mayor, according to the *Los Angeles Times*, could not "explain why Palmdale, whose population is almost 55% Latino and nearly 15% black, has elected only one Latino and no African Americans to its council."[22]

The state's rapidly surging Latino population has been a major driver of CVRA lawsuits.[23] The Southwest Voter Registration Project, a Latino voting rights organization, has been particularly aggressive in suing local governments that have at-large systems and an underrepresentation of Latinos as a legally protected minority class. If such jurisdictions fight in court and lose, as they almost always do, they often must pay large settlements and fees. Palmdale, for example, fought such a lawsuit, lost, and had to pay about $4.6 million in attorneys' fees. Fearing expensive lawsuits, officials in many jurisdictions have taken steps proactively to change from at-large to district systems. An example is the city of San Marcos, in which Latinos make up 37 percent of the population but have elected no Latinos to the city council in two decades.[24] Under the threat of such lawsuits, according to one report, more than 100 school and college districts throughout the state have also proactively decided to change their election systems.[25] Some advocates, like law professor Richard Hasen, see the CVRA as a "bright spot" in an era when other states are erecting barriers to minority voter participation. "In California, you have a large Latino population that's growing," Hasen told a reporter. "And you couple that with a Democratic majority in a state legislature that is willing to protect minority voting rights, then you get a very different situation than in Texas, where Republican legislators are making it harder for Latinos to vote."[26]

Most recently, the city of Santa Clara adopted district elections in response to a lawsuit brought on behalf of Asian American residents, who noted in their 2017 filing that all members of the council were white, despite a population that is just 34 percent non-Hispanic white and more than 40 percent Asian.

DIRECT DEMOCRACY At the local level of government, just as at the state level, ordinary citizens have access to the tools of **direct democracy** (the initiative, referendum, and recall) bequeathed to them by Progressive Era reformers. Specifically, if citizens gather the required number of valid signatures on formal petitions, they can accomplish the following:

- initiate direct legislation, including proposed ordinances and charter amendments, by placing such measures on the ballot for voter approval

- suspend implementation of council legislation until the voters approve it at a referendum election

- subject incumbent elected officials to a recall vote and possible dismissal before the next scheduled regular election

Local referenda are quite rare. Local recall elections are also rare, but they occur more often than do statewide recalls. For example, in the politically contentious town of Pacifica, voters have successfully petitioned for five recall elections over the last 40 years. The use of local ballot initiatives, however, is much more frequent and widespread, although not nearly to the extent observed at the state level. Direct legislation by citizen ballot initiative has become common in a few cities, especially larger and more diverse cities such as San Francisco, especially around land-use and housing issues. Citizen initiatives appear on ballots less frequently in most other cities, but they are not uncommon. A 2012 study found that there were only 212 city initiatives and 62 county initiatives in the 2001–08 period, an average of just half an initiative per jurisdiction over eight years.[27] A replication of that survey in 2018 would probably show a higher rate of citizen initiatives, given the rise of contentious politics and anti-establishment movements at all political levels.

Legal scholars Matthew Melone and George Nation III offer an important insight into the relationship between direct democracy and representative government:

> The importance of direct democracy is not diminished by the fact that representative democracy is the primary form of government because the importance of direct democracy is not determined by the frequency of its use. . . . [T]he mere fact that the tools of direct democracy are readily available in a state prevents many of the abuses associated with representative government despite the fact that such tools are actually used infrequently. . . . The institutions of representative democracy and the representatives themselves function better due to the possibility of the voters' resort to direct democracy.[28]

Some of the cases discussed later in this chapter will illustrate this point.

Also see Box 9.1 on the Brown Act, the "open meetings law" that gives citizens yet another tool of direct democracy to help them become more informed about the decision-making process and to hold their local government officials accountable.

BOX 9.1 ● California's Open Meetings Law
(The Brown Act)

The Ralph M. Brown Act of 1953 required that "all meetings of the legislative body of a local agency shall be open and public, and all persons shall be permitted to attend any meeting of the legislative body of a local agency, except as otherwise provided in this chapter." The intent of the Brown Act, also known as the "open meetings law," was to support transparency and prevent secret meetings and backroom dealings of local government officials conducting public business. (The Bagley-Keene Act of 1967 later extended the same open-meetings requirement to state government agencies.) The Brown Act allows closed meetings for personnel decisions and the like to protect community and individual rights. This also includes 1) city council or board of supervisors meetings discussing litigation, 2) labor relations, 3) disciplinary action, and 4) property acquisitions such as use of eminent domain. These meetings must be noticed and results reported out after a decision is made, but the public can be excluded from the discussion in an executive session.

The rules were further broadened in the 1990s to include meetings negotiating local collective-bargaining agreements, which the public may see only after they are signed—often too late to raise hard questions and objections about the financial implications. Further extensions were approved in 2008 and 2009 in order to ban serial meetings (in which Official A conveys a view privately to Official B who conveys it to Official C to reach a majority consensus). A majority of members of an elected body cannot communicate via any means outside a public meeting.

The Little Hoover Commission, the state's independent oversight agency, noted in a 2015 report that the state's open meeting acts have "hindered government decision-making processes and created less transparency instead of more." They further noted that the rules have isolated decision makers, "reduced their collective understanding of issues and opened them to greater manipulation out of public view." In 2017 columnist Joe Mathews opined, "The act's requirements of advance notice before local officials hold a meeting has mutated into strict limitations on the ability of local officials to have frank conversations with one another. Brown Act requirements that we, the public, can weigh in at meetings have been turned against us, by way of a standardized three-minute-per-speaker limit that encourages rapid rants and discourages real conversation with our representatives."

SOURCE: League of California Cities, *Open & Public IV: A Guide to the Ralph M. Brown Act* (2007); Peter Scheer, "Public Employee Unions: Losing the Image Battle," *San Francisco Chronicle*, June 13, 2010, p. N5; www.lhc.ca.gov /sites/lhc.ca.gov/files/Reports/227/Report227.pdf; www.sacbee.com/opinion/op-ed/article140151118.html (accessed 8/24/18).

LOCAL VOTER TURNOUT AND POLITICAL REPRESENTATION Despite the surge in voter turnout in the 2008 presidential election, with 62.2 percent of eligible voters going to the polls, the overall trend in voter participation since 1960 has been gradually downward in national elections (see Chapter 4). That trend continued in the 2016 presidential election, with just 60.2 percent of eligible voters going to the polls—an improvement from the 58.6 percent turnout in 2012. Turnout in California mirrors national trends, with 61.7 percent turnout in 2008, 55.7 percent turnout in 2012, and 58.4 percent turnout in 2016.[29] Voter turnout rates in California's local elections tend to be much lower. A study by Melissa Marschall and John Lappie of mayoral elections between 1995 and 2014 found that turnout was only 21 percent, decreasing to just over 16 percent if a single candidate for mayor was running unopposed (of the mayoral elections they examined, nearly a quarter were uncontested).[30] Boosting turnout in these elections thus to a certain extent depends on the candidates and whether they are running unopposed; however, rescheduling local nonconcurrent elections to coincide with high-turnout presidential and midterm congressional elections would likely result in significantly higher participation rates.

Similar reasoning lies behind one of the arguments for ranked-choice voting, also known as the alternative vote or "instant runoff voting," which San Francisco adopted in 2002 (soon followed by Berkeley, Oakland, and San Leandro). Under ranked-choice voting, voters in the November general election rank the candidates for an office by order of preference (first choice, second choice, and so on). When all the ballots are counted, if no candidate receives a majority of first-choice preferences, the candidate receiving the fewest is dropped from the list and his or her ballots are transferred to the remaining candidates according to voters' rankings. (If a voter's lower-ranked candidates aren't among the survivors, his or her ballot is classified as "exhausted" and removed from the transfer flow of "continuing" ballots to be counted again in the next round.) Another tally is taken of continuing ballots, and if there is still no majority winner, the process is repeated until a majority winner is declared.

This system presents an alternative to the typical local election in California, in which the top two vote-getters face off in a typically low-turnout, low-interest runoff election in December if no candidate receives a majority of the votes cast in November. Under the ranked-choice system, these December runoff elections can be avoided.

Some critics of ranked-choice voting argue that many voters actually prefer December runoffs because they winnow the field of candidates and sharpen the voter's focus on only two choices. Further, voter turnout for mayoral elections and other high-profile local contests is sometimes even higher in the December runoff than in the November general election. These kinds of debates about the merits of ranked-choice voting and other proposed electoral reforms will continue.[31] This is considered a benefit by scholars who view local governments as ideal "laboratories of democracy" where innovations like ranked-choice voting can be tried and tested before being recommended to a wider public.[32]

California has implemented a number of reforms to its voter registration and electoral processes in recent years with the aim of increasing participation among eligible voters. In 2017, California began to allow 16- and 17-year olds to preregister to vote, although they cannot actually participate in elections until they are 18 years old. In 2018 the state rolled out an automatic voter registration policy that automatically registers eligible citizens when they go to the DMV for their drivers license. Also in 2018 selected counties (Madera, Napa, Nevada, Sacramento, and San Mateo) began to implement the California Voter's Choice Act of 2016, which replaces traditional community polling places with mailed ballots and vote centers. Instead of requiring registered voters to only vote by mail or at their local polling place, the VCA allows citizens within a participating county to vote at any of the county's vote centers.[33]

Finally, and more controversially, a case can be made for greater political representation of noncitizens in local government. Noncitizens are not only tolerated but respected in many California cities, and their voices are heard and heeded by local officials. Leaders of immigrant-serving nonprofit agencies, community-based organizations, and worker centers are highly politically active in self-declared sanctuary cities such as San Francisco, where their efforts have led to assured equal access to city services regardless of immigrant status, the provision of municipal identification cards, and passage of wage-theft legislation to deter the economic exploitation of this vulnerable population. In 2004 advocacy groups and a broad coalition of supporters advanced a ballot measure giving noncitizen parents of children enrolled in public schools the right to vote in the city's school board elections. That measure failed, just barely, and it failed again in 2010 by a slightly larger margin. The third time was a charm, however. In the November 8, 2016, election, the city's voters approved the measure by an 8-point margin, 54-to-46 percent.[34] The measure was then unanimously adopted by the San Francisco Board of Supervisors in May 2018, paving the way for noncitizen parents to vote in November 2018 school board elections. According to Hong Mei Pang, director of advocacy at the San Francisco–based nonprofit Chinese for Affirmative Action, about one-third of the students in the district come from immigrant households, so the measure will give many parents a rightful voice.[35] That said, few noncitizens chose to take advantage of the opportunity to vote in November 2018.

Special Districts

Special districts are limited-purpose local governments. They fill the need or desire for services that general-purpose governments such as counties and cities cannot or will not provide. If residents or landowners desire new or better services, they can take steps to establish a special district to pay for them. As a popular guide to special districts notes: "Special districts *localize* the costs and benefits of public services. Special districts allow local citizens to obtain the services they want at a price they are willing to pay."[36] Examples of special districts include fire protection districts, cemetery districts, water districts, recreation and park districts, storm water drainage and conservation districts, irrigation districts, and mosquito abatement districts.

School and Community College Districts

California's **school and community college districts** are a unique type of special district. As of 2017–18 there were 1,026 K–12 school districts in the state, serving over 6.2 million students.[37] School districts derive their authority from the California Education Code and are governed by locally elected school boards. Each board sets general policies and appoints a superintendent as chief executive officer, who serves at the pleasure of the board. The superintendent has overall responsibility for managing the system and its various schools and programs. In 2018 the state's community college system of two-year public institutions comprised 114 colleges organized into 72 districts. Serving more than 2.1 million students, it is the largest system of higher education in the nation.[38] In 1988 the California legislature enacted Assembly Bill 1725, giving community colleges status as institutions of higher education. AB 1725 also strengthened the advisory role of local academic senates and of the Student Senate for California Community Colleges in working with state government officials to make higher-education policy. Each community college district is governed by a locally elected board of trustees that sets general policies and appoints a chancellor as chief executive officer. As discussed elsewhere in this book, the state of California's K–14 public education system, and especially the financial crises that surround it, continue to be a major focus of policy debate and political battle.

In recent years, community colleges in California have come under fire for their poor graduation rates. A 2010 report by the Institute for Higher Education Leadership & Policy at Cal State Sacramento found that 70 percent of students seeking degrees at California community colleges did not attain them or transfer to four-year universities within six years. In 2018 new rules went into effect that tie each college's funding to how well it serves students (as measured by graduation and transfer rates), and especially to how well it serves poor students.[39]

Nonschool Special Districts

Excluding the school districts, the state had 4,884 special districts in 2017.[40] These special districts can be classified in three different ways: single-purpose versus multiple-purpose, enterprise versus nonenterprise, and independent versus dependent.

- About 85 percent of the state's special districts perform a single function, such as sewage management, water management, fire protection, or mosquito abatement. The others are multifunctional, such as the state's more than 800 County Service Areas (CSAs), which provide two or more services, such as enhanced recreation services and extended police protection.

- About one in four special districts are **enterprise districts**, which are run like businesses and charge **user fees** for services. Nearly all airport, harbor and port, transit, water, waste, and hospital districts are enterprise districts of this sort. In fiscal year 2015–16, the state's enterprise districts generated a total of $21.98 billion in user fees.[41] The state's many nonenterprise districts provide public services such as fire protection and pest control that benefit the entire community, not just individual residents. Typically, property taxes rather than user fees pay the costs.

- About two-thirds of the state's special districts are **independent districts**. An independent district is governed by its own separate board of directors appointed by an authorizing agency or elected directly by the district's voters. Dependent districts are governed by existing legislative bodies. Nearly all CSAs, for example, are governed by a county board of supervisors.

These three ways of classifying special districts are not mutually exclusive, and examples of all possible combinations exist.

Legal Framework

Like all local governments in the state, special districts must conform to the state constitution and to the legislature's government code. Statutory authority for special districts derives from either a principal act or a special act of the state legislature. A *principal act* is a general law that applies to all special districts of a given type. For example, the Fire Protection District Law of 1987 in the California Health and Safety Code governs all 386 fire districts. About 60 of these principal law statutes are on the books and can be used to create a special district anywhere in the state. Another 120 or so *special acts* have been passed by the legislature to adapt a special district's structure, financing, and authority to unique local circumstances. The Alameda County Flood Control and Water District, for example, was formed under such a special act.

How Special Districts Are Created

To form a special district, the voters in the proposed district must apply to their county's LAFCo. After the LAFCo reviews and approves the proposal, it moves to an election in which only the voters residing inside the proposed district boundaries may vote. A simple majority is required for approval in most cases. A two-thirds majority is required if new special taxes are involved. As of August 2018 there were 3,776 special districts in California.

The Advantages and Disadvantages of Special Districts

The advantages of special districts include the following:

- the flexibility that such districts allow in tailoring the level and quality of service to citizen demands

- the linking of costs to benefits, so that those who don't benefit from a district's services don't have to pay for them

- the greater responsiveness of special districts to their constituents, who often reside in smaller geographic areas of larger city and county jurisdictions

The disadvantages of special districts include the following:

- the overlapping of jurisdictions and the resulting duplication of services already provided by cities and counties or by other special districts

- the reduced incentives for needed regional planning, especially in providing water, sewer, and fire protection services, which are typically offered by a host of special districts governed by independent boards without any central coordination

- the decreased accountability that results from the sheer multiplicity of limited special districts, which overwhelms the average citizen's ability to find out who is in charge of delivering specific services

Some critics think special districts should be abolished, their functions redistributed to established general-purpose city and county governments. One contends that special districts "make a mockery of the natural connections that people have with a specific place. Special districts lie beyond the commonsense experience of most citizens; their very purpose is to divorce a narrow element of policy from the consideration of those charged with the maintenance of the common interest."[42] Advocates for special districts counter that special districts "focus on providing one service, or sometimes a small suite of services, to a community. It is this focused service that leads to efficiency and effectiveness. By focusing on doing one thing really well, special districts excel at innovation. It also allows them to plan ahead, think long-term, and practice sustainable decision-making."[43]

Regional Governments

A number of **regional governments** have formed in California to cope with problems such as air pollution, waste management, growth control, affordable housing production, and transportation gridlock—problems that affect large geographical areas and millions of people living in many different city and county jurisdictions. Some of these regional bodies have strong regulatory powers. Others are mainly advisory in function.

Regulatory Regional Governments

Examples of state **regulatory regional governments** include the California Coastal Commission, the South Coast Air Quality Management District, and the San Francisco Bay Conservation and Development Commission.

CALIFORNIA COASTAL COMMISSION (CCC) Appointed by the governor and the state legislature, the 12-member CCC has state-empowered regulatory authority to control all development within the 1,000-yard-wide shoreline zone along the entire California coast. Exercising its powers to grant or withhold permits for development, the CCC has succeeded over the years in opening public access to beaches, protecting scenic views, and restoring wetlands. Sometimes, the commission's mission to protect public access to California's coast brings prolonged legal battles. In 2008, Sun Microsystems cofounder Vinod Khosla bought an 89-acre

The South Coast Air Quality Management District, one of California's regional regulatory governments, uses its rule-making authority to promote the welfare of citizens like those here, who supported the closure of a well that leaked massive amounts of gas into the atmosphere outside LA.

property south of Half Moon Bay that included public Martins Beach. Khosla closed access to the beach and posted "do not enter" signs, launching what became a 10-year battle with the CCC to force him to restore public access, which they eventually won. Similarly, in 2005 music producer David Geffen lost a 22-year fight with the commission to unlock access to an area of beach next to his Malibu home.[44]

SOUTH COAST AIR QUALITY MANAGEMENT DISTRICT (SCAQMD) The 12-member SCAQMD board has state-granted regulatory authority to control emissions from stationary sources of air pollution such as power plants, refineries, and gas stations in the state's south coast air basin. This region encompasses all of Los Angeles and Orange Counties and parts of Riverside and San Bernardino Counties, an area of 12,000 square miles and home to more than 12 million people, nearly half the state's total population. This area also has the worst smog problem in the nation. Over the years, the board, which is appointed by city governments in the basin area, has conducted many studies, monitored air pollution levels, developed regional pollution abatement plans, and vigorously enforced federal and state air pollution laws. Thanks in large part to its efforts, the maximum level of ozone in the basin has been cut to less than half of what it was in the 1950s, despite the tripling of the population and quadrupling of vehicles in the region over that same period.

SAN FRANCISCO BAY CONSERVATION AND DEVELOPMENT COMMISSION (BCDC) The 27-member BCDC was created by the state legislature in 1965 in response to growing public concern about the future of San Francisco Bay, which was being dredged and polluted at an alarming rate by landfill projects. The commission includes members appointed by the governor, legislature, and various state and federal agencies; four city representatives appointed by the Association of Bay Area Governments; and nine county supervisors—one from each of the nine Bay Area counties. The commission is charged with regulating all filling and dredging in the bay; protecting the Suisun Marsh, the largest wetlands in California; regulating proposed new development within the first 100 feet inland from the bay to ensure maximum public access; enforcing the federal Coastal Zone Management Act; and other regulatory functions. By exercising its permit powers, BCDC not only stopped development that could have reduced the bay to a pond but also added hundreds of acres of new open water.

TAHOE REGIONAL PLANNING AGENCY (TRPA). The TRPA is a unique bi-state compact between California and Nevada, formed in 1969 with the mandate to protect the environment of the Lake Tahoe Basin. It includes seven members from California, seven from Nevada, and a fifteenth nonvoting member chosen by the president of the United States. Working in cooperation with other organizations, agencies, and private property owners, the TRPA works to heal past damage to the area's ecosystem through restoration projects and to minimize the impact of developed properties on the Lake Tahoe watershed. Board members work to maintain and expand recreational use of the lake and it's 72-mile shoreline, while also protecting air and water quality and minimizing the introduction of invasive species.[45]

Advisory Regional Governments

In addition to regional regulatory bodies, the state also has a number of regional planning, research, and advisory institutions called **advisory regional governments**.

The most important are various regional **councils of government (COGs)**. COGs are assemblies of delegates representing a region's counties and cities who join voluntarily and meet regularly to discuss common problems and regional issues. The state's two most prominent COGs are the Southern California Association of Governments (SCAG), which is the nation's largest COG, and the Association of Bay Area Governments (ABAG).

SCAG's regional jurisdiction encompasses 15 million people living in an area of more than 38,000 square miles, while ABAG's boundaries include 6 million people living in an area of 7,000 square miles. Both SCAG and ABAG have general assemblies that represent the broad membership of counties and cities located in each region. In both COGs, the serious work is done by smaller executive committees, a 75-member regional council in the case of SCAG and a 38-member executive board in the case of ABAG. Like most COGs, both SCAG and ABAG have professional staffs that conduct extensive research and planning studies of regional problems. Both regularly host regional conferences and forums on a range of substantive issues. And both have been designated by the federal government as metropolitan planning organizations for their regions, with the mandate to draw up plans for regional transportation, air quality, growth management, hazardous waste management, and production of affordable housing.

Both SCAG and ABAG have raised public awareness of regional problems and issues. They have also encouraged more regional planning and collaborative decision making. Neither COG, however, has the effective power or authority to enforce its policy recommendations on other local governments in their regions. Many Bay Area local officials, for example, pay lip service to ABAG's recommended fair-share quotas for production of affordable housing but then routinely ignore them when making decisions. Recent research has found that members of both political parties, and both conservatives and liberals, oppose new housing in their own neighborhoods.

Occasionally, a serious organized effort is made to create a truly comprehensive regional government with broad regulatory authority and strong enforcement powers. In the early 1990s, for example, an attempt was made to establish a powerful Bay Area regional government under the banner of BayVision 2020.[46] That proposal failed, like all the others, because most of the region's local governments were unwilling to surrender local autonomy and delegate some of their powers to a new, higher authority.

Local Government: Where Are We Now?

Ten years after the Great Recession of 2008, California's local governments have survived a gauntlet of economic and political crises. The Great Recession had severely weakened local economies and hit most of the state's city and county governments hard as tax revenues plummeted, which resulted in austerity in the form of slashed budgets, staff layoffs, and cutbacks in services. The cities of Vallejo (in 2008), Stockton (in 2012), and San Bernardino (in 2012) had been forced to declare bankruptcy, and other cities had teetered on the brink. As discussed earlier in this chapter, the state's newest city, Jurupa Valley, had barely survived a near-death experience. No financial rescue had come from the federal government, nor had the state government been of much help during the worst of it. Faced with its own budget crisis, the state had abolished California's 435 redevelopment agencies to extract new revenues to help make ends meet.

Today, California's finances have shifted dramatically thanks to the improving economy and to an increase in taxes that voters approved in 2012 (Proposition 30) and reauthorized in 2016. From a low point in 2011 when the state carried a $25 billion deficit, the state since 2013 has enjoyed surpluses, peaking in 2018 to a $14.8 billion surplus. The surplus funds allowed former governor Brown and the state legislature to give back to the cities and other local governments rather than taking from them. Funding was restored for public schools, health care, and social services. Plans for creating sustainable communities, improving transportation infrastructure, producing more affordable housing, and controlling greenhouse gas emissions—all of which had been placed on hold during hard times—were reactivated. Brown also set aside significant amounts from the surplus years into a rainy day fund, to help mitigate the need for another round of cuts the next time the economy hits a downturn.

At the local government level, post-recession economic recovery continues in most cities, especially in the San Francisco Bay Area and Los Angeles metropolitan region. In some cities, such as San Francisco, the tech-driven economic boom has created the problem of too much growth too fast, which has resulted in a housing affordability crisis, evictions and displacement, and growing political protest. In other cities, however, recovery from the recession still lags. The cities of Vallejo, Stockton, and San Bernardino are now released from bankruptcy, but all three continue to struggle with the same kinds of problems that forced them into bankruptcy in the first place: underfunded pension plans; limited tax revenues from slowly recovering businesses; and growing demands from citizens for better services, security, and employment opportunities. While cities in the state's coastal regions are once again thriving, many in the Central Valley and Inland Empire regions are still striving to attain prerecession levels of financial stability and economic well-being.

Illustrating the problems of the housing crisis and income inequality, San Francisco's homeless resorted to tent camps while the median price of homes in the city reached over $1,000,000 in 2018.

The Housing Crisis

Housing is perhaps the biggest crisis now facing California local governments. The median price of a home sale in June 2018 was over $600,000, double the U.S. median home price and a price only 30 percent of Californians can afford.[47] The upward pressure on prices is caused by a major shortage of housing supply, particularly lower-priced houses. From 2017 to 2018, the availability of homes priced below $200,000 fell by nearly 29 percent, while the supply of homes priced at $1 million or more increased by more than 18 percent. The housing shortage is particularly acute in the San Francisco Bay Area, where the median price of homes hit $1,088,000 in May 2018. The pace of new building is simply not keeping up with demand. Between 2008 and 2017, an average of 24.7 new housing permits were filed for every 100 new residents in California, well below the national average of 43.1 permits per 100 people.[48] See Figure 9.5 for details on this trend in recent years. At least 30 percent of people in every metropolitan area of the state cannot afford local rents, and that proportion increases to nearly 60 percent in some areas, as shown in Figure 9.6. The crisis has led to increased housing insecurity and homelessness. In the impacted areas of Silicon Valley and Los Angeles, more and more residents are living in trucks and RVs, parked along public streets, or in tents.

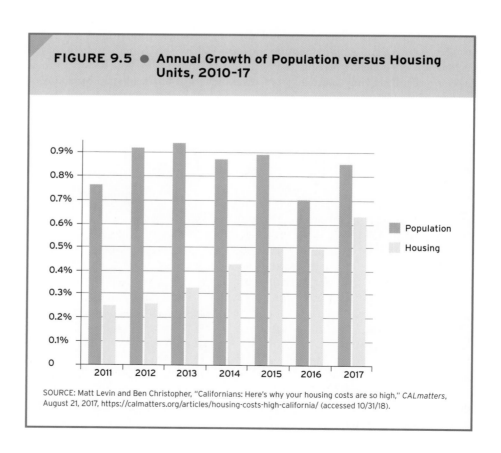

FIGURE 9.5 ● Annual Growth of Population versus Housing Units, 2010-17

SOURCE: Matt Levin and Ben Christopher, "Californians: Here's why your housing costs are so high," *CALmatters*, August 21, 2017, https://calmatters.org/articles/housing-costs-high-california/ (accessed 10/31/18).

FIGURE 9.6 ● Percentage of People Who Cannot Afford Local Rents by Metropolitan Area

In one report, it was shown that in every metropolitan area included in the study at least 30 percent of people were unable to afford local rent, with that figure being in some areas almost as high as 60 percent.

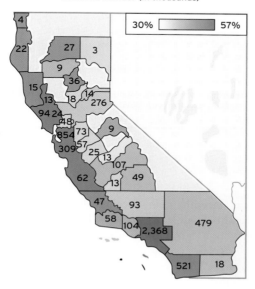

Households unable to afford rent as percent and total number (in thousands)

SOURCE: Data from U.S. Census Bureau; Zillow; McKinsey Global Institute analysis, and graph from www.artplusmarketing .com/california-needs-a-housing-first-agenda-my-2018-housing-package-1b6fe95e41da (accessed 9/7/2018).

NOTE: Shaded regions represent 98 percent of state population; unshaded regions represent 2 percent of state population and lacked sufficient data for analysis.

In September 2017, Governor Brown signed a set of 15 bills meant to ease the housing crunch, including a new tax on real estate transactions and a $4 billion bond that was approved by the voters in November 2018. Yet even the 14,000 new homes to be built each year with those funds will not put much of a dent in the problem, as shown in Figure 9.7. Developers would need to build well over 100,000 new homes more than planned each year to keep pace with California's population growth.[49]

Given simple economic rules of supply and demand, why don't developers simply build more housing? Part of the answer is that there is not enough affordable land to build on, particularly in the most impacted areas such as the San Francisco Bay Area. There is also a shortage of construction labor; California's unemployment rate in July 2018 was just 4.2 percent, the lowest rate since 1976.[50] Finally, there is the challenge of NIMBYism (Not In My Back Yard). Existing homeowners don't want new housing built near them, especially lower-priced housing, and this is true across political lines.[51]

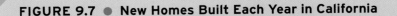

FIGURE 9.7 ● New Homes Built Each Year in California

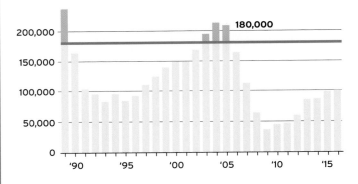

180,000

To keep up with a growing population, California needs 180,000 new homes each year. New legislation could add about 14,000 new homes each year.

SOURCE: Liam Dillon, "Gov. Brown just signed 15 housing bills. Here's how they're supposed to help the affordability crisis," *Los Angeles Times*, Sept 29, 2017, http://www.latimes.com/politics/la-pol-ca-housing-legislation-signed-20170929-htmlstory.html (accessed 10/31/18).

Another pressing issue faced by many local governments is the issue of growing income inequality and economic injustice. Following the lead of many local governments who adopted a $15 minimum wage policy, including San Francisco, Oakland, San Jose, Los Angeles County, and San Diego, in April 2016, Governor Brown signed a bill that made California the first state government in the country to adopt the $15 minimum wage along with the most generous paid-sick-leave policy in the United States. The increased minimum wage rules will take effect gradually, increasing $.50 to $1 each year for small and large businesses, and reaching $15 by 2022 for larger businesses and 2023 for smaller businesses.[52]

Conflict between California and the federal government has increased during the Donald Trump administration. Led by Attorney General Xavier Becerra, California has pushed back against Trump administration policies to roll back greenhouse gas emissions regulations. The state has also sought to protect marijuana markets, immigrants, and voting rights. As of October 2018, California has filed 44 lawsuits against the federal government. In September 2018, Governor Brown signed a bipartisan bill to block Trump's plan to expand offshore oil drilling off the California coast.[53] Battles between the state and federal government are also being waged over the 2020 Census and immigration.

Of all the lessons learned from the Great Recession, perhaps the most important is that local governments cannot solve economic and housing problems alone. Empowered business leadership, public-private partnerships, and market-based initiatives have the potential to help, but the private sector also is limited in its capacity to solve public problems. Local governments and their business partners require the power and resources of the federal and state governments to cope with such issues effectively. The years immediately ahead are certain to be politically turbulent and contentious, especially at the national level, and the future of California's state and local governments under the Trump administration is as yet unclear.

Study Guide

FOR FURTHER READING

Baldassare, Mark. *A California State of Mind: The Conflicted Voter in a Changing World*. Berkeley: University of California Press, 2002.

Bridges, Amy. *Morning Glories: Municipal Reform in the Southwest*. Princeton, NJ: Princeton University Press, 1997.

DeLeon, Richard Edward. *Left Coast City: Progressive Politics in San Francisco, 1975–1991*. Lawrence, KS: University Press of Kansas, 1992.

Hajnal, Zoltan L., Paul G. Lewis, and Hugh Louch. *Municipal Elections in California: Turnout, Timing, and Competition*. San Francisco: Public Policy Institute of California, 2002.

Rodriguez, Daniel B. "State Supremacy, Local Sovereignty: Reconstructing State/Local Relations under the California Constitution." In *Constitutional Reform in California: Making State Government More Effective and Responsive*, edited by Bruce E. Cain and Roger G. Noll, 401–29. Berkeley: Institute of Governmental Studies Press, University of California, 1995.

Sonenshein, Raphael J. *Politics in Black and White: Race and Power in Los Angeles*. Princeton, NJ: Princeton University Press, 1993.

ON THE WEB

California Department of Finance. www.dof.ca.gov. Accessed 8/24/18. The Department of Finance produces detailed and up-to-date statistical reports and studies on local government finances, the state budget process and its impacts on localities, and a wide range of demographic and economic information on cities and counties.

California Employment Development Department. www.edd.ca.gov. Accessed 8/24/18. Valuable source of up-to-date statewide and county-level information on employment and labor market conditions.

California Secretary of State. www.sos.ca.gov/elections. Accessed 8/24/18. Excellent source of information on county-level election results for statewide candidate races and ballot propositions.

California Special Districts Association. www.csda.net. Accessed 8/24/18.

California State Association of Counties. www.csac.counties.org. Accessed 8/24/18. Useful source of wide-ranging news and information on California's counties, with a main focus on policy and administration.

Institute for Local Government. www.ca-ilg.org. Accessed 8/24/18. The research arm and affiliate of the League of California Cities and the California State Association of Counties. Good source for in-depth studies of key policy issues facing the state's local governments.

League of California Cities. www.cacities.org. Accessed 8/24/18. An excellent source of news, information, and data on all aspects of governing California's cities.

U.S. Conference of Mayors. www.usmayors.org. Accessed 8/24/18.

SUMMARY

I. Overview of California local governments.
   A. California has more than 5,000 local governments of various types, including general-purpose governments such as those in counties and cities, specific-purpose governments such as those for school districts and special districts, and regional governments.
   B. Local governments provide essential services, ranging from law enforcement and fire protection to waste management and street maintenance to air- and water-quality control.

II. Legal framework for local government: the state has ultimate authority over local governments.
   A. Under Dillon's Rule, local governments are "creatures of the state" and have no inherent rights or powers except those given to them by the state constitution or legislature.
   B. California, like most states, gives counties and cities significant powers to govern themselves, make policies, enforce laws, raise revenues, borrow, and generally control local affairs as long as their decisions don't conflict with state or federal laws.
   C. The more populous cities and counties have adopted home-rule charters, which allow maximum local autonomy in self-governance.
   D. The other cities and counties operate as general-law counties and cities, which have to abide more strictly by the state legislature's local government code.

III. County governments.
   A. California's 58 counties are extremely diverse in terms of territorial extent, population size, demographic characteristics, and political culture.

B. Except for the unique case of San Francisco's consolidated county/city government, all counties are governed by five-member boards of supervisors that exercise both legislative and executive powers.

C. Counties perform important functions, many of them required by state government laws and mandates.

D. Counties also provide essential services, especially in unincorporated areas outside the cities and other jurisdictions, and they are major arenas for making large-scale land-use and development policies.

E. Each county also has a local agency formation commission (LAFCo), which plays a critical role in creating, merging, or dissolving new local governments, such as those in cities and special districts, and resolving disputes among competing jurisdictions.

IV. City governments.
A. The state has 482 cities, most of them general-law cities; the rest are charter cities with significant home-rule powers and local autonomy.

B. Cities are legally created through a process of municipal incorporation that requires LAFCo review and approval as well as a final majority vote of the community seeking formal city status.

C. Nearly all cities have a form of government modeled on the vision of Progressive Era reformers. Called reform cities, most of them have strong city managers, weak mayors, nonpartisan elections, at-large council elections, nonconcurrent elections, and direct democracy procedures (the initiative, referendum, and recall). Important exceptions to such reform cities are cities such as Los Angeles and San Francisco, which have strong mayors and district elections.

V. Citizen participation in local government.
A. The Brown Act of 1953, known as the "open meetings law," requires that all meetings of local legislative bodies be open and public unless specifically exempted, and that all citizens be permitted to attend such meetings.

B. Voter turnout in city elections has been steadily declining in recent years.
1. Those who do vote in city elections tend to be whiter, older, richer, and more educated than those who don't.
2. In particular, the state's growing population of noncitizens has little political voice or formal representation in local government.
3. Certain electoral reforms, such as a shift from nonconcurrent to concurrent elections, could markedly increase voter turnout levels.

VI. Special districts.
A. Special districts are limited-purpose local governments.

B. Excluding the state's 1,028 K–12 school districts and 72 community-college districts, California has nearly 5,000 special districts.

C. Special districts provide a range of services—for example, irrigation, pest abatement, parks and recreation, water, and fire protection—which are not provided at all (or in insufficient amounts) by general-purpose governments such as those for counties and cities.

D. Special districts are created by a LAFCo-approved citizen petition and a majority vote.

E. Most special districts are independent agencies that provide one type of service received and paid for by residents in smaller territories of larger jurisdictions, like counties.

F. Some special districts are enterprise districts that charge individual user fees for service.

G. Most special districts are funded by taxes or special assessments from service recipients.

H. The advantages of special districts include greater flexibility and responsiveness in tailoring service and requiring only the beneficiaries to pay the costs.

I. The disadvantages of special districts include duplication of services, lack of coordination, and unclear structures of authority and accountability.

VII. Regional governments.
A. The state's regional governments address problems such as air pollution and population growth that affect large areas and multiple local government jurisdictions.

B. Some regional governments, such as the San Francisco Bay Conservation and Development Commission and the California Coastal Commission, have strong regulatory authority and enforcement powers.

C. Other regional governments, such as the Southern California Association of Governments, the Association of Bay Area Governments, and other councils of government (COGs), mainly perform research, planning, and advisory functions and have little or no power or authority to impose their decisions on local jurisdictions.

VIII. The housing crisis.
A. Higher-priced homes have been increasing while more affordable homes are scarcer.

B. Building more housing has been impeded by increasing land costs, a shortage of construction labor, and homeowner obstruction.

C. Income inequality in cities has been addressed by a $15 minimum wage first instituted by localities then by the state.

PRACTICE QUIZ

1. Cities and counties that have home-rule charters have the authority to make their own laws even if they violate state and federal laws.
   a) true
   b) false

2. The U.S. Constitution gives local governments inherent rights and powers that cannot be taken away by state governments.
   a) true
   b) false

3. County boards of supervisors have both legislative and executive authority.
   a) true
   b) false

4. Most cities are governed by council-manager systems.
   a) true
   b) false

5. At the local government level, citizens cannot petition for a referendum or recall election.
   a) true
   b) false

6. Which of the following is *not* a characteristic of reform government at the local level?
   a) at-large council elections
   b) nonpartisanship
   c) city manager plan
   d) concurrent elections

7. Which of the following counties operates under a single charter as a consolidated city and county?
   a) Los Angeles
   b) Sacramento
   c) San Francisco
   d) Orange

8. Which of the following elected officials can be found only in county governments?
   a) sheriff
   b) mayor
   c) council member
   d) manager

9. ABAG is an example of a COG.
   a) true
   b) false

10. Despite decreasing availability of affordable homes in California's urban areas, the pace of new building has kept up with demand, averting a housing shortage.
    a) true
    b) false

CRITICAL-THINKING QUESTIONS

1. Do you think the Progressive Era reform vision for local governments is still a good one today? Should the state's local governments continue to be run by professional managers and insulated as much as possible from state and national party politics? Why or why not?

2. Should local governments, such as cities, be given more home-rule powers and greater local autonomy free of state interference? Test case: Would you support all California cities asserting their home-rule powers and local autonomy to the extent that San Francisco has? Why or why not?

3. Do you agree with some critics that most special districts should be abolished and their functions centralized under the control of county and city governments? Why or why not?

4. Do you agree with some observers that California needs more and stronger regional governments? Why or why not? If you agree, what are some of the problems facing those who seek to form such governments, and what steps would you take to create them? How would you balance your recommendations with the principles of home rule and local autonomy?

5. Do you support or oppose the rebellion of local governments against the state as a response to the state's attempt to use local government property tax revenues to solve its budget deficit problems? Why or why not?

KEY TERMS

Public Policy in California

WHAT CALIFORNIA GOVERNMENT DOES AND WHY IT MATTERS

California's housing crisis has been one of economics throughout its history. The climate and the state's abundance have drawn people to California since before its statehood. By the late twentieth century, the effects of housing costs were still mostly felt by those who were low-income or living in densely populated areas where property values had skyrocketed and Proposition 13's effects were deeply rooted. The impact of this problem has shifted in recent years and now affects many more groups in the population and many more areas within the state.

Recent problems in Riverside County, east of Los Angeles, illustrate the complexity of this problem well. The county has over 300 trailer parks, many inhabited by migrant agricultural workers who pick the vegetables and fruit that grow abundantly in the county's irrigated valleys. In 1999 the county accused several trailer parks that catered to migrant workers of substandard and dangerous conditions and subsequently shut them down. Harvey Duro, Sr., a member of the Torres Martinez Desert Cahuilla Indian Reservation, spread the word of a new trailer park on reservation land where the displaced workers could reside. Many farmworkers moved in, paying about $500 a month per trailer to live there.[1]

The conditions weren't good. The trailer park, officially called Desert Mobile Home Park but unofficially known as Duroville or Duros, was located next to a dump that burned from time to time. Heaps of tires and construction debris littered the area, the streets were dusty (and muddy when it rained), and the area's sewage flowed into a pond next door. In 2002 the teachers in the local schools noticed that many of their students who lived in the park were suffering from asthma and rashes, and they determined that the dump was the likely cause. The Bureau of Indian Affairs, which had jurisdiction because the trailer park was on the reservation, moved to close the park because of the unsanitary conditions. In 2009 the local U.S. attorney cited in court the park's "leaking sewage, 800 feral dogs, piles of debris and fire hazards," as well as 5,000 tenants. The cost of bringing it into compliance would be more than $4 million, which the owner could not afford.

After several years of litigation, in 2009 a federal judge decreed that since there was no other place for the residents to go, the park could stay open. The population of the park numbered between 2,000 to 6,000 people, depending on the time of year and economic conditions. Many residents were undocumented. Many earned less than $10,000 per year. And many of them were Purépechas, an indigenous people from Michoacán, Mexico. Many, in fact, were from a single town in Michoacán.

By 2010 most of the people who sold drugs in the park were gone, the feral dog problem was substantially reduced, and the rotting garbage had been cleared. But there was still no place for the residents to move, and the quality of the trailers was also still no better. Riverside County then completed a public housing project for the residents, Mountain View Estates, six miles away from Duroville and composed of 181 units.[2] Duroville finally closed in June 2014, 15 years after it opened. Public housing projects require that residents be in the United States legally, so many undocumented former residents of Duroville moved to other trailer parks in the area.

While Duroville was open, articles about the community occasionally appeared in the *New York Times* and the *Los Angeles Times* as well as in the local newspapers. It even had its own Wikipedia entry. And although Duroville had new-resident councils and representatives to help ensure residents' adherence to the rules and was eventually cleaned up because of legal intervention, a lack of quality housing and living conditions persisted and continues to persist for many farmworkers, particularly the undocumented. For example, the *Los Angeles Times* reported in October 2015 that some families who work in the Coachella Valley have "pooled resources" to create livable trailer parks. Given their limited resources, the end result is that "they [have] jury-rigged almost everything. Electricity was tapped from a post meant to power one well, the dirt road was covered in rugs to keep down the choking dust." Similar trailer parks dot the area, and most are vulnerable to power outages, storm damage, and sewage overflow. Residents are sometimes left with no option but to sleep in tents because of the heat index during the summer. Riverside County has responded to this problem by proposing $3.4 million dollars to pave dirt roads in a number of the trailer parks, and the county has "authorized the use of temporary construction power lines to return power."[3]

Duroville is one of many extremes that illustrate how the least enfranchised in the state have been among those most affected by this problem. But as stated in the beginning of this chapter, in the twenty-first century the housing crisis has impacted many groups. The state has attempted to respond to this crisis. In 2017, former governor Jerry Brown signed 15 bills that were created by the legislature to address housing issues in the state. Some of the bills included incentives for developers who dedicated a proportion of their projects to low-income housing, and one bill was a bond measure proposing fees, including real estate transaction fees. While these kinds of policies are intended to help ameliorate the housing crisis, the *Los Angeles Times* has reported that they likely will be insufficient. The problem is such that the supply cannot possibly meet the demand given the severity of the shortage.[4] The legislature is aware of this and recently proposed several additional bills. One of these, SB 1227, is aimed at student housing. It provides incentives to developers who build housing dedicated to students and, more importantly, set aside 20 percent of the units for students who are very low-income or homeless.[5]

The issue of housing, along with many other policy areas in California politics, exemplifies the challenges posed throughout this book—challenges related to California's enormous diversity and unique institutions. Sites such as Duroville can exist on Indian reservations, which have jurisdiction over most governmental areas except law enforcement. If not for this jurisdiction, the zoning and other laws in effect in most areas of California would have shut Duroville down much sooner.

You may have concluded by now that California is a land of contrasts. The same state that includes Beverly Hills and Silicon Valley also has its Durovilles. Public policy in California governs areas that are like Duroville—that is, areas that are not doing so well—and other areas that are in better shape. California's high degree of heterogeneity is evident in the proposal to divide California into six states, an initiative that failed to collect enough signatures in 2014 to make the ballot. It was attempted again in 2018. This plan would have created the richest state in the United States (the state that would have encompassed Silicon Valley), as well as the poorest (the state that would have included the Central Valley).

We know from earlier chapters in this book that California has come close to being ungovernable during the last two decades. We have a public that demands a high level of services but consistently refuses to pay for them. Many members of the public feel that the free tuition and low fees in higher education during the Pat Brown era are still possible at a time when the state's people and politics have changed profoundly. Proposition 30, passed in November 2012, is one of the few exceptions—a small sales tax increase and larger temporary income tax increases on the wealthy (these increases were set to expire in 2018, but were extended by Proposition 55 until 2025). The public is sometimes willing to approve initiatives to undertake new projects that lack funding. It is also willing to pass special taxes earmarked for special purposes, many of which benefit the interests sponsoring the relevant initiative.

The lack of consensus among the public is reflected in our institutions, which in some cases barely function. However, major steps have been taken to improve the quality of the political process in California. While the legislature has been unable to change the state's tax structure, now over 50 years old, some new institutional changes—most notably the top-two primary system and the new nonpartisan legislative redistricting system—are designed to improve the functioning of our political system. The 50 percent majority now necessary to pass a budget has ended the budget haggling that used to paralyze Sacramento all summer and for part of the fall, but the cost of limited revenues in 2011 and 2012 was a substantial reduction in funds for the state's public schools. The top-two primary, the 50 percent rule for passing the state's budget in the legislature, and the commission to handle redistricting every 10 years in a neutral and nonpartisan fashion may be just the beginning of a wave of reform, though these reforms will take years to assess.

Meanwhile, our focus in this chapter is on the current state of public policy in California. The term **public policy** means what government actually does or "produces" in various policy areas such as health, welfare, education, higher education, water, and the like. The policies in each of these areas are different in each state. For the California of the 1950s and 1960s, education and water policy were proud, if politically difficult, achievements, and the state was one of the nation's leaders in solving its problems and supporting its schools and colleges. For the California of the 2000s, these are areas of profound disappointment.

For example, even with Proposition 98 (1988) "guaranteeing" the public schools some 40 percent of the general fund, California's finances have been so tight that K-12 spending is below average, sometimes ranking in the bottom 40 percent of states.[6] *Education Week*, a national newspaper that covers issues in K-12 public education, gave California a C– for its "overall quality" of education. The grade includes evaluations of financial support, probabilities of success, and measures of student achievement. Only 10 other states received lower marks in early 2016.[7] Like 46 other states and the District of Columbia, California has adopted the Common Core Standards. Although the state adopted these standards in 2010, they were not implemented until 2012-13, so it is a bit soon to evaluate whether the Common Core Standards have improved student learning and achievement. According to Tom Torlakson, the State Superintendent of Public Instruction, it is hopeful that the Common Core Standards will improve college readiness. Results of the 2018 statewide standardized testing of students across all grades found that 49.83 percent met or exceeded the English language arts/literacy standard. Eleven percent fewer (38.65 percent) met or exceeded the standard for mathematics.[8] It is obvious from these measures that there is significant need for improvement. Advocates of the Common Core argue that over time the scores should improve because of the rigorous curriculum. One of the biggest problems facing public education in California is the achievement gap. It remains to be seen whether the Common Core will help narrow this gap given the many factors that need to be addressed, especially funding.

Likewise, the University of California, the California State University, and the state's extensive community college system have all seen cutbacks in faculty pay and course offerings as well as substantially higher costs for tuition and fees. How much higher these can go is a major, unanswered question, but there were few alternatives in the severe recession of 2009-10.

One could write several books about California public policy, so in this chapter we have confined ourselves to three areas of interest. They are typical in the sense that they show some of the best and worst areas in which the state is involved. The first of these is water policy. The second is health insurance. The third is the state's infrastructure, which has experienced spending issues similar to those endured by K-12 education.

Water Policy

Of the water used in California, 20 percent is for households, business, and industry, while 80 percent is for agricultural purposes, including irrigation. Farm production and food processing compose about 2 percent of the California economy, down from 5 percent in 1960. Over the past decade or more, higher revenue perennial crops that require annual watering, such as grapes, nuts, and other fruits, have increased as a proportion of California's total agricultural output (as compared to annual crops, which enable land to be left fallow in times of drought). As a consequence, **agricultural water use** has been creeping up.

Household water use is dominated by the two megalopolises of California: the San Francisco Bay region and Southern California. Residential and commercial water use is split 50–50 between use inside the house and landscaping outside. Total urban water usage has declined significantly in recent years. For example, 2013–15 witnessed an additional reduction of 25 percent in residential use according to the Public Policy Institute of California (PPIC).[9] Water districts have instituted water conservation programs that have aided in this effort despite increases in the state's population. Some of these are tiered pricing programs, so that large users pay more per unit, and some incorporate legal requirements to install low-flow toilets and showerheads. Even so, substantial differences among similar cities exist, depending on their closeness to the Pacific coast, density of the population, typical climate, and amount of industry. Coastal cities use less water; a dense population means smaller yards. Hot weather means more watering, and more industry can skew statistics because some industries may use a lot more water than others. A 2004 law requires that water meters be installed statewide by 2025. As of 2018 there were still cities with some unmetered customers; generally they are billed a flat rate each month.[10]

The major **2013–14 drought** exposed the problems of water rights and uses in the existing system. Governor Jerry Brown proclaimed a statewide water emergency in January 2014, and local water agencies, depending on their particular situations, gradually imposed measures to restrict the use of water.

The drought has also highlighted problems in the water supply. A study by several University of California researchers released in 2014 pinpointed the central problem: California's freshwater runoff in an average year is about 70 million acre-feet, but since 1914 the state has handed out water rights totaling 370 million acre-feet. That's five times more water than nature, on average, produces.[11] An acre-foot of water (one foot of water in depth on an acre of land) is sufficient for two average households for a year. There is tension here, however, between what are known as *riparian* vs. *appropriative* water rights. **Riparian rights** are water rights that people have because they own property on a lake or stream, for example. There are restrictions on exercising these rights such as "natural flow" of the water source and requirements that the water source be adjacent to the smallest piece of the property. California and Oklahoma are the only "western" states to recognize riparian rights. Granting water rights to private persons obviously makes California's water problems more complex. In addition, there are what are known as *appropriative* rights. These rights are given to persons who use water that is not on riparian land or to persons who are on riparian land but do not have riparian rights. People are given permits by the State's Division of Water Rights.[12] If this sounds a bit confusing, it is. And it exacerbates the state's water problems because the number of permits issued under **appropriated rights** exceeds the amount of water available.[13]

Many solutions have been proposed, among them the following: building two 35-mile tunnels around the Sacramento–San Joaquin Delta to bring water to the California aqueduct, importing water from new sources, increasing water conservation efforts, and using rainwater or gray water at home. Four practical solutions were suggested in major studies released in June 2014 by Oakland's Pacific Institute, the Natural Resource Defense Council, and researchers from UC Santa Barbara. Taken together, these four solutions, listed below, point to the future of water supply.[14]

1. Increasing efficiency in homes and industries by replacing or improving inefficient appliances, reducing waste and leaks, and replacing traditional landscapes with low-water-use plants and gardens. The potential savings are 2.9 to 5.2 million acre-feet per year.
2. Increasing efficiency in agriculture through better irrigation techniques and practices, with potential savings of 5.6 to 6.6 million acre-feet per year.
3. Reusing treated wastewater for irrigation, landscapes, industry, and recharging groundwater basins. Savings here could total 1.2 to 1.8 million acre-feet per year.
4. Capturing storm water at homes and businesses, using it locally or to recharge groundwater basins. Savings could total 0.4 to 0.6 million acre-feet per year.[15]

At a minimum, the new sources over time could add 10 million acre-feet of water.

The other side of the water quantity problem is the water *quality* problem, involving problems of **groundwater management**, naturally occurring minerals such as arsenic in California's water, and, in the eyes of many Californians, hardness. (The latter isn't a water quality issue, but many feel that it is.)

Thirty-five percent of the total water used in California in an average year is groundwater. In a drought year, pumping groundwater increases as users attempt to compensate for the lack of rain. While surface water is regulated in California, until September 2014 groundwater was largely unregulated. Some groundwater basins have been so heavily used that the amount taken out each year exceeds what can reasonably be replenished, even in El Niño years with relatively heavy rainfall totals. When groundwater declines, the energy costs of pumping water from deeper wells increase, and the additional pumping can cause land to sink, damaging surface infrastructure such as roads and canals.[16]

Contamination of groundwater is a growing problem in California. Some basins are contaminated from fertilizers and manure, and others suffer because of salinity. Changes in water-use practices will help in the future, but some existing basins will need to be cleaned up.

Until 2014, California was the only western state in the United States without some level of state regulation of groundwater. The state took a major step in this direction as a result of the 2013–14 drought: the Assembly and state Senate passed three bills to compel water-basin managers in certain areas of the state to design groundwater management plans that would prevent overdrafting. All three bills were signed into law by Governor Brown. Together, they make up the Sustainable Groundwater Management Act (SGMA). The SGMA includes not only guidelines and regulations for the management of groundwater, but also regulatory language for areas that may not have groundwater basin managers.

In addition, a water bond issue of more than $7 billion was placed on the November 2014 ballot, as the drought provided the catalyst for the legislature to agree on a series of projects in the water policy area. The bond issue had previously been stalled in the legislature for several years. The water bond was approved by almost 67 percent of the voters.

Health Insurance

While many Californians are still without health insurance coverage, President Obama's Affordable Care Act (ACA) has already had a significant impact in California. During the first six months of enrollment, 1.4 million people purchased a policy on Covered California, the state's health insurance exchange.[17] Another 1.9 million people enrolled in Medi-Cal, now open to single adults and couples without children who qualify on the basis of poverty. These enrollments should reduce the number of people without health insurance in California by about 3 million; the exact number is unclear because some new enrollees replaced their private insurance plans with insurance through the exchange or Medi-Cal. Gallup polls taken in 2013 and in mid-2014 showed a reduction in those without health insurance in California from 21.6 percent to 16.3 percent, which is "in the ballpark" of what can reasonably be expected—a good start toward reducing the very high proportion of people in California without health insurance. More recently, a 2015 Gallup poll indicated that the trend has continued—only 11.8 percent of Californians were uninsured.

While the number of uninsured has declined steadily since the ACA's adoption and implementation, there are three major reasons why the number of uninsured has been so high in California. One is that many people in California, more than the national average, work in small firms, and small firms tend not to offer health insurance nearly as often as large firms do. The second is that the state's population has a large proportion of immigrants, and immigrants are much less likely to have health insurance than are native-born Americans. The third reason is that undocumented immigrants are not eligible to enroll in Medicaid (Medi-Cal is California's Medicaid program, discussed later in this section), nor are they eligible to purchase health insurance through the ACA exchanges. (See the "Who Are Californians?" feature on p. 275 for more information on who is uninsured in the state.) About 2.5 million people are undocumented in California, a figure that has remained constant for over a decade. These statistics are unlikely to improve given the 2016 presidential election outcome. Donald Trump called for the repeal of the ACA in his campaign, and this position was a very popular one for many of his supporters and other conservatives. In 2017 he attempted to replace the ACA with his own health care reform plan. Trump's plan would have significantly impacted those who are eligible to participate as well as those who will remain uninsured because of their undocumented status. One proposed change was a tax deduction for the insured. The working poor or those who have a lower income would have been unlikely to benefit from a tax deduction in the way that wealthier Californians would, however.

After a bill proposing single payer health care stalled in the California Assembly, members of the California Nurses Association rallied at the Capitol in June 2017 to bring the bill to a vote.

Employer-Sponsored Insurance

In 2015 about 50 percent of Californians under age 65 had **employer-sponsored insurance (ESI)**—that is, they obtained their insurance through their employer, who typically subsidized some of the cost. ESI has been declining nationally, and the recession of 2008–09 accelerated the process. In California, ESI has historically been lower than in other states because of the size and structure of California's employers and the number of undocumented workers in the state. After the first round of enrollment in the ACA, there was some decline in ESI numbers for eligible lower-income workers with families, who may have chosen not to enroll in ESIs given the more affordable alternatives under the ACA.[18]

Single Payer Proposal

SB 562, known as the Healthy California Act, was proposed in the state Senate in 2017. The scope of the act was very broad. It included health care as a right to California residents and guaranteed universal health care with substantial government subsidies and potentially no out-of-pocket expenses for all Californians. The Healthy California Act became very controversial very quickly. A report issued by the state projected the cost of SB 562 to be approximately 400 billion dollars per year. Proponents of the bill argued that at least half of the cost would be offset by funds from other existing plans at the federal, state, and local levels. Paying for the other 200 billion per year became a larger sticking point. A proposed increase in payroll taxes would have helped to cover this, but the percentage of the necessary increase became an issue of political debate.[19]

In June 2017 the bill hit a roadblock in the state Assembly. The state Assembly shelved the bill because of what members thought were significant problems with funding and implementing the legislation. **Single payer health care** remains an important political issue despite the fact that SB 562 was stalled in the Assembly. In fact, it was one of the most important issues in the 2018 governor's race, dividing candidates and the electorate alike along party lines. Democrats are in support, and Republicans are in opposition. According to a May 2018 survey conducted by the Public Policy Institute of California, 41 percent of likely voters in the gubernatorial race favored single payer while 41 percent opposed it. Another 12 percent responded that they favored single payer as long as it didn't increase taxes.[20] Political support among Democratic candidates for single payer, as well as public support for such plans, means that single payer will remain on the public policy agenda in California for the near future.

Individual Health Insurance Marketplace

In California's state **individual insurance marketplace**, people purchase a health insurance policy directly from the insurance company. This is the market expected to be most directly affected by the ACA. Several provisions in the act reformed this market, which has been characterized in the past by extremely large price increases from year to year (one large insurer asked for a 39 percent price increase from 2010 to 2011) and by **rescissions**, cases in which insurers have dropped policyholders who have become sick and filed large claims, on the grounds that their applications were not truthful. The extent of these price increases and rescissions enabled by California's pre-ACA marketplace meant that it was a model other states would not want to emulate. The ACA now prohibits companies that provide insurance on the marketplace from charging higher rates for preexisting conditions, rescinding policies after policyholders file insurance claims, rating users by health status so that those with fair or poor health pay a higher rate, and enforcing lifetime limits on policies. In 2016 about 1.5 million Californians participated in this market. Most of the people in the market should eventually be receiving their health insurance through Covered California, the state's health insurance exchange.

Medi-Cal

Medi-Cal is California's version of the federal Medicaid plan for the poor. The federal government sponsors two large federal health insurance programs, **Medicare** and **Medicaid**. Medicare, aimed primarily at senior citizens, is paid for with federal funds, a tax on workers and their employers, and beneficiary premiums, deductibles, and co-pays. Medicaid, in contrast, is aimed at low-income people, and the financing is split between the federal government and the states. The federal government provides an average of 57 percent of the funding and some national standards, and the states provide the other 43 percent of the funding plus basic program administration and decision making. The proportion of the funding that each state provides is determined by a formula based on state per-capita income, and because California is a relatively rich state, it receives 50 percent federal funding, the minimum rate. Mississippi received the maximum federal funding rate at 73.6 percent in fiscal year 2015.

Under the ACA, Medicaid/Medi-Cal will expand by dropping requirements that excluded single individuals and couples without children and by accepting Medi-Cal enrollees solely on the basis of their income. These changes resulted in 1.9 million people signing up for Medi-Cal during the first enrollment period for the ACA, from November 2013 to March 2014. Medi-Cal now covers more than 13 million Californians, one-third of the population.[21]

The downside to this expansion is that California's average cost per Medi-Cal recipient is the lowest of any state, mostly because provider payments—the payment to each hospital and doctor for providing a service covered by Medi-Cal—are the lowest in the country. Consequently, access to doctors, particularly specialists, is limited for Medi-Cal beneficiaries in many parts of the state. This is because, for financial reasons, many medical practices either will not take Medi-Cal beneficiaries at all or limit the number of Medi-Cal patients they will see.[22]

Medicare

Approximately 12.5 percent of Californians are over 65, and almost all of the 4.5 million people in that category are on Medicare. In addition, 2.4 percent of Californians under 65 also qualify for Medicare. All those under 65 who are on Medicare have a disability of some kind (although not all those with disabilities are eligible for Medicare): anyone with ALS (Lou Gehrig's disease) or end-stage renal disease is immediately eligible for Medicare, and those who are on Social Security disability are eligible for Medicare after a two-year wait. The Medicare numbers are not expected to be affected by the ACA.

TRICARE

TRICARE and other military-related programs are the health care programs for military retirees and their dependents, including some members of the military reserves, with some civilian health benefits for military personnel as well. The category also includes those who receive their health care from the U.S. Department of Veterans Affairs (VA). About 2.4 percent of those under 65, some 800,000 Californians, are on TRICARE. The ACA does not affect TRICARE.

The Uninsured

The California Health Care Foundation, using census data from the federal government, calculated the proportion of uninsured Californians under age 65 at 21.2 percent in 2010 to 2012. Gallup, using its own surveys and a much simpler question, calculated the proportion as 21.6 percent in 2013 and 16.3 percent in mid-2014, and less than 9 percent in 2016.[23] See the "Who Are Californians?" section on the facing page about who the 3 million uninsured Californians were in 2018. Clearly, the implementation of the ACA in early 2014 has resulted in a major drop in the number and proportion of the uninsured. Just as surely, there is still a long way to go. Basic information about those without insurance follows, although any specific numbers cited are from *before* the ACA.

- Some 23 percent of workers lacked insurance in California, compared with 19 percent in the nation.

- Most heads of household without insurance have a job, and most of those jobs are full-time.

Who Are California's 3 Million Uninsured?

California has a large degree of income inequality, and it has struggled with providing equal access to health insurance. While American citizens and permanent residents have access to government-provided health insurance through Medicare at the age of 65, many Californians under that age are unable to gain insurance either through employer-based, individual, or public programs. Before the passage of the Affordable Care Act in 2010, California had one of the highest uninsured rates in America for people between the ages of 0–64 (24.3 percent in 2009), but since then the uninsured rate has dropped significantly (7 percent in 2018) across the state.

Though coverage has expanded, approximately 3 million Californians under the age of 65 remain uninsured. For those who qualify for one of these government heath care programs but chose not to apply, it may be for a variety of reasons including they do not want to enroll in a government program, they do not know they are eligible for one of these programs, or the programs, despite subsidies, are still cost prohibitive.

Why are Californians Uninsured?

■ Immigration Status   ■ Eligible for Covered CA WITH Subsidies

■ Eligible for Medi-Cal   ■ Eligible for Covered CA with NO Subsidies

👤 = 2% of total population

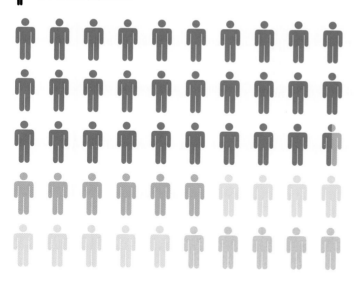

Percentage of Uninsured by County

■ Less than 1% uninsured   ■ 6–10% uninsured

■ 1–5% uninsured   ■ Greater than 10% uninsured

SOURCE: http://healthpolicy.ucla.edu/publications/Documents/PDF/California%27s%20 Uninsured%20by%20County2.pdf (accessed 07/27/2018); "2008–2016 Small Area Health Insurance Estimates (SAHIE) using the American Community Survey (ACS)," United States Census Bureau, www.census.gov/data/datasets/time-series/demo/sahie/estimates-acs.html (accessed 07/27/2018); "How Many in Your Area Are Uninsured–and Why?," California Health Care Foundation, www.chcf.org/publication/how-many-area-uninsured-why/ (accessed 07/27/2018); "Child Uninsured Rate In California Ranks Lowest In Nation," Georgetown University Health Policy Institute: Center for Children and Families, ccf.georgetown.edu/2016/11/01/child-uninsured-rate-in-california-ranks-lowest-in-nation/ (accessed 07/27/2018).

forcriticalanalysis

1. Why do some regions of California have higher rates of uninsured than others? What drives the different rates shown in the map?

2. What other strategies might California use to lower the uninsured rate further?

- It is estimated that most *children* without insurance are eligible for Medi-Cal or Healthy Families, California's State Children's Health Insurance Program (SCHIP, which is a federal program aimed at those whose incomes are just above the Medicaid/Medi-Cal eligibility levels).

- 25- to 34-year-olds are the largest age group represented among the uninsured (26 percent), but every age group under 65 is represented. So-called pre-retirees, 55- to 64-year-olds, make up 9 percent of the total.

- In terms of ethnicity, of those without health insurance in California most are Latino (about 58 percent). Whites represent the next most frequent group, at 24 percent. Asians compose 11 percent of the total, and African Americans 5 percent.

- Of those without health insurance, 63 percent are American citizens and 37 percent are not.

California's Infrastructure

Infrastructure is the part of government with which citizens come into contact the most—highways, schools, universities, commuter buses, and railways. California's infrastructure deteriorated significantly from the 1970s into the 2000s, although recently the state has made some progress toward improving the system. One factor complicating the successful maintenance of the state's infrastructure is what Bruce Cain of UC Berkeley's Institute of Governmental Studies calls California's "infrastructure ambivalence." On the one hand, Californians want modern facilities and infrastructure, but "we don't want what often comes with those things. There are, for instance, unavoidable environmental costs. Water projects can endanger fisheries in the Delta. New roads and housing can separate and destroy ecosystems."[24] And, of course, we don't want to pay for them. Consider the following examples.

Highways

California's highway system was close to the best in the nation after World War II and into the 1950s and 1960s. Beginning in the 1970s, however, it declined severely. The "California Infrastructure Report Card 2018," issued by the American Society of Civil Engineers, gave California's infrastructure a grade of C−, which is a bit better than the D grade for the nation as a whole.[25] A 2011 report on pavement conditions in the United States found 37 percent of California's roads to be "poor," with only 21 percent "good," making California the state ranked sixth from the bottom of the list.[26] A study of the structural quality of California's bridges found an improvement overall from 2007 to 2013. In 2007, 3,249, or 13.4 percent, of California's 24,189 bridges were structurally deficient; this number declined to 2,769, or 11.1 percent, in 2013.[27] There has been progress, partly the result of bond issues that were approved by the voters during the Schwarzenegger administration, but there is still much to be done.

The rebuilding of the Bay Bridge connecting San Francisco and Oakland is an extreme example of the substantial problems that have plagued the California state government's management of infrastructure projects. A 2014 report published in the *Sacramento Bee* indicated that the state agency responsible for the bridge construction chose a Chinese contractor who had never built parts for a bridge before to fabricate the steel structure of the bridge. The contractor ignored quality requirements built into the contract and fell behind schedule, necessitating the expenditure of hundreds of millions of dollars above the contract level. The result was a bridge built years behind schedule, costing more than twice the original price, and inspiring significant doubts about its quality.[28]

The management of California's transportation funds is clearly an issue. Dan Walters, who has been writing about California politics and management issues for the *Sacramento Bee* for several decades, points to "the labyrinth of interlocking transportation accounts" that direct money to infrastructure projects as the root of the mismanagement.[29] Others locate the problem in the increase in hybrid automobiles that use less gasoline, resulting in less income for the state from the gasoline tax. Another factor is the politicians who find few political benefits from maintaining infrastructure compared with building new projects. Additionally, there are governance problems. In a recent op-ed piece for the *Los Angeles Times*, George Skelton identified Proposition 13 as another factor that has affected potential revenues for California's highways and bridges. As noted in earlier chapters, Proposition 13 requires a two-thirds vote in both houses of the state legislature for any statewide tax increases. Governor Brown called for a special session of the legislature to address infrastructure problems. Representatives from Northern California, Senator Jim Beall and Assemblyman Jim Frazier, both Democrats, co-sponsored a bill that would increase the gas tax on regular fuel by 17 cents a gallon and on diesel fuel by 30 cents a gallon. The bill would also require zero-emission vehicles to pay an annual fee of $165. Skelton noted that it is unlikely for this 7.4 billion-dollar plan to pass, however, because of the two-thirds vote requirements and because of the current majorities in the state legislature.[30] But despite these obstacles, it did pass in 2017 (see related discussion of Proposition 6, an attempt to reverse this increase, in Chapter 4). One bright note in all of this is a change in California's car culture. As noted in the "Who Are Californians?" feature on p. 278, recent survey results from the state's department of transportation show that increasing numbers of Californians are choosing public transportation, biking, and walking to get around over driving personal cars. Transportation is not the only persistent infrastructure problem that is confronted with political obstacles. When a water main broke in Los Angeles in 2014, it turned out that the main was 100 years old and that water rates were too low to keep up with the cost of maintenance. This was because the city council, not a water agency, set the rates. Although California's infrastructure is clearly beset by numerous problems, few people consider the maintenance of California's infrastructure, so critical to the movement of citizens, to be a top priority.

Levees

In 1986 a levee along the Yuba River broke and inundated the small town of Linda in the Central Valley, causing several hundred million dollars' worth of damage. In 2004, 18 years later, the state Supreme Court ratified a court of appeal decision that found the state of California liable because it had not repaired the broken stretch of levee. While the state resisted liability for the break and its consequences, the courts have determined that the state must pay for the consequences of its neglect.[31]

The *Sacramento Bee* published a series of articles detailing several governmental agencies that were responsible for flood control and maintenance of the levees

How Do Californians Get Around?

Every 10 years, the California Department of Transportation conducts the California Household Travel Survey. The most recent survey covers the 2010–12 period and includes responses from 42,431 California households. Though the average household owns 1.8 cars, nearly 8 percent of California residents said that they don't own a car. When comparing the most recent survey data to the previous survey, conducted in 2000, we see that the percentage of people driving a car dropped by 11 percentage points, while the percentage of people walking, biking, and taking public transit doubled to 23 percent.

Percentage of All Trips by Travel Mode

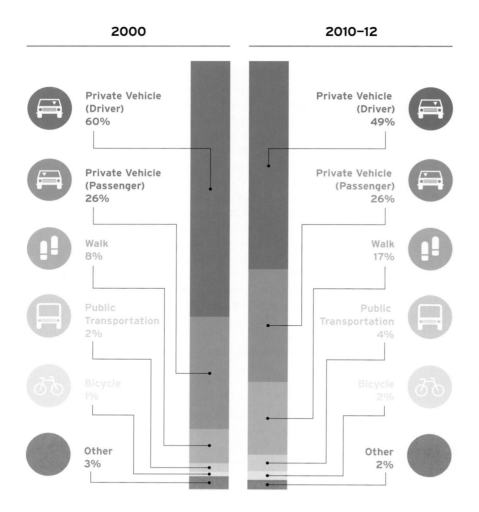

2000

Private Vehicle (Driver) 60%

Private Vehicle (Passenger) 26%

Walk 8%

Public Transportation 2%

Bicycle 1%

Other 3%

2010–12

Private Vehicle (Driver) 49%

Private Vehicle (Passenger) 26%

Walk 17%

Public Transportation 4%

Bicycle 2%

Other 2%

SOURCE: U.S. California Department of Transportation, Statewide Travel Analysis Branch, www.dot.ca.gov/hq/tpp/offices/omsp/statewide_travel_analysis/ (accessed 10/31/18).

forcriticalanalysis

1. How do you travel to school? What role does the government play in your commute?

2. What, if anything, should government do to encourage people to use methods other than private cars to get where they need to go?

along the Sacramento River. Although the agencies have not been able to find the funds to repair more than 150 sites where the levees could fail during a major flood, builders and developers have continued to construct large developments in the Central Valley near Sacramento in areas where levees hold back rivers that are capable of flood damage to thousands of homes and businesses.[32]

In mid-2004, just after the publication of the *Sacramento Bee* series, a dirt levee broke suddenly in the Delta region, instantly changing 12,000 acres of farmland into a 12,000-acre lake. Officials found that a second levee was in danger of breaking, and a third needed to be shored up to prevent a road from being flooded and cutting off the only connection to two islands housing 178 residents.[33] The total damage amounted to $35 million in damages to buildings and crops, plus another $36.5 million to fix the levees. Some of this changed when California lawmakers prioritized levee reconstruction after the destruction wreaked by Hurricane Katrina on the Gulf Coast and the subsequent failure of government in many places to fulfill its emergency responsibilities. The public-works package of bond issues approved by the voters in November 2006 included Proposition 1E, the Disaster Preparedness and Flood Prevention Act, which authorized $4.1 billion in bonds to rebuild flood-control structures, including the Delta levees. The authorized money has provided a starting point for rebuilding the eroding facilities.

In late 2013, Governor Jerry Brown proposed a $25 billion plan to build two 35-mile-long tunnels to carry water under and around the Delta and to rebuild the Delta levees, with construction starting in 2017. The plan would restore wetlands and, in the eyes of supporters, would provide a more reliable source for the 25 million Californians who use the Delta's water. Opponents, however, are concerned about the cost of the tunnels, the possible ecological damage from the additional water pumped out of the Delta, and the project's questionable financing. In April 2016 the *Los Angeles Times* reported that the previously projected impact of this project, now called California WaterFix, may have been overstated. According to the article, some federal agencies that have reviewed the plan are skeptical about its ability to do more than sustain the status quo of water delivery.[34] This skepticism is predicated on factors such as the complicated irrigation and other water delivery systems that currently exist in and adjacent to the Delta, as well as the existing federal regulatory policies that protect endangered fish species that would be affected by the proposed tunnel system. Water is obviously essential to California in myriad ways. It is a public policy problem that deserves to be at the top of the state's agenda. It illustrates, however, the challenges to solving critical public problems even when there is a consensus to act.[35]

In April 2018 the Delta tunnels or "twin tunnels" project was given a major boost with a $10.8 billion funding commitment from the Metropolitan Water District of Southern California. The project still faces other obstacles, according to the *Sacramento Bee*. These include water rights and access, and legal challenges. It is estimated that the project won't begin until 2019, even if these hurdles are overcome, and that it will still take at least 15 years to complete it.[36]

The Future of California's Infrastructure

In addition to the Delta tunnels, Governor Brown's second long-term infrastructure priority is the high-speed rail system that would connect San Francisco, Sacramento, and Los Angeles. A ground-breaking ceremony was held in Fresno on January 6, 2015. Construction has been delayed by numerous lawsuits over the system's funding and other design and implementation problems. The plan was projected to cost $68 billion, and the voters have authorized about $10 billion in bonds for the first phase of construction, along with federal stimulus funds from the 2009 recession. However, in March 2018 the state revealed that the projected cost would now be at least $77.3 billion and may even exceed $98 billion by its completion. Moreover, it was expected that it wouldn't be fully operational until 2033.[37] In April, California High-Speed Rail Authority's chief executive, Jeff Morales, resigned. His departure and those of others in this agency have reinforced concerns that the project is too problematic to be realized.[38] Since its inception, many have argued that the state cannot afford a project this large on top of its other needs.

The neglect of the state's infrastructure over time is obvious. There are many reasons why infrastructure repair and upkeep are not more pressing concerns, but the priorities of both politicians and the public are clearly part of the problem. Infrastructure is a long-term problem, and our political system, based on two- and four-year terms of office, thinks short-term. This factor is magnified by the term limits imposed on the legislature, traditionally a body in which legislators spend several decades of their careers and can think in longer terms than the governor and the executive-branch officials, who are elected for only one or two four-year terms. Now with term limits, the members of the legislature are subject to the same short-term time constraints.

Conclusion

The Duroville case study illustrates the problems that arise in California because of fractured interests, complications of land (Indian reservations) that the state cannot control or regulate, and problems resulting from the number of undocumented immigrants. That a disgraceful trailer park finally closed after many years of dysfunction is good. That it took so many years to find a substitute location for the people who lived in the park is not good. That some families who work in this area are still residing in inadequate housing and lack basic amenities that are widely available to most Californians remains a problem. One characteristic of contemporary California is that years or decades can pass before even modest starts are made on solving problems.

Water policy and health insurance are two issues that illustrate how external changes, such as climate fluctuations or new federal policy, can dramatically affect state policy. When these kinds of catalysts do not exist, California is often slow or unable to make headway. For example, the health insurance situation only worsened in the two decades before the passage of the ACA, and the last great pieces of legislation affecting water policy were decided upon during the administration of Governor Edmund G. "Pat" Brown, from 1959 to 1967. Recent external events have finally prompted movement in both policy areas. The 2013–14 drought stimulated California's state government to pass path breaking legislation in August 2014, making it the last western state to enact groundwater regulations. Regarding health insurance, the passage of the federal Affordable Care Act gave California the opportunity to insure a substantial proportion of its uninsured population at the minimum cost. California was wise to take advantage of this opportunity. Single payer was an important issue in the gubernatorial race. How to fund it without increasing existing taxes and fees will determine public support for single payer plans in the future.

Water policy has become immensely more complicated with the growth of the environmental movement since the first Earth Day in 1969. But even under the senior Governor Brown in the early 1960s, the decisions made on water were not easy and involved prolonged political conflict. We often hear commentators discussing the "cultural breakup" of the old political consensus in the state, but the truth is that we are better for the multiplicity of voices that continually debate the best course of action for California to pursue. These differing voices make it more difficult to achieve public policy consensus and to make decisions, some long overdue, but water policy and health insurance are two important interests that need to be considered in the present day. We have begun the long road to reform on many issues discussed in this chapter and the book as a whole, and there is hope that California will be more governable in the future. But more steps have to be taken, and we need both visionary leadership and voters who pay attention and are interested in change. We hope the readers of this book will be those voters.

A federal judge ordered the closure of Duroville, a mobile park residence in Thermal, California, where a large population of undocumented immigrants resided.

Study Guide

FOR FURTHER READING

"Arnold's Big Chance: A Survey of California." *The Economist*, May 1, 2004, pp. 1–16.

Barrera, E. A. "A Firestorm of Controversy—Still No County Fire Department Five Years after Cedar Blaze." *East County Magazine*, August 2008. www.eastcountymagazine.org. Accessed 8/17/12.

"The Drying of the West." *The Economist*, February 22, 2014, pp. 22–23.

Gleick, Peter H. "Solving California's Water Problems." *Huffington Post*, June 10, 2014. www.huffingtonpost.com/peter -h-gleick/solving-californias-water_b_5479569.html. Accessed 9/3/14.

Hanak, Ellen, Jeffrey Mount, and Caitrin Chappelle. "Just the Facts: California's Latest Drought." Public Policy Institute of California, February 2014. www.ppic.org. Accessed 9/3/14.

Hill, Laura E., Magnus Lofstrom, and Joseph M. Hayes. "Immigrant Legalization: Assessing the Labor Market Effects." Public Policy Institute of California, 2010. www.ppic.org /content/pubs/report/R_410LHR.pdf. Accessed 8/17/12.

Johnson, Hans, and Laura Hill. "At Issue: Illegal Immigration." Public Policy Institute of California, July 2011. www .ppic.org/content/pubs/atissue/AI_711HJAI.pdf. Accessed 8/17/12.

Khazan, Olga, "Are You Sure You Want Single Payer?" *The Atlantic*, August 21, 2017. https://www.theatlantic.com /health/archive/2017/08/are-you-sure-you-want-single -payer/537456. Accessed 9/18/18.

Lustig, R. Jeffrey. *Remaking California, Reclaiming the Public Good*. Berkeley: Heyday Books, 2010.

Matthews, Joe, and Mark Paul. *California Crack-Up, How Reform Broke the Golden State and How We Can Fix It*. Berkeley: University of California, 2010.

Pear, Robert. "Lacking Papers, Citizens Are Cut from Medicaid." *New York Times*, March 12, 2007, p. A1.

Piller, C. "Bay Bridge's Troubled China Connection," *Sacramento Bee*, June 8, 2014.

Rogers, Paul. "Is Jerry Brown's Delta Tunnels Plan Repeating the Errors of High-Speed Rail?" *San Jose Mercury-News*, December 9, 2013.

Schrag, Peter. *California: America's High-Stakes Experiment.* Berkeley: University of California Press, 2006.

Simmons, Charlene Wear. *Gambling in the Golden State, 1998 Forward.* Sacramento: California Research Bureau, California State Library, May 2006.

"Special Report: Democracy in California, The People's Will." *The Economist*, April 23, 2011.

State of California, Legislative Analyst's Office. *A Primer: The State's Infrastructure and the Use of Bonds.* Sacramento: Legislative Analyst's Office, January 2006.

Walters, Dan. "Politicians Often Ignore California's Aging Infrastructure." *Sacramento Bee*, August 9, 2014.

ON THE WEB

American Association of State Highway and Transportation Officials. www.transportation.org. Accessed 10/17/16.

American Society of Civil Engineers (ASCE). https://www.asce.org/report_cards (accessed 9/28/18).

California Health Care Foundation. www.chcf.org. Accessed 9/3/14.

Huffington Post. www.huffingtonpost.com. Accessed 9/3/14.

Kaiser Family Foundation. http://kff.org. Accessed 9/3/14. Health insurance information.

Pacific Institute. http://pacinst.org/ or www.californiadrought.org. Accessed 9/3/14.

Public Policy Institute of California. www.ppic.org. Accessed 9/3/14.

State of California, Legislative Analyst's Office. www.lao.ca.gov. Accessed 9/3/14.

SUMMARY

I. Duroville was a trailer park located on an Indian reservation in Riverside County. Many of its residents were agricultural workers, and they experienced particularly squalid conditions during the 12 years of the park's existence.

   A. The federal government filed suit to close Duroville, but federal and state efforts to do so were stymied by the lack of an alternative location that the park's several thousand residents could afford.

   B. The state and county have constructed a new trailer park/public housing complex using redevelopment funds, and the Duroville trailer park was finally closed in 2014.

II. The 2013–14 drought worsened California's water supply problem.

   A. Twenty percent of the water used in California is for household and business consumption, half of which is used for landscaping. The other 80 percent is for agriculture.

   B. Urban water use has been constant despite increases in population, evidence of the conservation programs implemented in water districts in California.

   C. California water agencies have vastly overpromised the average amount of water that runs off each year in California.

   D. Practical solutions to increase the amount of water available for people to use in California include increased efficiency at home or in industry, increased efficiency in agriculture, reusing treated wastewater on landscapes and recharging groundwater basins, and capturing storm water.

E. Water quality is also an issue in California because of pollution and naturally occurring minerals such as arsenic in the groundwater.

F. Groundwater makes up 35 percent of the water used in an average year, and the percentage is higher in drought years. Until 2014, California was the only western state that did not regulate its groundwater. In August of that year, the legislature passed a bill that allows the state to review groundwater management plans to be produced by many water districts in the state.

III. The lack of health insurance among Californians is a major problem, but President Obama's Affordable Care Act has had a major impact in the state, with 1.4 million people purchasing health insurance policies and another 1.9 million enrolling in Medi-Cal, California's Medicaid program during the first six months of enrollment.

   A. Employers insure a lower proportion of people in California compared with other states because there are more small firms in California and the state is home to many noncitizens.

   B. Proportionally, more people in California buy their own health insurance than people in other states do. The California health insurance market has been characterized by large price increases from year to year and by "rescissions," the cancellation of policies because of inaccurate applications (from the perspective of the insurance companies) or because high claims have been filed (from the perspective of the state). These are the areas that the Affordable Care Act will affect the most, by more closely standardizing policies and eliminating rescissions.

C. Medi-Cal covers 30 percent of Californians, a larger proportion than are covered by Medicaid in other states. California's average cost per beneficiary is among the lowest of the states because provider payments are so low. As a result, access to providers is a major problem in some areas of the state.

D. In California, Medicare covers some 600,000 persons under 65 with disabilities. A similar number is covered by TRICARE or the Department of Veterans Affairs (VA).

E. Although we do not have good quality data on the statistics at this point, it appears that because of the Affordable Care Act, the percentage of uninsured adult Californians under 65 has fallen to 16 percent or less, down from 21 percent.

IV. California's infrastructure has noticeably deteriorated in the last 50 years.

A. The state's highways were in poor condition but are being gradually upgraded through bond issues passed in 2006 at Governor Schwarzenegger's urging and through federal Recovery Act funds.

B. The management of transportation funds is an issue, with the major contemporary example being the problems with the new San Francisco–Oakland Bay Bridge.

C. The levees in the Delta and the Central Valley of California are the subject of a major and controversial plan that Governor Jerry Brown pushed for in 2014. Some levee work is being attended to by state funds provided in bond issues passed in 2006.

PRACTICE QUIZ

1. Medicaid is
   a) a national program, administered by the federal government, with little state input.
   b) a state program, administered with little federal government guidance or funds.
   c) a federal/state program, with over half the money coming from the federal government.
   d) a federal/state program, with over half the money coming from the states.

2. Duroville was a particularly difficult public policy problem because
   a) the trailer park was located on an Indian reservation, where the state has little jurisdiction.
   b) many of the residents were undocumented, meaning they will have a difficult time qualifying for public housing.
   c) the many other trailer parks in Riverside County indicate that the problems symbolized by Duroville may be widespread.
   d) all of the above

3. In California, employer-sponsored health insurance or ESI
   a) has historically been higher proportionately than in other states because of the size and structure of California's employers and the number of noncitizens in the state.
   b) has historically been about the same as in other states.
   c) has historically been lower than in other states because of the size and structure of California's employers and the number of noncitizens in the state.
   d) has historically been higher than in other states because of the generosity of the state's medical programs.

4. The individual health insurance market in California, prior to the implementation of the Affordable Care Act, was a model that other states might emulate.
   a) true
   b) false

5. California's basic water allocation is as follows:
   a) Most is used for households and businesses, and only a small amount for agriculture. The water for household and business use is divided roughly 50–50 between inside and outside use.
   b) About half is used for households and businesses, with the other half for agriculture. The household and business portion is dominated by inside use, which is the greater proportion.
   c) Most is used in agriculture. The portion used for households and businesses is divided about 50–50 between inside and outside use.
   d) Most is used in agriculture. The portion used for households and businesses is mostly used outside for landscape watering.

6. The most likely solution for increasing California's water supply relies on
   a) reusing treated wastewater.
   b) capturing storm water.
   c) increased efficiency at homes, businesses, and in agriculture.
   d) all of the above

7. California's infrastructure has been neglected for all *except* which of the following reasons?
   a) Most recent budgets have had to cut expenses, and infrastructure is among the easier items to cut.

b) The state legislature does not put a high priority on infrastructure issues.
c) Most politicians in California have long-term horizons.
d) California's transportation funds are often mismanaged.

8. The amount of groundwater pumped during a drought is higher than the average amount pumped in most years.
a) true
b) false

9. The example of the new San Francisco–Oakland Bay Bridge illustrates the following problem:
a) Not nearly enough money was spent on the bridge.
b) The management of bridge construction is a major problem for California state government.
c) The bridge was built far too quickly, although by competent construction workers.
d) The governor of the state should not be involved in constructing major projects such as the new Bay Bridge.

CRITICAL-THINKING QUESTIONS

1. Discuss the condition of California's highways, both in your experience and as presented in the book. What do you think is the nature of the problem at the most fundamental level?
2. Issues such as housing scarcity and health care costs continue to be significant problems for California's residents. Do you think these are solvable problems?

3. What future reforms of California state government might help with the public policy problems illustrated in this chapter?

KEY TERMS

2013–14 drought (p. 269)
agricultural water use (p. 269)
appropriated rights (p. 270)
employer-sponsored insurance (ESI) (p. 272)
groundwater management (p. 270)

household water use (p. 269)
individual insurance marketplace (p. 273)
infrastructure (p. 276)
Medicaid (p. 273)
Medi-Cal (p. 273)

Medicare (p. 273)
public policy (p. 268)
riparian rights (p. 269)
rescissions (p. 273)
single payer health care (p. 273)

Answer Key

Chapter 1
1. a
2. b
3. d
4. b
5. b
6. d
7. c
8. a
9. c
10. b
11. a

Chapter 2
1. b
2. c
3. a
4. c
5. c
6. c
7. a
8. c
9. d
10. b

Chapter 3
1. c
2. b
3. a
4. c
5. b
6. c
7. a
8. d
9. b
10. b

Chapter 4
1. a
2. b

3. d
4. a
5. a
6. d
7. a
8. b
9. a
10. b

Chapter 5
1. a
2. a
3. d
4. c
5. d
6. c
7. a
8. c
9. a
10. d

Chapter 6
1. a
2. b
3. d
4. c
5. d
6. d
7. d
8. b
9. a
10. b

Chapter 7
1. a
2. b
3. a
4. b
5. b
6. a

7. b
8. c
9. a
10. d

Chapter 8
1. a
2. a
3. c
4. b
5. d
6. a
7. a
8. b
9. d
10. b
11. b

Chapter 9
1. b
2. b
3. a
4. a
5. b
6. d
7. c
8. a
9. a
10. b

Chapter 10
1. c
2. d
3. c
4. b
5. c
6. d
7. c
8. a
9. b

Notes

Chapter 1

1. Joe Matthews, "What Is the California Dream? Commentary," Zocalo Public Square, January 14, 2015, http://curious.kcrw.com/2015/01/what-is-the-california-dream (accessed 7/7/16). Matt Levin, "Digging Into the Data: How Attainable is the 'California Dream' Today?" Calmatters, February 15, 2018, https://goo.gl/iSfqAA (accessed 6/18/18).
2. James Q. Wilson, "A Guide to Schwarzenegger Country," Commentary (December 2003): 45–49. Field Institute, "Legislation by Initiative vs. through Elected Representatives," November 1999, https://web.archive.org/web/20160306150856/ (accessed 9/10/18).
3. Ballotpedia, "History of the Initiative and Referendum in California," https://ballotpedia.org/History_of_Initiative_and_Referendum_in_California (accessed 6/29/18).
4. Initiative and Referendum Institute, "Initiative Use," University of Southern California Gould School of Law, September 2010, www.iandrinstitute.org (accessed 7/2/18).
5. United States Census Bureau, "Quick Facts, California," www.census.gov/quickfacts/table/PST045215/06 (accessed 7/2/18).
6. United States Census Bureau, "Quick Facts, California; United States," https://www.census.gov/quickfacts/fact/table/CA,US/EDU685216 (accessed 7/2/18). Public Policy Institute of California, "Higher Education in California, 2016, http://www.ppic.org/content/pubs/report/R_0416HEBKR.pdf (accessed 6/14/18).
7. Public Policy Institute of California (PPIC), "Just the Facts, Immigrants in California," San Francisco, PPIC, May 2018, http://www.ppic.org/publication/immigrants-in-california/ (accessed 7/2/18).
8. Public Policy Institute of California, "Just the Facts: Poverty in California," San Francisco, PPIC, July 2018, http://www.ppic.org/publication/poverty-in-california/ (accessed 9/10/18).
9. Sarah Bonn and Caroline Danielson, "Income Inequality and the Safety Net in California," Public Policy Institute of California, May 2016, http://ppic.org/main/publication.asp?i=1190 (accessed 7/2/18).
10. Philip Reese, "California high school grads increasingly leave state for college. Here's where they go," Sacramento Bee, June 16, 2018, https://www.sacbee.com/news/local/education/article212922549.html (accessed 6/18/18).
11. Public Policy Institute of California, "Just the Facts: Immigrants in California," May 2018, http://www.ppic.org/publication/immigrants-in-california/ (accessed 7/2/18).
12. Jeffrey S. Passel, Randy Capps, and Michael Fix, "Undocumented Immigrants: Facts and Figures," Urban Institute Immigration Studies Program, January 12, 2004, www.urban.org/UploadedPDF/1000587_undoc_immigrantsfacts.pdf (accessed 7/2/18). Public Policy Institute of California, "Just the Facts: Undocumented Immigrants," March 2017, http://www.ppic.org/publication/undocumented-immigrants-in-california/ (accessed 7/2/18).
13. Dan Walters, "Ex-Governors Miss Chance to Discuss Complexities," Santa Barbara News-Press, February 21, 2004, p. A11.

Chapter 2

1. California Secretary of State, Ballot Measures, "Qualified Statewide Ballot Measures," http://www.sos.ca.gov/elections/ballot-measures/qualified-ballot-measures/ (accessed 9/6/2018).
2. Paddison, Joshua, "1848–1865: Gold Rush, Statehood, and the Western Movement," Calisphere, https://calisphere.org/exhibitions/essay/4/gold-rush/ (accessed 6/1/2018).
3. In March 1848 there were about 157,000 people in the California territory; fewer than 800 were non-native Americans, 150,000 were California Indians, and 6,500 were Californios of Spanish/Mexican descent. Congress required 60,000 residents to apply for statehood. http://users.humboldt.edu/ogayle/hist383/GoldRush.html.
4. Joe Matthews and Mark Paul, California Crackup: How Reform Broke the Golden State and How We Can Fix It (Berkeley: University of California Press, 2010), 21.

5. Carl Brent Swisher, *Motivation and Political Technique in the California Constitutional Convention: 1878–79* (New York: Da Capo Press, 1969).

6. The U.S. Constitution can also be amended by passage in a constitutional convention called by two-thirds of the states, followed by ratification by three-fourths of the states. This method has never been used, however. See Article V of the U.S. Constitution.

7. Spencer C. Olin, Jr., *California's Prodigal Sons: Hiram Johnson and the Progressives, 1911–1917* (Berkeley: University of California Press, 1968), 70.

8. John M. Allswang, *The Initiative and Referendum in California, 1898–1998* (Stanford, CA: Stanford University Press, 2000), 15.

9. George Mowry, *The California Progressives* (Chicago: Quadrangle Paperbacks, 1963), 9, 12–13.

10. Kevin Starr, *Inventing the Dream: California through the Progressive Era* (New York: Oxford University Press, 1985), 242–43.

11. Dean R. Cresap, *Party Politics in the Golden State* (Los Angeles: The Haynes Foundation, 1954), 12.

12. Mowry, *The California Progressives*, 12.

13. Mowry, *The California Progressives*, 15.

14. Quoted in Mowry, *The California Progressives*, 65.

15. Starr, *Inventing the Dream*, 254.

16. Many recalls take place at the local level; volunteer groups organize recalls of city council or school board members because they feel strongly about a particular issue. Statewide recalls, however, are rare.

17. California Secretary of State, "History of California Initiatives," www.sos.ca.gov/elections/ballot-measures/resources-and-historical-information/history-california-initiatives/ (accessed 11/15/16).

18. Allswang, *The Initiative and Referendum in California*, 33.

19. Allswang, *The Initiative and Referendum in California*, 75.

20. National Conference of State Legislatures, "Initiative, Referendum, and Recall," www.ncsl.org/research/elections-and-campaigns/initiative-referendum-and-recall-overview.aspx (accessed 6/23/16).

21. California Secretary of State, "Referendum," www.sos.ca.gov/elections/ballot-measures/referendum/ (accessed 11/15/16).

22. Jim Puzzanghera, "History of Recall Adds Fuel to Both Sides," *San Jose Mercury News*, June 18, 2003, http://digital.library.ucla.edu/websites/2003_999_022/latest.news/94/index.htm (accessed 6/23/16).

Chapter 3

1. Jay Michael, Dan Walters, and Dan Weintraub, *The Third House: Lobbyists, Power, and Money in Sacramento* (Berkeley: Berkeley Public Policy Press, 2002), 13.

2. Sam Delson, "Some Call Spending Money to Get Money Regrettable but Necessary for Inland Cities and Schools," *Riverside Press Enterprise*, July 6, 1997, A2.

3. California Secretary of State, "Employers of Lobbyists, 2015–16," http://cal-access.sos.ca.gov/Lobbying/Employers/list.aspx?session=2015 (accessed 6/7/18).

4. Mark Sappenfield, "Why Clout of Lobbyists Is Growing," Christian Science Monitor, July 23, 2003, www.csmonitor.com/2003/0722/p01s02-uspo.html (accessed 6/7/18).

5. Benjamin Ginsberg, Theodore J. Lowi, Margaret Weir, and Caroline J. Tolbert, *We the People, An Introduction to American Politics*, 11th ed. (New York: Norton, 2016), 424–25.

6. California Secretary of State, The Lobbying Directory 2015–2016, http://prd.cdn.sos.ca.gov/pdf/2015-2016-lobbying-directory.pdf (accessed 6/7/18).

7. Stephen Ansolabehere, James Snyder, Jr., and Mickey Tripathi, "Are PAC Contributions and Lobbying Linked? New Evidence from the 1995 Lobby Disclosure Act," *Business and Politics* 4, no. 2 (2002): 131–55, www.tandfonline.com/doi/abs/10.1080/13695250220000155866#preview (accessed 6/7/18).

8. National Institute on Money in State Politics, "California 2016 Elections," www.followthemoney.org/tools/election-overview?s=CA&y=2016 (accessed 6/7/18).

9. National Institute on Money in State Politics, "Independent Spending in California 2016, Offices," www.followthemoney.org/show-me?dt=2&is-s=CA&is-y=2016#[{1|gro=is-r-ot; Independent Spending in California 2016, Ballot Measures, www.followthemoney.org/show-me?dt=2&is-s=CA&is-y=2016#[{1|gro=is-t-beid (accessed 6/7/18).

10. National Institute on Money in State Politics, "California 2016 Elections, Parties," www.followthemoney.org/tools/election-overview?s=CA&y=2016 (accessed 6/7/18).

11. National Institute on Money in State Politics, "Ballot Measures," www.followthemoney.org/show-me?s=CA&y=2016&m-exi=1#[{1|gro=y (accessed 6/7/18).

12. The discussion of incumbent and open elections is based on data from the National Institute on Money in State Politics, Senate, www.followthemoney.org/show-me?s=CA&y=2016&c-exi=1&c-r-ot=S#[{1|gro=c-t-ico,c-t-sts; Assembly, www.followthemoney.org/show-me?s=CA&y=2016&c-exi=1&c-r-ot=H#[{1|gro=c-t-ico,c-t-sts (accessed 6/7/18).

13. National Institute on Money in State Politics, "Incumbency Status 2015–16," www.followthemoney.org/research/institute-reports/money-incumbency-in-2015-and-2016-state-legislative-races (accessed 6/7/18).

14. Robert Salladay, "Why Money Is Important," *Los Angeles Times*, September 11, 2006.

15. National Institute on Money in State Politics, www.followthemoney.org/entity-details?eid=3286 and www.followthemoney.org/show-me?dt=3&lby-f-fc=2#[{1|gro=lby-f-eid (accessed 6/7/18).

16. Maria Lagos, "Result of Furloughs—$1 Billion Liability," *San Francisco Chronicle*, April 23, 2011, www.sfgate.com/cgi-bin/article.cgi?f=/c/a/2011/03/07/MNSQ1I2ASB.DTL&ao=all (accessed 6/7/18).

17. Steven Malanga, "The Beholden State," *City Journal* 20 (Spring 2010), www.city-journal.org/2010/20_2_california-unions.html (accessed 6/7/18).

18. Mark Baldassare et al., "The Initiative Process in California," October 2013, Public Policy Institute of California, http://www.ppic.org/publication/the-initiative-process-in-california/ (accessed 6/7/18).

19. Elisabeth R. Gerber, "Interest Group Influence in the California Initiative Process," Public Policy Institute of California, 1998, www.ppic.org/main/publication.asp?i=49 (accessed 6/7/18).

20. Carey McWilliams, *California: The Great Exception* (Berkeley: University of California Press, 1999), 213.

21. Arthur H. Samish and Bob Thomas, *The Secret Boss of California* (New York: Crown Publishers, 1971), 13.

22. California Secretary of State, "History of the Political Reform Division," 2004, http://ss.ca.gov/campaign-lobbying/history -political-reform-division (accessed 6/7/18).

23. Patrick McGreevy and Nancy Vogel, "Senate Travel Perks for Sale," *Los Angeles Times*, March 16, 2008.

24. Pew Research Center for the People and the Press, "State of News Media 2016," http://assets.pewresearch.org/wp-content /uploads/sites/13/2016/06/30143308/state-of-the-news-media -report-2016-final.pdf (accessed 6/7/18).

25. Susan F. Rasky, "Covering California: The Press Wrestles with Diversity, Complexity, and Change," in *Governing California: Politics, Government, and Public Policy in the Golden State*, ed. Gerald C. Lubenow and Bruce E. Cain (Berkeley: Institute of Governmental Studies Press, University of California, 1997), 157–88.

26. Amy Mitchell et al., "The Modern News Consumer," July 7, 2016, Pew Research Center, http://assets.pewresearch.org/wp -content/uploads/sites/13/2016/07/07104931/PJ_2016.07 .07_Modern-News-Consumer_FINAL.pdf (accessed 6/7/18).

27. Rasky, "Covering California," 182.

28. Kristen Bialik and Katerina Eva Matsa, "Key trends in social and digital news media," Pew Research Center, http://www .pewresearch.org/fact-tank/2017/10/04/key-trends-in-social -and-digital-news-media/, October 4, 2017 (accessed 6/7/18).

29. David Pricco, "How Political Crowdfunding Killed Traditional Campaign Financing," http://crowdexpert.com/articles/crowd funding-in-politics/ (6/7/18).

30. Assemblyman Mike Gatto, press release, January 6, 2015, http://asmdc.org/members/a43/news-room/press-releases /assemblyman-mike-gatto-continues-groundbreaking-wiki -bill-project-invites-public-to-directly-draft-privacy-legislation (access 6/7/18).

31. Innovate Your State, "Prop 54: The Online Crowdsourced Ini- tiative, http://www.innovateyourstate.org/crowdsourced_initia tive_approved_by_californians (accessed 6/7/18).

32. Joe Garofoli, "Labor Beat Prop. 32 via Social Media," *SFGate*, December 25, 2012, www.sfgate.com/politics/joegarofoli/arti cle/Labor-beat-Prop-32-via-social-media-4145607.php (accessed 6/7/18).

33. Jim Rutenberg, "Distrust of Media Takes a Role in Campaigns," *New York Times*, October 12, 2003, http://209.157.64.201 /focus/f-news/999985/posts (accessed 6/7/18).

Chapter 4

1. Spencer C. Olin, *California's Prodigal Sons: Hiram Johnson and the Progressives, 1911–1917* (Berkeley: University of California Press, 1968).

2. Brian F. Schaffner, Matthew Streb, and Gerald Wright, "Teams without Uniforms: The Nonpartisan Ballot in State and Local Elections," *Political Research Quarterly* 54, no. 1 (2001): 7–30.

3. Matt Barreto, "The Prop 187 Effect: How the California GOP lost their way and implications for 2014 and beyond," Latino Decisions, October 17, 2013, www.latinodecisions.com/blog /2013/10/17/prop187effect/.

4. Lopez, Gustavo, Neil G. Ruiz, and Eileen Patten, "Key facts about Asian Americans, a diverse and growing population,"

http://www.pewresearch.org/fact-tank/2017/09/08/key-facts -about-asian-americans/ (accessed 10/18/18).

5. Javier Panzar, "It's Official: Latinos Now Outnumber Whites in California," *Los Angeles Times*, July 8, 2015, www.latimes .com/local/california/la-me-census-latinos-20150708-story .html (accessed 9/26/16).

6. John Myers, "Tens of Thousands Have Left California's Ameri- can Independent Party in the Last Month," *Los Angeles Times*, May 20, 2016, www.latimes.com/politics/la-pol-ca-american -independent-voters-registration-20160520-snap-story.html (accessed 9/26/16).

7. Michael Finnegan, "The Race for the White House," *Los Ange- les Times*, September 8, 2004, p. A1.

8. Mark Baldassare, "World Apart: California's Partisan Divide and the 2016 Election," *Viewpoints* (blog), Public Policy Insti- tute of California, June 14, 2016, www.ppic.org/main/blog _detail.asp?i=2073#.V32JZcEPuII.email (accessed 9/26/16).

9. Roper Center for Public Opinion Research, *Social Capital Com- munity Benchmark Survey: Methodology and Documentation*, February 17, 2001, http://ropercenter.cornell.edu/2000-social -capital-community-benchmark-survey/ (accessed 9/26/16).

10. Mark Baldassare, *A California State of Mind: The Conflicted Voter in a Changing World* (Berkeley: University of California Press, 2002), 47.

11. Stanford Law School Justice Advocacy Project, "Three Strikes Basics," law.stanford.edu/stanford-justice-advocacy-project/three -strikes-basics/ (accessed 9/26/16).

12. Richard Edward DeLeon, *Left Coast City: Progressive Politics in San Francisco, 1975–1991* (Lawrence: University Press of Kansas, 1992).

13. Eric McGhee, "Political Reform and Moderation in California's Legislature: Did Electoral Reforms Make State Representa- tives More Moderate?" Public Policy Institute of California, May 2018, http://www.ppic.org/publication/political-reform -and-moderation-in-californias-legislature-did-electoral-reforms -make-state-representatives-moderate/.

14. Christine Mai-Duc, "Get signatures, make money: How some gatherers are making top dollar in this year's flood of ballot initiatives," *Los Angeles Times*, August 10, 2016, www.latimes .com/politics/la-pol-ca-signature-gatherers-ballot-initiatives -california-20160627-snap-htmlstory.html (accessed 12/5/16).

15. "The Mormon Money behind Proposition 8," *The Atlantic*, October 23, 2008, www.theatlantic.com/daily-dish/archive /2008/10/the-mormon-money-behind-proposition-8/20 9748/ (accessed 8/13/12).

16. Reid Wilson, "The Most Expensive Ballot Initiatives," *GovBeat* (blog), *Washington Post*, May 17, 2014, www.washingtonpost .com/blogs/govbeat/wp/2014/05/17/the-most-expensive-bal lot-initiatives/?utm_term=.4f950116984b (accessed 12/5/16).

17. Carla Javier, "California's biggest ever election guide might not actually help voters decide," *Fusion*, September 22, 2016, fusion.net/story/349469/california-voter-guide-decide/?utm _source=emailshare&utm_medium=email&utm_campaign =socialshare&utm_content=theme_bottom_mobile (accessed 9/25/16).

18. Susan Rasky, "Introduction to 'An Antipolitician, Anti- establishment Groundswell Elected the Candidate of Change,'" in *California Votes: The 2002 Governor's Race and the Recall That Made History*, ed. Gerald Lubenow (Berkeley: Berkeley Public Policy Press, 2003).

19. Rasky, "Introduction."
20. Catherine Decker, "State's Shifting Political Landscape," *Los Angeles Times*, November 6, 2008, p. A1.
21. "Young Voters Help Secure Obama Victory, Passage of Progressive Ballot Measures," *Huffington Post*, November 7, 2012, http://www.huffingtonpost.com/2012/11/07/young-voters-2012-obama_n_2089789.html (accessed 9/26/16).
22. Phil Willon, "GOP Loses Grip on Inland Empire," *Los Angeles Times*, November 11, 2012, p. A37.
23. George Skelton, "Time for Initiative Reforms," *Los Angeles Times*, November 15, 2012, p. A2.
24. P. St John, "Prop. 47 would cut penalties for 1 in 5 criminals in California," *Los Angeles Times*, October 11, 2014, www.latimes.com/local/politics/la-me-ff-pol-proposition47-2014 1012-story.html (accessed 9/26/16).
25. "Exit Polls," *CNN*, November 9, 2016, www.cnn.com/election/results/exit-polls/california/president (accessed 11/17/2016).
26. A. Vesoulis, "The 2018 Elections Saw Record Midterm Turnout," *Time*, November 13, 2018, http://time.com/5452258/midterm-elections-turnout (accessed 11/30/18).
27. Jorge L. Ortiz, "Orange Is the New Blue: California Democrats Sweep 7 House Seats in Former GOP Stronghold," *USA Today*, November 18, 2018, www.usatoday.com/story/news/politics/elections/2018/11/18/california-democrats-sweep-house-seats-orange-county/2048696002/ (accessed 11/30/18).
28. D. P. Osorio, "The Cost of Winning a Senate Race," https://dposorio.com, May 9, 2012, http://dposorio.com/blog/822/the-cost-of-winning-a-senate-race (accessed 7/20/12).
29. Rasky, "Introduction."
30. William Booth, "In Calif. Governor's Race, It's Ads Infinitum," *Washington Post*, May 29, 1998, p. A1.
31. Carol A. Cassel, "Hispanic Turnout: Estimates from Validated Voting Data," *Political Research Quarterly* 55, no. 2 (June 2002): 391–408. Michael A. Jones-Correa and David L. Leal, "Political Participation: Does Religion Matter?" *Political Research Quarterly* 54, no. 4 (2001): 751–70.
32. Carl Bialik, "Voter Turnout Fell, Especially in States that Clinton Won," FiveThirtyEight, November 11, 2016, http://fivethirtyeight.com/features/voter-turnout-fell-especially-in-states-that-clinton-won (accessed 11/11/2016).

Chapter 5

1. Field Research Corporation, "California Voter Views of the State Legislature Turn Negative after the Arrest of State Senator Leland Yee," Poll release #2464, April 10, 2014, https://www.scribd.com/document/217499631/Field-Poll-California-Views-Of-The-State-Legislature (accessed 7/9/2018). Field Research Corporation, "Mixed View of the State Legislature . . . ," Poll release #2500, February 25, 2015, https://www.sacbee.com/site-services/newsletters/capitol-alert-news letter/article11125130.ece/BINARY/Field%20Poll%20results:%20Legislature%20job%20performance%20and%20program%20funding (accessed 7/9/2018). Field Research Corporation, "Californians Hold Divergent Views . . . ," Poll release #2552, September 29, 2016, https://www.politico.com/states/f/?id=00 000157-72c9-d370-addf-73cf03460000 (accessed 7/9/2018).

Mark Baldassare et al., "Californians and the Environment," Public Policy Institute of California, July 2018, http://www.ppic.org/wp-content/uploads/ppic-statewide-survey-july-2018.pdf (accessed 9/7/2018). Information on previous PPIC polls can be found at http://www.ppic.org/wp-content/uploads/timetrends-alladults0518.pdf (accessed 7/10/2018).
2. Andrew Dugan, "Congressional Approval Rating Languishes at low Level," Gallup Politics, July 15, 2014, www.gallup.com/poll/politics.aspx?ref=b (accessed 8/11/14). Gallup, "Congress and the Public," www.gallup.com/poll/1600/congress-public.aspx (accessed 7/9/2018).
3. Jeremy B. White, "Chevron Spends $1 Million to Boost Assembly Democrat Cheryl Brown," *Sacramento Bee*, April 14, 2016, www.sacbee.com/news/politics-government/capitol-alert/article71852047.html (accessed 7/9/2018). Patrick McGreevy and Chris Megerian, "With a record $24 million spent on the election so far, are special interests trying to buy their way into the Legislature?" *Los Angeles Times*, May 30, 2016, www.latimes.com/politics/la-pol-sac-california-independent-spending-20160530-snap-story.html (accessed 8/24/2016). Laurel Rosenhall, "Money Rains from Perfect Storm of Politics," *CALmatters*, June 16, 2016, https://calmatters.org/articles/money-rains-from-perfect-storm-of-politics/ (accessed 7/9/2018).
4. Editorial Board, "Editorial: Stop Disgrace of 'Gut and Amend' in Legislature," *Sacramento Bee Capitol Alert*, April 30, 2013, https://www.dailynews.com/2013/05/01/another-view-stop-disgrace-of-gut-and-amend-in-legislature/ (accessed 9/15/16).
5. Lou Cannon, *Governor Reagan: His Rise to Power* (New York: Public Affairs, 2003), 166.
6. Peter Schrag, *Paradise Lost: California's Experience, America's Future* (New York: New Press, 1998), 244.
7. Institute of Governmental Studies, "IGS Goes to Sacramento to Assess Ten Years of Term Limits," *Public Affairs Report* 42, no. 3 (Fall 2001).
8. National Association of Latino Elected and Appointed Officials Education Fund, *National Directory of Latino Elected and Appointed Officials 2017*, https://d3n8a8pro7vhmx.cloudfront.net/naleo/pages/1402/attachments/original/1512779367/2017_National_Directory_of_Latino_Elected_Officials.pdf#page=16 (accessed 7/9/2018). The National Conference of State Legislatures, 2015 Latino Legislators, http://www.ncsl.org/research/about-state-legislatures/latino-legislators.aspx (accessed 7/9/2018). The National Conference of State Legislatures, Women in State Legislatures for 2018, http://www.ncsl.org/legislators-staff/legislators/womens-legislative-network/women-in-state-legislatures-for-2018.aspx (accessed 7/9/2018). Leadership California Institute, *Women: The Status of Women in California State and Local Government*, http://www.leadershipcaliforniainstitute.org/ (accessed 7/9/2018).
9. Schrag, *Paradise Lost*, 143.
10. Adam Nagourney, "Political Shift in California Trips Brown," *New York Times*, September 20, 2011, www.nytimes.com/2011/09/21/us/politics/brown-says-california-gop-is-harder-to-work-with-decades-later.html?pagewanted=all (accessed 7/9/2018).
11. Anthony York, "Brown and Obama Find Bipartisanship a Difficult Goal to Reach," *Los Angeles Times*, February 24, 2012, http://articles.latimes.com/2012/feb/24/local/la-me-jerry-brown-20120224 (accessed 7/9/2018).
12. Nagourney, "Political Shift in California Trips Brown."

13. George Skelton, "California's Capitol—the Long View: A Columnist Looks Back on 50 Years Covering the Ups and Downs of Sacramento," *Los Angeles Times*, December 1, 2011, p. A2.
14. John Meyers, Melanie Mason and Liam Dillon, "Chaos Helps Avert Ballot Battles," *Los Angeles Times*, July 1, 2018, p. B1. George Skelton, "Voters Spared 3 Ballot Battles," *Los Angeles Times*, July 2, 2018, p. B1.
15. Laurel Rosenhall, "Special Interests Win As Lawmakers Cut Last-Minute Deals To Pull Initiatives Off Your Ballot," *CALmatters*, June 29,2018, https://calmatters.org/articles/special-interests-win-as-lawmakers-cut-last-minute-deals-to-pull-initiatives-off-your-ballot/ (accessed 7/8/2018).
16. Melanie Mason, "Hard View on Soft Drinks," *Los Angeles Times*, July 3, 2018, p. B1.
17. Adam Nagourney, "How Control of Congress Could Hinge on a 12-Cent Tax on Gasoline," *New York Times*, July 8, 2018, p. A18.
18. We Said Enough, "The Silence Breakers," https://www.wesaidenough.com/silence-breakers/ (accessed 7/8/2018); for more on this issue visit https://wesaidenough.com.
19. Melanie Mason, "Panel OKs New Policy on Capitol Harassment Complaints," *Los Angeles Times*, June 27, 2018 p. B3.
20. Melanie Mason, "Panel OKs New Policy on Capitol Harassment Complaints."
21. John Meyers, "Jerry Brown's Budget Legacy," *Los Angeles Times*, July 1, 2018, p. A1.

Chapter 6

1. This figure is calculated from 154,000 employees from the UC system, 150,000 from the California State University system, and 230,000 other state employees. www.universityofcalifornia.edu/infocenter/employee-fte; www2.calstate.edu/csu-system/about-the-csu/facts-about-the-csu; www.sco.ca.gov/ppsd_empinfo_demo.html (accessed 7/5/18).
2. Thomas E. Cronin and Michael A. Genovese, *The Paradoxes of the American Presidency* (New York: Oxford University Press, 1998).
3. Public Policy Institute of California, "PPIC Statewide Survey: Time Trends for Job Approval Ratings for Governor Schwarzenegger," http://www.ppic.org/data-set/ppic-statewide-survey-time-trends-for-job-approval-ratings/ (accessed 8/30/18).
4. Public Policy Institute of California, "Californians and Their Government," May 2018, www.ppic.org/wp-content/uploads/crosstabs-alladults0518.pdf (accessed 7/5/18).
5. Andy Kroll, "The Last Days of Jerry Brown," *The California Sunday Magazine*, March 18, 2018, https://story.californiasunday.com/jerry-brown-last-days (accessed 7/5/18).
6. Mark Truppner, "Brown's Plan to Streamline State Government," MyMotherlode.com, https://www.mymotherlode.com/news/local/63810/browns-plan-to-streamline-state-government.htm (accessed 10/29/18).
7. Office of Governor, "Governor Brown Takes Action to Increase Zero-Emission Vehicles, Fund New Climate Investments," January 26, 2018, www.gov.ca.gov/2018/01/26/governor-brown-takes-action-to-increase-zero-emission-vehicles-fund-new-climate-investments/ (accessed 7/5/18).
8. John Myers, "Gov. Jerry Brown agrees to National Guard border efforts, but not 'a mission to round up women and children,'" *Los Angeles Times*, April 11, 2018, www.latimes.com/politics/la-pol-ca-jerry-brown-national-guard-20180411-story.html (accessed 7/5/18).
9. Joshua Stark, "New Report Calls for Radical Reform of Caltrans," *TransForm*, February 4, 2014, www.transformca.org/trblogpost/report-calls-radical-reform-caltrans (accessed 8/24/16). Debra J. Saunders, "Jerry Brown on Bay Bridge: Don't Worry, Be Happy," *SFGate*, May 16, 2014, https://blog.sfgate.com/djsaunders/2014/05/16/jerry-brown-on-bay-bridge-dont-worry-be-happy/ (accessed 8/30/18).
10. Jeff McDonald, "Brown signs bills to reform CPUC, urges administrative fixes too," *San Diego Union-Tribune*, September 29, 2016, www.sandiegouniontribune.com/news/watchdog/sd-me-watchdog-cpuc-20160929-story.html (accessed 7/5/2018).
11. Dan Weikel and Kim Christensen, "How a Ban on Ex Parte Communications by the Coastal Commission Could Change the Balance of Power," *Los Angeles Times*, May 14, 2016, www.latimes.com/local/california/la-me-adv-coastal-commission-20160515-story.html (accessed 8/24/16). Steve Lopez, "Cover Your Ears: Coastal Commissioner Martha McClure's on the Phone," *Los Angeles Times*, May 14, 2016, www.latimes.com/local/california/la-me-lopez-commission-sleepover-20160514-column.html (accessed 8/24/2016).
12. California Senate Office of Research, "How Often Do Governors Say No?" October 16, 2017, https://sor.senate.ca.gov/sites/sor.senate.ca.gov/files/Governors%20Vetoes%202017_Senate%20Office%20of%20Research.pdf (accessed 8/31/18). John Meyers, "Political Roadmap: There's a Reason Why Jerry Brown Signs so Many Bills," *Los Angeles Times*, October 2, 2016, http://www.latimes.com/politics/la-pol-sac-roadmap-jerry-brown-signs-bills-20161002-snap-story.html (accessed 8/31/2018).
13. Eric McGhee and Paul Warren, "The Vanishing Line-Item Veto," *Viewpoints: The PPIC Blog*, Public Policy Institute of California, June 26, 2014, www.ppic.org/main/blog_detail.asp?i=1551 (accessed 8/24/16).
14. Steven Harmon, "Gov. Brown Warns Democratic Lawmakers Not to Overreach, Overspend," *Vallejo Times-Herald*, January 24, 2013, www.timesheraldonline.com/ci_22439612/gov-brown-warns-democratic-lawmakers-not-overreach-overspend (accessed 8/24/16).
15. Liam Dillon, "More than a Dozen Assembly Members Flipped Their Votes from Last Year to Support Climate Change Bill," *LA Times Essential Politics*, August 23, 2016, www.latimes.com/politics/essential/la-pol-sac-essential-politics-updates-more-than-a-dozen-assemblymembers-1471987788-html story.html (accessed 9/24/16). Jessica Calefati, "California Climate Change Law: Extension of Greenhouse Gas Goals OK'd by Assembly," *The Mercury News*, August 23, 2016, www.mercurynews.com/2016/08/23/california-climate-change-law-extension-of-greenhouse-gas-goals-okd-by-assembly/ (accessed 9/24/16).
16. George Skelton, "Governor Hits Back at Big Oil," *Los Angeles Times*, August 25, 2016, p. B1.
17. James Fallows, "Jerry Brown's Political Reboot," *The Atlantic Monthly*, June 2013, https://www.theatlantic.com/magazine/archive/2013/06/the-fixer/309324/ (accessed 10/20/18).
18. Fallows, "Jerry Brown's Political Reboot." Egan, "Jerry Brown's Revenge." Lou Cannon, "Calif. Comeback: Jerry Brown Leads a Turnaround," *Real Clear Politics*, June 25, 2013, www.real

clearpolitics.com/articles/2013/06/25/calif_comeback_jerry _brown_leads_a_turnaround_118943.html (accessed 8/24/16).

19. Dan Walters, "Could Anne Gust Brown Be the Next Governor," *Sacramento Bee*, March 8, 2015, www.sacbee.com/news /politics-government/politics-columns-blogs/dan-walters/arti cle13044824.html (accessed 8/24/16).

20. Times Editorial Board, "Designating an active governor when the actual governor leaves California is an archaic and pointless tradition," *Los Angeles Times*, July 29, 2006, http://www .latimes.com/opinion/editorials/la-ed-acting-governor-2016 0728-snap-story.html.

21. Reports can be viewed at www.auditor.ca.gov.

Chapter 7

1. Patrick McGreevy, "California has sued the Trump administration 38 times. Here's a look at the legal challenges," *Los Angeles Times*, July 22, 2018, www.latimes.com/politics/la-pol-ca-cali fornia-sues-trump-20180722-story.html (accessed 8/20/18).

2. Massoud Hayoun, "A Judge Ruled Against Trump's Challenge to California's Sanctuary Law. But That Doesn't Mean the Immigration Battle Is Over," *Pacific Standard*, July 6, 2018, psmag.com/news/judge-ruled-against-trump-challenge-to -california-sanctuary-law (accessed 8/20/18).

3. Court Statistics Report (2017), "Statewide Caseload Trends, 2006–2007 Through 2015–2016," www.courts.ca.gov/docu ments/2017-Court-Statistics-Report.pdf (accessed 8/20/18).

4. www.courts.ca.gov.

5. Bob Egelko, "In Starbucks case, California court says workers owed for off-the-clock time," July 26, 2018, www.sfchronicle .com/bayarea/article/in-suit-against-starbucks case (accessed 8/20/18).

6. See *Anderson v. Mt. Clemons Pottery Co*, 328 U.S. 680 (1946).

7. Court Statistics Report (2017).

8. *People v. Colvin*, 203 Cal.App.4th 1029 (2012).

9. *Unpublished* means that the memorandum may not be used for purposes of legal citation or precedent. gpo.gov/fdsys/pkg /USCOURTS-caed-2_11-cv-02939. The memorandum can be found here: U.S. Government Printing Office, *11-2939—Sacramento Nonprofit Collective et al v. Holder et al.*, cdn.ca9.us courts.gov/datastore/memoranda/2014/01/15/12-15991.pdf (accessed 8/20/18).

10. "SB-643 Medical marijuana," California Legislative Information, https://leginfo.legislature.ca.gov/faces/billNavClient.xhtml ?bill_id=201520160SB643 (accessed 9/7/18).

11. The act can be found here: www.congress.gov/bill/113th-con gress/house-bill/83/text (accessed 8/20/18).

12. Bob Egelko, "California Supreme Court Nomination a 'Statement' to U.S.," *SF Gate*, July 22, 2014, www.sfgate.com/poli tics/article/Brown-nominates-Stanford-professor-to-state-high -5638237.php (accessed 8/20/18).

13. David Siders, "Gov. Jerry Brown Names Obama Administration Lawyer to California Supreme Court," *Sacramento Bee*, November 24, 2014, www.sacbee.com/news/politics-govern ment/capitol-alert/article4123447.html (accessed 8/20/18).

14. Prebloe Stolz, *Judging Judges: The Investigation of Rose Bird and the California Supreme Court* (New York: Free Press, 1981).

15. California Courts, "Judicial Council," www.courts.ca.gov/policy admin-jc.htm?genpubtab (accessed 8/20/18).

16. Carmen Lo, Katie Londenberg, and David Nims, "Spending in Judicial Elections: State Trends in the Wake of *Citizens United*," http://gov.uchastings.edu/public-law/docs/judicial-elections -report-and-appendices-corrected.pdf (accessed 8/20/18).

17. 2017 Court Statistics Report.

18. Unlimited jurisdiction civil cases are disputes that involve more than $25,000. Limited jurisdiction civil cases are disputes that involve amounts from $10,000 to $25,000. See Court Statistics Report (2017), "Statewide Trends," 2017.

19. "California Courts Wrestle with Budget Cuts Old and New," *Los Angeles Times*, June 19, 2012, latimesblogs.latimes .com/california-politics/2012/06/california-court.html (accessed 8/20/18).

20. Maria Dinzeo, "IT Project Sinks in Sea of Criticism," *Courthouse News Service*, March 27, 2012, www.courthousenews .com/2012/03/27/45079.htm (accessed 8/20/18).

21. Cheryl Miller, "Judges Criticize Court Bureaucracy in Blistering Report," inlandpolitics.com/blog/2012/05/30/the-rec order-judges-criticize-court-bureaucracy-in-blistering-report/ (accessed 8/20/18).

22. Cheryl Miller, "What's Taking Jerry Brown So Long to Pick a Supreme Court Justice?" *The Recorder*, March 5, 2018, www .law.com/therecorder/2018/03/05/whats-taking-jerry-brown -so-long-to-pick-a-supreme-court-justice/.

Chapter 8

1. Legislative Analyst's Office, "2016–17 Budget: Higher Education Analysis," February 25, 2016, www.lao.ca.gov (accessed 7/31/18).

2. Rosanna Xia, "State Funding Cuts During the Recession Still Shortchanging Cal State Students, Officials Say," *Los Angeles Times*, July 21, 2016, www.latimes.com/local/lanow/la-me-cal -state-executive-compensation-20160719-snap-story.html (accessed 7/31/18).

3. Marla Dickerson, "State Fiscal Woes Threaten Cities' Budgets and a Leading Job Engine," *Los Angeles Times*, January 17, 2003, pp. C1+.

4. California Department of Finance, "Historical Budget Publications," February 24, 1998, www.dof.ca.gov (accessed 7/31/18).

5. California Department of Finance, "Historical Budget Publications."

6. George Skelton, "The 'Budget Nun' Earns Her Pay and Bipartisan Respect," *Los Angeles Times*, May 26, 2003, p. B5.

7. Public Finance Division, "California's Current Credit Ratings," California State Treasurer, www.treasurer.ca.gov/ratings/current .asp (accessed 7/31/18). Dan Walters, "Moody's Raises California's Credit Rating," *Sacramento Bee*, June 25, 2014, https:// inlandpolitics.com/blog/2014/06/26/sacbee-moodys-raises -californias-bond-credit-rating (accessed 9/22/18). Moody's Investors Service, "Moody's Fiscal Test of Most Populous States Show Texas Best Prepared for Next Recession, California Least Ready," April 21, 2016, www.moodys.com/research /Moodys-Fiscal-test-of-most-populous-states-show-Texas-best —PR_347649, April 21, 2016 (accessed 7/31/18).

8. William Chen, "Who Pays Taxes in California?" April 2015, calbudgetcenter.org/wp-content/uploads/Who-Pays-Taxes-in-CA_Issue-Brief_04.14.2015.pdf (accessed 7/31/18). Justin Garosi and Jason Sisney, "'Top 1 Percent' Pays Half of State Income Taxes," Legislative Analyst's Office, December 4, 2014, lao.ca.gov/LAOEconTax/Article/Detail/7 (accessed 7/31/18).

9. Tax Foundation, "Facts & Figures, How Does Your State Compare?" Washington, DC: Tax Foundation, 2018, files.taxfoundation.org/20180411102900/Facts-Figures-2018-How-Does-Your-State-Compare.pdf (accessed 7/20/18).

10. Katherine Barrett, Richard Greene, Michele Mariani, and Anya Sostek, "The Way We Tax," *Governing*, February 2003, p. 20.

11. Franchise Tax Board, State of California, "2012 Annual Report," Table C-8, Corporation Tax, Tax Liability by Net Income Class, Franchise Tax Board, 2011, www.ftb.ca.gov/aboutFTB/Tax_Statistics/Reports/2012/2012_C-8.pdf (accessed 7/31/18). See also Chen, "Who Pays Taxes in California?"

12. Oliver Libaw, "Where Does Lottery Revenue Go?" ABC News, August 26, 2001, abcnews.go.com/US/story?id=92595&page=1 (accessed 7/31/18). See also Valerie Strauss, "Mega Millions: Do Lotteries Really Benefit Public Schools?" *Washington Post*, March 30, 2012, www.washingtonpost.com/blogs/answer-sheet/post/mega-millions-do-lotteries-really-benefit-public-schools/2012/03/30/gIQAbTUNlS_blog.html (accessed 7/31/18).

13. Barrett et al., "The Way We Tax."

14. Council on State Taxation, "The Best and Worst of State Tax Administration," December 2013, www.cost.org (accessed 7/31/18).

15. California Taxpayers Association, "Cal-Tax: Taxes Are a Heavy Burden in California," digital.library.ucla.edu/websites/2004_999_003/dynamic/downloads/individual_download_file_link_1_english_10.pdf (accessed 7/31/18).

16. Tax Foundation, "State-Local Tax Burden Rankings FY 2012," taxfoundation.org/article/state-local-tax-burden-rankings-fy-2012 (accessed 7/31/18).

17. Chen, "Who Pays Taxes in California?"

18. Betty T. Yee and the Controller's Council of Economic Advisors on Tax Reform, "Comprehensive Tax Reform in California: A Contextual Framework," June 2016, www.sco.ca.gov/eo_cea_contextual_framework.html (accessed 7/31/18).

19. Carson Bruno, "California: CEOs Rate It Worst U.S. Business Climate for 8 Years Running," March 21, 2014, www.realclearmarkets.com/articles/2014/03/21/california_ceos_rate_it_worst_us_business_climate_for_8_years_running_100963.html (accessed 7/31/18).

20. Institute for Taxation and Economic Policy, "'High Rate' Income Tax States Are Outperforming No-Tax States," February 2012, www.itepnet.org (accessed 7/31/18).

21. Hans Johnson, "Defunding Higher Education" (San Francisco: Public Policy Institute of California, 2012), 4.

22. Phil Oliff, Vincent Palacios, Ingrid Johnson, and Michael Leachman, "Recent Deep State Higher Education Cuts May Harm Students and the Economy for Years to Come" (Washington, DC: Center on Budget and Policy Priorities, May 2013).

23. James D. Savage, "California's Structural Deficit Crisis," *Public Budgeting and Finance* 12, no. 2 (Summer 1992): 82–97.

24. California Forward, "Curing Deficits and Creating Value: Principles for Improving State Fiscal Decisions," s3.amazonaws.com/zanran_storage/www.caforward.org/ContentPages/1903423.pdf (accessed 7/31/18).

25. California Forward, "Curing Deficits and Creating Value."

26. Peter Nicholas and Virginia Ellis, "Budget Signals Narrowed Ambitions," *Los Angeles Times*, February 18, 2004, p. A1.

Chapter 9

1. Bernard H. Ross and Myron A. Levine, *Urban Politics: Power in Metropolitan America*, 6th ed. (Itasca, IL: F.E. Peacock, 2001), p. 90.

2. Dale Krane, Platon N. Rigos, and Melvin B. Hill Jr., *Home Rule in America: A Fifty-State Handbook* (Washington, DC: CQ Press, 2001).

3. Daniel B. Rodriguez, "State Supremacy, Local Sovereignty: Reconstructing State/Local Relations under the California Constitution," in *Constitutional Reform in California: Making State Government More Effective and Responsive*, eds. Bruce E. Cain and Roger G. Noll (Berkeley: Institute of Governmental Studies Press, University of California, 1995), pp. 401–29; Krane, Rigos, and Hill, *Home Rule in America*; Melvin B. Hill, *State Laws Governing Local Government Structure and Administration* (Washington, DC: U.S. Advisory Commission on Intergovernmental Relations [ACIR], 1993).

4. Ross and Levine, *Urban Politics*, p. 91.

5. John Taylor, "What Happened to Branciforte County?" in California State Association of Counties, *Introduction to California Counties*, www.counties.org/sites/main/files/file-attachments/tab_1_intro_to_california_counties.pdf (accessed 9/7/18).

6. County of Los Angeles, *2018–19 Recommended Budget*, April 10, 2018, https://www.lacounty.gov/budget (accessed 9/22/16).

7. Aaron Claverie and David Downey, "Pechanga to Buy Quarry Site," *The Californian*, November 15, 2012, www.sandiegouniontribune.com/sdut-region-pechanga-to-buy-quarry-site-2012nov15-story.html (accessed 9/7/18).

8. For an excellent study of the 1963 Knox-Nisbet Act, which created LAFCos to impose order and control on the post–World War II explosion of new cities and annexations in California, see Tom Hogen-Esch, "Fragmentation, Fiscal Federalism, and the Ghost of Dillon's Rule: Municipal Incorporation in Southern California, 1950–2010," *California Journal of Politics & Policy* 3, no. 2 (2011): 1–22.

9. California Senate Governance and Finance Committee, "City Fact Sheet," September 2016, https://sgf.senate.ca.gov/sites/sgf.senate.ca.gov/files/city_facts_2016.pdf (accessed 11/30/18).

10. Voters in these elections may, of course, choose not to incorporate as a city and run their own show. The prospect of rapid growth and development, for example, scared many of the 57,000 residents of Castro Valley. In November 2002 they voted three to one against incorporation, opting to remain Northern California's largest unincorporated community and governed locally by the Alameda County Board of Supervisors.

11. League of California Cities, "California Residents and Basic Geography," http://www.cacities.org/Resources/Learn-About-Cities (accessed 10/30/18).

12. See John H. Knox and Chris Hutchinson, "Municipal Disincorporation in California," *Public Law Journal* 32, no. 4 (Fall 2009), californiacityfinance.com/DisincorporationKnox2010.pdf (accessed 8/23/14).

13. Sandra Stokley, "Understanding the Disincorporation Issue," *The Press Enterprise*, September 18, 2013, www.pe.com/2013/09/18/jurupa-valley-understanding-the-disincorporation-issue (accessed 10/7/16). For more background on Jurupa Valley's tribulations, see Rick Rojas, "For Jurupa Valley, Cityhood Isn't What It Expected," *Los Angeles Times*, December 1, 2013, http://articles.latimes.com/2013/dec/01/local/la-me-jurupa-valley-20131202 (accessed 8/25/14); Sandra Stokley, "'Bitter' Announcement on Disincorporation," *The Press Enterprise*, December 18, 2013, www.pe.com/articles/city-682062-valley-jurupa.html (accessed 8/21/14); Irvin Dawid, "Puff! There Goes California's Newest City," *Planetizen*, January 18, 2014, www.planetizen.com/node/66954 (accessed 10/7/16).

14. Sandra Stokley, "Jurupa Valley: City Says It Will Survive, After All," *The Press Enterprise*, September 29, 2015, www.pe.com/articles/county-781898-city-jurupa.html (accessed 10/12/15).

15. Zoltan L. Hajnal, Paul G. Lewis, and Hugh Louch, *Municipal Elections in California: Turnout, Timing, and Competition* (San Francisco: Public Policy Institute of California, 2002), pp. 23–24.

16. Ross and Levine, *Urban Politics*, pp. 165–78.

17. Amy Bridges, *Morning Glories: Municipal Reform in the Southwest* (Princeton, NJ: Princeton University Press, 1997).

18. International City/County Management Association (ICMA), "Officials in U.S. Municipalities 2,500 and Over in Population," in *The Municipal Year Book 2003* (Washington, DC: ICMA, 2003), pp. 195–200.

19. Bruce E. Cain, Megan Mullin, and Gillian Peele, "City Caesars? An Examination of Mayoral Power in California," presented at the 2001 annual meeting of the American Political Science Association, August 29–September 2, San Francisco.

20. Hajnal et al., *Municipal Elections in California*, p. 25.

21. Richard DeLeon, *Left Coast City: Progressive Politics in San Francisco, 1957–1991* (Lawrence, KS: University Press of Kansas, 1992). A recent study of over 7,000 U.S. cities found that district systems were better than at-large systems at achieving diverse city councils only in areas where underrepresented groups were highly concentrated geographically and constituted a sizable share of the population. See Jessica Trounstine and Melody Ellis Valdini, "The Context Matters: The Effects of Single-Member Versus At-Large Districts on City Council Diversity," *American Journal of Political Science* 52, no. 3 (July 2008): 554–69.

22. Jean Merl, "Voting Rights Act Leading California Cities to Dump At-Large Elections," *Los Angeles Times*, September 14, 2013, www.latimes.com/local/la-me-local-elections-20130915-story.html#axzz2tt5grBf9 (accessed 8/27/14).

23. Javier Panzar, "It's Official: Latinos Now Outnumber Whites in California," *Los Angeles Times*, July 8, 2015, www.latimes.com/local/california/la-me-census-latinos-20150708-story.html (accessed 5/4/16).

24. Teri Figueroa, "City Poised to Shake Up Voting System," *San Diego Union-Tribune*, June 21, 2016, www.sandiegouniontribune.com/news/2016/jun/21/san-marcos-considering-district-elections (accessed 6/30/16).

25. Austin Walsh, "Redwood City Elementary School District Looking at Shifting Election System," *San Mateo Daily Journal*, January 13, 2016, https://www.smdailyjournal.com/news/local/redwood-city-elementary-school-district-looking-at-shifting-election-system/article_ff79167d-2b6c-58d9-b6e3-f8e6046a058f.html (accessed 6/30/16).

26. Spencer Woodman, "How California Is Solving Its Voting Rights Problem," *VICE Magazine*, May 26, 2016, www.vice.com/read/how-california-is-solving-its-voting-rights-problem (accessed 6/30/16). For a critical perspective on the CVRA as a boondoggle for lawyers at taxpayers' expense, see Carolyn Schuk, "California Voting Rights Act: $14 Million Legal Bill for Taxpayers," *Santa Clara Weekly*, December 2, 2015, www.santaclaraweekly.com/2015/Issue-49/city-observer.html (accessed 6/30/16).

27. Brian E. Adams. "Citizens, Interest Groups, and Local Ballot Initiatives" *Politics & Policy* 41, 1 (2012): 43–68.

28. Matthew A. Melone and George A. Nation III, "'Standing' on Formality: *Hollingsworth v. Perry* and the Efficacy of Direct Democracy in the United States" (unpublished paper), March 2014, p. 289, http://works.bepress.com/matthew_melone/2 (accessed 5/3/14).

29. "Voter Turnout," United States Election Project, www.electproject.org/home/voter-turnout/voter-turnout-data (accessed 9/7/18).

30. Melissa Marschall and John Lappie. "Turnout in Local Elections: Is Timing Really Everything?" *Election Law Journal: Rules, Politics, and Policy* (July 2018).

31. FairVote, a nonprofit advocacy group that promotes ranked-choice voting and other electoral reforms, provides useful background research and discussion of the pros and cons on its website at www.fairvote.org.

32. For example, see Richard Briffault, "Home Rule and Local Political Innovation," *Journal of Law and Politics* 22 (Winter 2006): 1–32, which uses San Francisco's ranked-choice voting system as a case study exemplifying the idea that local government can act as "laboratories of democracy."

33. California Secretary of State, "About California Voter's Choice Act," www.sos.ca.gov/elections/voters-choice-act/about-vca (accessed 9/7/18).

34. These are the unofficial results reported November 23, 2016. For more background on this measure and the outcome, see the Ballotpedia entry for "Local Measure N–Non-Citizen Voting in School Board Elections," https://ballotpedia.org/San_Francisco,_California,_Non-Citizen_Voting_in_School_Board_Elections_Amendment,_Proposition_N_(November_2016) (accessed 11/23/16).

35. Kimberly Yam, "San Francisco Now Allows Noncitizens to Vote in School Board Elections," *Huffington Post*, July 18, 2018, www.huffingtonpost.com/entry/san-francisco-now-allows-non-citizens-to-vote-in-school-board-elections_us_5b4e301ee4b0de86f48775d0 (accessed 9/7/18).

36. Senate Local Government Committee, *What's So Special about Special Districts? A Citizen's Guide to Special Districts in California*, 3rd ed. (Sacramento: California State Senate, 2002), p. 3.

37. California Department of Education, "Fingertip Facts on Education in California," www.cde.ca.gov/ds/sd/cb/ceffingertipfacts.asp (accessed 9/7/18).

38. California Community Colleges, www.cccco.edu (accessed 9/7/18).

39. David Kirp, "California to Community Colleges: Graduate More Students or Lose Your Funding," *Los Angeles Times*, August 22, 2018, www.latimes.com/opinion/op-ed/la-oe-kirp

-california-community-college-graduation-rates-20180822
-story.html (accessed 9/7/18).

40. California State Controller, "Special Districts Listing," https://
bythenumbers.sco.ca.gov/Special-Districts-Other/Special
-Districts-Listing/fv6y-3v29 (accessed 9/7/18).

41. California State Controller's Office, *Special Districts Annual
Report 2011–2012*, p. vii, www.sco.ca.gov/Files-ARD-Local
/LocRep/1112_special_districts.pdf (accessed 10/7/16).

42. Brian P. Janiskee, "The Problem of Local Government in California," *Nexus* (Spring 2001): 219–33.

43. Neil McCormick, Chief Executive Officer, and Kyle Pack-
ham, Advocacy and Public Affairs Director, California Special Districts Association, written testimony to Little Hoover
Commission Review of Special Districts, August 8, 2016,
lhc.ca.gov/sites/lhc.ca.gov/files/Reports/239/WrittenTestimony
/CSDAAug2016.pdf (accessed 9/22/18).

44. Rosanna Xia, "With Supreme Court challenge, tech billionaire could dismantle beach access rights—and a landmark
coastal law," *Los Angeles Times*, March 6, 2018, www.latimes
.com/local/lanow/la-me-martins-beach-supreme-court-2018
0306-story.html (accessed 9/7/18).

45. Tahoe Regional Planning Agency, www.trpa.org (accessed
9/7/18).

46. Gabriel Metcalf, "An Interview with Joe Bodovitz," SPUR
report no. 378 (September 1999).

47. California Association of Realtors, "Market at a Glance,"
www.car.org/en/marketing/chartsandgraphs/marketglance
(accessed 9/7/18).

48. Andrea Riquier, "California exodus gathers strength, as home
prices continue upward march," *Market Watch*, June 1, 2018,
www.marketwatch.com/story/with-no-letup-in-home-prices
-the-california-exodus-surges-2018-05-03 (accessed 9/7/18).

49. For more about the CA housing crisis, go to calmatters.org
/articles/housing-costs-high-california.

50. California Employment Development Department, "July
2018 California Employment Highlights," www.labormarket
info.edd.ca.gov/file/lfmonth/Employment-Highlights.pdf (accessed 9/7/18).

51. Emily Badger, "The Bipartisan Cry of 'Not in My Backyard,'"
New York Times, August 21, 2018, www.nytimes.com/2018
/08/21/upshot/home-ownership-nimby-bipartisan.html
(accessed 9/7/18).

52. California Department of Industrial Relations, "Minimum
Wage," www.dir.ca.gov/dlse/faq_minimumwage.htm (accessed
9/7/18).

53. Paul Rogers, "Jerry Brown signs new laws to block Trump's
California offshore oil drilling plans," *Mercury News*, September 8, 2018, www.mercurynews.com/2018/09/08/jerry-brown
-signs-new-laws-to-block-trumps-california-offshore-oil-drill
ing-plans.

Chapter 10

1. Dan Barry, "Beside a Smoldering Dump, a Refuge of Sorts,"
New York Times, October 21, 2007, www.nytimes.com/2007
/10/21/us/21land.html?_r=1 (accessed 9/17/18).

2. David Olson, "Duroville: Slum Mobile Home Park Finally
Closes," *Riverside Press-Enterprise*, June 26, 2014, www.pe.com
/articles/duroville-678572-park-mobile.html (accessed 9/17/18).

See also Phil Willon, "Farmworkers' New Home Is Near Duroville, Yet a World Away," *Los Angeles Times*, March 25, 2013,
www.latimes.com/news/local/la-me-duroville-20130325
,0,5395710.story (accessed 9/17/18).

3. Paloma Esquivel, "Farmworkers Find a Bumper Crop of
Squalor in Coachella Valley Trailer Parks," *Los Angeles Times*,
October 5, 2015, www.latimes.com/local/california/la-me
-farmworker-trailers-20151006-story.html (accessed 9/17/18).

4. Liam Dillon, "Gov. Brown just signed 15 housing bills. Here's
how they're supposed to help the affordability crisis," *Los
Angeles Times*, September 29, 2017, www.latimes.com/poli
tics/la-pol-ca-housing-legislation-signed-20170929-htmlstory
.html (accessed 9/17/18).

5. This bill can be found at: leginfo.legislature.ca.gov/faces/bill
TextClient.xhtml?bill_id=201720180SB1227.

6. California Budget Project, "School Finance Facts, a Decade
of Disinvestment: California Education Spending Nears the
Bottom," October 2011, calbudgetcenter.org/wp-content
/uploads/111012_Decade_of_Disinvestment_%20SFF.pdf
(accessed 9/17/18). See also National Education Association, "Rankings and Estimates, Rankings of the States 2013
and Estimates of School Statistics 2014," NEA Research
(March 2014), www.nea.org/home/rankings-and-estimates-2013
-2014.html (accessed 9/17/18).

7. "Quality Counts 2016: State Report Cards Map," *Education Week*, www.edweek.org/ew/qc/2016/2016-state-report
-cards-map.html (accessed 9/17/18).

8. California Department of Education, "State Schools Chief
Tom Torlakson Announces Results of California Assessment
of Student Performance and Progress Online Tests," October 2, 2018, https://www.cde.ca.gov/nr/ne/yr18/yr18rel62
.asp (accessed 10/31/18).

9. "Managing Droughts," Public Policy Institute of California
Water Policy Center, www.ppic.org/wp-content/uploads/cali
fornias-water-managing-droughts-november-2018.pdf
(accessed 11/30/18).

10. Paul Rogers and Nicholas St. Fleur, "California Drought:
Database Shows Big Difference Between Water Guzzlers
and Sippers," *Mercury News*, February 7, 2014, www.mercury
news.com/2014/02/07/california-drought-database-shows
-big-difference-between-water-guzzlers-and-sippers (accessed
9/17/18).

11. Matt Weiser, "California Allocates Vastly More Water Than
Supplies Allow, Study Shows," *Sacramento Bee*, August 19,
2014, www.sacbee.com/news/local/article2607102.html
(accessed 9/17/18).

12. "Water Rights: Frequently Asked Questions," California Water
Boards, www.waterboards.ca.gov/waterrights/board_info/faqs
.html#toc178761090 (accessed 9/17/18).

13. George Skelton, "In California, rights to water exceed the
supply," *Los Angeles Times*, April 12, 2015, www.latimes.com
/local/politics/la-me-cap-drought-water-20150413-column
.html (accessed 9/17/18).

14. Peter H. Gleick, "Solving California's Water Problems," *Huffington Post*, June 10, 2014, www.huffingtonpost.com/peter
-h-gleick/solving-californias-water_b_5479569.html (accessed
9/17/18).

15. Gleick, "Solving California's Water Problems."

16. Caitrin Chappelle and Ellen Hanack, "Just the Facts: Groundwater in California," Public Policy Institute of California,

May 2017, www.ppic.org/publication/groundwater-in-california (accessed 9/17/18). Chappelle, Hanack, and Mount, "Just the Facts: California's Latest Drought," Public Policy Institute of California, July 2016, www.ppic.org/publication/californias -latest-drought (accessed 9/17/18).

17. "Lessons Learned: Covered California Open Enrollment 2013–2014," Covered California, October 2014, www.coveredca .com/PDFs/10-14-2014-Lessons-Learned-final.pdf (accessed 9/17/18).

18. Ken Jacobs, "Employer-Sponsored Insurance in California," UC Berkeley Labor Center, October 23, 2017, healthcare.assembly .ca.gov/sites/healthcare.assembly.ca.gov/files/employer-based coverage_kenjacobs_chair_ucberkeley.pdf (accessed 9/17/18).

19. Tracy Seipel, "Healthy California Act annual price tag: $400 billion," *Mercury News*, May 22, 2017, www.mercurynews.com /2017/05/22/healthy-california-act-annual-price-tag-400-billion (accessed 9/17/18).

20. Alyssa Dykman, "Single-Payer Health Care and the Governor's Race," Public Policy Institute of California, June 4, 2018, http://www.ppic.org/blog/single-payer-health-care-and-the -governors-race (accessed 9/17/18).

21. California Health Care Foundation. "Medi-Cal Facts and Figures: An Evolving Program," December 21, 2017, www.chcf .org/publication/medi-cal-facts-and-figures-a-program-trans forms (accessed 9/28/18).

22. For more information about Medi-Cal, see the many publications of the California Health Care Foundation at their website, www.chcf.org (accessed 9/17/18), or the Kaiser Family Foundation, www.kff.org (accessed 9/17/18).

23. California Health Care Foundation, "California's Uninsured: Progress Toward Universal Coverage," August 6, 2018, https:// www.chcf.org/publication/californias-uninsured-progress-uni versal-coverage (accessed 9/28/18).

24. Bruce E. Cain, "Searching for the Next Pat Brown: California Infrastructure in the Balance," in "California's Future in the Balance," *California Policy Issues Annual*, special edition (Los Angeles: Edmund G. "Pat" Brown Institute of Public Affairs, November 2001).

25. "Report Card for California's Infrastructure 2018," The American Society of Civil Engineers, October 2018, http://asceca reportcard.org/wp-content/uploads/2018/10/2018-ASCE -California-Surface-Transportation-Report-Card.pdf (accessed 10/31/18).

26. Gary Stoller, "U.S. Roads, Bridges Are Decaying Despite Stimulus Influx," *USA Today*, July 29, 2013.

27. Daniel C. Vock, "Under Scrutiny, States Trim List of Bad Bridges," *Governing Magazine*, June 4, 2014.

28. C. Piller, "Bay Bridge's Troubled China Connection," *Sacramento Bee*, June 8, 2014.

29. Dan Walters, "California's Hefty Fuel Tax Buys Poor Roads," *Sacramento Bee*, July 2, 2013, www.sacbee.com/news/politics -government/politics-columns-blogs/dan-walters/article2577 987.html (accessed 9/17/18).

30. George Skelton, "On Road Repairs, Legislators Still in the Driveway," *Los Angeles Times*, August 22, 2016.

31. Stuart Leavenworth, "Logjam May Break on Mending Levees," *Sacramento Bee*, April 2, 2004.

32. Stuart Leavenworth, "Defenses Decayed: Neglected Levees Pushed Past Limits," *Sacramento Bee*, March 28, 2004.

33. Sara Lin and William Wan, "Crews Shore Up Levees as Concerns Rise over Upkeep," *Los Angeles Times*, June 10, 2004, pp. B1+.

34. Bettina Boxall, "A Delta Tunnel Project's Lofty Ambitions Have Been Scaled Back," *Los Angeles Times*, April 4, 2016, www.la times.com/science/la-me-delta-pumps-20160404-story.html (accessed 9/17/18).

35. Denny Walsh, "State Supreme Court Rules in State's Favor on Delta Property Rights," *Sacramento Bee*, July 21, 2016, www .sacbee.com/news/state/california/water-and-drought/delta /article91048507.html (accessed 9/17/18).

36. Ryan Sabalow and Dale Kasler, "Massive Delta tunnels project took a giant step forward—here's what you need to know," *Sacramento Bee*, April 11, 2018, www.sacbee.com/news/state /california/water-and-drought/delta/article208576299.html (accessed 9/17/18).

37. Ryan Sabalow and Dale Kasler, "Massive Delta tunnels project."

38. Ralph Vartabedian, "Leadership Turnover at the California High-Speed Rail Authority Could Signal Shakeup," *Los Angeles Times*, May 1, 2017, www.latimes.com/local/california/la -me-bullet-turmoil-20170428-story.html (accessed 9/17/18).

Credits

Chapter 1

Page 4: AP Photo/Rich Pedroncelli; Pg. 14: Max Whittaker/Reuters/Newscom.

Chapter 2

Pg. 27: Joy Jia-Shiuan Boston. Pg. 34: The Wasp, F850. W18, Volume 9, Number 316, pp 520–521. Courtesy of The Bancroft Library, University of California, Berkeley. Pg. 41: AP Photo/J. Scott Applewhite.

Chapter 3

Pg. 57: Monte Wolverton/Cagle Cartoons/PoliticalCartoons.com. Pg. 65: AP Photo/Rich Pedroncelli.

Chapter 4

Pg. 83: Figure from "The Prop 87 Effect: How the California GOP lost their way and implications for 2014 and beyond," by Matt Barreto. Latino Decisions, October 17, 2013. Reprinted by permission of Latino Decisions. Pg. 92: left: AP Photo/Chris Carlson, right: K.C. Alfred/San Diego Union-Tribune/ZUMA Wire/Alamy Live News. Pg. 114: Lucy Nicholson/Reuters/Newscom.

Chapter 5

Pg. 132: AP Photo/Rich Pedroncelli. Pg. 137: AP Photo/Rich Pedroncelli.

Chapter 6

Pg. 163: AP Photo/Rich Pedroncelli. Pg. 180: AP Photo/Rich Pedroncelli.

Chapter 7

Pg. 189: Sipa USA via AP. Pg. 190: "Flow of Cases through the California State Judicial System." Copyright © 2014, Judicial Council of California, used by permission. Pg. 196: Courtesy of the Supreme Court of California. Photo by Bob Knapik.

Chapter 8

Pg. 210: "Spending on Corrections and Higher Education" from the California Department of Finance, Chart C-1: Program Expenditures by Fund. Public Policy Institute of California Blog, August 4, 2016. Reprinted by permission of the Public Policy Institute of California. Pg. 220: Ben Margot/AP Photo. Pg. 224: Ken Wolter/Alamy Stock Photo.

Chapter 9

Pg. 254: Mark Boster/Los Angeles Times via Getty Images. Pg. 257: Gabrielle Lurie/The New York Times/Redux. Pg. 258: Figure from "Californians: Here's why your housing costs are so high," by Matt Levin and Ben Christopher. CALmatters, Aug. 21, 2017. Reprinted with permission. Pg. 259: Exhibit from "A Tool Kit to Close California's Housing Gap: 3.5 Million Homes by 2025," October 2016, McKinsey Global Institute, www.mckinsey.com. Copyright © 2018 McKinsey & Company. All rights reserved. Reprinted by permission. Pg. 260: Figure from "Gov. Brown just signed 15 housing bills. Here's how they're supposed to help the affordability crisis," by Liam Dillon. Los Angeles Times, Sep. 29, 2017. Copyright © 2017. Reprinted by permission of the Los Angeles Times.

Chapter 10

Pg. 272: AP Photo/Rich Pedroncelli. Pg. 281: AP Photo/Damian Dovarganes.

Index

Page numbers followed by *b*, *f*, or *t* refer to boxes, figures, and tables respectively. Italic page numbers refer to photos.